Program Advisors

Janice Brown
Houston ISD
Houston, Texas

Kay Licona
Franklin High School
El Paso, Texas

Beverly Ann Chin
University of Montana
Missoula, Montana

William Ray
Lincoln-Sudbury Regional High School
Sudbury, Massachusetts

Rosa Fonseca
Franklin High School
El Paso, Texas

Jacqueline Jones Royster
Ohio State University
Columbus, Ohio

Acknowledgments

"The Man with the Saxophone" from *Sin*, by Ai. Copyright © 1986 by Ai. Reprinted by permission of the author.

"The Diameter of the Bomb" by Yehuda Amichai, from *The Selected Poetry of Yehuda Amichai*, translated/edited by Chana Bloch and Stephen Mitchell. Copyright © 1996

The Regents of the University of California. Reprinted by permission of the University of California Press.

"The Elephants Are in the Yard" by Indran Amirthanayagam. Reprinted by permission of the author.

❖ *cont. on page 394*

Glencoe/McGraw-Hill

A Division of The **McGraw·Hill** Companies

Send all inquiries to:
Glencoe/McGraw-Hill
8787 Orion Place
Columbus, Ohio 43240-4027

ISBN 0-07-822929-4

Printed in the United States of America

1 2 3 4 5 6 7 8 9 10 071 05 04 03 02 01 00

GLENCOE

Asian American Literature

 **Glencoe McGraw-Hill**

New York, New York   Columbus, Ohio   Woodland Hills, California   Peoria, Illinois

Contents

❖

Theme One: Origins

Theme Two: People

Contents

❖

Contents

❖

America, 1985. Diana Ong. Computer graphic. Diana Ong/SuperStock.

Theme One

Origins

Life is like a vast, long dream

—*from Songs of Gold Mountain*

Before You Read

Water Names

Lan Samantha Chang
Born 1965

"I'm interested in exploring the solaces and tragedies that are interwoven with family love."

About Chang

Lan Samantha Chang was born in Appleton, Wisconsin. She says that she started writing as a child because she felt like an outsider in this small city. Her parents urged her to pursue a career involving science or math. Chang took premedical courses at Yale University and studied economics in graduate school. However, she could not forget her dream of becoming a writer. She enrolled at the Iowa Writer's Workshop, a decision that greatly upset her parents.

In 1998 Chang published *Hunger: A Novella and Stories*. The book received excellent reviews, and Chang's parents are now proud of her writing. Chang says that for years she delayed showing stories to publishers: "I wanted to be old enough to be certain of my artistic vision, to be able to withstand whatever happened when my first book came out."

Ghost Stories

In "Water Names," Chang retells a Chinese ghost story. Ghosts are common in folklore throughout the world. Belief in ghosts is based on the idea that the human spirit exists separately from the body and survives after a person's death. A ghost may take on a cloudy form or appear the same as he or she did when alive, or it may remain invisible. They make their presence known through laughter, shrieks, and other strange noises, or by moving objects around. Most ghosts are tied to a specific place, such as a house or graveyard. They often return to these places because they didn't receive proper burial.

The Chang Jiang described in the story is also known as the Yangtze River. It is Asia's longest river and the third longest in the world.

Water Names

— Lan Samantha Chang

Summertime at dusk we'd gather on the back porch, tired and sticky from another day of fierce encoded quarrels, nursing our mosquito bites and frail dignities, sisters in name only. At first we'd pinch and slap each other, fighting for the best—least ragged—folding chair. Then we'd argue over who would sit next to our grandmother. We were so close together on the tiny porch that we often pulled our own hair by mistake. Forbidden to bite, we planted silent toothmarks on each others' wrists. We ignored the bulk of house behind us, the yard, the fields, the darkening sky. We even forgot about our grandmother. Then suddenly we'd hear her old, dry voice, very close, almost on the backs of our necks.

"*Xiushila*! Shame on you. Fighting like a bunch of chickens."

And Ingrid, the oldest, would freeze with her thumb and forefinger right on the back of Lily's arm. I would slide my hand away from the end of Ingrid's braid. Ashamed, we would shuffle our feet while Waipuo calmly found her chair.

On some nights she sat with us in silence, the tip of her cigarette glowing red like a distant stoplight. But on some nights she told us stories, "just to keep up your Chinese," she said, and the red dot flickered and danced, making ghostly shapes as she moved her hands like a magician in the dark.

"In these prairie crickets I often hear the sound of rippling waters, of the Yangtze River," she said. "Granddaughters, you are descended on both sides from people of the water country, near the mouth of the great Chang Jiang, as it is called, where the river is so grand and broad that even on clear days you can scarcely see the other side.

"The Chang Jiang runs four thousand miles, originating in the Himalaya mountains where it crashes, flecked with gold dust, down steep cliffs so perilous and remote that few humans have ever seen them. In central China, the river squeezes through deep gorges, then widens in its last thousand miles to the sea. Our ancestors have lived near the mouth of this river, the ever-changing delta, near a city called Nanjing, for more than a thousand years."

"A thousand years," murmured Lily, who was only ten. When she was younger she had sometimes burst into nervous crying at the thought of so many years. Her small insistent fingers grabbed my fingers in the dark.

"Through your mother and I, you are descended from a line of great men and women. We have survived countless floods and seasons of ill-fortune because we have the spirit of the river in us. Unlike mountains, we cannot be powdered down or broken apart. Instead, we run together, like raindrops. Our strength and spirit wear down mountains into sand. But even our people must respect the water."

She paused, and a bit of ash glowed briefly as it drifted to the floor.

"When I was young, my own grandmother once told me the story of Wen Zhiqing's daughter. Twelve hundred years ago the civilized parts of China still lay to the north, and the Yangtze valley lay unspoiled. In those days lived an ancestor named Wen Zhiqing, a resourceful man, and proud. He had been fishing for many years with trained cormorants, which you girls of course have never seen. Cormorants are sleek, black birds with long, bending necks which the fishermen fitted with metal rings so the fish they caught could not be swallowed. The birds would perch on the side of the old wooden boat and dive into the river." We had only known blue swimming pools, but we tried to imagine the sudden shock of cold and the plunge, deep into water.

"Now, Wen Zhiqing had a favorite daughter who was very beautiful and loved the river. She would beg to go out on the boat with him. This daughter was a restless one, never contented with their catch, and often she insisted they stay out until it was almost dark. Even then, she was not satisfied. She had been spoiled by her father, kept protected from the river, so she could not see its danger. To this young woman, the river was as familiar as the sky. It was a bright, broad road stretching out to curious lands. She did not fully understand the river's depths.

"One clear spring evening, as she watched the last bird dive off into the blackening waters, she said, 'If only this catch would bring back something more than another fish!'

"She leaned over the side of the boat and looked at the water. The stars and moon reflected back at her. And it is said that the spirits living underneath the water looked up at her as well. And the spirit of a young man who had drowned in the river many years before saw her lovely face."

Water Names

We had heard about the ghosts of the drowned, who wait forever in the water for a living person to pull down instead. A faint breeze moved through the mosquito screens and we shivered.

"The cormorant was gone for a very long time," Waipuo said, "so long that the fisherman grew puzzled. Then, suddenly, the bird emerged from the waters, almost invisible in the night, Wen Zhiqing grasped his catch, a very large fish, and guided the boat back to shore. And when Wen reached home, he gutted the fish and discovered, in its stomach, a valuable pearl ring."

"From the man?" said Lily.

"Sshh, she'll tell you."

Waipuo ignored us. "His daughter was delighted that her wish had been fulfilled. What most excited her was the idea of an entire world like this, a world where such a beautiful ring would be only a bauble! For part of her had always longed to see faraway things and places. The river had put a spell on her heart. In the evenings she began to sit on the bank, looking at her own reflection in the water. Sometimes she said she saw a handsome young man looking back at her. And her yearning for him filled her heart with sorrow and fear, for she knew that she would soon leave her beloved family.

"'It's just the moon,' said Wen Zhiqing, but his daughter shook her head. 'There's a kingdom under the water,' she said. 'The prince is asking me to marry him. He sent the ring as an offering to you.' 'Nonsense,' said her father, and he forbade her to sit by the water again.

"For a year things went as usual, but the next spring there came a terrible flood that swept away almost everything. In the middle of a torrential rain, the family noticed that the daughter was missing. She had taken advantage of the confusion to hurry to the river and visit her beloved. The family searched for days but they never found her."

Her smoky, rattling voice came to a stop.

"What happened to her?" Lily said.

"It's okay, stupid," I told her. "She was so beautiful that she went to join the kingdom of her beloved. Right?"

"Who knows?" Waipuo said, "They say she was seduced by a water ghost. Or perhaps she lost her mind to desiring."

"What do you mean?" asked Ingrid.

"I'm going inside," Waipuo said, and got out of her chair with a creak. A moment later the light went on in her bedroom window. We knew she stood before the mirror, combing out her long, wavy silver-gray hair, and we imagined that in her youth she too had been beautiful.

We sat together without talking, breathing our dreams in the lingering smoke. We had gotten used to Waipuo's abruptness, her habit of creating a question and leaving without answering it, as if she were disappointed in the question itself. We tried to imagine Wen Zhiqing's daughter. What did she look like? How old was she? Why hadn't anyone remembered her name?

While we weren't watching, the stars had emerged. Their brilliant pinpoints mapped the heavens. They glittered over us, over Waipuo in her room, the house, and the small city we lived in, the great waves of grass that ran for miles around us, the ground beneath as dry and hard as bone.

Responding to the Selection

Questions for Discussion

1. How did you react to the last three paragraphs of "Water Names"? Why might Chang have decided to include a description of Waipuo combing her hair?

2. A frame story is a story that surrounds another story or that serves to link several stories together. Compare the styles of the frame story and the story of Wen Zhiqing's daughter in "Water Names." Do you think that the frame story makes "Water Names" more interesting? Why or why not?

3. Describe the personality traits of Wen Zhiqing's daughter. How do these traits help us understand what happens to her?

4. What explanations does Waipuo offer at the end of her tale? Which one seems most satisfying to you?

5. Waipuo tells her grandchildren that her stories are intended "just to keep up your Chinese." What other reasons might an immigrant such as Waipuo have for telling her story?

Activities

Writing from a Different Point of View

1. Write a version of the story of Wen Zhiqing's daughter from the water ghost's point of view.

Reading Ghost Stories

2. Find another Asian ghost story and read it aloud to a group of classmates.

Listening to Music

3. Choose a piece of music that could accompany a reading of "Water Names." Play the music for the class and explain why you feel it is appropriate for the story.

Before You Read

A Lost Memory of Delhi

Agha Shahid Ali
Born 1949

> *"One of the few things I don't lie about is poetry."*

About Ali

Agha Shahid Ali is a Kashmiri poet who draws on Eastern and Western literary traditions. Born in New Delhi, India, he was raised as a Muslim in Kashmir, a region that is now divided between India and neighboring Pakistan. In 1976 he moved to the United States, where he teaches literature and creative writing.

Cultural Influences

Ali often uses a surreal approach to writing—one that frequently involves combining or overlapping events from the past and the present, or elements from both Indian and American culture. Ali's style of writing is similarly a combination of cultural elements, since he sometimes mixes a traditional Indian poetic form with a contemporary American manner of speech. He has written several acclaimed volumes of verse, including *The Half-Inch Himalayas* and *The Country Without a Post Office*, and has also translated other Kashmiri poetry into English.

In his writing, Ali is preoccupied by a sense of loss, which he says is part of his "emotional coloring." He often writes about death, exile, and longing for the past. Yet there is also much playfulness and joy in his writing. In some poems he addresses the problems of Kashmir, which has been the scene of many violent clashes between Muslims and the Indian government.

A LOST MEMORY OF DELHI

— Agha Shahid Ali

I am not born
it is 1948 and the bus turns
onto a road without name

There on his bicycle
5   my father
He is younger than I

At Okhla where I get off
I pass my parents
strolling by the Jamuna River

10   My mother is a recent bride
her sari a blaze of brocade
Silverdust parts her hair

She doesn't see me
The bells of her anklets are distant
15   like the sound of china from

teashops being lit up with lanterns
and the stars are coming out
ringing with tongues of glass

They go into the house
20   always faded in photographs
in the family album

but lit up now
with the oil lamp
I saw broken in the attic

25   I want to tell them I am their son
older much older than they are
I knock keep knocking

but for them the night is quiet
this the night of my being
30   They don't they won't

hear me they won't hear
my knocking drowning out
the tongues of stars

Responding to the Selection

Questions for Discussion

1. What thoughts went through your mind as you were reading "A Lost Memory of Delhi"?

2. What event is described in the poem? Why might this be considered a "lost memory"?

3. How would you describe the speaker's attitude toward the past?

Activities

Writing an Imaginative Essay

1. If you could go back to an earlier time in your life, which experience would you revisit? Write a brief essay explaining your choice.

Reporting on Kashmir

2. Kashmir is famous for its incredible natural beauty as well as its violent past and present. Prepare a report for your class on Kashmir that includes photographs and analysis of its history since 1947, when the clashes between pro-India Hindus and pro-Pakistan Muslims began. Also include a selection of Agha Shahid Ali's poems about the conflict in Kashmir.

Before You Read

Hambun-Hambun

Susan Ito
Born 1959

> **"I have always had a heightened awareness of my 'otherness.'"**

About Ito

When Susan Ito was an infant, her mother gave her up for adoption to a Japanese American couple who had waited ten years for a child. Her adoptive parents were often confronted with questions about her racial background, which Ito describes as "fifty percent Japanese, and fifty percent . . . unknown." Because of her experiences, Ito is fascinated by literature that explores the complexities of adoption, especially in cases involving a mixed-race child.

Ito has co-edited an anthology called *A Ghost at Heart's Edge: Stories and Poems*

about Adoption. She lives in Oakland, California, where she teaches creative writing. Ito's stories, poems, and essays have appeared in numerous publications.

Ethnic Identity

At the opening of Ito's essay "Hambun-Hambun," she wonders which racial category she should choose to identify herself on a census form. In the 1990s, a growing number of people in the United States shared her anxiety. It is estimated that seven percent of United States residents could be considered multiracial or multiethnic. In California fifteen percent of births fall into more than one category. In response to lobbying, the U.S. Census Bureau allowed people to choose more than one category to describe their racial or ethnic background on the 2000 census form. In Ito's essay, *nisei* (literally "second generation") refers to children born to Japanese immigrants, while *issei* ("first generation") is the term used for the immigrants themselves.

Hambun-
Hambun

— *Susan Ito*

The census form came today. I saw the dreaded instructions, the stern admonishment to *check only one box*. White. Japanese. Other. There is the blank space to fill in, a half inch in which to claim identity. I am other. Hambunhambun, or half-and-half. *Hapa*. Biologically, genetically, I'm fifty percent Japanese, and fifty percent . . . unknown. Adopted as an infant into a Japanese American family, I have always had a heightened awareness of my "otherness."

"Your parents, they're so good, they treat you just like you were their own." I've heard this a lot.

Then is it true, that I am not "their own"? If not to them, to whom do I belong? From where do I come? From out there. From them, those phantom parents. Am I a part of this family, or not? I cling to their name, to *my* name, Ito, as one holds an amulet. I fasten it around my throat. Yes. *I do belong*. And yet, there is that question, that other name, burned into the black plastic of microfiche, buried in the catacombs of hospital storage like the name of a dead person. The life I never lived.

I've met the woman who gave birth to me; she is a nisei like my parents. I hunted her down when I was in college, searched the underground of buried information until I arrived at her door. She wasn't happy about being discovered, but when she learned that I had grown up a sansei, a third-generation Japanese American, something inside her softened. She had let me go into the world, destination unknown, and I could have turned up anywhere. But I grew up as the daughter of Masaji and Kikuko, who brought me to visit relatives in Japan when I was nine, who taught me to sing "Sakura," the cherry blossom song.

They get along well now, the three of them. They fall easily into a natural camaraderie, their shared culture, their linked parentage of me. We have all eaten sushi together, chopsticks clicking comfortably. None of them will mention that missing link, that *other* part of the equation, the one out of four parents who is not Japanese at all.

This invisible one, my nameless birth father, shows up to haunt me every time I look in the mirror. I see his freckles, his pink skin that doesn't tan easily. His dark furry forearms, and legs that need to be shaved every day. His nose, twice as long and more defined than my Japanese kin, is an unmistakable flag on my profile. But what color is that flag? What country? What people?

When my second daughter was born with blonde-red hair and blue eyes, those recessive genes surfaced like an earthquake in our family. Who are those fair freckled blondes, her great-grandparents? My birth mother has remained silent to my questions, and I have become tired of asking.

These questions of origin and identity have been circling around like stubborn moths in my head ever since I was small. They beat their wings, bumping up against my brain, dumbly searching for answers. What? Who? Why? I started writing when I was six, making up stories that always ended with astonishing surprises: The cat was really a turtle in disguise. A girl found a rabbit under her bed, and they became sisters. The questions and answers surfaced as fables in my green marbled notebooks before I knew how to speak them out loud. I wrote incessantly for years and years, words bleeding uncontrollably onto the page. When I searched for and found my birth mother, people would say, "You ought to make this into a story. Your life is such a soap opera." It seemed like a ludicrous idea to me; Japanese people don't show up on soap operas.

My adoptive parents, both nisei, are solidly cemented into the Japanese American community. They have their friends from half a century now, who all grew up together in New York City public schools, all with immigrant parents, mothers who were picture brides, fathers who didn't speak English. They stick together. I grew up between them, bolstered by their unflinching love for me, the way they never questioned my "authenticity." My parents' people took me in, called me "Susie-chan." Yet without my parents, I feel shy, self-conscious about joining the Japanese community in California. I worry that they'll look at me sideways, saying, "What is she doing here?"

Whenever I was out with one parent, new acquaintances would always assume that the other parent was white. And why wouldn't they? They were innocent questions, innocent assumptions, but the years of constant questions, the curiosity, the nosiness, have left me with a bitter taste that won't go away.

I am fourteen or fifteen years old, my body bursting into adolescence, all bright flowers and elastic in my new halter top. I am helping my father set up one of his merchandise booths and another salesman comes up, slaps him on the back.

"Mr. Ito! This is *your* daughter?"

My father beams and reaches out to ruffle my hair. "Yes, this is Susan."

Hambun-*Hambun*

"Why, you old dog. I never woulda known!" An elbow in the ribs, another slap, a wink. "Well, your wife must be *some beauty* then." Meaning: you snagged a white woman, you crafty little Jap.

My father and I busy ourselves with our work, not looking at each other.

I am thirty-five years old, teaching English at community college. A colleague invites me to join an Asian American faculty organization and, as I am introduced to the group, a nisei man does a double take, looks at me sideways.

"You don't *look* like an Ito."

What does an Ito look like? What does it mean to be Japanese American, to be "real"? I try to keep my voice steady, to find a balance between a humiliated whisper and outraged shouting. "Well, I am. I am." I don't offer an explanation.

I go to a conference of mixed-race people and am moved and astounded to see the hundreds of people who, in a peculiar way, all look like me, even as we are singularly different. It is a relief to be among so many who know this life, this *hapa* seesaw, but as I meet and share stories with other biracial people, I realize that once again I am on the periphery. Everyone seems to come from a family with two identifiable parents. Even those whose parents have split up have photos, stories of the one that isn't around. They see themselves reflected in this dual mirror: "I get my blue eyes from *him* but my black hair is from *her*." They get to see the source of their mixture, their differences split by their blended roots. It is as if half of my mirror is covered up.

Even among this peculiar group of people with whom I have so much in common, I feel separate. They talk about the cultural wars between parents: Mom wanted to fix won tons, but Dad insisted on corned beef. I had none of that bifurcated experience. So maybe I'm not really a *hapa*, not really part of the club. It was a homogeneous front, my all-Japanese family. Yet sometimes, when I caught a glimpse of my own reflection, or saw a portrait of the three of us together, I felt dizzy.

My junior high school friend Cathy laughed when she saw the framed family photo on our piano. "What's wrong with this picture?" she giggled, pointing at me. It was like a children's puzzle, a song my own daughters have learned from *Sesame Street*: *One of these things is not like the others, one of these things just doesn't belong. . . .*

Not long after we met, my birth mother and I began to wage an emotional tug-of-war. I pulled and pulled at her, trying to extract information, stories, memories. *Tell me where I came from. Tell me who I am.* She begrudgingly let go of tiny fragments of her history, a small tidbit or anecdote every few years, but never much about that pale Midwestern man who helped to create me. Years of struggle, of tears and demands and refusal, and finally a silence that has turned into a stiff, saccharine cordiality. We don't bring it up any more.

Is information something that can be owned, hoarded, desired? Is it really possible to guard the truth as she has? After years of raging, pleading, begging, and threatening, I must finally accept the truth: We are not going to sit down together, a pot of green tea between us, talking about the past, flipping pages of a photo album, while I soak up a sense of identity. We are not going to appear on *Oprah*, an ecstatic mother-daughter reunion. If I am going to have a birth story, a chronicle of my roots, it is going to be up to me.

I write down all that I know of my beginnings, and these scanty notes barely fill one side of an index card. My birthdate. Birthplace. The place where they met. The few precious details that she has let slip into conversations, the small specks that I have been gathering like dust in my pocket.

I take my birthday, count back nine months, calculating my conception to be somewhere around Christmas in 1958. I close my eyes for several minutes, pulling myself back there. A cold month, a month full of snow. Then I begin writing. I imagine him, red-cheeked in the bitter wind, stomping ice from his boots. I see her in her cat's-eye glasses, a school-teacher with black hair and red lipstick. The only Japanese woman in the tiny Midwestern town. I give them outfits, like paper dolls, and winter colds. He carries a linen handkerchief in his pocket. I write them closer and closer together, until their paths cross and I give them eye contact. This is the beginning of my story. This is where my life begins.

I write, not to provide a screenplay for *Days of Our Lives*, but to fill in the holes of this tale that I don't know, but which exists in my blood, my skin, my bones. Pages accumulate, and like the velveteen rabbit of childhood, I feel myself becoming real.

Five years ago, I had a bookshelf full of green marbled notebooks and a wild, aching need to write that I fed every day like a drug habit. The notebooks simmered on the shelf like radioactive material. A certain point came when it wasn't enough to produce chaos; I wanted to write a story. I took a class in creative writing, terrified of what I might find out. It would be a trite, predictable soap opera. I would be laughed out of the room.

Nobody laughed. The first story was published. Seeing the familiar letters of my own name, in black typography in a published book, was like seeing my birth mother's face for the first time. *There I am.*

Autobiography comes in different forms: the what-if of my creation tale, and then the this-happened-and-I-need-to-tell-it witness kind. It is different to take memory and to turn it into fiction, into the not quite tangible world of literature. This can be more vulnerable. Writing about actual life is a many-layered process. First you dig and dig with your pencil until something is unearthed. Is this what I was looking for? The dusting-off, the close examination. Yes, this is something I can use. Once its value is acknowledged, then comes the task of disguising it. Some memories must be enrolled in the witness protection program, given false mustaches and dyed hair. They pretend to live in cities that they have never visited.

I sweat as I write my author's bio for a particularly risky story, wondering who will see it. Someone suggests using a pseudonym, and my reaction is swift and furious: Unacceptable. My name was already taken from me once, and I won't let it happen again. I am not going to hide or lie about who I am.

But then the irony strikes me: in *some* ways it is fine, even necessary, to take on a disguise, to dress up the truth. This is what writing fiction is all about. But fiction is about being in control, about choosing the particular camouflage myself. When I sense a mask being fastened over my face by some external force, or a label slapped onto my shoulder, I balk. *Don't tell me who I am.*

A life once removed. It has felt, for much of these thirty-some-odd years, like a stigma, an unfair weight strapped to my shoulders. Always being held in question. Having that fear of not being whole, not being enough. Living a life neither here nor there, perpetually sitting on a fence and waiting to fall one way or another.

Yet this is what the essence of being a writer is; to remove oneself, to set a story down on a page and shape it from above. I am grateful to language, the place where I went in my greatest confusion, where the question "Who am I?" ricocheted around and around, making me dizzy. Writing became the ladder stacked of words, allowing me to climb hand over hand out of the chaos, out of the confusion. The answer is finally clear. I may be half-and-half of many other things, but I am entirely a writer.

Writers live in that space that is neither here nor there; that is both being and seeing at once. I used to be afraid of that space, for it offered no solid ground. But now I gladly step into it, as if I am letting myself out of the door of a moving airplane. I walk out onto a cloud that has no shape, and it doesn't feel like falling. I can see everything, and I'm flying.

Responding to the Selection

Questions for Discussion

1. What is the meaning of the essay's title? How does it relate to Susan Ito?

2. How would you have responded to the questions and assumptions of strangers that Ito describes in "Hambun-Hambun"?

3. Ito says that "Writers live in that space that is neither here nor there; that is both being and seeing at once." How do you interpret this statement? What impact has writing had on Ito's perception of herself?

4. Have you ever had questions or concerns about your origins? How did you deal with these questions or concerns?

Activities

Writing a Persuasive Essay

1. How important is it for adopted children to be placed with parents who share the child's racial or ethnic background? Take a position on this question and support it in a brief essay.

Writing a Dialogue

2. Ito writes about her conversation with her birth mother about her father and other family issues. Write a dialogue that could have taken place between the two people.

Researching Race and Ethnicity

3. Research the statistical results on race and ethnicity in the 2000 census. Find out whether there was any controversy surrounding the census questions on this topic. Report your findings to the class.

Having a Debate

4. Arrange a class debate on the topic of open adoption and the question of whether an adopted child has a right to learn who his or her birth parents are, even if the parents wish to keep their identity secret.

Before You Read

from *China Men*

Maxine Hong Kingston
Born 1940

"When I wrote these books, I was claiming the English language and the literature to tell our story as Americans."

About Kingston

Maxine Hong Kingston grew up in Stockton, California. Her parents ran a laundry, where Kingston spent much of her time. She flunked kindergarten because she refused to say a word at school. "The other Chinese girls did not talk either, so I knew the silence had to do with being a Chinese girl," she later wrote. Although Kingston continued to feel uncomfortable speaking in English, she became an excellent student and won scholarships to attend college.

Kingston's mother, trained as a doctor in China, was a gifted storyteller. She provided Kingston with much of the material for her first two books, *The Woman Warrior* and *China Men.* In these highly acclaimed memoirs, Kingston offers an imaginative account of her family's experiences in China and the United States.

History and Legends

Kingston's two memoirs, *The Woman Warrior* and *China Men,* were originally supposed to be one book. Kingston decided to separate the men's and women's stories because her male and female ancestors led such different lives. For Kingston, there is no definite line between fiction and nonfiction: she weaves together legends, history, and family stories in her memoirs. The selection you will read is about Kingston's grandfather Ah Goong, who helped build the Transcontinental Railroad in the 1860s. Over ten thousand Chinese were employed by the Central Pacific Railroad to complete the project's western section, which linked up with the eastern section in Utah in 1869. Their work included difficult and dangerous tunneling through the Sierra Mountains.

from China Men

— *Maxine Hong Kingston*

Slow as usual, Ah Goong arrived in the spring; the work had begun in January 1863. The demon that hired him pointed up and up, east above the hills of poppies. His first job was to fell a redwood, which was thick enough to divide into three or four beams. His tree's many branches spread out, each limb like a little tree. He circled the tree. How to attack it? No side looked like the side made to be cut, nor did any ground seem the place for it to fall. He axed for almost a day the side he'd decided would hit the ground. Halfway through, imitating the other lumberjacks, he struck the other side of the tree, above the cut, until he had to run away. The tree swayed and slowly dived to earth, creaking and screeching like a green animal. He was so awed, he forgot what he was supposed to yell. Hardly any branches broke; the tree sprang, bounced, pushed at the ground with its arms. The limbs did not wilt and fold; they were a small forest, which he chopped. The trunk lay like a long red torso; sap ran from its cuts like crying blind eyes. At last it stopped fighting. He set the log across sawhorses to be cured over smoke and in the sun.

He joined a team of men who did not ax one another as they took alternate hits. They blew up the stumps with gunpowder. "It was like uprooting a tooth," Ah Goong said. They also packed gunpowder at the roots of a whole tree. Not at the same time as the bang but before that, the tree rose from the ground. It stood, then plunged with a tearing of veins and muscles. It was big enough to carve a house into. The men measured themselves against the upturned white roots, which looked like claws, a sun with claws. A hundred men stood or sat on the trunk. They lifted a wagon on it and took a photograph. The demons also had their photograph taken.

Because these mountains were made out of gold, Ah Goong rushed over to the root hole to look for gold veins and ore. He selected the shiniest rocks to be assayed later in San Francisco. When he drank from the streams and saw a flash, he dived in like a duck; only sometimes did it turn out to be the sun or the water. The very dirt winked with specks.

He made a dollar a day salary. The lucky men gambled, but he was not good at remembering game rules. The work so far was endurable. "I could take it," he said.

The days were sunny and blue, the wind exhilarating, the heights god-like. At night the stars were diamonds, crystals, silver, snow, ice. He had never seen diamonds. He had never seen snow and ice. As spring turned into summer, and he lay under that sky, he saw the order in the stars. He recognized constellations from China. There—not a cloud but the Silver River, and there, on either side of it—Altair and Vega, the Spinning Girl and the Cowboy, far, far apart. He felt his heart breaking of loneliness at so much blue-black space between star and star. The railroad he was building would not lead him to his family. He jumped out of his bedroll. "Look! Look!" Other China Men jumped awake. An accident? An avalanche? Injun demons? "The stars," he said. "The stars are here." "Another China Man gone out of his mind," men grumbled. "A sleepwalker." "Go to sleep, sleepwalker." "There. And there," said Ah Goong, two hands pointing. "The Spinning Girl and the Cowboy. Don't you see them?" "Homesick China Man," said the China Men and pulled their blankets over their heads. "Didn't you know they were here? I could have told you they were here. Same as in China. Same moon. Why not same stars?" "Nah. Those are American stars."

Pretending that a little girl was listening, he told himself the story about the Spinning Girl and the Cowboy: A long time ago they had visited earth, where they met, fell in love, and married. Instead of growing used to each other, they remained enchanted their entire lifetimes and beyond. They were too happy. They wanted to be doves or two branches of the same tree. When they returned to live in the sky, they were so engrossed in each other that they neglected their work. The Queen of the Sky scratched a river between them with one stroke of her silver hairpin—the river a galaxy in width. The lovers suffered, but she did devote her time to spinning now, and he herded his cow. The King of the Sky took pity on them and ordered that once each year, they be allowed to meet. On the seventh day of the seventh month (which is not the same as July 7), magpies form a bridge for them to cross to each other. The lovers are together for one night of the year. On their parting, the Spinner cries the heavy summer rains.

Ah Goong's discovery of the two stars gave him something to look forward to besides meals and tea breaks. Every night he located Altair and Vega and gauged how much closer they had come since the night before. During the day he watched the magpies, big black and white birds with round bodies like balls with wings; they were a welcome sight, a promise of meetings. He had found two familiars in the wilderness: magpies and stars. On the meeting day, he did not see any magpies nor hear their chattering jaybird cries. Some black and white birds flew overhead, but they may have been American crows or late magpies on their way. Some men laughed at him, but he was not the only China Man to collect water in pots, bottles, and canteens that day. The water would stay fresh forever and cure anything. In ancient days the tutelary gods of the mountains sprinkled corpses with this water and brought them to life. That night, no women to light candles, burn incense, cook special food, Grandfather watched for the convergence and bowed. He saw the two little stars next to Vega—the couple's children. And bridging the Silver River, surely those were black flapping wings of magpies and translucent-winged angels and faeries. Toward morning, he was awakened by rain, and pulled his blankets into his tent.

The next day, the fantailed orange-beaked magpies returned. Altair and Vega were beginning their journeys apart, another year of spinning and herding. Ah Goong had to find something else to look forward to. The Spinning Girl and the Cowboy met and parted six times before the railroad was finished.

When cliffs, sheer drops under impossible overhangs, ended the road, the workers filled the ravines or built bridges over them. They climbed above the site for tunnel or bridge and lowered one another down in wicker baskets made stronger by the lucky words they had painted on four sides. Ah Goong got to be a basketman because he was thin and light. Some basketmen were fifteen-year-old boys. He rode the basket barefoot, so his boots, the kind to stomp snakes with, would not break through the bottom. The basket swung and twirled, and he saw the world sweep underneath him; it was fun in a way, a cold new feeling of doing what had never been done before. Suspended in the quiet sky, he thought all kinds of crazy thoughts, that if a man didn't want to live any more, he could just cut the ropes or, easier, tilt the basket, dip, and never have to worry again. He could spread his arms, and the air would momentarily hold him before he fell past the buzzards, hawks, and eagles, and landed impaled on the tip of a sequoia. This high and he didn't see any gods, no Cowboy, no Spinner. He knelt in the basket though he was not bumping his head against the sky. Through the wickerwork, slivers of depths darted like needles, nothing between him and air but thin rattan. Gusts of wind spun the light basket. "Aiya," said Ah Goong. Winds came up under the basket, bouncing it. Neighboring baskets swung together and parted. He and the man next to him looked at each other's faces. They laughed. They might as well have gone to Malaysia to collect bird nests. Those who had done high work there said it had been worse; the birds screamed and scratched at them. Swinging near the cliff, Ah Goong stood up and grabbed it by a twig. He dug holes, then inserted gunpowder and fuses. He worked neither too fast nor too slow, keeping even with the others. The basketmen signaled one another to light the fuses. He struck match after match and dropped the burnt matches over the sides. At last his fuse caught; he waved, and the men above pulled hand over hand hauling him up, pulleys creaking. The scaffolds stood like a row of gibbets. Gallows trees along a ridge. "Hurry, hurry," he said. Some impatient men clambered up their ropes. Ah Goong ran up the ledge road they'd cleared and watched the explosions, which banged almost synchronously, echoes booming like war. He moved his scaffold to the next section of cliff and went down in the basket again, with bags of dirt, and set the next charge.

This time two men were blown up. One knocked out or killed by the explosion fell silently, the other screaming, his arms and legs struggling. A desire shot out of Ah Goong for an arm long enough to reach down and catch them. Much time passed as they fell like plummets. The shreds of baskets and a cowboy hat skimmed and tacked. The winds that pushed birds off course and against mountains did not carry men. Ah Goong also wished that the conscious man would fall faster and get it over with. His hands gripped the ropes, and it was difficult to let go and get on with the work. "It can't happen twice in a row," the basketmen said the next trip down. "Our chances are very good. The trip after an accident is probably the safest one." They raced to their favorite basket, checked and double-checked the four ropes, yanked the strands, tested the pulleys, oiled them, reminded the pulleymen about the signals, and entered the sky again. . . .

After tunneling into granite for about three years, Ah Goong understood the immovability of the earth. Men change, men die, weather changes, but a mountain is the same as permanence and time. This mountain would have taken no new shape for centuries, ten thousand centuries, the world a still, still place, time unmoving. He worked in the tunnel so long, he learned to see many colors in black. When he stumbled out, he tried to talk about time. "I felt time," he said. "I saw time. I saw world." He tried again, "I saw what's real. I saw time, and it doesn't move. If we break through the mountain, hollow it, time won't have moved anyway. You translators ought to tell the foreigners that."

Summer came again, but after the first summer, he felt less nostalgia at the meeting of the Spinning Girl and the Cowboy. He now knew men who had been in this country for twenty years and thirty years, and the Cowboy's one year away from his lady was no time at all. His own patience was longer. The stars were meeting and would meet again next year, but he would not have seen his family. He joined the others celebrating Souls' Day, the holiday a week later, the fourteenth day of the seventh month. The supply wagons from San Francisco and Sacramento brought watermelon, meat, fish, crab, pressed duck. "There, ghosts, there you are. Come and get it." They displayed the feast complete for a moment before falling to, eating on the dead's behalf.

from China Men

In the third year of pounding granite by hand, a demon invented dynamite. The railroad workers were to test it. They had stopped using gunpowder in the tunnels after avalanches, but the demons said that dynamite was more precise. They watched a scientist demon mix nitrate, sulphate, and glycerine, then flick the yellow oil, which exploded off his fingertips. Sitting in a meadow to watch the dynamite detonated in the open, Ah Goong saw the men in front of him leap impossibly high into the air; then he felt a shove as if from a giant's unseen hand—and he fell backward. The boom broke the mountain silence like fear breaking inside stomach and chest and groin. No one had gotten hurt; they stood up laughing and amazed, looking around at how they had fallen, the pattern of the explosion. Dynamite was much more powerful than gunpowder. Ah Goong had felt a nudge, as if something kind were moving him out of harm's way. "All of a sudden I was sitting next to you." "Aiya. If we had been nearer, it would have killed us." "If we were stiff, it would have gone through us." "A fist." "A hand." "We leapt like acrobats." Next time Ah Goong flattened himself on the ground, and the explosion rolled over him.

He never got used to the blasting; a blast always surprised him. Even when he himself set the fuse and watched it burn, anticipated the explosion, the bang—*bahng* in Chinese—when it came, always startled. It cleaned the crazy words, the crackling, and bingbangs out of his brain. It was like New Year's, when every problem and thought was knocked clean out of him by firecrackers, and he could begin fresh. He couldn't worry during an explosion, which jerked every head to attention. Hills flew up in rocks and dirt. Boulders turned over and over. Sparks, fires, debris, rocks, smoke burst up, not at the same time as the boom (*bum*) but before that— the sound a separate occurrence, not useful as a signal.

The terrain changed immediately. Streams were diverted, rockscapes exposed. Ah Goong found it difficult to remember what land had looked like before an explosion. It was a good thing the dynamite was invented after the Civil War to the east was over.

The dynamite added more accidents and ways of dying, but if it were not used, the railroad would take fifty more years to finish. Nitroglycerine exploded when it was jounced on a horse or dropped. A man who fell with it in his pocket blew himself up into red pieces. Sometimes it combusted merely standing. Human bodies skipped through the air like puppets and made Ah Goong laugh crazily as if the arms and legs would come together again. The smell of burned flesh remained in rocks.

In the tunnels, the men bored holes fifteen to eighteen inches deep with a power drill, stuffed them with hay and dynamite, and imbedded the fuse in sand. Once, for extra pay, Ah Goong ran back in to see why some dynamite had not gone off and hurried back out again; it was just a slow fuse. When the explosion settled, he helped carry two-hundred-, three-hundred-, five-hundred-pound boulders out of the tunnel.

As a boy he had visited a Taoist monastery where there were nine rooms, each a replica of one of the nine hells. Lifesize sculptures of men and women were spitted on turning wheels. Eerie candles under the suffering faces emphasized eyes poked out, tongues pulled, red mouths and eyes, and real hair, eyelashes, and eyebrows. Women were split apart and men dismembered. He could have reached out and touched the sufferers and the implements. He had dug and dynamited his way into one of these hells. "Only here there are eighteen tunnels, not nine, plus all the tracks between them," he said.

One day he came out of the tunnel to find the mountains white, the evergreens and bare trees decorated, white tree sculptures and lace bushes everywhere. The men from snow country called the icicles "ice chopsticks." He sat in his basket and slid down the slopes. The snow covered the gouged land, the broken trees, the tracks, the mud, the campfire ashes, the unburied dead. Streams were stilled in mid-run, the water petrified. That winter he thought it was the task of the human race to quicken the world, blast the freeze, fire it, redden it with blood. He had to change the stupid slowness of one sunrise and one sunset per day. He had to enliven the silent world with sound. "The rock," he tried to tell the others. "The ice." "Time."

The dynamiting loosed blizzards on the men. Ears and toes fell off. Fingers stuck to the cold silver rails. Snowblind men stumbled about with bandannas over their eyes. Ah Goong helped build wood tunnels roofing the track route. Falling ice scrabbled on the roofs. The men stayed under the snow for weeks at a time. Snowslides covered the entrances to the tunnels, which they had to dig out to enter and exit, white tunnels and black tunnels. Ah Goong looked at his gang and thought, If there is an avalanche, these are the people I'll be trapped with, and wondered which ones would share food. A party of snowbound barbarians had eaten the dead.

Cannibals, thought Ah Goong, and looked around. Food was not scarce; the tea man brought whiskey barrels of hot tea, and he warmed his hands and feet, held the teacup to his nose and ears. Someday, he planned, he would buy a chair with metal doors for putting hot coal inside it. The magpies did not abandon him but stayed all winter and searched the snow for food.

The men who died slowly enough to say last words said, "Don't leave me frozen under the snow. Send my body home. Burn it and put the ashes in a tin can. Take the bone jar when you come down the mountain." "When you ride the fire car back to China, tell my descendants to come for me." "Shut up," scolded the hearty men. "We don't want to hear about bone jars and dying." "You're lucky to have a body to bury, not blown to smithereens." "Stupid man to hurt yourself," they bawled out the sick and wounded. How their wives would scold if they brought back deadmen's bones. "Aiya. To be buried here, nowhere." "But this is somewhere," Ah Goong promised. "This is the Gold Mountain. We're marking the land now. The track sections are numbered, and your family will know where we leave you." But he was a crazy man, and they didn't listen to him.

Spring did come, and when the snow melted, it revealed the past year, what had happened, what they had done, where they had worked, the lost tools, the thawing bodies, some standing with tools in hand, the bright rails. "Remember Uncle Long Winded Leong?" "Remember Strong Back Wong?" "Remember Lee Brother?" "And Fong Uncle?" They lost count of the number dead; there is no record of how many died building the railroad. Or maybe it was demons doing the counting and chinamen not worth counting. Whether it was good luck or bad luck, the dead were buried or cairned next to the last section of track they had worked on. "May his ghost not have to toil," they said over graves. (In China a woodcutter ghost chops eternally; people have heard chopping in the snow and in the heat.) "Maybe his ghost will ride the train home." The scientific demons said the transcontinental railroad would connect the West to Cathay. "What if he rides back and forth from Sacramento to New York forever?" "That wouldn't be so bad. I hear the cars will be like houses on wheels." The funerals were short. "No time. No time," said both China Men and demons. The railroad was as straight as they could build it, but no ghosts sat on the tracks; no strange presences haunted the tunnels. The blasts scared ghosts away.

Responding to the Selection ────────

Questions for Discussion

1. Does this selection seem more like a work of fiction or history to you? Explain your answer.

2. Why do you think Ah Goong pays so much attention to the stars?

3. An **external conflict** exists when a character struggles against an outside force. What outside forces does Ah Goong struggle against in this selection?

4. How do the men generally respond to the sight of dying or dead coworkers? Why might they respond in this manner?

5. At the beginning of this essay, Kingston describes how Ah Goong found the stars a familiar and comforting sight in a strange land. Describe a similar experience you have had, in which something familiar reminded you of home when you were away.

Activities

Analyzing Imagery

1. In the selection, Maxine Hong Kingston gives readers a vivid sense of how big things are in the Sierras. Choose a descriptive passage and analyze the techniques she used to convey this impression.

Writing in a Diary

2. Imagine that you are working alongside Ah Goong. Write a diary entry in which you express your feelings about one of the experiences described in the selection.

Researching the Transcontinental Railroad

3. Do research to learn more about the building of the Transcontinental Railroad. Find out why the Central Pacific Railroad decided to employ Chinese immigrants and compare the treatment of Chinese and white laborers. Present your findings to the class.

MEDIA connection

The Iron Road

Web Site

This Web site is about *The Iron Road*, part of *The American Experience*, an award-winning television documentary that aired on the Public Broadcasting System.

http://www.pbs.org

The Iron Road, produced by Neil Goodwin of Peace River Films, is the story of the building of the first railroad link connecting the East to the West.

Even before the Civil War, the nation had been divided. In the West, the rich and expansive territory of California was a continent's-length away from the existing United States. To reach California's fabled gold mines meant months of dangerous sailing around Cape Horn, or traveling 2,000 miles overland across mountains and deserts through Indian territories. Many believed that a railroad to the Pacific would be the key to westward expansion and the future of the country.

. . . In 1862, the Congress passed the first of several Railroad Acts, choosing a route which went from Omaha to Sacramento—much of it an old pioneer trail—and naming the two companies to be responsible for the construction of the railroad: the Central Pacific, building from the West, and the Union Pacific, building from the East.

The Central Pacific was founded by Theodore Judah, a brilliant young civil engineer who found a way to lay tracks across the Sierra Nevada Mountains of California, the traditional stumbling block to a transcontinental railroad. For financing, Judah teamed up with four shrewd Sacramento businessmen—Charley Crocker, Mark Hopkins, Leland Stanford, and Collis Huntington—otherwise known as the "Big Four."

The Union Pacific was run by Thomas C. Durant, who got involved for the glory and the easy money. When the operation began, he was already accepting kickbacks from construction subcontractors. After three years under Durant, the Union Pacific had laid only 40 miles of track. To salvage the fortunes of the Union Pacific, Durant brought in Grenville Dodge, a civil engineer who, during the Civil War, had built railroads so fast they used to say of him, "We don't know where he is, but we can see where he has been."

The real heroes of the railroad, however, were the 20,000 men who labored to build the iron road with their bare hands. Most of the workers were immigrants. The Central Pacific employed almost 10,000 Chinese workers; Union Pacific laborers were mainly from Europe—Irishmen, Germans, Dutch, and Czechoslovakians. Thousands of Civil War veterans also worked on the Union Pacific.

Conditions were harsh for employees of both companies. Union Pacific laborers endured brutal 12-hour shifts, searing summer heat, Indian attacks, and most dangerous of all, the lawless and violent end-of-the-track towns called "hell-on-wheels."

The Central Pacific Chinese crews endured equally long shifts made worse by extremely dangerous conditions: avalanches striking without warning throughout winter—carrying whole crews over the mountainsides—and premature explosions of black powder and nitroglycerine.

"One of the strongest images the Chinese-Americans have of working on the railroad is Chinese workers being hung over cliffs in baskets which they wove themselves," says writer and historian Connie Yu in the film. "They planted charges and had to scramble up the lines if the charges were short, or be pulled up very quickly by their comrades. Then they were lowered down to drill again. But when they were pulled up, frequently the explosions would be right under them."

As the railroad was nearing completion, competition grew between the two companies. There were no settlements between Sacramento and Omaha except for the prosperous Mormon communities of the Salt Lake Valley. It became clear that whichever company got to Salt Lake first could establish a depot and capture the lucrative Salt Lake business. There was no finish line to this race, so the Central Pacific and Union Pacific surveyed and graded right past each other across the high desert of Northern Utah. Congress finally intervened and forced the two companies to agree on a meeting point. They settled on Promontory, Utah, on the north rim of Salt Lake. It was here they finally met on May 10, 1869, six years after beginning the project.

Questions for Discussion

1. How did travelers cross the country before the building of the railroad?

2. What modern development in transportation or communication do you consider comparable to the transcontinental railroad? Explain.

Before You Read

Winterblossom Garden

David Low
Born 1952

"My parents assumed that as long as I ate well, everything in my life would be fine."

About Low

David Low is the son of Chinese immigrants. He grew up in a predominantly German neighborhood in New York City, where his parents owned a Chinese restaurant. Low is a book editor and writer. His stories have appeared in a variety of literary magazines and anthologies.

Business Opportunities

After dealing with harsh immigration restrictions, Chinese Americans faced discriminatory laws that limited their employment opportunities. During the California gold rush—when the West Coast was largely populated by miners and frontiersmen—many Chinese American workers seized the opportunity to work as cooks.

Although the restaurants they opened often served as the anchor for scattered communities of Chinese Americans throughout the West, they also attracted large numbers of non-Chinese patrons. As with many such businesses, these restaurants were often family owned and operated, and were subsequently passed from one generation to the next.

As the popularity of Chinese food spread, restaurant owners could open businesses in areas where there wasn't a large Chinese community. The most common type of Chinese American food is called Cantonese, named after a port city where many early immigrants embarked for the United States. In recent years, other cooking styles such as Szechwan and Hunan have become popular. Diners in the United States are accustomed to ending a Chinese meal with fortune cookies. This dessert was actually invented in the United States; a worker in a San Francisco noodle factory came up with the idea to satisfy tourists.

Winterblossom Garden

— *David Low*

I

I have no photographs of my father. One hot Saturday in June, my camera slung over my shoulder, I take the subway from Greenwich Village to Chinatown. I switch to the M local, which becomes an elevated train after it crosses the Williamsburg Bridge. I am going to Ridgewood, Queens, where I spent my childhood. I sit in a car that is almost empty; I feel the loud rumble of the whole train through the hard seat. Someday, I think, wiping the sweat from my face, they'll tear this el down, as they've torn down the others.

I get off at Fresh Pond Road and walk the five blocks from the station to my parents' restaurant. At the back of the store in the kitchen, I find my father packing an order: white cartons of food fit neatly into a brown paper bag. As the workers chatter in Cantonese, I smell the food cooking: spareribs, chicken lo mein, sweet and pungent pork, won ton soup. My father, who has just turned seventy-three, wears a wrinkled white short-sleeve shirt and a cheap maroon tie, even in this weather. He dabs his face with a handkerchief.

"Do you need money?" he asks in Chinese as he takes the order to the front of the store. I notice that he walks slower than usual. Not that his walk is ever very fast; he usually walks with quiet assurance, a man who knows who he is and where he is going. Other people will just have to wait until he gets there.

"Not this time," I answer in English. I laugh. I haven't borrowed money from him in years but he still asks. My father and I have almost always spoken different languages.

"I want to take your picture, Dad."

"Not now, too busy." He hands the customer the order and rings the cash register.

"It will only take a minute."

He stands reluctantly beneath the green awning in front of the store, next to the gold-painted letters on the window:

Winterblossom Garden

WINTERBLOSSOM GARDEN
CHINESE-AMERICAN RESTAURANT
WE SERVE THE FINEST FOOD
I look through the camera viewfinder.
"Smile," I say.

Instead my father holds his left hand with the crooked pinky on his stomach. I have often wondered about that pinky; is it a souvenir of some street fight in his youth? He wears a jade ring on his index finger. His hair, streaked with gray, is greased down as usual; his face looks a little pale. Most of the day, he remains at the restaurant. I snap the shutter.

"Go see your mother," he says slowly in English.

According to my mother, in 1929 my father entered this country illegally by jumping off the boat as it neared Ellis Island and swimming to Hoboken, New Jersey; there he managed to board a train to New York, even though he knew no English and had not one American cent in his pockets. Whether or not the story is true, I like to imagine my father hiding in the washroom on the train, dripping wet with fatigue and feeling triumphant. Now he was in America, where anything could happen. He found a job scooping ice cream at a dance hall in Chinatown. My mother claims that before he married her, he liked to gamble his nights away and drink with scandalous women. After two years in this country, he opened his restaurant with money he had borrowed from friends in Chinatown who already ran their own businesses. My father chose Ridgewood for the store's location because he mistook the community's name for "Richwood." In such a lucky place, he told my mother, his restaurant was sure to succeed.

When I was growing up, my parents spent most of their days in Winterblossom Garden. Before going home after school, I would stop at the restaurant. The walls then were a hideous pale green with red numbers painted in Chinese characters and Roman numerals above the side booths. In days of warm weather huge fans whirred from the ceiling. My mother would sit at a table in the back where she would make egg rolls. She began by placing generous handfuls of meat-and-cabbage filling on squares of thin white dough. Then she delicately folded up each piece of dough, checking to make sure the filling was totally sealed inside, like a mummy wrapped in bandages. Finally, with a small brush she spread beaten egg on the outside of each white roll. As I watched her steadily produce a tray of these uncooked creations, she never asked me about school; she was more concerned that my shirt was sticking out of my pants or that my hair was disheveled.

Winterblossom Garden

"Are you hungry?" my mother would ask in English. Although my parents had agreed to speak only Chinese in my presence, she often broke this rule when my father wasn't in the same room. Whether I wanted to eat or not, I was sent into the kitchen, where my father would repeat my mother's question. Then without waiting for an answer, he would prepare for me a bowl of beef with snow peas or a small portion of steamed fish. My parents assumed that as long as I ate well, everything in my life would be fine. If I said "Hello" or "Thank you" in Chinese, I was allowed to choose whatever dish I liked; often I ordered a hot turkey sandwich. I liked the taste of burnt rice soaked in tea.

I would wait an hour or so for my mother to walk home with me. During that time, I would go to the front of the store, put a dime in the jukebox and press the buttons for a currently popular song. It might be D3: "Bye Bye, Love." Then I would lean on the back of the bench where customers waited for takeouts; I would stare out the large window that faced the street. The world outside seemed vast, hostile and often sad.

Across the way, I could see Rosa's Italian Bakery, the Western Union office and Von Ronn's soda fountain. Why didn't we live in Chinatown? I wondered. Or San Francisco? In a neighborhood that was predominantly German, I had no Chinese friends. No matter how many bottles of Coca-Cola I drank, I would still be different from the others. They were fond of calling me "Skinny Chink" when I won games of stoop ball. I wanted to have blond curly hair and blue eyes; I didn't understand why my father didn't have a ranch like the rugged cowboys on television.

Now Winterblossom Garden has wood paneling on the walls, Formica tables and aluminum Roman numerals over the mock-leather booths. Several years ago, when the ceiling was lowered, the whirring fans were removed; a huge air-conditioning unit was installed. The jukebox has been replaced by Muzak. My mother no longer makes the egg rolls; my father hires enough help to do that.

Some things remain the same. My father has made few changes in the menu, except for the prices; the steady customers know they can always have the combination plates. In a glass case near the cash register, cardboard boxes overflow with bags of fortune cookies and almond candies that my father gives away free to children. The first dollar bill my parents ever made hangs framed on the wall above the register. Next to that dollar, a picture of my parents taken twenty years ago recalls a time when they were raising four children at once, paying mortgages and putting in the bank every cent that didn't go toward bills. Although it was a hard time for them, my mother's face is radiant, as if she has just won the top prize at a beauty pageant; she wears a flower-print dress with a large white collar. My father has on a suit with wide lapels that was tailored in Chinatown; he is smiling a rare smile.

My parents have a small brick house set apart from the other buildings on the block. Most of their neighbors have lived in Ridgewood all their lives. As I ring the bell and wait for my mother to answer, I notice that the maple tree in front of the house has died. All that is left is a gray ghost; bare branches lie in the gutter. If I took a picture of this tree, I think, the printed image would resemble a negative.

"The gas man killed it when they tore up the street," my mother says. She watches television as she lies back on the gold sofa like a queen, her head resting against a pillow. A documentary about wildlife in Africa is on the screen; gazelles dance across a dusty plain. My mother likes soap operas but they aren't shown on weekends. In the evenings she will watch almost anything except news specials and police melodramas.

"Why don't you get a new tree planted?"

"We would have to get a permit," she answers. "The sidewalk belongs to the city. Then we would have to pay for the tree."

"It would be worth it," I say. "Doesn't it bother you, seeing a dead tree every day? You should find someone to cut it down."

My mother does not answer. She has fallen asleep. These days she can doze off almost as soon as her head touches the pillow. Six years ago she had a nervous breakdown. When she came home from the hospital she needed to take naps in the afternoon. Soon the naps became a permanent refuge, a way to forget her loneliness for an hour or two. She no longer needed to work in the store. Three of her children were married. I was away at art school and planned to live on my own when I graduated.

"I have never felt at home in America," my mother once told me.

Now as she lies there, I wonder if she is dreaming. I would like her to tell me her darkest dream. Although we speak the same language, there has always been an ocean between us. She does not wish to know what I think alone at night, what I see of the world with my camera.

My mother pours two cups of tea from the porcelain teapot that has always been in its wicker basket on the kitchen table. On the sides of the teapot, a maiden dressed in a jade-green gown visits a bearded emperor at his palace near the sky. The maiden waves a vermilion fan.

"I bet you still don't know how to cook," my mother says. She places a plate of steamed roast pork buns before me.

"Mom, I'm not hungry."

Winterblossom Garden

"If you don't eat more, you will get sick."

I take a bun from the plate, but it is too hot. My mother hands me a napkin so I can put the bun down. Then she peels a banana in front of me.

"I'm not obsessed with food like you," I say.

"What's wrong with eating?"

She looks at me as she takes a big bite of the banana.

"I'm going to have a photography show at the end of the summer."

"Are you still taking pictures of old buildings falling down? How ugly! Why don't you take happier pictures?"

"I thought you would want to come," I answer. "It's not easy to get a gallery."

"If you were married," she says, her voice becoming unusually soft, "you would take better pictures. You would be happy."

"I don't know what you mean. Why do you think getting married will make me happy?"

My mother looks at me as if I have spoken in Serbo-Croatian. She always gives me this look when I say something she does not want to hear. She finishes the banana; then she puts the plate of food away. Soon she stands at the sink, turns on the hot water and washes dishes. My mother learned long ago that silence has a power of its own.

She takes out a blue cookie tin from the dining-room cabinet. Inside this tin, my mother keeps her favorite photographs. Whenever I am ready to leave, my mother brings it to the living room and opens it on the coffee table. She knows I cannot resist looking at these pictures again; I will sit down next to her on the sofa for at least another hour. Besides the portraits of the family, my mother has images of people I have never met: her father, who owned a poultry store on Pell Street and didn't get a chance to return to China before he died; my father's younger sister, who still runs a pharmacy in Rio de Janeiro (she sends the family an annual supply of cough drops); my mother's cousin Kay, who died at thirty, a year after she came to New York from Hong Kong. Although my mother has a story to tell for each photograph, she refuses to speak about Kay, as if the mere mention of her name will bring back her ghost to haunt us all.

My mother always manages to find a picture I have not seen before; suddenly I discover I have a relative who is a mortician in Vancouver. I pick up a portrait of Uncle Lao-Hu, a silver-haired man with a goatee who owned a curio shop on Mott Street until he retired last year and moved to Hawaii. In a color print, he stands in the doorway of his store, holding a bamboo Moon Man in front of him, as if it were a bowling trophy. The statue, which is actually two feet tall, has a staff in its left hand, while its right palm balances a peach, a sign of long life. The top of the Moon

Winterblossom Garden

Man's head protrudes in the shape of an eggplant; my mother believes that such a head contains an endless wealth of wisdom.

"Your Uncle Lao-Hu is a wise man, too," my mother says, "except when he's in love. When he still owned the store, he fell in love with his women customers all the time. He was always losing money because he gave away his merchandise to any woman who smiled at him."

I see my uncle's generous arms full of gifts: a silver Buddha, an ivory dragon, a pair of emerald chopsticks.

"These women confused him," she adds. "That's what happens when a Chinese man doesn't get married."

My mother shakes her head and sighs.

"In his last letter, Lao-Hu invited me to visit him in Honolulu. Your father refuses to leave the store."

"Why don't you go anyway?"

"I can't leave your father alone." She stares at the pictures scattered on the coffee table.

"Mom, why don't you do something for yourself? I thought you were going to start taking English lessons."

"Your father thinks it would be a waste of time."

While my mother puts the cookie tin away, I stand up to stretch my legs. I gaze at a photograph that hangs on the wall above the sofa: my parents' wedding picture. My mother was matched to my father; she claims that if her own father had been able to repay the money that Dad spent to bring her to America, she might never have married him at all. In the wedding picture she wears a stunned expression. She is dressed in a luminous gown of ruffles and lace; the train spirals at her feet. As she clutches a bouquet tightly against her stomach, she might be asking, "What am I doing? Who is this man?" My father's face is thinner than it is now. His tuxedo is too small for him; the flower in his lapel droops. He hides his hand with the crooked pinky behind his back.

I have never been sure if my parents really love each other. I have only seen them kiss at their children's weddings. They never touch each other in public. When I was little, I often thought they went to sleep in the clothes they wore to work.

Before I leave, my mother asks me to take her picture. Unlike my father, she likes to pose for photographs as much as possible. When her children still lived at home, she would leave snapshots of herself all around the house; we could not forget her, no matter how hard we tried.

She changes her blouse, combs her hair and redoes her eyebrows. Then I follow her out the back door into the garden, where she kneels down next to the rose bush. She touches one of the yellow roses.

Winterblossom Garden

"Why don't you sit on the front steps?" I ask as I peer through the viewfinder. "It will be more natural."

"No," she says firmly. "Take the picture now."

She smiles without opening her mouth. I see for the first time that she has put on a pair of dangling gold earrings. Her face has grown round as the moon with the years. She has developed wrinkles under the eyes, but like my father, she hardly shows her age. For the past ten years, she has been fifty-one. Everyone needs a fantasy to help them stay alive: my mother believes she is perpetually beautiful, even if my father has not complimented her in years.

After I snap the shutter, she plucks a rose.

As we enter the kitchen through the back door, I can hear my father's voice from the next room.

"Who's he talking to?" I ask.

"He's talking to the goldfish," she answers. "I have to live with this man."

My father walks in, carrying a tiny can of fish food.

"You want a girlfriend?" he asks, out of nowhere. "My friend has a nice daughter. She knows how to cook Chinese food."

"Dad, she sounds perfect for you."

"She likes to stay home," my mother adds. "She went to college and reads books like you."

"I'll see you next year," I say.

That evening in the darkroom at my apartment, I develop and print my parents' portraits. I hang the pictures side by side to dry on a clothesline in the bathroom. As I feel my parents' eyes staring at me, I turn away. Their faces look unfamiliar in the fluorescent light.

II

At the beginning of July my mother calls me at work.

"Do you think you can take off next Monday morning?" she asks.

"Why?"

"Your father has to go to the hospital for some tests. He looks awful."

We sit in the back of a taxi on the way to a hospital in Forest Hills. I am sandwiched between my mother and father. The skin of my father's face is pale yellow. During the past few weeks he has lost fifteen pounds; his wrinkled suit is baggy around the waist. My mother sleeps with her head tilted to one side until the taxi hits a bump on the road. She wakes up startled, as if afraid she has missed a stop on the train.

"Don't worry," my father says weakly. He squints as he turns his head toward the window. "The doctors will give me pills. Everything will be fine."

Winterblossom Garden

"Don't say anything," my mother says. "Too much talk will bring bad luck."

My father takes two crumpled dollar bills from his jacket and places them in my hand.

"For the movies," he says. I smile, without mentioning it costs more to go to a film these days.

My mother opens her handbag and takes out a compact. She has forgotten to put on her lipstick.

The hospital waiting room has beige walls. My mother and I follow my father as he makes his way slowly to a row of seats near an open window.

"Fresh air is important," he used to remind me on a sunny day when I would read a book in bed. Now after we sit down, he keeps quiet. I hear the sound of plates clattering from the coffee shop in the next room.

"Does anyone want some breakfast?" I ask.

"Your father can't eat anything before the tests," my mother warns. "What about you?"

"I'm not hungry," she says.

My father reaches over to take my hand in his. He considers my palm.

"Very, very lucky," he says. "You will have lots of money."

I laugh. "You've been saying that ever since I was born."

He puts on his glasses crookedly and touches a curved line near the top of my palm.

"Be patient," he says.

My mother rises suddenly.

"Why are they making us wait so long? Do you think they forgot us?"

While she walks over to speak to a nurse at the reception desk, my father leans toward me.

"Remember to take care of your mother."

The doctors discover that my father has stomach cancer. They decide to operate immediately. According to them, my father has already lost so much blood that it is a miracle he is still alive.

The week of my father's operation, I sleep at my parents' house. My mother has kept my bedroom on the second floor the way it was before I moved out. A square room, it gets the afternoon light. Dust covers the top of my old bookcase. The first night I stay over I find a pinhole camera on a shelf in the closet; I made it when I was twelve from a cylindrical Quaker Oats box. When I lie back on the yellow comforter that covers my bed, I see the crack in the ceiling that I once called the Yangtze River, the highway for tea merchants and vagabonds.

Winterblossom Garden

At night I help my mother close the restaurant. I do what she and my father have done together for the past forty-three years. At ten o'clock I turn off the illuminated white sign above the front entrance. After all the customers leave and the last waiter says goodbye, I lock the front door and flip over the sign that says "Closed." Then I shut off the radio and the back lights. While I refill the glass case with bottles of duck sauce and packs of cigarettes, my mother empties the cash register. She puts all the money in white cartons and packs them in brown paper bags. My father thought up that idea long ago.

In the past when they have walked the three blocks home, they have given the appearance of carrying bags of food. The one time my father was attacked by three teenagers, my mother was sick in bed. My father scared the kids off by pretending he knew kung fu. When he got home, he showed me his swollen left hand and smiled.

"Don't tell your mother."

On the second night we walk home together, my mother says, "I could never run the restaurant alone. I would have to sell it. I have four children and no one wants it."

I say nothing, unwilling to start an argument.

Later my mother and I eat Jell-O in the kitchen. A cool breeze blows through the window.

"Maybe I will sleep tonight," my mother says. She walks out to the back porch to sit on one of the two folding chairs. My bedroom is right above the porch; as a child I used to hear my parents talking late into the night, their paper fans rustling.

After reading a while in the living room, I go upstairs to take a shower. When I am finished, I hear my mother calling my name from downstairs.

I find her dressed in her bathrobe, opening the dining-room cabinet.

"Someone has stolen the money," she says. She walks nervously into the living room and looks under the lamp table.

"What are you talking about?" I ask.

"Maybe we should call the police," she suggests. "I can't find the money we brought home tonight."

She starts to pick up the phone.

"Wait. Have you checked everywhere? Where do you usually put it?"

"I thought I locked it in your father's closet but it isn't there."

"I'll look around," I say. "Why don't you go back to sleep?"

She lies back on the sofa.

"How can I sleep?" she asks. "I told your father a long time ago to sell the restaurant but he wouldn't listen."

Winterblossom Garden

I search the first floor. I look in the shoe closet, behind the television, underneath the dining-room table, in the clothes hamper. Finally after examining all the kitchen cupboards without any luck, I open the refrigerator to take out something to drink. The three cartons of money are on the second shelf, next to the mayonnaise and the strawberry jam.

When I bring the cartons to the living room, my mother sits up on the sofa, amazed.

"Well," she says, "how did they ever get *there?*"

She opens one of them. The crisp dollar bills inside are cold as ice.

The next day I talk on the telephone to my father's physician. He informs me that the doctors have succeeded in removing the malignancy before it has spread. My father will remain in intensive care for at least a week.

In the kitchen my mother irons a tablecloth.

"The doctors are impressed by Dad's willpower, considering his age," I tell her.

"A fortune teller on East Broadway told him that he will live to be a hundred," she says.

That night I dream that I am standing at the entrance to Winterblossom Garden. A taxi stops in front of the store. My father jumps out, dressed in a bathrobe and slippers.

"I'm almost all better," he tells me. "I want to see how the business is doing without me."

In a month my father is ready to come home. My sister Elizabeth, the oldest child, picks him up at the hospital. At the house the whole family waits for him.

When Elizabeth's car arrives my mother and I are already standing on the front steps. My sister walks around the car to open my father's door. He cannot get out by himself. My sister offers him a hand but as he reaches out to grab it, he misses and falls back in his seat.

Finally my sister helps him stand up, his back a little stooped. While my mother remains on the steps, I run to give a hand.

My father does not fight our help. His skin is dry and pale but no longer yellow. As he walks forward, staring at his feet, I feel his whole body shaking against mine. Only now, as he leans his weight on my arm, do I begin to understand how easily my father might have died. He seems light as a sparrow.

When we reach the front steps, my father raises his head to look at my mother. She stares at him a minute, then turns away to open the door. Soon my sister and I are leading him to the living-room sofa,

Winterblossom Garden

where we help him lie back. My mother has a pillow and a blanket ready. She sits down on the coffee table in front of him. I watch them hold each other's hands.

III

At the beginning of September my photography exhibit opens at a cooperative gallery on West Thirteenth Street. I have chosen to hang only a dozen pictures, not much to show for ten years of work. About sixty people come to the opening, more than I expected; I watch them from a corner of the room, now and then overhearing a conversation I would like to ignore.

After an hour I decide I have stayed too long. As I walk around the gallery, hunting for a telephone, I see my parents across the room. My father calls out my name in Chinese; he has gained back all his weight and appears to be in better shape than many of the people around him. As I make my way toward my parents, I hear him talking loudly in bad English to a short young woman who stares at one of my portraits.

"That's my wife," he says. "If you like it, you should buy it."

"Maybe I will," the young woman says. She points to another photograph. "Isn't that you?"

My father laughs. "No, that's my brother."

My mother hands me a brown paper bag.

"Left over from dinner," she tells me. "You didn't tell me you were going to show my picture. It's the best one in the show."

I take my parents for a personal tour.

"Who is that?" my father asks. He stops at a photograph of a naked woman covered from the waist down by a pile of leaves as she sits in the middle of a forest.

"She's a professional model," I lie.

"She needs to gain some weight," my mother says.

A few weeks after my show has closed, I have lunch with my parents at the restaurant. After we finish our meal, my father walks into the kitchen to scoop ice cream for dessert. My mother opens her handbag. She takes out a worn manila envelope and hands it to me across the table.

"I found this in a box while I was cleaning the house," she says. "I want you to have it."

Inside the envelope, I find a portrait of my father, taken when he was still a young man. He does not smile, but his eyes shine like wet black marbles. He wears a polka-dot tie; a plaid handkerchief hangs out of the front pocket of his suit jacket. My father has never cared about his clothes matching. Even when he was young, he liked to grease down his hair with brilliantine.

Winterblossom Garden

"Your father's cousin was a doctor in Hong Kong," my mother tells me. "After my eighteenth birthday, he came to my parents' house and showed them this picture. He said your father would make the perfect husband because he was handsome and very smart. Grandma gave me the picture before I got on the boat to America."

"I'll have it framed right away."

My father returns with three dishes of chocolate ice cream balanced on a silver tray.

"You want to work here?" he asks me.

"Your father wants to sell the business next year," my mother says. "He feels too old to run a restaurant."

"I'd just lose money," I say. "Besides, Dad, you're not old."

He does not join us for dessert. Instead, he dips his napkin in a glass of water and starts to wipe the table. I watch his dish of ice cream melt.

When I am ready to leave, my parents walk me to the door.

"Next time, I'll take you uptown to see a movie," I say as we step outside.

"Radio City?" my father asks.

"They don't show movies there now," my mother reminds him.

"I'll cook dinner for you at my apartment."

My father laughs.

"We'll eat out," my mother suggests.

My parents wait in front of Winterblossom Garden until I reach the end of the block. I turn and wave. With her heels on, my mother is the same height as my father. She waves back for both of them. I would like to take their picture, but I forgot to bring my camera.

Responding to the Selection

Questions for Discussion

1. What thoughts went through your mind as you finished reading this essay?
2. **Foreshadowing** is the use of clues to prepare readers for events that will happen in a literary work. How does Low foreshadow his father's illness in the first scene? In a later scene?
3. What circumstances in the mother's life may have led to her nervous breakdown?
4. On page 36 Low says, "I have never been sure if my parents really love each other." Do you think that this uncertainty is resolved by the end of the essay? Explain.
5. In the essay, Low expresses views that conflict with those of his parents. What kinds of differences would you say are most likely to occur between immigrants and their children? Why?

Activities

Writing a Paragraph

1. Do you think that Low's relationship with his parents changes during the period he describes in the essay? Write a paragraph in response to this question.

Writing a Dialogue

2. Write a dialogue between Low's mother and the cousin who convinces her to marry Low's father.

Sharing Recipes

3. Find a recipe for your favorite Chinese dish and share it with the class.

Focus on . . .
Angel Island

The Angel Island Immigration Station opened in 1910 to handle people entering the United States from Pacific routes. Located in San Francisco Bay, it was often compared to Ellis Island in New York harbor, which welcomed immigrants from Europe. Most immigrants processed through Angel Island were Chinese or other Asians, and most were detained for days or months. Some were detained nearly two years. For them, it was more of a prison than a welcoming center. "When we arrived," said one immigrant, "they locked us up like criminals in compartments like the cages in the zoo."

The Chinese Exclusion Act of 1882 was supposed to solve the "problem" of Chinese immigration. Congress declared that only relatives of Chinese American citizens—and there were few of those—could enter the country. However, this loophole became important after the San Francisco Earthquake of 1906. Many Chinese residents claimed that their citizenship papers were among those destroyed in the city's records. Some took the opportunity to bring over wives and children. Others, in exchange for a fee, helped strangers come to the United States by falsely testifying that they were relatives. Angel Island was designed to weed out these "paper sons" and "paper daughters."

Officials interrogated Chinese arrivals at great length, asking questions such as "How many steps are in your house in China?" The same questions were posed separately to all relatives. If their answers did not match closely, then the arrivals were deported. To pass this examination, paper sons would study "coaching papers" full of family information. Because the questions were so detailed, even genuine relatives relied on coaching papers. Immigrants could also be deported for having fairly common diseases. The least fortunate immigrants of all never left Angel Island, having chosen suicide.

As they waited for a decision, immigrants lived in crowded and unsanitary wooden barracks. Families had to be split up because men were isolated from women. Each detention room might house a hundred people, with bunks stacked three high. Immigrants could only leave the rooms for meals, interrogation sessions, and exercise periods. The facility was finally closed in 1940 after one of its buildings burned down. Three years later, Congress passed laws that made it easier for Chinese to come here. Angel Island is now a popular tourist destination, where visitors can tour restored detention buildings and learn about immigration history. There, visitors can still see on the barracks walls the poems that immigrants wrote about their hopes and fears, as they waited to learn their fates in "Gold Mountain," their name for California.

Linking to . . .
• Think about how the experience of staying on Angel Island affected the lives of people in the Chinese American community.

Before You Read

The World of Our Grandmothers

Connie Young Yu
Born 1941

"I needed . . . to put our history back in its place in American history."

About Yu

Connie Young Yu was raised mainly in San Francisco, where her father ran a soy sauce company. Her grandparents lived with the family, and they also had frequent visits from elderly men who lacked wives because of immigration restrictions. This contact with older people helped Yu gain a strong sense of her Chinese heritage.

While raising three children, Yu began to write short articles for Asian American publications. After she published an article about Chinese railroad workers in a San Francisco newspaper, she became committed to uncovering the Chinese American history that was missing from textbooks. In addition to her historical work, Yu writes poetry and fiction. She is one of the founders of Asian Americans for Community Involvement, an organization that advocates social justice. Yu is also devoted to the ancient sport of fencing; she has taught it for many years.

Immigration Law

In "The World of Our Grandmothers," Yu discusses how her ancestors were affected by immigration laws. As the United States economy deteriorated during the 1870s, Chinese immigrants became scapegoats for rising unemployment. Congress passed the Chinese Exclusion Act of 1882 to choke off the supply of Chinese labor. Under the act, only Chinese merchants, teachers, students, travelers, and relatives of Chinese American citizens were allowed into the United States. Any Chinese resident who left the country needed a special permit to reenter. The act, which remained in effect until 1943, also made it impossible for Chinese immigrants to gain U.S. citizenship. Additional restrictions were placed on the Chinese and other Asian ethnic groups by the Immigration Act of 1924.

The World of Our Grandmothers

— *Connie Young Yu*

In Asian America there are two kinds of history. The first is what is written about us in various old volumes on immigrants and echoed in textbooks, and the second is our own oral history, what we learn in the family chain of generations. We are writing this oral history ourselves. But as we research the factual background of our story, we face the dilemma of finding sources. Worse than burning the books is not being included in the record at all, and in American history—traditionally viewed from the white male perspective—minority women have been virtually ignored. Certainly the accomplishments and struggles of early Chinese immigrants, men as well as women, have been obscured.

Yet for a period in the development of the West, Chinese immigration was a focus of prolonged political and social debate and a subject of daily news. When I first began searching into the background of my people, I read this nineteenth-century material with curious excitement, grateful for any information on Chinese immigration.

Looking for the history of Chinese pioneer women, I began with the first glimpses of Chinese in America—newspaper accounts found in bound volumes of the *Alta California* in the basement of a university library. For Chinese workers, survival in the hostile and chaotic world of Gum San, or Gold Mountain, as California was called by Chinese immigrants, was perilous and a constant struggle, leaving little time or inclination for reflection or diary writing. So for a look into the everyday life of early arrivals from China, we have only the impressions of white reporters on which to depend.

The newspapers told of the comings and goings of "Chinamen," their mining activities, new Chinese settlements, their murders by claim-jumpers, and assaults by whites in the city. An item from 17 August 1855 reported a "disgraceful outrage": Mr. Ho Alum was setting his watch under a street clock when a man called Thomas Field walked up and deliberately dashed the time-piece to the pavement. "Such unprovoked assaults upon unoffending Chinamen are not of rare occurrence. . . ." On the same day the paper also reported the suicide of a Chinese prostitute. In this item no name, details, or commentary were given, only a stark announcement. We can imagine the tragic story behind it: the short miserable life of a young girl sold into slavery by her impoverished parents and taken to Gum San to be a prostitute in a society of single men.

An early history of this period, *Lights and Shades in San Francisco* by B. E. Lloyd (1878), devoted ten chapters to the life of California Chinese, describing in detail "the subjects of the Celestial Kingdom." Chinese women, however, are relegated to a single paragraph:

> Females are little better than slaves. They are looked upon as merchantable property, and are bought and sold like any other article of traffic, though their value is not generally great. A Chinese woman never gains any distinction until after death. . . . Considering the humble position the women occupy in China, and the hard life they therefore lead, it would perhaps be better (certainly more merciful) were they all slain in infancy, and better still, were they never born.

Public opinion, inflamed by lurid stories of Chinese slave girls, agreed with this odious commentary. The only Chinese women whose existence American society acknowledged were the prostitutes who lived miserable and usually short lives. Senate hearings on Chinese immigration in 1876 resounded with harangues about prostitutes and slave girls corrupting the morals of young white boys. "The Chinese race is debauched," claimed one lawyer arguing for the passage of the Chinese Exclusion Law: "They bring no decent women with them." This stigma on the Chinese immigrant woman remained for many decades, causing unnecessary hardship for countless wives, daughters, and slave girls.

Chinese American society finally established itself as families appeared, just as they did in the white society of the forty-niners who arrived from the East Coast without bringing "decent women" with them. Despite American laws intended to prevent the "settlement" of Chinese, Chinese women did make the journey and endured the isolation and hostility, braving it for future generations here.

Even though Chinese working men were excluded from most facets of American society and their lives were left unrecorded, their labors bespoke their existence—completed railroads, reclaimed lands, and a myriad of new industries. The evidence of women's lives seems less tangible. Perhaps

The World *of Our* Grandmothers

the record of their struggles to immigrate and overcome discriminatory barriers is their greatest legacy. Tracing that record therefore becomes a means of recovering our history.

Our grandmothers are our historical links. As a fourth-generation Chinese American on my mother's side, and a third-generation on my father's, I grew up hearing stories about ancestors coming from China and going back and returning again. Both of my grandmothers, like so many others, spent a lot of time waiting in China.

My father's parents lived with us when I was growing up, and through them I absorbed a village culture and the heritage of my pioneer Chinese family. In the kitchen my grandmother told repeated stories of coming to America after waiting for her husband to send for her. (It took sixteen years before Grandfather could attain the status of merchant and only then arrange for her passage to this country.) She also told stories from the village about bandits, festivals, and incidents showing the tyranny of tradition. For example, Grandma was forbidden by her mother-in-law to return to her own village to visit her mother: A married woman belonged solely within the boundaries of her husband's world.

Sometimes I was too young to understand or didn't listen, so my mother—who knew all the stories by heart—told me those stories again later. We heard over and over how lucky Grandpa was to have come to America when he was eleven—just one year before the gate was shut by the exclusion law banning Chinese laborers. Grandpa told of his many jobs washing dishes, making bricks, and working on a strawberry farm. Once, while walking outside Chinatown, he was stoned by a group of whites and ran so fast he lost his cap. Grandma had this story to tell of her anger and frustration: "While I was waiting in the immigration shed, Grandpa sent in a box of *dim sum*. I was still waiting to be released. I would have jumped in the ocean if they decided to deport me." A woman in her position was quite helpless, but she still had her pride and was not easily pacified. "I threw the box of *dim sum* out the window."

Such was the kind of history I absorbed. I regret deeply that I was too young to have asked the questions about the past that I now want answered; all my grandparents are now gone. But I have another chance to recover some history from my mother's side. Family papers, photographs, old trunks that have traveled across the ocean several times filled with clothes, letters, and mementos provide a documentary on our immigration. My mother—and some of my grandmother's younger contemporaries—fill in the narrative.

A year before the Joint Special Committee of Congress to investigate Chinese immigration met in San Francisco in 1876, my great-grandmother,

The World *of Our* Grandmothers

Chin Shee, arrived to join her husband, Lee Wong Sang, who had come to America a decade earlier to work on the transcontinental railroad. Chin Shee arrived with two brides who had never seen their husbands. Like her own, their marriages had been arranged by their families. The voyage on the clipper ship was rough and long. Seasick for weeks, rolling back and forth as she lay in the bunk, Chin Shee lost most of her hair. The two other women laughed, "Some newlywed you'll make!" But the joke was on them as they mistakenly set off with the wrong husbands, the situation realized only when one man looked at his bride's normal-sized feet and exclaimed, "But the letter described my bride as having bound feet!" Chin Shee did not have her feet bound because she came from a peasant family. But her husband did not seem to care about that nor that the back of her head was practically bald. He felt himself fortunate just to be able to bring his wife to Gum San.

Chin Shee bore six children in San Francisco, where her husband assisted in the deliveries. They all lived in the rear of their grocery store, which also exported dried shrimp and seaweed to China. Great-Grandma seldom left home; she could count the number of times she went out. She and other Chinese wives did not appear in the streets even for holidays, lest they be looked upon as prostitutes. She took care of the children, made special cakes to sell on feast days, and helped with her husband's work. A photograph of her shows a middle-aged woman with a kindly, but careworn face, wearing a very regal brocade gown and a long, beaded necklace. As a respectable, well-to-do Chinese wife in America, married to a successful Chinatown merchant, with children who were by birthright American citizens, she was a rarity in her day. (In contrast, in 1884 Mrs. Jew Lim, the wife of a laborer, sued in federal court to be allowed to join her husband, but was denied and deported.)

In 1890 there were only 3,868 Chinese women among 103,620 Chinese males in America. Men such as Lee Yoke Suey, my mother's father, went to China to marry. He was one of Chin Shee's sons born in the rear of the grocery store, and he grew up learning the import and export trade. As a Gum San merchant, he had money and status and was able to build a fine house in Toishan. Not only did he acquire a wife but also two concubines. When his wife became very ill after giving birth to an infant who soon died, Yoke Suey was warned by his father that she was too weak to return to America with him. Reminding Yoke Suey of the harsh life in Gum San, he advised his son to get a new wife.

In the town of Foshan, not far from my grandfather's village, lived a girl who was recommended to him by his father's friend. Extremely capable, bright, and with some education, she was from a once prosperous family that had fallen on hard times. A plague had killed her two older brothers, and her heartbroken mother died soon afterwards. She was an

The World *of Our* Grandmothers

excellent cook and took good care of her father, an herb doctor. Her name was Jeong Hing Tong, and she was pretty, with bound feet only three and a half inches long. Her father rejected the offer of the Lee family at first; he did not want his daughter to be a concubine, even to a wealthy Gum San merchant. But the elder Lee assured him this girl would be the wife, the one who would go to America with her husband.

So my maternal grandmother, bride of sixteen, went with my grandfather, then twenty-six, to live in America. Once in San Francisco, Grandmother lived a life of confinement, as did her mother-in-law before her. When she went out, even in Chinatown, she was ridiculed for her bound feet. People called out mockingly to her, *"Jhat!"* meaning bound. She tried to unbind her feet by soaking them every night and putting a heavy weight on each foot. But she was already a grown woman, and her feet were permanently stunted, the arches bent and the toes crippled. It was hard for her to stand for long periods of time, and she frequently had to sit on the floor to do her chores. My mother comments: "Tradition makes life so hard. My father traveled all over the world. There were stamps all over his passport—London, Paris—and stickers all over his suitcases, but his wife could not go into the street by herself."

Their first child was a girl, and on the morning of her month-old "red eggs and ginger party" the earth shook 8.3 on the Richter scale. Everyone in San Francisco, even Chinese women, poured out into the streets. My grandmother, babe in arms, managed to get a ride to Golden Gate Park on a horse-drawn wagon. Two other Chinese women who survived the earthquake recall the shock of suddenly being out in the street milling with thousands of people. The elderly goldsmith in a dimly lit Chinatown store had a twinkle in his eye when I asked him about the scene after the quake. "We all stared at the women because we so seldom saw them in the streets." The city was soon in flames. "We could feel the fire on our faces," recalls Lily Sung, who was seven at the time, "but my sister and I couldn't walk very fast because we had to escort this lady, our neighbor, who had bound feet." The poor woman kept stumbling and falling on the rubble and debris during their long walk to the Oakland-bound ferry.

That devastating natural disaster forced some modernity on the San Francisco Chinese community. Women had to adjust to the emergency and makeshift living conditions and had to work right alongside the men. Life in America, my grandmother found, was indeed rugged and unpredictable.

As the city began to rebuild itself, she proceeded to raise a large family, bearing four more children. The only school in San Francisco admitting Chinese was the Oriental school in Chinatown. But her husband felt, as did most men of his class, that the only way his children could get a good education was for the family to return to China. So they lived in China and my grandfather traveled back and forth to the United States for his trade business. Then suddenly, at the age of forty-three, he died of an illness on board a ship returning to China. After a long and painful mourning, Grandmother decided to return to America with her brood of now seven children. That decision eventually affected immigration history.

At the Angel Island immigration station in San Francisco Bay, Grandmother went through a physical examination so thorough that even her teeth were checked to determine whether she was the age stated on her passport. The health inspector said she had filariasis, liver fluke, a common ailment of Asian immigrants which caused their deportation by countless numbers. The authorities thereby ordered Grandmother to be deported as well.

While her distraught children had to fend for themselves in San Francisco (my mother, then fifteen, and her older sister had found work in a sewing factory), a lawyer was hired to fight for Grandmother's release from the detention barracks. A letter addressed to her on Angel Island from her attorney, C. M. Fickert, dated 24 March 1924, reads: "Everything I can legitimately do will be done on your behalf. As you say, it seems most inhuman for you to be separated from your children who need your care. I am sorry that the immigration officers will not look at the human side of your case."

Times were tough for Chinese immigrants in 1924. Two years before, the federal government had passed the Cable Act, which provided that any woman born in the United States who married a man "ineligible for citizenship" (including the Chinese, whose naturalization rights had been eliminated by the Chinese Exclusion Act) would lose her own citizenship. So, for example, when American-born Lily Sung, whom I also interviewed, married a Chinese citizen she forfeited her birthright. When she and her four daughters tried to re-enter the United States after a stay in China, they were denied permission. The immigration inspector accused her of "smuggling little girls to sell." The Cable Act was not repealed until 1930.

The year my grandmother was detained on Angel Island, a law had just taken effect that forbade all aliens ineligible for citizenship from landing in America. This constituted a virtual ban on the immigration of all Chinese, including Chinese wives of U.S. citizens.

Waiting month after month in the bleak barracks, Grandmother heard many heart-rending stories from women awaiting deportation. They spoke of the suicides of several despondent women who hanged themselves in the shower stalls. Grandmother could see the calligraphy carved on the walls by other detained immigrants, eloquent poems expressing homesickness, sorrow, and a sense of injustice.

The World *of Our* Grandmothers

Meanwhile, Fickert was sending telegrams to Washington (a total of ten the bill stated) and building up a case for the circuit court. Mrs. Lee, after all, was the wife of a citizen who was a respected San Francisco merchant, and her children were American citizens. He also consulted a medical authority to see about a cure for liver fluke.

My mother took the ferry from San Francisco twice a week to visit Grandmother and take her Chinese dishes such as salted eggs and steamed pork because Grandmother could not eat the beef stew served in the mess hall. Mother and daughter could not help crying frequently during their short visits in the administration building. They were under close watch of both a guard and an interpreter.

After fifteen months the case was finally won. Grandmother was easily cured of filariasis and was allowed—with nine months probation—to join her children in San Francisco. The legal fees amounted to $782.50, a fortune in those days.

In 1927 Dr. Frederick Lam in Hawaii, moved by the plight of Chinese families deported from the islands because of the liver fluke disease, worked to convince federal health officials that the disease was noncommunicable. He used the case of Mrs. Lee Yoke Suey, my grandmother, as a precedent for allowing an immigrant to land with such an ailment and thus succeeded in breaking down a major barrier to Asian immigration.

My most vivid memory of Grandmother Lee is when she was in her seventies and studying for her citizenship. She had asked me to test her on the three branches of government and how to pronounce them correctly. I was a sophomore in high school and had entered the "What American Democracy Means To Me" speech contest of the Chinese American Citizens Alliance. When I said the words "judicial, executive, and legislative," I looked directly at my grandmother in the audience. She didn't smile, and afterwards, didn't comment much on my patriotic words. She had never told me about being on Angel Island or about her friends losing their citizenship. It wasn't in my textbooks either. I may have thought she wanted to be a citizen because her sons and sons-in-law had fought for this country, and we lived in a land of freedom and opportunity, but my guess now is that she wanted to avoid any possible confrontation—even at her age—with immigration authorities. The bad laws had been repealed, but she wasn't taking any chances.

I think a lot about my grandmother now and can understand why, despite her quiet, elegant dignity, an aura of sadness always surrounded her. She suffered from racism in the new country, as well as from traditional cruelties in the old. We, her grandchildren, remember walking very slowly with her, escorting her to a family banquet in Chinatown, hating the stares of tourists at her tiny feet. Did she, I wonder, ever feel like the victim of a terrible hoax, told as a small weeping girl that if she tried to untie

The World *of Our* Grandmothers

the bandages tightly binding her feet she would grow up ugly, unwanted, and without the comforts and privileges of the wife of a wealthy man?

We seemed so huge and clumsy around her—a small, slim figure always dressed in black. She exclaimed once that the size of my growing feet were "like boats." But she lived to see some of her granddaughters graduate from college and pursue careers and feel that the world she once knew with its feudal customs had begun to crumble. I wonder what she would have said of my own daughter who is now attending a university on an athletic scholarship. Feet like boats travel far?

I keep looking at the artifacts of the past: the photograph of my grandmother when she was an innocent young bride and the sad face in the news photo taken on Angel Island. I visit the immigration barracks from time to time, a weather-beaten wooden building with its walls marked by calligraphy bespeaking the struggles of our history. I see the view of sky and water from the window out of which my grandmother gazed. My mother told me how, after visiting hours, she would walk to the ferry and turn back to see her mother waving to her from this window. This image has been passed on to me like an heirloom of pain and of love. When I leave the building, emerging from the darkness into the glaring sunlight of the island, I too turn back to look at my grandmother's window.

Responding to the Selection

1. Which historical detail in this essay made the biggest impression on you? Explain your response.

2. What obstacles did Yu's grandmothers face that were not shared by women of other ethnic groups who immigrated to the United States?

3. Yu guesses that her grandmother applied for citizenship in the 1950s because she wanted to avoid confrontation with immigration authorities rather than for idealistic reasons. Do you agree with her conclusion? Why or why not?

4. A **theme** is a message or idea that a literary work conveys. What do you consider the main theme of this essay?

5. In your opinion, how well do current history textbooks cover the struggles and achievements of early immigrants from Asia? Of women in general?

Activities

Having a Debate

1. Should the government place any restrictions on immigration? What would be the fairest way to limit the number of people coming to this country? Plan and conduct a class debate on this topic.

Writing a Speech

2. C. M. Fickert was the attorney who represented Yu's grandmother as she was detained on Angel Island. Write a speech for him to deliver to the immigration board about her case.

Giving an Oral Report

3. Do research to find out more about one of the topics discussed in Yu's essay, such as the practice of binding women's feet, exclusionary immigration laws, or life in a big-city Chinatown. Present your findings to the class in an oral report.

Before You Read

from *Songs of Gold Mountain*

Background

For early Chinese immigrants, California was *Gum San,* or Gold Mountain. As this name would imply, they saw the United States as a land of opportunity. Yet their hopes often collided with the reality of racial discrimination, injustice, and poverty.

Angel Island Poetry

The first three poems in this selection come from the Angel Island Immigration Station in San Francisco Bay (see pages 44–45). While waiting to find out whether they would be deported back to China, detainees carved or wrote down hundreds of poems on the wooden walls of their barracks. The style of these unsigned poems is generally simple and direct. Angel Island stopped receiving immigrants in 1940. Thirty years later, the buildings were scheduled for demolition. However, a park ranger noticed poems on the walls and brought them to public attention. The station is now a historical landmark.

Poems by Chinese Laborers

The last three poems in the selection were written by immigrants who came to the United States before Angel Island existed. Some Chinese laborers grew crops in California fields. Others panned for gold or helped build the Transcontinental Railroad. The work was hard, and almost all the laborers remained cut off from their families. Their poems express longing and disappointment, but they also reveal a remarkable determination to make the promise of Gold Mountain come true.

from *Songs* of *Gold Mountain*

— Translated by Marlon K. Hom

2

The moment I hear
   we've entered the port,
I am all ready:
   my belongings wrapped in a bundle.
5   Who would have expected joy to become sorrow:
Detained in a dark, crude, filthy room?
What can I do?
Cruel treatment, not one restful breath of air.
Scarcity of food, severe restrictions—all
   unbearable.
10   Here even a proud man bows his head low.

3

In search of a pin-head gain,
I was idle in an impoverished village.
I've risked a perilous journey to come to the Flowery
    Flag Nation.
Immigration officers interrogated me;
5   And, just for a slight lapse of memory,
I am deported, and imprisoned in this barren
    mountain.
A brave man cannot use his might here,
And he can't take one step beyond the confines.

from **Songs** of **Gold Mountain**

7

Detention is called "awaiting review."
No letter or message can get through to me.
My mind's bogged down with a hundred frustrations
    and anxieties,
My mouth balks at meager meals of rice gruel.
5   O, what can I do?
Just when can I go ashore?
Imprisoned in a coop, unable to breathe,
My countrymen are made into a herd of cattle!

from *Songs* of *Gold Mountain*

21

Come to think of it, what can I really say?
Thirty years living in the United States—
Why has life been so miserable and I, so frail?
I suppose it's useless to expect to go home.
5   My heart aches with grief;
My soul wanders around aimlessly.
Unable to make a living here, I'll try it in the East,
With a sudden change of luck, I may make it back to
    China.

from *Songs* of *Gold Mountain*

23

I have walked to the very ends of the earth,
A dusty, windy journey.
I've toiled and I'm worn out, all for a miserable lot.
Nothing is ideal when I am down and out.
5   I think about it day and night—
Who can save a fish out of water?
From far away, I worry for my parents, my wife,
    my boy:
Do they still have enough firewood, rice, salt, and
    cooking oil?

30

Life is like a vast, long dream
Why grieve over poverty?
A contented life soothes ten thousand matters.
Value the help from other people.
5   In all earnest, just endure:
You can forget about cold and hunger, as you
    see them often.
After lasting through winter's chill and snow's
    embrace,
You will find joy in life when happiness comes
    and sorrow fades.

Responding to the Selection

Questions for Discussion

1. Which of these poems did you find the most moving? Why did it have this effect on you?
2. **Irony** is a conflict between expectations and reality. Describe an irony that appears in the first poem.
3. What grievances are expressed in the first three poems? What problem seems most burdensome for the Angel Island detainees?
4. Compare how the speakers of the last two poems respond to their predicament. Which speaker's attitude toward life seems closest to your own?

Activities

Writing an Imaginative Report

1. Imagine that you are an official sent to inspect the Angel Island Immigration Station. Using details from the first three poems in this selection, write a report on the treatment of Chinese detainees. Include suggestions for improving conditions at Angel Island.

Adapting Poetry to Music

2. With a partner, set one of the poems in this selection to music. You may adapt the lines to fit whichever style of music you are working in.

Before You Read

Tanka

Ki no Tsurayuki *(c. 872–c. 945)*   Lady Ise *(c. 875–c. 938)*
Ono no Komachi *(c. 833–c. 857)*   Saigyō *(1118–1190)*

> *"[P]oetry, without effort,*
> *moves heaven and earth, . . .*
> *smoothes the relations of men*
> *and women, and calms the*
> *hearts of fierce warriors."*
> — Tsurayuki (from the preface
> to *Kokinshū*)

About the Tanka Poets

One of the most important anthologies of Japanese verse is the *Kokinshū*, a collection gathered around A.D. 905 for Japan's emperor. Ki no Tsurayuki, an official in the imperial court and a celebrated poet, critic, and diarist, was largely responsible for compiling this anthology. His opinions about poetry helped define Japanese verse for years to come.

Two prominent Kokinshū women poets were the novelist Lady Ise and Ono no Komachi. According to legend Komachi was often cruel to others, but she suffered as well, as time diminished her beauty.

The twelfth-century poet Saigyō was a guardian of the imperial palace who renounced court life to become a Buddhist monk. He traveled throughout Japan, often living in the mountains as a recluse. His poems reflect his devotion to Buddhism and to nature.

Tanka

These four poems are examples of the *tanka*, an unrhymed Japanese verse form that consists of five lines. The first and third lines have five syllables each, while the other lines have seven syllables each. From the 700s to the 1500s, the tanka was the dominant form in Japanese poetry. Poets viewed the tanka as ideal for capturing a fleeting emotion or experience. Two frequent themes in tanka are the splendors of nature and the passage of time. Poets wrote about the changing seasons, both to reflect on nature's beauty and to express sorrow about the passage of time.

Poetry was often combined with painting on Japanese screens. Often, poems were written on the screen to complement the art; many Kokinshū poems were used this way.

Tanka

— Translated by Geoffrey Bownas and Anthony Thwaite

When I Went to Visit
— Ki no Tsurayuki

When I went to visit
The girl I love so much,
That winter night
The river blew so cold
That the plovers were crying.

Forsaking the Mists
— Lady Ise

Forsaking the mists
That rise in the spring,
Wild geese fly off.
They have learned to live
In a land without flowers.

Tanka

Was It That I Went to Sleep
— Ono no Komachi

Was it that I went to sleep
Thinking of him,
That he came in my dreams?
Had I known it a dream
I should not have wakened.

Trailing on the Wind
— Saigyō

Trailing on the wind,
The smoke from Mount Fuji
Melts into the sky.
So too my thoughts—
Unknown their resting place.

Responding to the Selection

Questions for Discussion

1. Which group of poems, the tanka or the Gold Mountain poems, would you describe as more emotional? Why?

2. Select one of these tanka and one of the songs of Gold Mountain that you feel share a mood or communicate a similar message. Compare the two poems.

3. Both the tanka and the Gold Mountain poems contain striking images of nature. What might be the reasons for this attention to nature? Could the authors of the two kinds of poems have had different reasons for emphasizing nature? Explain.

Activities

Writing an Essay

1. Which of these nine poems is your favorite? Write a short essay explaining your reasons.

Writing a Dialogue

2. Write an imaginary dialogue on a subject of your choice between one of the tanka poets and one of the Gold Mountain poets.

Creating an Illustration

3. Create an illustration to accompany one of these poems. Share your illustration with the class and explain how you arrived at your idea for the illustration.

Before You Read

Linked and *My Father and the Figtree*

Naomi Shihab Nye
Born 1952

"When you have a loved one on the other side of the world, it is hard to look at that world as divided."

About Nye

Naomi Shihab Nye grew up in a nurturing, creative household in St. Louis. Her Palestinian father and American mother both encouraged her to express herself. Nye says that even as a child she was "fascinated by the power of words on the page to make us look differently at our lives, to help us see and connect." A children's magazine accepted one of her poems when she was seven, and she has been publishing steadily ever since.

Nye has won many awards for her poetry collections. Early in her career, she taught creative writing in Texas public schools. She began writing stories for children after the birth of her son. Her simple, straightforward style allows her to appeal to audiences of all ages. "Ultimately I look at writing as a form of discovery," she told an interviewer. "I hope my words reach out to the reader and they can say yes to them."

Making Connections

Nye often writes about connections between people separated by time or distance. She originally felt connected to the Middle East through the folktales her father told at bedtime. When she was fourteen, Nye and her family spent about a year in Jerusalem, where she was able to meet the Palestinian side of her family. She grew especially close to her grandmother, who appears in many of her poems. Nye also wrote a children's book called *Sitte's Secrets* that is based on her relationship with her grandmother.

Linked

— *Naomi Shihab Nye*

My American grandmother said, I don't know,
oh I don't know, and my grandfather said, You'd better.
She took a little bow backwards: whatever you say.
Luckily I had two others across the sea who were mysteries.

5   My mother wrote her own early story down
in a red book which I found.
Saw movie. New dress.
When I was ten, I wanted her to complete the sentence.

We lived in the grayest city on earth
10   with a broom and a frazzled mop.
My daddy kept his passport in his pocket.
My daddy had a long eye and a manner of speaking.

Where are you from? people asked him.
He liked to tease. *I am from the land of stones.*
15   *I fell down from the tallest, oldest tree.*
In school, we were all from our own families.

I wanted a common name—Debbie, or Karen.
But the rest of it was good for me.
We had hummos, pine nuts.
20   We had olive oil tipped from a shiny can.

Who wanted to go to the Methodist Church
or the neighborhood fish fry? We tried it all.
We didn't have to belong. Our parents took us seriously.
They took us everywhere they went.

Linked

25   Our days were studded with attention,
    shadowed by twin cherry trees, thick.
    We had umbrellas and boots.
    We used good sense.

    Our teachers said, Excuse me, how do you
30   pronounce this? Our teachers said, Welcome.
    I don't know much about it, but tell me.
    Do they still ride camels over there?

    Whenever I think about the small white house,
    our father is pitching sticks into a flaming barrel
35   in the backyard. It's as tall as I am. He sings as he stirs it.
    His old country smelled like smoke.

    What day can ever feel more real?
    I'm linked to the jingling sound of keys
    in someone else's pocket. I'm following behind.
40   I'll come in when they tell me to.

My Father and the Figtree

— Naomi Shihab Nye

For other fruits my father was indifferent.
He'd point at the cherry trees and say,
"See those? I wish they were figs."
In the evenings he sat by my bed

5   weaving folktales like vivid little scarves.
They always involved a figtree.
Even when it didn't fit, he'd stick it in.
Once Joha was walking down the road and he saw a figtree.
Or, he tied his camel to a figtree and went to sleep.

10   Or, later when they caught and arrested him,
his pockets were full of figs.

At age six I ate a dried fig and shrugged.
"That's not what I'm talking about!" he said,
"I'm talking about a fig straight from the earth—

15   gift of Allah!—on a branch so heavy it touches the ground.
I'm talking about picking the largest fattest sweetest fig
in the world and putting it in my mouth."
(Here he'd stop and close his eyes.)

Years passed, we lived in many houses, none had fig trees.

20   We had lima beans, zucchini, parsley, beets.
"Plant one!" my mother said, but my father never did.
He tended garden half-heartedly, forgot to water,
let the okra get too big.
"What a dreamer he is. Look how many things he starts

25   and doesn't finish."

My Father and the Figtree

The last time he moved, I got a phone call.
My father, in Arabic, chanting a song I'd never heard.
"What's that?" I said.
"Wait till you see!"
He took me out back to the new yard.
There, in the middle of Dallas, Texas,
a tree with the largest, fattest, sweetest figs in the world.
"It's a figtree song!" he said,
plucking his fruits like ripe tokens,
emblems, assurance
of a world that was always his own.

Responding to the Selection ─────────

1. What impression of childhood do you get from reading these poems?

2. Why do you think figs are so important to the father in "My Father and the Figtree"? Which phrases or lines in the poem support your interpretation?

3. **Mood** is the overall feeling that a work of literature creates for readers. How would you describe the mood of "My Father and the Figtree"?

4. In "Linked," how do people in the speaker's community react to her ethnic identity? How does the speaker seem to feel about her Middle Eastern background?

5. In what ways does your own ethnic identity make you feel like an outsider? In what ways does it help you feel connected to others?

6. In an interview Nye said about her childhood, "I always knew I had a private place to go to, an interior haven that was all mine." She was referring to both her mixed cultural background and her ability to step back and observe life. Do you have a "private place" to go to? Why might such a place be valuable to a person?

Activities

Writing About Your Ancestry

1. What sort of links do you feel with your ancestors or relatives living far away from you in time or space? Write a brief essay in response to this question.

Discussing Literature

2. Nye says that one of the powers of words and literature is to help us "see and connect." Think of a novel, story, or poem that helped you see and connect in some way. Explain to a partner what the work helped you see and connect to and why you think it succeeded.

A Sunny Day with a Gentle Breeze, 1993. Zifen Qian. Oil on canvas, 42 × 56 in. SuperStock.

Theme Two

People

Ma, hear me now, tell me your story again and again.

— Nellie Wong

Before You Read

Bad Luck Woman

Chitra Divakaruni
Born 1956

"I hope people who read my book will not think of the characters as Indians, but feel for them as people."

About Divakaruni

Raised in India, Chitra Divakaruni came to the United States when she was nineteen. Immigration broadened her opportunities, but it also left her feeling like an outsider in two cultures: "It is such a powerful and poignant experience when you live away from your original culture and this becomes home, but never quite, and then you can't go back and be quite at home there either."

Divakaruni began to write poetry after earning her Ph.D. in English literature. She later turned to fiction because she wanted to reach a wider audience. Her novels, short stories, and poems have won numerous awards. In addition to writing and teaching, Divakaruni has founded an organization that helps Indian women adjust to life in the United States.

Religious Influences

India, the birthplace of Buddhism, Hinduism, and other religions, has long been associated with spirituality. According to Divakaruni, "There is a certain spirituality, not necessarily religious—the essence of spirituality—that is at the heart of the Indian psyche, that finds the divine in everything. . . ." The narrator of "Bad Luck Woman" travels with a group of women to Hindu shrines in Kashmir, a region divided between India and Pakistan.

Bad Luck Woman

— *Chitra Divakaruni*

"Unlucky. I tell you, that woman's plain unlucky, and she'll bring bad luck to anyone that comes near her." Aunt Seema's loud whisper carried across the dining room and ricocheted off the peeling walls of the Nataraj Hotel of Pahalgaon, where they had arrived just an hour ago.

"Aunt Seema, please!" Lila hissed.

"Yes, yes, I know, you modern girls don't believe in these things, especially you, living in America for ten years now and working in that science laboratory cutting up rats and what-not, but I tell you, it's true! Something evil is bound to happen to us all because of her if we aren't careful. You just watch and see!"

"Aunt Seema!" Lila's face burned with embarrassment. She wished her aunt wouldn't always say exactly what she thought—and so loudly, too. Although she was fond of her aunt and generally tolerant of her ways, today she felt impatient because she was struggling with a secret disappointment of her own.

Aunt Seema and she were part of a pilgrimage group that was now on its way back from Lord Shiva's shrine in Amarnath, in the mountains of Kashmir. It had been a strenuous trip, four days on foot over an icy terrain. When they had finally reached the cave shrine, Lila had waited expectantly. All around her pilgrims were weeping in joy, touching their foreheads to the ground in thanksgiving. Many sang out, their faces bright with ecstasy. Lila waited for something similar to touch her, for grace to pierce her like a ray of light, perhaps, as in old religious movies. Wasn't that the unspoken promise that had sustained all of them through the rigorous climb? But she had felt nothing except a vague awe at the sight of the immense granite cave roof receding into darkness, and she had wondered if she had made a mistake coming all the way from America for this. It was a question that haunted her still as she stared out across the dining room.

The subject of their conversation sat hunched alone at a rickety table, her back towards them. She must have heard what they said. She said nothing, but Lila thought that her shoulders drooped a little more as she drew the edge of her sari tighter around her. Against the dirty white of the

Bad Luck Woman 77

Bad Luck Woman

hotel wall splotched with garish touristy art, she appeared small, shrunken, childlike. Lila noticed how the bones on the back of her thin neck stuck out like knobs beneath a sparse knot of grey hair, and in spite of her own disappointment, she felt a rush of pity.

Everyone in the Jai Guru Pilgrimage Party, which consisted mostly of middle-aged women, knew about Mrs Ghosh, although most of them had not spoken to her. The woman had truly had the worst luck, not only during the pilgrimage but throughout her life. On the very second day of the trip, the doctor's wife, who always seemed to know these things, had informed all the women who cared to listen that at the age of twenty Mrs Ghosh had lost her husband in an accident. Worse, his property had been seized by his brothers, who declared the marriage—and the children of that marriage—illegitimate.

"Can you imagine that?" The doctor's wife had raised her eyes to the ceiling to indicate the magnitude of the calamity. "She went to court, of course, but her lawyer was no good. Or maybe her brothers-in-law bribed him. She lost everything. Everything! That's when her hair turned white. She had to go to work as a clerk in some office, unfortunate soul, and struggle for years to bring up her two sons. And then, just last year, when she finally quit her job, hoping her sons would take care of her, the older one, an air force pilot, was killed in a crash. Burnt to death. Nothing left of his body. Nothing at all."

A chorus of groans had come from the listeners, but the doctor's wife had not finished yet.

"So now she's forced to live with her youngest, whose wife treats her no better than a maid. I've heard she makes her cook and clean the house. Even the bathrooms!"

As another chorus of exclamations rose, Lila couldn't stand it any more. She had to leave the room. She hated all this gossip, this mindless superstition. She remembered watching these women at Parvati's temple only the day before, offering coconuts to the goddess, praying fervently. How she had admired them. "This is the kind of thing I miss in the U.S.," she had said to Aunt Seema a bit enviously as she saw them devoutly placing flowers at the deity's feet, "this sense of spiritual community that all of you share." Yet now those same women were like vultures, delighting in picking poor Mrs Ghosh's private life apart. And the worst thing was that they had no sense of wrongdoing. Is this what my culture really is? thought Lila. This cruel ignorance, instead of the rich fullness I had hoped to discover on this journey? As though in answer she heard a voice behind her, suspiciously like her aunt's exclaiming, "She was surely born under an unlucky star, that one!"

Bad Luck Woman

But as she walked away, Lila could not deny to herself that Mrs Ghosh *had* experienced an amazing number of difficulties. On the train to Kashmir, she had developed a bad case of heat rash which, together with motion sickness, had confined her to her bunk all through the scenic ride. At Pahalgaon, the dandi bearers engaged to carry her up to the shrine had not shown up, and the inexperienced substitutes had slipped on the ice, dropping the dandi so that she had fallen and injured her back. Of all the bedrolls, hers alone had been lost during the trek. If a couple of pilgrims had not lent her blankets, she couldn't have managed through the freezing nights. Finally, the dandi bearers had refused to carry her up the last stretch of stairs to the shrine until she promised them her gold ring, her one piece of jewelry. On the way back, the trauma of the last few days had caught up with her, and she had been sick with fever. Only this day was she sufficiently recovered to come downstairs for a meal.

Could all this really be coincidence? a small insidious voice had asked inside Lila's head, but she had pushed the thought quickly away.

Now, sitting with Aunt Seema, Lila watched the lone figure picking at her food in silence. No one was sitting at Mrs Ghosh's table, although space was scarce in the cramped dining area and the other tables were overcrowded. What idiocy, thought Lila in sudden anger. Perhaps a bit of the anger was directed at the small voice which had appeared from a place within her that she hadn't known about.

"These people are treating the poor woman like a leper just because of some unfortunate occurrences. Much good going on a pilgrimage has done to them!" she said to herself. "My friends in America would be amazed if I told them about this." She tried to picture the expression on the face of her lab mates, Ron and Carolina, when they heard her story. But to her consternation she found that she couldn't recall their features. The crisp white rustle of their lab coats seemed to come from very far away, from a receding world. She fought against a sudden panic, a sense of being dragged headlong into mysteries she couldn't fathom.

"I don't care what these women think," she told herself defiantly. "I'm going to be as kind as I possibly can to Mrs Ghosh as soon as I get an opportunity."

Lila's chance arrived sooner than she had anticipated. She and her aunt had just settled down, with much complaining on Aunt Seema's part, in the dilapidated three-cot room they had been assigned on the top storey of the hotel when there was a hesitant knock at the door. Opening it, Lila came face to face with Mrs Ghosh.

"I've been assigned the same room as you. I hope you don't mind," she said, breathless and apologetic.

Bad Luck Woman

Lila noticed that the woman had a raised mole, very dark, to the left side of her upper lip. A couple of hairs sprouted from it, and it moved as though alive when she talked. It gave Lila an unpleasant sensation and for a moment she couldn't respond. Then she moved to screen Mrs Ghosh from the look that she knew must be on Aunt Seema's face and gave her the best smile she could summon.

"Of course not. We'll be most happy to have you with us. Here, let me help you."

Mrs Ghosh looked astonished and then pathetically gratified at this unexpected kindness. Together, she and Lila moved her bags and bedding to the cot on the far side of the room, while Aunt Seema watched with growing displeasure.

"No good will come of this, I can tell you that," she finally burst out. "Heaven only knows what's going to happen to us now, stuck in the same room with her!"

Lila felt a moment of fear. Aunt sounded so certain. Then she looked at Mrs Ghosh, who was fiddling with the catch on her bag, her face turned away, her head bowed. The cheap white fabric of her widow's sari accentuated the grey in her hair. She looked so helpless, so accepting of Aunt Seema's outburst, that Lila's throat tightened in sympathy.

"Aunt Seema, that's a wicked, wicked thing to say! I'm so embarrassed. How can you be so cruel to someone, and right after a pilgrimage trip, too? Don't you remember how, when I was growing up, you always told me to treat others like I wanted them to treat me?"

Aunt Seema shook her head. "You don't understand. She isn't like other people," she said, stubbornly. "Can't you see, she's touched by Alakshmi, the deity of misfortune."

Lila walked over to her aunt and brought her face close to hers. Her voice had an angry tremor in it. "That's sheer nonsense, all this talk about Alakshmi. If you keep behaving like this, I don't think I want to come visit you again, and I certainly don't want to go with you on that trip you are planning to Rameshwar next month. In fact, I think I'll cut my stay short and return to the U.S. as soon as we get back to Calcutta."

"You're asking for trouble, being friendly with that one," Aunt Seema muttered, turning away. But she didn't say any more. Instead, she spent the rest of the afternoon on the far cot, her face turned to the wall, covers pulled up to her ears.

To counter her aunt's attitude, Lila made a special effort to be friendly with Mrs Ghosh, and the woman responded to it so thirstily that Lila guessed she must not have many friends. Before Lila knew it, Mrs Ghosh was telling her the story of her life, which was much as the doctor's wife had described it. When Mrs Ghosh spoke, though, her intensity weighted the events with an added tragedy, the sense of a menacing universe. The words welled from her with a desperation that made the young woman uncomfortable. But she didn't know how to stop her without hurting her feelings. So she listened as Mrs Ghosh talked about her sense of guilt at her son's death, the mole near her mouth trembling with agitation.

"Sometimes I really do wonder whether I was born unlucky, whether I'm fated to harm all those I come in contact with, all my loved ones."

"Nonsense!" Lila said, and she was, perhaps, speaking as much to herself as to the other woman. "You mustn't let other people's superstitions affect you. There's no such thing as being lucky or unlucky."

Mrs Ghosh mulled over this for a while, looking doubtful. "You really think so?"

"If you look back on your life carefully, for instance," Lila said, "you're sure to find lots of positive things there as well."

"Maybe you're right."

"Of course I am!" Lila's voice sounded adequately convincing, even to her own ears. "Now, how would you like to go shopping with me? I've heard that the Kashmiri shawls here are the best."

The outing did Mrs Ghosh a great deal of good. Her face lost some of its pinched look as she bargained spiritedly and finally purchased a beautiful rug embroidered with bright blue peacocks at half its original price. When it started raining and they had to ride back in an old horse carriage that lurched all over the road, she seemed to think it was quite an adventure. She laughed at every one of Lila's stories, even those that weren't particularly funny, and attempted a few weak jokes of her own.

When they reached the hotel, she grasped Lila's hand tightly as the young woman helped her down from the carriage. "You're like the daughter I never had," she said. But even as Lila smiled her thanks, she noticed how Mrs Ghosh's fingers felt dry and raspy, almost like a bird's claw on her arm, and she had to make an effort not to pull away.

At dinner Mrs Ghosh seemed to take it for granted that they would sit together. She talked animatedly to Lila throughout the meal, and it seemed that for once she didn't care about the pointed looks of disapproval that they were getting from the others. But Lila, catching Aunt Seema's unhappy expression, felt a pang of guilt, as though she had betrayed her aunt.

As they walked up the stairs together after the meal, Mrs Ghosh grew hesitant again. "I saw how they were looking at you because you sat with me at dinner. Maybe you shouldn't do it any more. I don't want them treating you badly just because . . ."

"Nonsense!" interrupted Lila, embarrassed because she had been thinking somewhat the same thoughts. "As though I care what they think! Besides, I like you. You're much nicer than most of them, and more intelligent, too!"

"Me? Intelligent? Why, no one's called me that!" said Mrs Ghosh, and her face glowed. She looked so happy that Lila felt a sudden lightness in her own heart. It was almost a physical sensation, and it made her dizzy for a moment. She felt as though she had been given a glimpse into the nature of goodness. This must be what grace is, she thought, and she did not let the glistening mole on Mrs Ghosh's face bother her as the woman leaned forward to give her a kiss.

This new sense of well-being buoyed Lila up through the rest of the evening, making her behave with extra sweetness to Mrs Ghosh. It was still raining, heavier now, the air getting colder. She sat curled up in a blanket on Mrs Ghosh's bed, sharing with her the spicy cashew nuts that she'd bought from a street vendor and telling her about life in the United States. Only once in a while, as Mrs Ghosh exclaimed in amazement over roads so wide that eight cars could travel on them side by side, or shop doors so intelligent that they knew to open when a customer came, did she let her eyes stray to Aunt Seema, who was lying on her cot in disapproving silence, her prayer beads clasped in one hand.

Just before they went to bed Mrs Ghosh handed her the peacock rug. "I want you to have it."

"No, no, I couldn't do that! That's such an expensive rug," said Lila, embarrassed.

"I want you to have it, so when you look at it you'll think of me."

Before Lila could respond, Aunt Seema cried from the other end of the room, "No! Don't take it! You mustn't take anything from her!"

Lila looked up, a little frightened by the urgency in her aunt's voice. Outside, a gust of wind shook the windows, menacing, sudden. Startled, she dropped the rug. It fell from her hand to the floor, unrolling, it seemed to Lila, in slow motion. The peacocks' eyes, embroidered in thread red as blood, gleamed in the dim light like a warning.

"I'm telling you," Aunt Seema continued, her voice high with agitation, "it'll bring you bad luck. Anything of hers will bring you bad luck."

Mrs Ghosh gathered up the rug and tried to fold it. Lila noticed that the mole on her lip was trembling, like something small and alive and trapped. Had she seen the brief moment of fear in Lila's eyes, guessed the small voice which had returned, whispering that perhaps her aunt was right? Shame made her voice harsh, louder than usual.

"Aunt Seema, that's enough! I *told* you I don't believe in all this nonsense. And I don't want to hear about it again."

Lila turned to Mrs Ghosh, who had retreated into the corner by her bed. Fear is the enemy of goodness, she said to herself, and took the clumsily folded rug from Mrs Ghosh's hands. "Thank you so much. I'll put it in my living room back in San Francisco, and every time I look at it I'll think of you."

Mrs Ghosh's face lighted up, and Lila could see the shimmer of tears in her eyes. The brightness that had left her heart returned with a rush. The air was intoxicating. Like sweet wine, she thought, pulling up the simile from a past that seemed too remote to belong to her.

When she fell asleep that night, listening to the rain, Lila still had a smile on her lips.

She was sinking, sinking into the glacier. There was no trail, only slush, because of the rain. She could feel her feet slipping. Nothing to hold on to. Blackness everywhere and the numbing weight of ice pressed against her chest. She opened her mouth to cry out for help, but her mouth, too, filled with ice. Ahead, there was a face, huge and pale, hanging in the darkness. It reminded her of someone, but who? Then she knew. It was Alakshmi, goddess of ill luck. We warned you, said the face, opening its cavernous mouth, we warned you. The mole on its upper lip trembled. Behind her, she heard the mountain break open with a thunderous crack, but her feet were too heavy to carry her to safety. And all around her, ceaselessly, the rain kept falling, falling . . .

Lila bolted upright in the dark, her heart pounding so loudly that she was amazed the others were not awakened by it. What a horrible, horrible dream! And so real! She could still hear the angry drumming of the rain, still feel the clammy moisture enveloping her like a shroud. Then with another start she realized it was no dream. She was weighed down by wet bedclothes, and the dripping sound which had now increased to the gurgling rush of a mountain stream was very real.

She jumped out of bed, calling her aunt and groping for the light, and found herself ankle-deep in freezing water. Bewildered, she clicked on the switch and looked around as the bulb swung crazily on its wire, barely missing her head. Part of the ceiling, rotted from lack of repair, had collapsed near the foot of her cot onto their suitcases, bringing with it a torrent of water. The floor was already covered, and more water kept pouring down the walls. Several other parts of the ceiling looked as though they could collapse at any moment.

Bad Luck Woman

Lila pushed her way through the debris to Aunt Seema, who slept on, covers drawn over her head, totally exhausted by the rigours of the last few days. She shook her as hard as she could.

"Aunt, wake up! Wake up! Come with me! Hurry, for God's sake!"

As the ceiling creaked ominously, she pushed her half-awake aunt to the door and jerked it open, loosening more plaster in the process. At that moment, her eyes fell on Mrs Ghosh, whom she had forgotten in the turmoil. She was sitting up, bedclothes bunched around her, eyes wide with shock, incapable of movement.

"Get out of the room! Fast!" Lila screamed, and as the ceiling began to crumble, she dashed in and grabbed the dazed woman's arms, and partly dragged her out through the wreckage. She had almost got them both through the door when something hit her head.

When Lila regained consciousness, she was lying on a bed in one of the other rooms in the hotel. Several women were gathered around her, and the doctor was bandaging her head, which ached dully and felt impossibly heavy.

"You cut your head open on a piece of falling sheetrock, young lady," he said in response to her questioning look. "Could have been worse. The bleeding's stopped, and you don't seem to have a concussion. I've put in a couple of stitches and given you a tetanus shot, just to be on the safe side."

He turned briskly to Aunt Seema, who was clutching at Lila's arm and weeping hysterically. "Now, stop that and get her out of these wet clothes fast, before she catches pneumonia. And try not to jerk the head."

Someone brought a towel, someone else donated a sari and a blouse, and Lila was made as comfortable as possible. But Aunt Seema kept on weeping, great gulping sobs shaking her frame.

"It's all her fault, that evil unlucky woman! You didn't know any better, how could you, but *I* should have been more careful. I shouldn't have let you get so friendly with her. I saw it, how she was casting a spell on you, turning you against all of us. Oh, how stupid I was not to insist on another room right away. Look at your poor dear head now! What am I going to tell your mother!"

"Aunt, do stop," Lila whispered tiredly, closing her eyes. Every little sound seemed to pierce her skull. But even through the pain, she could feel her aunt's anxiety, and she tried to make her voice gentle. "I'll be all right, but your crying makes my head ache."

There was relative silence around them, now that Aunt Seema had quieted down. The disturbing noise of gushing water was less, too, so it seemed to have stopped raining. Lila could hear the servants

Bad Luck Woman

clearing away the debris upstairs. Had the doctor given her a painkiller? Was that why she was having trouble focusing on her thoughts? They flashed through her head in a series of blinding, disconnected images: glaciers, Shiva's shrine, her living room in the U.S., cashews, a pale, huge face, a rug from which blue peacocks stared out with blood-red eyes.

There seemed to be some kind of commotion outside the room. It shattered the images like bright glass against her eyelids.

"I must go inside! I must! I must see her!"

The voice boomed into Lila's head, almost recognized, but her brain refused to place it.

"No, you can't," the doctor said, "no excitement. She must rest."

Who was the doctor's wife talking to?

"Go away! Haven't you done us enough harm already? Haven't you brought us enough bad luck? Or won't you be satisfied until you've killed her?"

That was Aunt Seema at the door, her voice breaking as it rose hysterically.

"Please! Please! I won't harm her in any way. I won't even talk to her or touch her," the half-known voice pleaded. "I just want to see for myself that she's all right."

"No thanks to you if she is!" Aunt Seema lashed out. "Over my dead body you'll come into this room!" She turned to the bed. "Lila, tell her! Tell her yourself!"

Reluctantly, Lila forced her eyes open, struggling against the weights that pinned them down. How the voices made her head ache! If only they would let her be! Against the harsh rectangle of light from the door, she saw Mrs Ghosh, a gash on her cheek intensifying her lack of colour, desperately trying to push her way past Aunt Seema and the doctor's wife. Her face, with the mole blooming on it like a black, blemished flower—it was the pale one of Lila's dream.

A dark coil of fear that had been waiting inside Lila came to life suddenly, twisting and growing until it filled her throbbing head. Aunt Seema was right. It *was* her fault! All her fault! She *was* touched by misfortune. She was misfortune itself. Lila could see it clearly now, in the pain that burned through her head like a hot red light. Everything had been fine until she had joined them. Until she had enmeshed them in her bad luck. And who knew what else she might do if she remained?

"You heard Aunt." Her voice came out thin and wavery, and she took a deep breath to strengthen it. "Go away. Leave me alone.

Bad Luck Woman

Leave me alone, bad luck woman!" Exhausted, she pulled the cover over her head, turning from the figure who stood at the door, suddenly very still.

In a few days Lila had recovered enough to join the group on its tour of Srinagar. "Lucky you're so healthy and strong, young lady," the doctor had said as he removed the bandage to check on the wound. "It's healing very nicely." She photographed the prize-winning roses at the historic Mughal gardens, offered milk at the shrine of Bhavani, according to tradition, and rode in a silk-lined shikara on the picturesque Dal lake. She graciously accepted all the attention her fellow travellers showered on her, the little gifts they brought.

Today, the last day of the trip, she sat in the most coveted seat on the bus, the one with the best view, right in front of the big double windows. The scar on her forehead was already beginning to fade to an interesting pink, and the doctor promised that it would be just about gone in a month. Meanwhile, it was certain to afford her special treatment at home. So there was no reason, surely, for this tight feeling in her chest, this heaviness that pushed out from inside and made breathing difficult.

"By the way, Aunt, whatever happened to Mrs Ghosh?" Lila made her voice sound very, very casual.

"Oh, *her!* Who knows? She disappeared that same day. The tour manager asked all the servants, but no one had seen her leave."

Lila felt a cold queasiness deep in the pit of her stomach. She didn't want to hear any more.

"Are you talking about that unlucky woman?" The doctor's wife leaned forward from the seat behind Seema. "Strange, wasn't it, how she went off all of a sudden, without even taking her luggage? The manager had to pay the sweeper to take away her bags. Anyway, good riddance is what I say!"

Lila remembered the brief happy look on Mrs Ghosh's face the evening of the accident and a pang went through her.

Aunt Seema and the doctor's wife were discussing the possible evil effects of having had Mrs Ghosh in their pilgrimage party. "I would do a special puja for purification, if I were you, as soon as I got home," said the doctor's wife, "seeing what-all happened to your niece," and Aunt Seema nodded agreement.

Stop, Lila wanted to shout. Don't talk like that. But she couldn't say a word. I don't have the right, she thought. She reached inside to touch that special lightness, like a folded wing, and wasn't surprised to find it gone.

"Yes, best not to think about people like that," Aunt Seema was saying now. "Lila dear, how about trying some of these delicious grapes? What?

Bad Luck Woman

Not feeling so good? It's probably car sickness. All these winding roads, they'd make anyone ill. Here, have a lemon drop."

Outside, the green and gold of trees and sunlight merged into a flashing kaleidoscope as the bus picked up speed. The peaks of the Himalayas shone calm and silver against a brilliant postcard-blue sky. But Lila, staring at the suddenly blurry windowpane through wet eyelashes, didn't see any of it.

Responding to the Selection

Questions for Discussion

1. Were you surprised by the outcome of the story? Explain your reaction.

2. Why is Lila especially disappointed at the way her aunt and the other pilgrims treat Mrs. Ghosh?

3. How does Lila's experience at the shrine influence her relationship with Mrs. Ghosh?

4. An **internal conflict** occurs within the mind of a character who is torn between opposing feelings or goals. What internal conflict does Lila experience in the story? Does she ever resolve this conflict?

5. Do you blame Lila for chasing away Mrs. Ghosh after her accident? Why or why not?

Activities

Interpreting the Story

1. How do you think Mrs. Ghosh would interpret the accident in the hotel room and Lila's subsequent behavior toward her? Write a paragraph in response to this question, supporting your opinions with evidence from the story.

Writing a Dialogue

2. Write a dialogue in which Lila describes her experience to her lab mates in the United States. Include both her comments and their questions about the experience.

Discussing a Statement

3. Meet in a small group to discuss this statement: "There is no such thing as luck; what happens to people is a result only of their or other people's actions." Give examples from real life or literature to support your position.

Before You Read

Elegy for a Woman of No Importance

Nāzik al-Malā'ikah
Born 1923

> *"Loneliness and the feeling of being unwanted is the most terrible poverty."*
> —Mother Teresa

About al-Mala'ikah

Writing poetry is a family tradition for Nāzik al-Malā'ikah. Both her father and her grandfather are known as distinguished poets in their native Iraq. Born in Baghdad, Iraq's capital city, Nāzik al-Malā'ikah studied Arabic literature at Baghdad University. She then traveled to the United States and earned an advanced degree in comparative literature at Princeton University. When she returned to Iraq, she accepted a position at Baghdad University, where she taught for many years.

Nāzik al-Malā'ikah is known as a leading proponent of the Arabic free-verse movement, which introduced modern poetic forms and informal diction to Arabic poetry. She currently lives in Kuwait, a Persian Gulf state that borders Iraq.

Muslim Women

Most of Iraq's population is Muslim. Traditionally, the identity of women in Muslim cultures has been shaped by family, husband, and home. Although the roles of Muslim women are changing in some countries, with many women achieving a greater degree of independence than in the past, an unmarried or widowed woman is still considered to be adrift in most Muslim cultures.

The Elegy

Named for an ancient Greek metrical form, the elegy is one of poetry's most enduring forms. This is not surprising, as its theme—human mortality and its emotional consequences—is a universal one. Poets in all times and cultures have written elegies.

ELEGY FOR A *Woman* OF NO IMPORTANCE

— Nāzik al-Malā'ikah
Translated by Chris Knipp and Mohammad Sadiq

When she died no face turned pale, no lips trembled
doors heard no retelling of her death
no curtains opened to air the room of grief
no eyes followed the coffin to the end of the road—
5   only, hovering in the memory, a vague form
          passing in the lane

The scrap of news stumbled in the alleyways
its whisper, finding no shelter,
lodged obscurely in an unseen corner.
The moon murmured sadly.

10   Night, unconcerned, gave way to morning
light came with the milk cart and the call to fasting
with the hungry mewing of a cat of rags and bones
the shrill cries of vendors in the bitter streets
the squabbling of small boys throwing stones
15   dirty water spilling along the gutters
smells on the wind
which played about the rooftops
playing in deep forgetfulness
playing alone

Responding to the Selection

Questions for Discussion

1. In what ways are the subject of Nāzik al-Malā'ikah's poem and Mrs. Ghosh of "Bad Luck Woman" similar? In what ways are they different?

2. Compare and contrast the attitudes of the speaker in the poem and those of Lila in "Bad Luck Woman" toward the events they experience. Cite details from the poem and story that justify your answer.

3. Which of these works did you like better? Why?

4. Could either of these situations have taken place in the United States today? Why or why not?

Activities

Writing an Essay

1. Write a short essay responding to this statement and how it relates to these two literary works: "Indifference to suffering is just as bad as active persecution of another person."

Having a Poetry Reading

2. Do research to find a collection of famous elegies. Arrange a poetry reading for your class featuring some of these poems. Prepare a short introduction to each poem, explaining the circumstances of its writing. You may want to include appropriate music to enhance the poetic experience.

Focus on . . .
The Internment
of Japanese
Americans

After Japan bombed Pearl Harbor on December 7, 1941, rumors spread that Japanese Americans in Hawaii had committed acts of sabotage. Investigators found no evidence to support these charges. However, most military and political leaders insisted that Japanese Americans would pose a threat if Japan attacked the U.S. mainland. On February 19, 1942, President Roosevelt signed an order allowing the army to evacuate all 110,000 people of Japanese descent from California, Hawaii, Oregon, and Washington.

The order applied to citizens (the *nisei*, or second generation) as well as immigrants (the *issei*). Japanese Americans were given seven days' notice for the evacuation. Since they could only bring small items such as clothes

and bedding, they had to sell other possessions quickly, often for ridiculously small sums. Families received a set of numbered tags to attach to their coat lapels and luggage. At first they were housed in stockyards, fairgrounds, and racetracks, where they slept in filthy stables. Then they boarded trains bound for internment camps.

The camps, mainly located in remote desert areas of the West, were surrounded by guard towers and barbed-wire fences. Each family occupied a small, sparsely furnished room in the wooden barracks. Internees had to use communal facilities for eating and bathing. During the day, most adults accepted low wages to perform manual labor or provide services. Children attended schools set up within the camps. "I was too young to understand," one internee later stated, "but I remember soldiers carrying rifles, and I remember being afraid."

Despite claims that they were a security threat, the government announced in 1943 that Japanese Americans were eligible for military service. Thousands of nisei enlisted or were drafted. Some went reluctantly, but many wanted a chance to prove their loyalty. The all-nisei 442nd regiment, which fought in Europe, won more medals than any other unit of its size.

At the end of the war, internees often returned to badly damaged homes and fields. The government compensated them for only a fraction of their losses. A full apology came in 1988, when Congress passed a bill offering $20,000 to each surviving internee. President Reagan, who signed the bill into law, admitted that the United States had committed a "grave wrong" against Japanese Americans during World War II.

Linking to . . .
- As you read the selections that follow, think about how the internment affected the lives of Japanese Americans.

Before You Read

Kubota

Garrett Hongo
Born 1951

"America is not the melting pot, but a meeting place, and that inspires me."

About Hongo

Garrett Hongo was born in a small Hawaiian town called Volcano. His family moved to the Los Angeles area when he was a baby. As a high school student, he became convinced that his generation of Japanese Americans had the responsibility to speak up about the mistreatment of their parents and grandparents during World War II. At the time he was interested in both photography and writing. Eventually he decided to focus on poetry because he felt that poets "were the truth-tellers, the passionate ones."

In addition to his two volumes of poetry and a memoir, Hongo has contributed to Asian American literature by editing important anthologies. His favorite place to work is Volcano. Hongo says that when he first returned to the beautiful town he was "astonished that a place like that existed and that I was from that place."

A Grandfather's Tale

In "Kubota," a grandfather recalls the days following Japan's attack on Pearl Harbor on December 7, 1941, when rumors circulated about acts of sabotage. Although the FBI found these rumors to be false, Navy Secretary Frank Knox proposed a plan for mass evacuation of Japanese Americans in Hawaii. Local officials resisted the plan, in part because this population of 158,000 was vital to the Hawaiian economy. The government ended up arresting 1,444 Hawaiians of Japanese descent. All Japanese Americans who lived in California, Oregon, and Washington were later rounded up and placed in internment camps (see pages 92–93).

Kubota

— Garrett Hongo

On December 8, 1941, the day after the Japanese attack on Pearl Harbor in Hawaii, my grandfather barricaded himself with his family—my grandmother, my teenage mother, her two sisters and two brothers—inside of his home in La'ie, a sugar plantation village on Oahu's North Shore. This was my maternal grandfather, a man most villagers called by his last name, Kubota. It could mean either "Wayside Field" or else "Broken Dreams," depending on which ideograms he used. Kubota ran La'ie's general store, and the previous night, after a long day of bad news on the radio, some locals had come by, pounded on the front door, and made threats. One was said to have brandished a machete. They were angry and shocked, as the whole nation was in the aftermath of the surprise attack. Kubota was one of the few Japanese Americans in the village and president of the local Japanese language school. He had become a target for their rage and suspicion. A wise man, he locked all his doors and windows and did not open his store the next day, but stayed closed and waited for news from some official.

He was a *kibei*, a Japanese American born in Hawaii (a U.S. territory then, so he was thus a citizen) but who was subsequently sent back by his father for formal education in Hiroshima, Japan, their home province. *Kibei* is written with two ideograms in Japanese: one is the word for "return" and the other is the word for "rice." Poetically, it means one who returns from America, known as the Land of Rice in Japanese (by contrast, Chinese immigrants called their new home Mountain of Gold).

Kubota was graduated from a Japanese high school and then came back to Hawaii as a teenager. He spoke English—and a Hawaiian creole version of it at that—with a Japanese accent. But he was well liked and good at numbers, scrupulous and hard working like so many immigrants and children of immigrants. Castle & Cook, a grower's company that ran the sugarcane business along the North Shore, hired him at first as a stock boy and then appointed him to run one of its company stores. He did well, had the trust of management and labor—not an easy accomplishment in any day—married, had children, and had begun to exert himself in community affairs and excel in his own recreations. He put together a Japanese community organization that backed a Japanese language school for children and sponsored teachers

Kubota

from Japan. Kubota boarded many of them, in succession, in his own home. This made dinners a silent affair for his talkative, Hawaiian-bred children, as their stern *sensei*, or teacher, was nearly always at table and their own abilities in the Japanese language were as delinquent as their attendance. While Kubota and the *sensei* rattled on about things Japanese, speaking Japanese, his children hurried through their suppers and tried to run off early to listen to the radio shows.

After dinner, while the *sensei* graded exams seated in a wicker chair in the spare room and his wife and children gathered around the radio in the front parlor, Kubota sat on the screened porch outside, reading the local Japanese newspapers. He finished reading about the same time as he finished the tea he drank for his digestion—a habit he'd learned in Japan—and then he'd get out his fishing gear and spread it out on the plank floors. The wraps on his rods needed to be redone, gears in his reels needed oil, and, once through with those tasks, he'd painstakingly wind on hundreds of yards of new line. Fishing was his hobby and his passion. He spent weekends camping along the North Shore beaches with his children, setting up umbrella tents, packing a rice pot and hibachi along for meals. And he caught fish. *Ulu'a* mostly, the huge surf-feeding fish known on the mainland as the jack crevalle, but he'd go after almost anything in its season. In Kawela, a plantation-owned bay nearby, he fished for mullet Hawaiian-style with a throw net, stalking the bottom-hugging, gray-backed schools as they gathered at the stream mouths and in the freshwater springs. In an outrigger out beyond the reef, he'd try for *aku*—the skipjack tuna prized for steaks and, sliced raw and mixed with fresh seaweed and cut onions, for *sashimi* salad. In Kahaluu and Ka'awa and on an offshore rock locals called Goat Island, he loved to go torching, stringing lanterns on bamboo poles stuck in the sand to attract *kumu'u*, the red goatfish, as they schooled at night just inside the reef. But in Lai'e on Laniloa Point near Kahuku, the northernmost tip of Oahu, he cast twelve-and fourteen-foot surf rods for the huge, varicolored, and fast-running *ulu'a* as they ran for schools of squid and baitfish just beyond the biggest breakers and past the low sand flats wadable from the shore to nearly a half mile out. At sunset, against the western light, he looked as if he walked on water as he came back, fish and rods slung over his shoulders, stepping along the rock and coral path just inches under the surface of a running tide.

When it was torching season, in December or January, he'd drive out the afternoon before and stay with old friends, the Tanakas or Yoshikawas, shopkeepers like him who ran stores near the fishing grounds. They'd have been preparing for weeks, selecting and cutting their bamboo poles, cleaning the hurricane lanterns, tearing up burlap sacks for the cloths they'd soak with kerosene and tie onto sticks they'd poke into the soft sand of the

Kubota

shallows. Once lit, touched off with a Zippo lighter, these would be the torches they'd use as beacons to attract the schooling fish. In another time, they might have made up a dozen paper lanterns of the kind mostly used for decorating the summer folk dances outdoors on the grounds of the Buddhist church during O-Bon, the Festival for the Dead. But now, wealthy and modern and efficient killers of fish, Tanaka and Kubota used rag torches and Colemans and cast rods with tips made of Tonkin bamboo and butts of American-spun fiberglass. After just one good night, they might bring back a prize bounty of a dozen burlap bags filled with scores of bloody, rigid fish delicious to eat and even better to give away as gifts to friends, family, and special customers.

It was a Monday night, the day after Pearl Harbor, and there was a rattling knock at the front door. Two FBI agents presented themselves, showed identification, and took my grandfather in for questioning in Honolulu. He didn't return home for days. No one knew what had happened or what was wrong. But there was a roundup going on of all those in the Japanese American community suspected of sympathizing with the enemy and worse. My grandfather was suspected of espionage, of communicating with offshore Japanese submarines launched from the attack fleet days before war began. Torpedo planes and escort fighters, decorated with the insignia of the Rising Sun, had taken an approach route from northwest of Oahu directly across Kahuku Point and on toward Pearl. They had strafed an auxiliary air station near the fishing grounds my grandfather loved and destroyed a small gun battery there, killing three men. Kubota was known to have sponsored and harbored Japanese nationals in his own home. He had a radio. He had wholesale access to firearms. Circumstances and an undertone of racial resentment had combined with wartime hysteria in the aftermath of the tragic naval battle to cast suspicion on the loyalties of my grandfather and all other Japanese Americans. The FBI reached out and pulled hundreds of them in for questioning in dragnets cast throughout the West Coast and Hawaii.

My grandfather was lucky; he'd somehow been let go after only a few days. Others were not as fortunate. Hundreds, from small communities in Washington, California, Oregon, and Hawaii, were rounded up and, after what appeared to be routine questioning, shipped off under Justice Department orders to holding centers in Leuppe on the Navaho reservation in Arizona, in Fort Missoula in Montana, and on Sand Island in Honolulu Harbor. There were other special camps on Maui in Ha'iku and on Hawaii—the Big Island—in my own home village of Volcano.

Many of these men—it was exclusively the Japanese American men suspected of ties to Japan who were initially rounded up—did not see their families again for more than four years. Under a suspension of due process that was only after the fact ruled as warranted by military necessity, they were, if only temporarily, "disappeared" in Justice Department prison camps scattered in particularly desolate areas of the United States designated as militarily "safe." These were grim forerunners of the assembly centers and concentration camps for the 120,000 Japanese American evacuees that were to come later.

I am Kubota's eldest grandchild, and I remember him as a lonely, habitually silent old man who lived with us in our home near Los Angeles for most of my childhood and adolescence. It was the fifties, and my parents had emigrated from Hawaii to the mainland in the hope of a better life away from the old sugar plantation. After some success, they had sent back for my grandparents and taken them in. And it was my grandparents who did the work of the household while my mother and father worked their salaried city jobs. My grandmother cooked and sewed, washed our clothes, and knitted in the front room under the light of a huge lamp with a bright three-way bulb. Kubota raised a flower garden, read up on soils and grasses in gardening books, and planted a zoysia lawn in front and a dichondra one in back. He planted a small patch near the rear block wall with green onions, eggplant, white Japanese radishes, and cucumber. While he hoed and spaded the loamless, clayey earth of Los Angeles, he sang particularly plangent songs in Japanese about plum blossoms and bamboo groves.

Once, in the mid-sixties, after a dinner during which, as always, he had been silent while he worked away at a meal of fish and rice spiced with dabs of Chinese mustard and catsup thinned with soy sauce, Kubota took his own dishes to the kitchen sink and washed them up. He took a clean jelly jar out of the cupboard—the glass was thick and its shape squatty like an old-fashioned. He reached around to the hutch below where he kept his bourbon. He made himself a drink and retired to the living room where I was expected to join him for "talk story," the Hawaiian idiom for chewing the fat.

I was a teenager and, though I was bored listening to stories I'd heard often enough before at holiday dinners, I was dutiful. I took my spot on the couch next to Kubota and heard him out. Usually, he'd tell me about his schooling in Japan where he learned judo along with mathematics and literature. He'd learned the *soroban* there—the abacus, which was the original pocket calculator of the Far East—and that, along with his strong, judo-trained back, got him his first job in Hawaii. This was the moral. "Study *ha-ahd*," he'd say with pidgin emphasis. "Learn read good. Learn speak da kine *good* English." The message is the familiar one taught to any children of immigrants: succeed through education. And imitation. But this time, Kubota reached down into his past and told me a different story. I was thirteen by then, and I suppose he thought me ready for it. He told me about

Kubota

Pearl Harbor, how the planes flew in wing after wing of formations over his old house in La'ie in Hawaii, and how, the next day, after Roosevelt had made his famous "Day of Infamy" speech about the treachery of the Japanese, the FBI agents had come to his door and taken him in, hauled him off to Honolulu for questioning, and held him without charge for several days. I thought he was lying. I thought he was making up a kind of horror story to shock me and give his moral that much more starch. But it was true. I asked around. I brought it up during history class in junior high school, and my teacher, after silencing me and stepping me off to the back of the room, told me that it was indeed so. I asked my mother and she said it was true. I asked my schoolmates, who laughed and ridiculed me for being so ignorant. We lived in a Japanese American community, and the parents of most of my classmates were the *nisei* who had been interned as teenagers all through the war. But there was a strange silence around all of this. There was a hush, as if one were invoking the ill powers of the dead when one brought it up. No one cared to speak about the evacuation and relocation for very long. It wasn't in our history books, though we were studying World War II at the time. It wasn't in the family albums of the people I knew and whom I'd visit staying over weekends with friends. And it wasn't anything that the family talked about or allowed me to keep bringing up either. I was given the facts, told sternly and pointedly that "it was war" and that "nothing could be done." "*Shikatta ga nai*" is the phrase in Japanese, a kind of resolute and determinist pronouncement on how to deal with inexplicable tragedy. I was to know it but not to dwell on it. Japanese Americans were busy trying to forget it ever happened and were having a hard enough time building their new lives after "camp." It was as if we had no history for four years and the relocation was something unspeakable.

But Kubota would not let it go. In session after session, for months it seemed, he pounded away at his story. He wanted to tell me the names of the FBI agents. He went over their questions and his responses again and again. He'd tell me how one would try to act friendly toward him, offering him cigarettes while the other, who hounded him with accusations and threats, left the interrogation room. Good cop, bad cop, I thought to myself, already superficially streetwise from stories black classmates told of the Watts riots and from my having watched too many episodes of *Dragnet* and *The Mod Squad*. But Kubota was not interested in my experiences. I was not made yet, and he was determined that his stories be part of my making. He spoke quietly at first, mildly, but once into his narrative and after his drink was down, his voice would rise and quaver with resentment and he'd make his accusations. He gave his testimony to me and I held it at first cautiously in my conscience like it was an heirloom too delicate to expose to strangers and anyone outside of the world Kubota made with his

Kubota

words. "I give you story now," he once said, "and you learn speak good, eh?" It was my job, as the disciple of his preaching I had then become, Ananda to his Buddha, to reassure him with a promise. "You learn speak good like the Dillingham," he'd say another time, referring to the wealthy scion of the grower family who had once run, unsuccessfully, for one of Hawaii's first senatorial seats. Or he'd then invoke a magical name, the name of one of his heroes, a man he thought particularly exemplary and righteous. "Learn speak dah good Ing-rish like *Mistah Inouye*," Kubota shouted. "He *lick* dah Dillingham even in debate. I saw on *terre-bision* myself." He was remembering the debates before the first senatorial election just before Hawaii was admitted to the Union as its fiftieth state. "You *tell* story," Kubota would end. And I had my injunction.

The town we settled in after the move from Hawaii is called Gardena, the independently incorporated city south of Los Angeles and north of San Pedro harbor. At its northern limit, it borders on Watts and Compton, black towns. To the southwest are Torrance and Redondo Beach, white towns. To the rest of L.A., Gardena is primarily famous for having legalized five-card draw poker after the war. On Vermont Boulevard, its eastern border, there is a dingy little Vegas-like strip of card clubs with huge parking lots and flickering neon signs that spell out "The Rainbow" and "The Horseshoe" in timed sequences of varicolored lights. The town is only secondarily famous as the largest community of Japanese Americans in the United States outside of Honolulu, Hawaii. When I was in high school there, it seemed to me that every *sansei* kid I knew wanted to be a doctor, an engineer, or a pharmacist. Our fathers were gardeners or electricians or nurserymen or ran small businesses catering to other Japanese Americans. Our mothers worked in civil service for the city or as cashiers for Thrifty Drug. What the kids wanted was a good job, good pay, a fine home, and no troubles. No one wanted to mess with the law— from either side—and no one wanted to mess with language or art. They all talked about getting into the right clubs so that they could go to the right schools. There was a certain kind of sameness, an intensely enforced system of conformity. Style was all. Boys wore moccasin-sewn shoes from Flagg Brothers, black A-1 slacks, and Kensington shirts with high collars. Girls wore their hair up in stiff bouffants solidified in hairspray and knew all the latest dances from the slauson to the funky chicken. We did well in chemistry and in math, no one who was Japanese but me spoke in English class or in history unless called upon, and no one talked about World War II. The day after Robert Kennedy was assassinated, after winning the California Democratic primary, we worked on calculus and elected class coordinators for the prom, featuring the 5th Dimension. We avoided grief. We avoided government. We avoided strong feelings and dangers of any kind. Once punished, we tried to maintain a concerted emotional and social discipline and would not willingly seek to fall out of the narrow margin of protective favor again.

But when I was thirteen, in junior high, I'd not understood why it was so difficult for my classmates, those who were themselves Japanese American, to talk about the relocation. They had cringed, too, when I tried to bring it up during our discussions of World War II. I was Hawaiian-born. They were mainland-born. Their parents had been in camp, had been the ones to suffer the complicated experience of having to distance themselves from their own history and all things Japanese in order to make their way back and into the American social and economic mainstream. It was out of this sense of shame and a fear of stigma I was only beginning to understand that the *nisei* had silenced themselves. And, for their children, among whom I grew up, they wanted no heritage, no culture, no contact with a defiled history. I recall the silence very well. The Japanese American children around me were burdened in a way I was not. Their injunction was silence. Mine was to speak.

Away at college, in another protected world in its own way as magical to me as the Hawaii of my childhood, I dreamed about my grandfather. Tired from studying languages, practicing German conjugations or scripting an army's worth of Chinese ideograms on a single sheet of paper, Kubota would come to me as I drifted off into sleep. Or I would walk across the newly mown ball field in back of my dormitory, cutting through a street-side phalanx of ancient eucalyptus trees on my way to visit friends off campus, and I would think of him, his anger, and his sadness.

I don't know myself what makes someone feel that kind of need to have a story they've lived through be deposited somewhere, but I can guess. I think about *The Iliad, The Odyssey, The Peloponnesian Wars* of Thucydides, and a myriad of the works of literature I've studied. A character, almost a *topoi* he occurs so often, is frequently the witness who gives personal testimony about an event the rest of his community cannot even imagine. The sibyl is such a character. And Procne, the maid whose tongue is cut out so that she will not tell that she has been raped by her own brother-in-law, the king of Thebes. There are the dime novels, the epic blockbusters Hollywood makes into miniseries, and then there are the plain, relentless stories of witnesses who have suffered through horrors major and minor that have marked and changed their lives. I myself haven't talked to Holocaust victims. But I've read their survival stories and their stories of witness and been revolted and moved by them. My father-in-law, Al Thiessen, tells me his war stories again and again and I listen. A Mennonite who set aside the strictures of his own church in order to serve, he was a Marine codeman in the Pacific

Kubota

during World War II, in the Signal Corps on Guadalcanal, Morotai, and Bougainville. He was part of the island-hopping maneuver MacArthur had devised to win the war in the Pacific. He saw friends die from bombs which exploded not ten yards away. When he was with the 298th Signal Corps attached to the Thirteenth Air Force, he saw plane after plane come in and crash, just short of the runway, killing their crews, setting the jungle ablaze with oil and gas fires. Emergency wagons would scramble, bouncing over newly bulldozed land men used just the afternoon before for a football game. Every time we go fishing together, whether it's in a McKenzie boat drifting for salmon in Tillamook Bay or taking a lunch break from wading the riffles of a stream in the Cascades, he tells me about what happened to him and the young men in his unit. One was a Jewish boy from Brooklyn. One was a foul-mouthed kid from Kansas. They died. And he *has* to tell me. And I *have* to listen. It's a ritual payment the young owe their elders who have survived. The evacuation and relocation is something like that.

Kubota, my grandfather, had been ill with Alzheimer's disease for some time before he died. At the house he'd built on Kamehameha Highway in Hau'ula, a seacoast village just down the road from La'ie where he had his store, he'd wander out from the garage or greenhouse where he'd set up a workbench, and trudge down to the beach or up toward the line of pines he'd planted while employed by the Work Projects Administration during the thirties. Kubota thought he was going fishing. Or he thought he was back at work for Roosevelt, planting pines as a windbreak or soilbreak on the windward flank of the Ko'olau Mountains, emerald monoliths rising out of sea and cane fields from Waialua to Kaneohe. When I visited, my grandmother would send me down to the beach to fetch him. Or I'd run down Kam Highway a quarter mile or so and find him hiding in the cane field by the roadside, counting stalks, measuring circumferences in the claw of his thumb and forefinger. The look on his face was confused or concentrated, I didn't know which. But I guessed he was going fishing again, I'd grab him and walk him back to his house on the highway. My grandmother would shut him in a room.

Within a few years, Kubota had a stroke and survived it, then he had another one and was completely debilitated. The family decided to put him in a nursing home in Kahuku, just set back from the highway, within a mile or so of Kahuku Point and the Tanaka Store where he had his first job as a stock boy. He lived there three years, and I visited him once with my aunt. He was like a potato that had been worn down by cooking. Everything on him—his eyes, his teeth, his legs and torso—seemed like it had been sloughed away. What he had been was mostly gone now and I was looking at the nub of a man. In a wheelchair, he grasped my hands and tugged on them—violently. His hands were still thick and, I believed, strong enough to lift me out of my own seat into his lap. He murmured something in Japanese—he'd long ago ceased to speak any English. My aunt and I cried a little, and we left him.

I remember walking out on the black asphalt of the parking lot of the nursing home. It was heat-cracked and eroded already, and grass had veined itself into the interstices. There were coconut trees around, a cane field I could see across the street, and the ocean I knew was pitching a surf just beyond it. The green Ko'olaus came up behind us. Somewhere nearby, alongside the beach, there was an abandoned airfield in the middle of the canes. As a child, I'd come upon it playing one day, and my friends and I kept returning to it, day after day, playing war or sprinting games or coming to fly kites. I recognize it even now when I see it on TV—it's used as a site for action scenes in the detective shows Hollywood always sets in the islands: a helicopter chasing the hero racing away in a Ferrari, or gun dealers making a clandestine rendezvous on the abandoned runway. It was the old airfield strafed by Japanese planes the day the major flight attacked Pearl Harbor. It was the airfield the FBI thought my grandfather had targeted in his night fishing and signaling with the long surf poles he'd stuck in the sandy bays near Kahuku Point.

Kubota died a short while after I visited him, but not, I thought, without giving me a final message. I was on the mainland, in California studying for Ph.D. exams, when my grandmother called me with the news. It was a relief. He'd suffered from his debilitation a long time and I was grateful he'd gone. I went home for the funeral and gave the eulogy. My grandmother and I took his ashes home in a small, heavy metal box wrapped in a black *furoshiki*, a large silk scarf. She showed me the name the priest had given to him on his death, scripted with a calligraphy brush on a long, narrow talent of plain wood. Buddhist commoners, at death, are given priestly names, received symbolically into the clergy. The idea is that, in their next life, one of scholarship and leisure, they might meditate and attain the enlightenment the religion is aimed at. "*Shaku Shūchi*," the ideograms read. It was Kubota's Buddhist name, incorporating characters from his family and given names. It meant "Shining Wisdom of the Law." He died on Pearl Harbor Day, December 7, 1983.

After years, after I'd finally come back to live in Hawaii again, only once did I dream of Kubota, my grandfather. It was the same night I'd heard HR 442, the redress bill for Japanese Americans, had been signed into law. In my dream that night Kubota was "torching," and he sang a Japanese song, a querulous and wavery folk ballad, as he hung paper lanterns on bamboo poles stuck into the sand in the shallow water of the lagoon behind the reef near Kahuku Point. Then he was at a work table,

Kubota

smoking a hand-rolled cigarette, letting it dangle from his lips Bogart-style as he drew, daintily and skillfully, with a narrow trim brush, ideogram after ideogram on a score of paper lanterns he had hung in a dark shed to dry. He had painted a talismanic mantra onto each lantern, the ideogram for the word "red" in Japanese, a bit of art blended with some superstition, a piece of sympathetic magic appealing to the magenta coloring on the rough skins of the schooling, night-feeding fish he wanted to attract to his baited hooks. He strung them from pole to pole in the dream then, hiking up his khaki worker's pants so his white ankles showed and wading through the shimmering black waters of the sand flats and then the reef. "The moon is leaving, leaving," he sang in Japanese. "Take me deeper in the savage sea." He turned and crouched like an ice racer then, leaning forward so that his unshaven face almost touched the light film of water. I could see the light stubble of beard like a fine, gray ash covering the lower half of his face. I could see his gold-rimmed spectacles. He held a small wooden boat in his cupped hands and placed it lightly on the sea and pushed it away. One of his lanterns was on it and, written in small neat rows like a sutra scroll, it had been decorated with the silvery names of all our dead.

Responding to the Selection ———————

Questions for Discussion

1. Do you think that the FBI agents had any good reasons to be suspicious of Kubota? Why or why not?

2. How much of Kubota's silence and loneliness later in his life would you attribute to bitterness over his experiences during World War II?

3. Compare the attitudes of Garrett Hongo and his classmates toward the treatment of Japanese Americans during the war. How would you explain the reaction of Hongo's classmates to his questions?

4. Garrett Hongo told an interviewer, "I share with so many Japanese Americans of my generation a feeling that we have a story to tell, that we have a responsibility. . . ." Do you feel that your generation has a story to tell? What is that story? Why is it important for your generation to tell it?

5. In your opinion, what is the best way for governments to make up for violating the rights of large groups of people?

Activities

Conducting an Interview

1. Interview someone who was an adult during World War II. Ask this person about his or her feelings regarding the wartime treatment of Japanese Americans. Then write a summary of your interview.

Discussing in a Group

2. Do you think that the injustices experienced by Japanese Americans could happen again in the United States if the country were attacked? What groups of people might be targets of similar hostility? What should the government do about it? Conduct a group discussion on this question.

Writing Creatively

3. In an interview, Garrett Hongo said, "I believe that people are basically good, not basically bad. So I believe that if they learn to trust their nature, something good will emerge out of it." Write a short story, poem, or essay in response to this statement.

Newspaper Article

This newspaper article describes a White House ceremony to present to Japanese American soldiers the nation's highest military honor.

Asian American WWII valor honored

by Naftali Bendavid—*Chicago Tribune*, June 22, 2000

WASHINGTON—Finding his platoon under blistering three-way crossfire, Sgt. Yukio Okutsu crawled under the bullets to hurl two grenades into one machine-gun nest, dashed to another and took it out also. Bullets slamming into his helmet briefly knocked him out, but he recovered and charged a third nest.

Okutsu should have won the Medal of Honor for that extraordinary bravery in Italy in April 1945, but he didn't. The military establishment was ambivalent about Japanese Americans; we were at war with Japan, after all, a conflict that had cost extensive U.S. casualties.

On Wednesday, 55 years after Okutsu's heroics, he walked across a stage in the White House, gray-haired now but still erect in bearing, to receive the Medal of Honor from President Clinton for what the military calls "conspicuous gallantry and intrepidity."

Okutsu was joined by six other Asian American World War II heroes and the relatives of 14 others no longer alive in a ceremony acknowledging American soldiers who fought with exceptional bravery even as their friends and relatives back home were held in detention centers.

The ceremony was part of a renewed focus on World War II at the beginning of a new century as the great war's veterans are increasingly dying out. Among other things, the re-examination has fostered a new determination to honor those who were overlooked, including minorities who fought against Hitler in a segregated military.

"We were not only fighting for freedom and equality abroad," Clinton said Wednesday. "We were also in a struggle here at home over whether America would be defined narrowly, on the basis of race, or broadly, on the basis of shared values and ideals."

Wartime military leaders at first had no use for Japanese-Americans because of "the universal distrust in which they are held," as one committee put it. They eventually relented, and young Japanese Americans in many cases volunteered directly from the detention camps, where they had been locked up after the attack on Pearl Harbor, to fight for the country that was imprisoning them.

"That is the amazing fact," said Kristine Miami, Washington representative of the Japanese American Citizens' League. "Some of them volunteered out of internment camps while their families were still there. They were intent on proving their loyalty. It was, 'The country doesn't believe I'm loyal, and I've got something to prove.'"

Few doubt that they did that. Many believe that the 442nd Regimental Combat Team, made up of Japanese-Americans, was intentionally dispatched to the most dangerous battles of the European theater.

The regiment became legendary, adopting the motto "Go for broke" and

becoming the most decorated unit in Army history. . . .

Yet even then prejudice was evident. On the corpse of one dead soldier, a chaplain found a letter from his father reporting that the family's house and barn had been burned down. . . .

Sen. Daniel Inouye (D-Hawaii), one of those decorated Wednesday, entered a barber shop shortly after returning home to Hawaii in full uniform, 15 medals dangling from his chest, missing the right arm he had lost in combat and was told that "we don't cut Jap hair." . . .

"I get choked up thinking about it," said Karen Narasaki, executive director of the National Asian Pacific American Legal Consortium, who was at the event and whose father fought in the 442nd. "That was a particularly painful time because of the internment. There is still a lot of pain. These things are important because it brings closure."

But she added, "What is remarkable about the United States is that it can say, 'OK, we made a mistake. We will acknowledge it, and then we will move on.'"

Questions for Discussion

1. Why did so many Japanese American soldiers fight so bravely during the war?

2. Do you think that Japanese Americans would have been justified in not fighting during the war? Why or why not?

Before You Read

Can't Tell and From a Heart of Rice Straw

Nellie Wong
Born 1934

> *"My poems feed my activism and my activism feeds my poetry."*

About Wong

Nellie Wong is the daughter of Chinese immigrants. She grew up in the Chinatown district of Oakland, California. When she began writing in her mid-thirties, she was employed as a secretary. At first she had many self-doubts, but she says that the act of writing motivated her to make changes in her own life and to work for change in society. Wong enrolled at San Francisco State University, where she earned a bachelor's degree. She also became involved in political and feminist organizations.

Wong often writes about her experiences in the workplace and about the lives of immigrants. She was featured in the documentary film, *Mitsuye and Nellie, Asian American Poets.* The author of three volumes of verse, Wong is especially proud that two of her poems are engraved, one in granite and one in bronze, on the streets of San Francisco as part of a public arts program.

Background

One of the poems you will read, "Can't Tell," portrays the experience of a Chinese American family after the Japanese attack on Pearl Harbor in 1941. Although the United States and China were allies during World War II, Chinese Americans were not immune to the "yellow peril" hysteria that erupted in this country. Some began to wear "I Am a Chinese" buttons because they were afraid of being mistaken for Japanese Americans and assaulted.

Can't Tell

— *Nellie Wong*

When World War II was declared
on the morning radio,
we glued our ears, widened our eyes.
Our bodies shivered.

5   A voice said
Japan was the enemy,
Pearl Harbor a shambles
and in our grocery store
in Berkeley, we were suspended

10   next to the meat market
where voices hummed,
valises, pots and pans packed,
no more hot dogs, baloney,
pork kidneys.

15   We children huddled on wooden planks
and my parents whispered:
We are Chinese, we are Chinese.
Safety pins anchored,
our loins ached.

20   Shortly our Japanese neighbors vanished
and my parents continued to whisper:
We are Chinese, we are Chinese.

We wore black arm bands,
put up a sign
25   in bold letters.

From a Heart of Rice Straw

— Nellie Wong

Ma, my heart must be made of rice straw,
the kind you fed a fire in Papa's home village
so Grandma could have hot tea upon waking,
so Grandma could wash her sleepy eyes. My heart
5   knocks as silently as that LeCoultre clock
that Papa bought with his birthday money.
It swells like a baby in your stomach.

Your tears have flooded the house, this life.
For Canton? No, you left home forty years ago
10   for the fortune Papa sought in Gum San.
In Gold Mountain you worked side by side
in the lottery with regular pay offs
to the Oakland cops. To feed your six daughters
until one day Papa's cousin shot him.

15   I expected you to fly into the clouds, wail
at Papa's side, but you chased cousin instead.
Like the cops and robbers on the afternoon radio.
It didn't matter that Papa lay bleeding.
It didn't matter that cousin accused Papa
20   of cheating him. You ran, kicking
your silk slippers on the street, chasing
cousin until you caught him, gun still in hand.
My sister and I followed you, crying.

If cousin had shot you, you would have died.
25   The cops showed up and you told them how cousin
gunned Papa down, trusted kin who smoked
Havana cigars after filling his belly with rice
and chicken in our big yellow house.

Papa lay in his hospital bed, his kidney removed.
30   Three bullets out. They couldn't find the last
bullet. A search was made, hands dove into Papa's
shirt pocket. A gold watch saved Papa's life.

Ma, you've told this story one hundred times.
The cops said you were brave. The neighbors said
35   you were brave. The relatives shook their heads,
the bravery of a Gold Mountain woman unknown
in the old home village.

The papers spread the shooting all over town.
One said Papa dueled with his brother like
40   a bar room brawl. One said it was the beginning
of a tong war, but that Occidental law
would prevail. To them, to the outside,
what was another tong war, another dead Chinaman?

But Papa fooled them. He did not die
45   by his cousin's hand. The lottery closed down.
We got food on credit. You wept.
I was five years old.

My heart, once bent and cracked, once
ashamed of your China ways.
50   Ma, hear me now, tell me your story
again and again.

Responding to the Selection

Questions for Discussion

1. Compare the styles of "Can't Tell" and the poem "From A Heart of Rice Straw." Why might the author have chosen to vary her style in these two poems?

2. Both poems describe childhood experiences. What sort of lasting impact did the experiences have on the speakers?

3. What does the title "Can't Tell" refer to?

4. The speaker of the poem "From A Heart of Rice Straw" compares her heart to rice straw. What does she seem to be suggesting about her present and past feelings with this metaphor?

Activities

Writing an Essay

1. In "Can't Tell," a Chinese American family does not publicly protest the treatment of their Japanese American neighbors. Why did they remain silent? Do you think that there is greater solidarity today among ethnic groups in the United States than there was during World War II? Write a brief essay in response to these questions.

Writing a Journal Entry

2. In your journal, describe a time when a parent or guardian did something that took you by surprise. How did the incident change your impression of this person?

Expressing Poetry Artistically

3. Both of these poems contain striking visual images. Using an art medium of your choice, represent one of the images.

Before You Read

Obasan in Suburbia

Susan Ito
Born 1959

> *"I am grateful to language, the place where I went in my greatest confusion, where the question 'Who am I?' ricocheted around and around, making me dizzy."*

About Ito

When Susan Ito was an infant, her mother gave her up for adoption to a Japanese American couple who had waited ten years for a child. Her adoptive parents were often confronted with questions about her racial background, which Ito describes as "fifty percent Japanese, and fifty percent . . . unknown." Because of her experiences, Ito is fascinated by literature that explores the complexities of adoption, especially in cases involving a mixed-race child.

Ito has co-edited an anthology called *A Ghost at Heart's Edge: Stories and Poems about Adoption.* She lives in Oakland, California, where she teaches creative writing. Ito's stories, poems, and essays have appeared in numerous publications.

Generations

The grandmother portrayed in "Obasan in Suburbia" is an *issei,* or first-generation Japanese immigrant. While growing up in Japan, she would have been taught to place a high value on family obligations. *Issei* were generally willing to make great sacrifices for their children. In return they expected appreciation and obedience. Most *issei* planned to live with their children when they grew old. The *nisei* (second generation) were exposed to American ways at an early age. Although many *nisei* showed considerable respect to their parents, there was often friction between the two generations. The more assimilated the *nisei* became, the more likely they were to reject traditional Japanese views about the roles of husbands and wives, parents and children.

Obasan in Suburbia

— *Susan Ito*

When my grandmother was eighty years old, she got kicked out of her house for leaving her nighttime *kimono* in the bathroom one time too many. I remember the day she moved; I was ten. I sat in the backseat of my parents' station wagon while my father loaded her things—they fit easily into three or four cartons. He wrapped her little black and white television in a white chenille bedspread and laid it on the floor by my feet. She sat next to me, looking out the window, with a Kleenex in her fist.

She was living with my uncle Taro, her youngest son, his wife and my little cousin Jenney, in the big pink house she and my grandfather had bought after the war. When Uncle Taro brought his bride, Michiko, down from Canada, my grandparents invited them to stay until their savings grew. They never got any savings. They bought a car, a big one with automatic windows. They bought a fur coat. They bought television sets for every room in the pink house, and when my grandfather died ten years later, it was clear that Uncle Taro and his family weren't going anywhere.

That was all right. Nana would have been sad if they'd left her alone in all that space. But by that time the house had filled up with their things, pushing my grandmother to the outer perimeters of the house. She slept in the attic, in a small room with a slanted ceiling. Even though she was tiny, not even five feet tall, she could only stand up in the center of the room. She took her meals in the basement, back behind the laundry room where my grandfather had built a small, second kitchen, a one-burner stove next to an industrial size freezer. Sometimes she rested her plate on the ping-pong table and watched the Lawrence Welk Show while she ate.

The rest of them ate above her, Jenney spilling her Spaghetti-O's on the linoleum floor. It was like a split screen television, America above, and Japan below. Upstairs, they called themselves Ray and Lillian. Lil. I think Michiko chose that name intentionally, knowing that my grandmother would never be able to pronounce it. "Lil-lian," she tried to say, but it always came out sounding like "Re-run." Changing their names never seemed right, anyway. Once, my mother told me that Aunt Michi's mother up in Canada never knew she was calling herself Lil. To me, they were always Uncle Taro and Aunt Michi. Ray and Lil sounded like something out of I Love Lucy. But there they were, upstairs, trying to fit that suburban life around them. He joined the volunteer fire department. She gave Tupperware parties.

In the downstairs kitchen, my grandmother shuffled on the cement floor in her rubber-soled *zoris*. She washed the rice in the sink where Lil's nylons hung, dripping. There was a pantry down there, next to the enormous refrigerator. One shelf was designated for her food, the cans she carried in a canvas bag on the subway from Manhattan. *Kamaboko,* and the stinky yellow *daikon.* White fish cakes with the hot pink coating. I stacked the cans and cellophane packages, neatly, on her shelf, playing Japanese grocer with my play money. *"Ikura?"* I asked my grandmother. "How much?" "Two hundred dollar, please," she laughed. Her teeth clicked in her mouth, and she covered her face with the back of her hand.

After a while they stopped letting her talk to Jenney. "She won't be able to learn English," said Aunt Michi. "When she goes to school, people will think she talks funny."

Ray and Lil gave barbecues in the backyard, my uncle wearing a red butcher's apron. They couldn't keep Nana locked in the attic, not on weekends with everyone around, so she sat in the cool basement, rolling logs of *sushi* on little bamboo mats. I helped her with the *nori*, thin sheets of green-black seaweed. You had to toast it first, holding it carefully over a gas flame or a candle. Nana didn't mind when I burned holes in it. "Don't worry. It's a window for the *gohan* to look out." We arranged the sushi pieces on a big round platter, and brought them out to the picnic table. Nana put it down right next to whatever Aunt Michi had made, green Jell-O or fruit cocktail with little marshmallows in it. Michi would make a face when she saw the *sushi,* like it was something strange and disgusting, so none of her friends would eat it either. She didn't tell them it was the same thing she loved to eat when she was a little girl. But sometimes I'd see her, after everyone went home, and she'd be standing next to the refrigerator, popping the little *norimaki* in her mouth when she thought no one was looking.

One of the problems with the house was that it only had one bathroom. Aunt Michi made it clear that it was *her* bathroom, and that other people, namely my uncle and cousin and Nana, were allowed to use it, but only because of her generosity. There were rules. The shampoo had to stay under the sink, not on the bathroom ledge. All her knick-knacks had to be arranged just so: the pink yarn sweater with the dog's head that covered the extra toilet tissue; the porcelain mermaid whose tail spread into a soap dish. Wet towels had to be taken directly down to the laundry room, and put in the dryer, set to high so that they'd fluff up. Wet towels were ugly.

One day, I was sitting in Nana's room, and the window was open. Michiko was out on the back patio with Kit. Kit was their next-door neighbor with red hair, who smoked, inhaling and exhaling like an accordion.

Aunt Michi said, "Tell me, Kit, what's it like to have your own house?" They were sitting in matching white Adirondack chairs, balancing glasses of iced tea on the armrests.

"Lil, believe me, it's no picnic. I've gotta clean up after the kids, after Mister Air-Conditioner King, with no help. At least you get a hand around here!" Kit took another long puff, and then let it out. "I don't think Ray's mother is so bad. What's the matter, she pick on you?"

I leaned against the window screen, not breathing.

After a pause, I heard Aunt Michi say, in her low gravelly voice, "She drives me nuts. She won't speak English. She won't eat anything that comes in an aluminum package. She shuffles around in those damn zoris like she's Mrs. Buddha. Kit, that woman has been here more than fifty years, and she acts like she just popped up out of a rice paddy!"

Kit laughed. "So she hasn't learned to say the Pledge of Allegiance yet. I think she's cute, Lil."

Aunt Michi snorted. "Cute. She's a pain in the *oshidi*."

"What?"

"You know what I mean."

Nana, at eighty years old, was still making a daily commute over the Hudson River to Manhattan, where she worked in a curtain factory. More than once, I watched her wrap Band-Aids around her fingers, which sometimes got caught under the machine's running needle. Her nails were purple and scarred, and each finger pad was a callous, but she liked her job. The sweatshop where she earned less than minimum wage was a place to feel busy, useful, a place to gossip with her Chinese lady friends.

My grandmother signed her paychecks, "Sadao Kitayama" in a long, snaky scrawl, the only English characters she knew. Then she turned them over to Uncle Taro for the mortgage payment. He went to the bank for her and deposited them in their joint account, keeping the little leather passbook in the locked drawer of his mahogany desk. It wasn't the money that mattered to her though, it was the work. Crossing the Hudson each morning on the big silver commuter bus gave her a sense of confidence, knowing that she could maneuver through places that Michi was afraid to go. She wandered by herself through the alleys of Chinatown, picking up unusual vegetables, carrying them in a bag made of plastic fishnet. Every night she came home, prepared dinner quietly by herself in the basement, and retired to her room in the attic.

Obasan in *Suburbia*

There was no sound to indicate her presence except the soft lilt of Lawrence Welk through the floor.

The crime that committed her to solitude though, the final insult, was the kimono, indigo and white in a bamboo pattern. She kept hanging it on the bathroom hook and forgetting to remove it in the morning. It riled my aunt; she didn't want to touch the thing, so she would leave it there and seethe all day. By the time Nana came home from work, Michi's face was set in steel. Two words only: "Kimono, Obasan."

No one ever told me the details of how it happened, how the family split that summer, like a tree struck by lightning. I imagined my aunt and uncle saying something to her about how there wasn't enough space for all of them. My parents offered up our spare room, told her she could move in with us right away. But Nana was too sad, and too proud to accept. She insisted that they help her find an apartment, something small enough to be rented on her paycheck. It was an old brick building, in the same complex where my parents had lived as newlyweds. There was talk of a legal battle, of my grandmother winning her house back, but she refused to do it. "Taro my smallest baby," she said, wiping her runny eyes. "No fight him with lawyer." She turned away from the pink house without a struggle.

After she moved, my parents and I drove to Nana's place every Wednesday night and took her out to dinner. It made me sad to see her whole life in such a tiny box, her studio apartment. One room held a miniature kitchen, a folding metal table which she used for meals, and to iron on. Underneath the window was her single bed, a plastic cube-shaped nightstand and a phonograph on a rolling tea cart. The bed was covered with the white chenille spread and two plain yellow throw pillows she had taken from my uncle's couch.

My father tried once, a few years later, to build a bridge to the other side, but it was already too late. He went to Uncle Taro's house and stood on the front step, shaking the quarters and pennies in his pockets. Taro talked to him from behind the screen door, repeating, "There's nothing to say." My father's effort collapsed like a thing made of old, hollow bones, and when he came back to our house that night, we knew there wouldn't be another try. He stood in the driveway and opened the door to the station wagon, and my mother and I got in. It was a Wednesday, fried chicken night at Howard Johnson's, and my grandmother was waiting for us.

Responding to the Selection

Questions for Discussion

1. Ito reveals the outcome of "Obasan in Suburbia" in the first paragraph. How did this affect your reading of the selection? Would you have preferred the outcome to be a surprise?

2. **Motivation** is the reason or reasons behind a character's actions. What seems to motivate Taro's and Michi's behavior toward the grandmother?

3. How is the conflict in the grandmother's house influenced by Japanese culture and tradition?

4. Do you think that the split in the family could have been avoided? Why or why not?

5. For whom in the story do you have more sympathy, Obasan, or Taro and Michi? Whose values do you feel are closer to your own?

Activities

Writing

1. Imagine that you are the narrator of "Obasan in Suburbia." Write a script of a conversation about the way your grandmother is treated by Taro and Michi. The conversation is between you and a radio talk show host who specializes in personal advice. Include the host's answers to your questions and comments.

Conducting a Survey

2. Conduct a survey on family values and living arrangements. Think of five questions you would like to ask friends and classmates. After you finish the survey, present your findings to the class. You might wish to use graphs or charts in the presentation.

Creating a Storyboard

3. Imagine that "Obasan in Suburbia" has been written and filmed as a TV show. Create a storyboard for a 15-second "trailer," or preview, for the show. What scene might you include? What would the voice-over announcer say about the show?

Before You Read

As the Crow Flies

David Henry Hwang
Born 1957

"Creating a mythology, creating a past for myself, involved going into Chinese history and Chinese-American history"

About Hwang

When he was growing up in California, David Henry Hwang thought that being Chinese American was "a minor detail, like having red hair." In college he became more interested in his heritage, and he also fell in love with theater. He explored the theme of assimilation in his play *FOB*, which he completed when he was twenty-two. The play had a successful run in New York City and launched his career. Wang became famous in 1988 for *M. Butterfly*, the first play by an Asian American to win a Tony Award, Broadway's equivalent of the movies' Oscar.

Hwang has been a strong supporter of Asian American theaters. Nevertheless, he feels that such institutions will eventually become obsolete as the United States grows increasingly multicultural. "The whole notion of what is ethnic as opposed to what is mainstream," he says, "is going to become more and more difficult to define."

Different Identities

According to Hwang, the characters of *As the Crow Flies* are based on his grandmother and her African American cleaning woman. The cleaning woman would switch between different identities, as a character does in the play. Hwang says that the fluid nature of identity is an important theme for him: "In a lot of my plays, from *FOB* to *M. Butterfly*, people become other people."

As the Crow Flies

— *David Henry Hwang*

CHARACTERS

HANNAH: a black woman in her 60s

MRS. CHAN: a Chinese woman in her 70s, sometimes called Popo (Grandma)

P.K.: a Chinese man in his 70s, sometimes called Gung Gung (Grandfather)

SANDRA: a black woman in her 40s

TIME and PLACE: *The living room of an upper middle-class home. The present.*

[*A living room in an upper middle-class home, owned by* MRS. CHAN, *a Chinese woman in her seventies, and her husband,* P.K. *Up right, a door leads out to the front driveway. Stage left is a door leading to the rest of the house.* MRS. CHAN *sits in a large chair, center stage, looking downstage out into a garden. Around her,* HANNAH, *a black woman in her late sixties, cleans. She has been their cleaning woman for over a decade.*]

HANNAH.   I guess I never told you this before, Mrs. Chan, but I think the time is right now. See, I'm really two different folks. You've been knowin' me as Hannah Carter, 'cuz when I'm over here cleanin', that's who I am. But at night, or when I'm outside and stuff, I turn into Sandra Smith. [*Beat.*] Is that all clear?

CHAN.   Um. Yeah.

HANNAH.   You got all that?

CHAN.   When you are here, you are Hannah Carter—

HANNAH.   Right.

CHAN.   And, then, you go outside, and you are . . . someone . . . someone . . .

HANNAH.   Sandra Smith.

CHAN. Um. Okay.

[*Pause.*]

HANNAH. You don't have any questions 'bout that?

CHAN. Hannah Carter, Sandra Smith—I understand.

HANNAH. Well, you know how you can tell the two apart?

CHAN. No. Because I have not seen Sandra—Sandra . . .

HANNAH. Smith. Well, when I'm Sandra Smith, see, I look different. First of all, I'm a lot younger.

CHAN. Good.

HANNAH. And, you know, since I'm younger, well, guess I'm looser, too. What I mean by that, is, when I talk, well, I use different words. Young words. And, Mrs. Chan, since I'm younger, my hair color's a lot different too. And I don't clean floors. 'Cuz young people nowadays, they don't clean floors. They stay up around the clock, and make themselves into lazy good-for-nothings, and drink a lot, and dance themselves into a state. Young people—I just don't know what's got into them. But whatever it is, the same thing's gotten into Sandra Smith. [*Pause.*] You don't think this is all a little strange?

CHAN. No.

HANNAH. Well, that's the first time . . . I remember when I told Mrs. Washburn about Sandra Smith—she just fell right over.

CHAN. So what? So you have two different people.

HANNAH. That's right. Living inside me.

CHAN. So what? My uncle had six!

HANNAH. Six people?

CHAN. Maybe even seven. Who can keep count?

HANNAH. Seven? All in one guy?

CHAN. Way back in China—my second uncle—he had seven, maybe even eight people—inside here. I don't . . . is hard to remember all their name.

HANNAH. I can believe that.

CHAN. Chan Yup Lee—he was, uh, I think, the businessman. He runs Uncle's import-export association. Good man. Very stingy. I like him. Then, I think there was another: ah, C. Y. Sing—he is the family man. Then, one man, Fat-Fingers Lew. Introduce this sport—what is the name? Ball goes through big hoop.

As the Crow Flies

HANNAH. Basketball?

CHAN. Yes, yes—introduce that to our village. Then, there is Big Ear Tong—collects debt for C.Y.'s company. Never talks, only fight. Then, also, one who has been to America—Morty Fong. He all the time warns us about Communists. And, then, oh, maybe two or three others that I hardly ever meet.

HANNAH. This is all one guy?

CHAN. Mmmmm.

HANNAH. Isn't that somethin'?

CHAN. No.

HANNAH. Huh?

CHAN. Whatever you can tell me—man with six persons inside, man with three heads, man who sees a flying ghost, a sitting ghost, a ghost disguise to look like his dead wife—none of these are so unusual.

HANNAH. No?

CHAN. I have lived a long time.

HANNAH. Well, so have I, Mrs. Chan, so have I. And I'm still scared of Sandra Smith.

CHAN. Scare? Why scare? Happens all the time.

HANNAH. I don't want Sandra comin' round to any of my houses that I clean.

CHAN. Aaah—do not worry.

HANNAH. Whaddya mean? Sandra's got no respect for authority.

CHAN. Do not worry. She will not come into any house.

HANNAH. What makes you so sure?

CHAN. You have to know how ghosts think. You say, Sandra appears outdoors. Therefore, she is the outside ghost. She cannot come inside.

HANNAH. Yeah? They got rules like that? In ghost-land?

CHAN. Yes—there are rules everyplace! Have you ever been someplace where there were none?

HANNAH. Well, no, but—

CHAN. You see? Ghosts cannot kill a man if there is a goldfish in the room. They will think the fish is gold, and take it instead. They cannot enter a house if there is a raised step in the doorway. Ghosts do not look, so they trip over it instead.

As the Crow Flies

HANNAH. These ghosts don't sound like they got a lot on the ball.

CHAN. Some ghosts, they are smart. But most ghosts, they are like most people. When alive, they were stupid. After death, they remain the same.

HANNAH. Well, I don't think Sandra's got much respect for those rules. That's probably why she showed up at Mrs. Washburn's.

CHAN. Inside the house?

HANNAH. 'Fraid so.

CHAN. Oh. Mrs. Washburn—does she have a goldfish?

HANNAH. No, no—I don't think so.

CHAN. There—you see?

HANNAH. Anyway, Mrs. Chan, I just thought I oughta tell you about her, on account of what happened to Mrs. Washburn. I been working for all you people ten, sometimes twenty years. All my clients—they're gettin' up there. We're all startin' to show our age. Can't compete with the young girls no more.

CHAN. I never try—even when I was one.

HANNAH. Well, the older I get, the more I see of Sandra, so I just thought I oughta be warnin' you.

CHAN. I am not afraid of Sandra Smith.

HANNAH. Well, good then. Good for you.

CHAN. She comes here, I will fight her. Not like these Americans. So stupid. Never think of these things. Never think of ghost. Never think of death. Never prepare for anything. Always think, life goes on and on, forever. And so, always, it ends.

HANNAH. Okay. Glad to hear it. Guess I'll go take the slime off the shower walls.

[HANNAH *exits, into the house.* CHAN *just stares downstage, from her chair. Silence.* P.K. *enters from the driveway, golf clubs slung over his shoulder.*]

P.K. Hi, Popo!

CHAN. Hello.

P.K. Do you have a beer?

CHAN. Look in 'frigerator.

P.K. Just return from a good game of golf!

CHAN. Ah! What are you talking about?

As the Crow Flies

P.K. Eighteen holes, Popo!

CHAN. Ai! You cannot remember anything anymore!

P.K. So? I remember that I go to golf!

CHAN. How can this be? You do not drive!

P.K. What do you mean? I drive the Eldorado.

CHAN. You cannot drive the Eldorado.

P.K. I do!

CHAN. Hanh! We sell it many years ago!

P.K. What?

CHAN. Yes! Remember? We sell it! To John, your nephew.

P.K. Huh? How much did he pay?

CHAN. Who cares?

P.K. I want to know!

CHAN. I always tell you, John buys the car; you always ask me, how much does he pay?

P.K. It is important! It is worth—lots of money!

CHAN. Ah, not so much money.

P.K. No! Lots!

CHAN. Not after Humphrey breaks the back window by trying to lower top while driving.

P.K. Yes! I tell Humphrey—cannot lower while driving. He says, "Of course! Can! This is a luxury car!" How come we sell the car?

CHAN. Ah! You cannot remember anything!

P.K. No. Gung Gung cannot remember anything anymore.

CHAN. We sell, because you can no longer drive.

P.K. I can! I can!

CHAN. You cannot pass the test.

P.K. Can Humphrey pass the test?

CHAN. Of course! Of course, he passes it.

P.K. How can? He is the one who lowers top while driving!

CHAN. Gung Gung! Because he is young, so he can pass the test!

P.K. Young, but not so smart.

CHAN. Stupid.

P.K. Sometimes, stupid.

CHAN. Stupid does not matter. Many stupid people drive.

[*Pause.*]

P.K. So I did not go to golf?

CHAN. No! How can you go to golf? You cannot go anyplace.

P.K. [*Points to clubs.*] Then, what are these?

CHAN. You just put them on your shoulder, then walk outside. Two hour later, you return.

P.K. Where did I go?

CHAN. I don't know! You tell me!

P.K. I cannot remember anything, anymore. I thought that I go to play eighteen-hole golf. But there is no golf course. So perhaps I walk into those hills. Maybe I shoot a few balls in the hills. Maybe I sink a putt into a gopher hole.

[*Pause.*]

CHAN. Gung Gung.

P.K. Yes, Popo?

CHAN. I saw a ghost today.

P.K. Popo! A ghost?

CHAN. Yes—a warning ghost.

P.K. Which is this?

CHAN. They warn that another ghost will soon come. Bigger. More dangerous. Fatter.

P.K. Oh! Popo! Why do they send this warning ghost?

CHAN. Because, they are stupid! This is how, they become dead to begin with. Because when they were living, they were too stupid to listen to the warning ghost!

P.K. Popo! Will you die? [*He starts to cry.*] What will Gung Gung do without you?

CHAN. No.

P.K. Without Popo, I will be completely all lost.

CHAN. No, Gung Gung.

P.K. I will walk around all day, not know where I am going, not know where I come from, only saying, "Popo? Where is Popo? Where is—?"

CHAN. No! Will you listen to me? You ask the question, then you will not listen to the answer! Talk, talk, talk! If I die, leave you alone, I would be lucky!

P.K. You mean, you will not die?

CHAN. No, I will not die.

P.K. How can this be?

CHAN. They are stupid enough to send the warning ghost. This is how I know, they will not defeat me.

P.K. But, when the ghost come, no one can resist.

CHAN. Who says this?

P.K. Ummm . . .

CHAN. See? Maybe, Gung Gung, *you* cannot resist.

P.K. No. I cannot resist.

CHAN. But you have no responsibilities. I have. I have responsibility. I cannot leave you alone, Gung Gung. And also, I must watch the grandchildren grow to adults.

P.K. Yes—this would be good.

CHAN. So, you see, I cannot die.

P.K. This makes me so happy.

CHAN. I will defeat the ghost.

P.K. Yes! Popo! You can do it! Popo is very smart!

CHAN. Yeah, yeah, yeah, we all know this already.

P.K. I am fortunate to marry such a smart wife.

CHAN. Not smart. Smart is not enough.

P.K. More than smart.

CHAN. Fight. Fight is more important. I am willing to fight. I like to fight.

[*Pause.*]

P.K. Why do I carry these golf clubs?

CHAN. I do not know! You ask so many times already!

P.K. Oh—I suppose—I must go to golf.

[*Pause.*]

CHAN. Yes—you must go to golf.

P.K. Okay. I will leave now. Take the Eldorado. Bye, Popo.

CHAN. Bye, Gung Gung.

As the Crow Flies

P.K. You will have a cold can of beer in the 'frigerator, for when I return?

CHAN. I will, Gung Gung. I will.

[*P.K. starts to exit out the upstage door.*]

Gung Gung!

P.K. Yes, Popo?

CHAN. Have a good game, okay, Gung Gung?

P.K. I will have a good game, okay, Popo. [*He exits.*]

CHAN. I arrive in America one day, June 16, 1976. Many times, I have come here before, to visit children, but on this day, I arrive to stay. All my friends, all the Chinese in the Philippine, they tell me, "We thought you are stupid when you send all your children to America. We even feel sorry for you, that you will grow old all alone—no family around you." This is what they tell me.

The day I arrive in America, I do not feel sorry. I do not miss the Philippine, I do not look forward live in America. Just like, I do not miss China, when I leave it many years ago—go live in Philippine. Just like, I do not miss Manila, when Japanese take our home during wartime, and we are all have to move to Baguio, and live in haunted house. It is all same to me. Go, one home to the next, one city to another, nation to nation, across ocean big and small.

We are born traveling. We travel—all our lives. I am not looking for a home. I know there is none. The day I was marry, my mother put many gold bracelets on my arm, and so many necklaces that the back of my head grows sore. "These," she tells me. "These are for the times when you will have to run."

[*The upstage door opens. HANNAH is standing there, dressed as SANDRA SMITH. SANDRA wears a bright orange fright wig and a tight dress, sports huge sunglasses, and swings a small purse.*]

SANDRA. Well, hello there! Howdy, howdy, howdy!

CHAN. Hi.

SANDRA. Say, you seen Hannah? Hannah Carter? I understand she works here on Wednesdays.

CHAN. I think, she just leave.

SANDRA. Oh, well, that's a shame. I usually don't get to visit where she works. We were supposed to go for dinner at Chicken on Fire, but, looks like we're just not connecting. Damn! Always happens, whenever I try to meet her at one of these houses.

As the Crow Flies

CHAN. So, would you like to go home, now?

SANDRA. Mmmm. Guess I could, but I wouldn't mind enjoying some of your hospitality.

CHAN. What is this, hospitality?

SANDRA. You know. What you show your guests.

CHAN. We do not have guests here! Only relatives, and, ah, servants.

SANDRA. Well, what do you do when someone comes over?

CHAN. They tell me what they want. Then, they leave.

SANDRA. No time to socialize?

CHAN. What is, socialize?

SANDRA. You know. You're not gonna offer me a tea, coffee, cake, Sanka?

CHAN. No.

SANDRA. I can't hardly believe this house.

CHAN. People—they are like cats. If you feed them, they will always return.

SANDRA. What ever happened to old-fashioned manners?

CHAN. My manners—they are very old. We act like this for centuries.

SANDRA. My name's Sandra. Sandra Smith.

CHAN. This is no surprise. Are you finish, now? Hannah is not here.

SANDRA. No—I can see that. [*Pause.*] You know, I've known Hannah—well, ever since she was a little girl. She wasn't very pretty. No one in Louisville paid much attention to her. Yeah, she's had five husbands and all, okay, that's true, but my personal guess is that most of 'em married her because she was a hard-working woman who could bring home the bacon week after week. Certain men will hold their noses for a free lunch. Hannah thinks the same thing, though she hardly ever talks about it. How can she think anything else when all five of them left her as soon as they got a whiff of some girl with pipe cleaners for legs? Hard for her to think she's much more than some mule, placed on this earth to work her back. She spends most of her life wanderin' from one beautiful house to the next, knowing intimately every detail, but never layin' down her head in any of 'em. She's what they call a good woman. Men know it, rich folks know it. Everyplace is beautiful, 'cept the place where she lives. Home is a dark room, she knows it well, knows its limits. She knows she can't travel nowhere without returnin' to that room once the sun goes down. Home is fixed, it does not move, even as the rest of the world circles 'round and 'round, picking up speed.

CHAN. You are a ghost.

As the Crow Flies

SANDRA. I have a good time, if that's what you mean.

CHAN. I was warned that you would come.

SANDRA. By Hannah? She's always tellin' people about me. Like I was some kinda celebrity or somethin'.

CHAN. I fight ghosts. I chase them.

SANDRA. Can't chase anything, unless you get it runnin' from ya first.

CHAN. In Baguio, we live in a haunted house.

SANDRA. In where?

CHAN. Baguio. In the Philippine.

SANDRA. I never been there.

CHAN. During the war, we live in a haunted house. I chase the ghost out, with pots and pan. So, I know I can defeat them.

SANDRA. Hannah—she lives in a haunted house right now.

CHAN. Yes—haunted with you.

SANDRA. I show her how to make her life a little easier. Someone's gotta do it, after all her sixty-some-odd years. How 'bout you? Anything I can help you with?

CHAN. Ha! I do not need a thing!

SANDRA. I'm not sure if I believe that, Mrs. . . . Mrs. . . . whatever. Hannah sees you sittin' here, day after day—

CHAN. I am old! Of course I sit!

SANDRA. —starin' out into that garden—

CHAN. So?

SANDRA. First off, it's mostly dirt.

CHAN. This way, easier to take care of.

SANDRA. But you stare like there's somethin' out there.

CHAN. Yes! The sun is out there!

SANDRA. Lookin' at the sun, Mrs.—ma'am? Gotta be careful you don't burn your eyeballs out.

CHAN. I only look outside because—sky, clouds, sun—they are all there— interesting to watch.

SANDRA. Real pretty, huh?

CHAN. Yes. Sometimes pretty.

SANDRA. Looks like home.

As the Crow Flies

CHAN. What is this? All the time, you talk about home, home, home?

SANDRA. Just like you do.

CHAN. I never talk about home. Barely talk at all.

SANDRA. You think, you keep your lips buttoned, that means all your secrets are safe inside? If they're strong enough, things make themselves known, one way or another. Hannah knows, she's not stupid. She'd never tell anyone but me. But me, I'd tell anybody. [*Pause.*] Want me to tell you?

CHAN. Tell me what?

SANDRA. What you're lookin' at out there?

   [*Pause.*]

CHAN. I can defeat you. I defeat ghost before.

SANDRA. Honey, it's not a fight no more. I've been around fifteen years. I already know you. You know me. We see the same thing. Out there. [*Pause.*] There's a crow sitting on a window sill. And two kids who chase it down a steep ravine. Their path grows darker and darker, but the crow continues, and the kids don't tire, even when the blisters start to show on their feet. Mud, sleet, rain, and snow, all try to make the kids give up the chase. The crow caws—mountains fall in its wake, but still the children continue. And then it becomes dark, so dark, and the crow throws disasters at their feet. Floods, droughts, wars. The children see nothing, now. They follow the crow only by the catastrophes it leaves in its path. Where there is famine, the crow must have been. Where there are earthquakes, it has rested. They run on faith now, passing through territories uncharted, following the sound of their suffering. And it is in this way that they pass through their lives. Hardly noticing that they've entered. Without stopping to note its passing. Just following a crow, with single dedication, forgetting how they started, or why they're chasing, or even what may happen if they catch it. Running without pause or pleasure, past the point of their beginning.

   [*Over the next section, MRS. CHAN's dress slowly rises into the air. She wears a white slip beneath. She stands up from the chair, for the first time in the play, and walks over to SANDRA.*]

I see it in the distance.

CHAN. It is waiting for me.

SANDRA. I cannot stop my running.

CHAN. I cannot rest, even for a second.

SANDRA. There's a field out in the distance.

CHAN. There's a wooden gate in that field.

As the Crow Flies

SANDRA.   There is a crow sitting on that gate.

CHAN.   It caws.

SANDRA.   It caws.

CHAN.   And disaster comes.

SANDRA.   Once again.

CHAN.   Nothing new.

SANDRA.   Nothing blue.

CHAN.   Only the scent of home.

SANDRA.   I don't know why I follow it.

CHAN.   I don't care to know.

SANDRA.   Not now.

CHAN.   Not here.

SANDRA.   Not ever. Perhaps someday.

CHAN.   Maybe to remember.

SANDRA.   Why I run.

CHAN.   Why I chase.

SANDRA.   Until I am so—

CHAN.   So tired.

SANDRA.   Another disaster.

CHAN.   Another lonely child.

SANDRA.   We follow the scent of home.

[SANDRA *removes her wig, glasses, tight dress. She too wears a white slip. She is* HANNAH *again.* MRS. CHAN *moves towards the door.* HANNAH *ever so slowly lowers herself into* MRS. CHAN's *chair.* HANNAH *sits in it, beams.*]

HANNAH.   Ooooh. Nice home, Mrs. Chan.

CHAN.   I see it.

HANNAH.   So do I, so do I.

CHAN.   I see all the way past those mountains.

HANNAH.   Welcome home, Mrs. Chan.

CHAN.   Welcome home, Hannah.

[MRS. CHAN *exits through the garden.* HANNAH *looks around her like a kid with a new toy. Upstage,* P.K. *enters with golf clubs. He cannot see* HANNAH *in the chair.*]

As the Crow Flies

P.K.   Hi, Popo! [*Pause.*] Where is my beer?

  [*HANNAH closes her eyes, a smile on her face.*]

You leave a beer in the 'frigerator? [*Pause.*] Popo? Popo?

  [*P.K. is walking towards the chair as lights fade to black.*]

End of Play

Responding to the Selection

Questions for Discussion

1. What did you find most comical in this play? Which lines or speeches were confusing to you? Explain your answers.

2. **Motivation** is the reason or reasons behind a character's actions. What seems to have motivated Hannah to transform herself at times into Sandra? Why might she have begun revealing this secret identity to her employers?

3. Chan describes her life before she arrived in the United States in the long speech beginning "I arrive in America . . ." What insight into her character does this speech give you?

4. How do you interpret Sandra's long speech about the children following the crow?

5. Is your personality always the same, or does it undergo changes depending on what situation you are in? Explain. What are some reasons that people's personalities sometimes seem to change, depending on their surroundings or situation?

Activities

Writing a Sketch

1. What do you predict will happen between Hannah and P.K. after Chan leaves the house? Write a brief sketch dramatizing this encounter.

Interpreting the Play

2. Why does Chan get up from her chair and exit into the garden? What sort of "home" is she moving toward? Write a paragraph in which you interpret her actions at the end of the play.

Drawing a Sketch

3. Hwang gives a short description of each character in the play. Choose one of the characters and sketch him or her. Use details from the play, as well as your imagination, to create your picture of the character.

Discussing the Play

4. Reread Hwang's comment in the second paragraph of the introduction about the merging of ethnic and mainstream literature and other art forms. Do you agree with this statement? Discuss it with a partner, giving reasons for your agreement or disagreement.

Before You Read

My Rough Skinned Grandmother

Tina Chang
Born 1969

"Tina Chang's images rise and rush through the page like iridescent rivers."

—Gloria Anzaldua

About Chang

Tina Chang was born in Stillwater, Oklahoma. She studied creative writing at State University of New York-Binghamton and Columbia University. In many of her poems, the speaker reflects on her early life and on the loss of her father. Chang has also written imaginatively about war-torn China in the late 1930s and early 1940s.

China in Turmoil

The first half of the twentieth century was a turbulent era for China, and life was difficult for its citizens. At the turn of the century, China was looking for ways to free itself from political manipulation by foreign powers and to modernize its culture. In the span of forty years, these efforts resulted in severe political upheaval—including three revolutions and a series of civil wars and peasant revolts. China reluctantly participated in World War I after being pressured by Europe into joining the Allied Powers. In the 1920s, regional warlords took advantage of this instability and began fighting each other for control of the country. In 1931, Japan invaded from the east, and China went to war in order to keep the Japanese from seizing the nation's capitol in Beijing. The ensuing war with Japan, which lasted until 1945, all but destroyed the Chinese economy. Many Chinese who immigrated to the United States in the early part of the century did so in order to escape the social and political turmoil in their native land.

My Rough Skinned Grandmother

— Tina Chang

My rough skinned grandmother
woke me up in the morning by
stroking my face with a warm
callused hand, scrubbed my skin clean
5   off when I took a bath. She would say, "Here
more dirt, there on your ankle, more
dirt." Her thumb rubbed soiled
flesh like thick brown wood
carvings off my body, until my skin
10   was a tender pink slate. When I ate dinner
she grabbed chicken legs from me
and scolded me for not sucking the meat
down to the bare bone. Eating
my leftovers, she'd tell me stories
15   of when she was my age and had to
eat fried roaches like crisp candy,
on her birthdays, a boiled egg
on a chipped plate.

My rough skinned grandmother told
20   me not to cry when she tore my baby teeth
out of my mouth. I could hear them rip from
their root; she said crying should be
saved for death, happiness, or any other good
reason but not for the loss of teeth.

25   My rough skinned grandmother
washed the rice with a quick
whooshing hand, rinsing the grains
again and again until the water
was clear. When she cooked, she beat

30 the tough meat tender with a fist
and sang nursery rhymes at the same time.
In the summer, she dropped
live, snapping crabs into a vat of hissing
water. Their pink shells turned a freckled
35 red as their arms became limp, drifting downward.

My rough skinned grandmother had a
chunk of skin missing from her arm
as if a pair of teeth had bitten straight
through her bicep. She carved her own muscle
40 with a butcher knife to make a healing
broth for her father. She never felt the pierce
of blade as he lay dying by daylight.

My rough skinned grandmother walked with me
past grown men sitting on crates in front
45 of convenience stores, holding
a cool St. Paulie Girl in their chapped
white hands as they yelled,
"ching chong ching chong"
like hot bells ejaculating
50 in my ear. She pretended
not to understand: she didn't speak
English but she understood
thunderous voices
from the gentle kind,
55 and she knew when to cross a street.
But she was no meek grandmother
Once on a night walk across a dark overpass,
she had me tucked beneath her
elbow. A man began to
60 follow the wind behind us. She shifted
her plump body around and roared Chinese curses,
her voice booming like a long string
of lit, flailing firecrackers. After
he ran away, she stroked my forehead
65 with her warm, callused hand,
my rough skinned grandmother.

❖

Responding to the Selection

Questions for Discussion

1. What memories did "My Rough Skinned Grandmother" stir up in you?

2. What is your impression of the grandmother? What are some words you would choose to describe her?

3. **Style** is the expressive qualities that distinguish an author's work. How would you characterize the style of this poem?

4. What do you think is the **symbolic** significance of the grandmother's rough skin? What information is given in the poem that supports your conclusion?

Activities

Comparing Characters

1. Write a paragraph comparing the "rough skinned grandmother" with another grandmother portrayed in this anthology. What do these Asian American grandmothers have in common? Are they portrayed as stereotypes, or do they each have an individual identity?

Illustrating a Poem

2. Choose one of the episodes from the poem and illustrate it.

Before You Read

Anchorage

Sylvia Watanabe
Born 1952

"I like to explore the forces which bring individual human beings of different cultures together, and to imagine the private struggles which arise from such meetings."

About Watanabe

Sylvia Watanabe was born in Maui, Hawaii, the daughter of Japanese American parents. She says that she began writing to show what life was like on the island before commercial development and tourism transformed it: "I wanted to tell how the Lahaina coast looked before it was covered with resorts, how the old-time fishermen went torching at night out on the reefs, and how the iron-rich earth of the canefields smelled in the afternoon sun. I wanted to save my parents' and grandparents' stories."

In addition to writing fiction and essays, Watanabe has edited anthologies and taught creative writing. Her first collection of stories, *Talking to the Dead,* came out in 1992. Some of the stories were inspired by "naming walks" that she has taken with her father since childhood. "Even now," she says, "when we go for walks he tells me the names of things—of plants, and birds, and trees. . . . He has a reminiscence about every spot we pass."

Memory

The "forgetting sickness" described in "Anchorage" is Alzheimer's disease. People with Alzheimer's suffer from memory loss, confusion, and personality changes. The symptoms get worse over time. Patients eventually find it hard to communicate and lose the ability to care for themselves.

Anchorage

— *Sylvia Watanabe*

The needle glinted in my grandmother's hand as she appliquéd Bird Tracks onto a square of white cotton. She glanced from Father, dozing in his lawn chair, to Aunt Pearlie with her head buried in the *County News,* to me, then began, "Last night I dreamed . . ."

Little Grandma was always having dreams. She said the spirits of our kin watched from the shrine on her bedroom dresser and spoke to her while she was sleeping. She said they told her when to go down to the beach to harvest seaweed, and where to look when Cousin Makoto misplaced his store teeth, and what chicken to bet on at the chicken fights.

"In my dream, it was dark," she said. "There was no sun, no moon, no speck of light in the whole sky. Then a hole opened somewhere on the other side of the darkness, and it opened, and opened, and opened . . ."

"I think we get the picture." Aunt Pearlie yawned.

Father snored softly, his mouth slightly open as if in surprise.

It was a hot summer afternoon, and we were cooling off under the poinciana tree in Little Grandma's front yard. I had just graduated from the university and was visiting home a few weeks before leaving for Anchorage and my first real job as an art teacher in a public high school. I had never been away from the islands before, and was caught between the anticipation of a new, independent life and the sensation of being cast adrift, with everything familiar slipping further and further away. I shivered as I smoothed the blank page of the sketchpad lying open on my lap, and Little Grandma reached over to squeeze my hand.

"Would you look at this." Aunt Pearlie gestured at the item she'd been reading. The headline said, "Rise in Peeping Tom Incidents." Before I could read further, she folded the paper away, then declared, "But it doesn't surprise me one bit, considering the depraved goings-on right here under our very noses."

If there was anyone who'd given much consideration to that particular subject, it was my aunt Pearlie. Among the members of the Buddhist Mission's Ladies Auxiliary, she took an especially keen interest in the moral, and immoral, affairs of the community. Each morning, after seeing her husband Freddy Woo off to the sugar mill and putting her house in order, she set out for Little Grandma's. There, strategically positioned at the top of the lane overlooking the rest of the village, she carried out her surveillance work from the front yard.

"Why, just the other day," she continued now, "Emiko McAllister was telling me that the Laundry Burglar is on the loose again. What do you suppose Someone Like That would want with our clean wash?"

"All it takes is a bit of imagination," Little Grandma said. "Now, Hana, where was I?"

I fidgeted with the wire binding on my sketchbook but didn't answer. Aunt Pearlie scowled.

"Hana, do you remember?" Little Grandma repeated.

"Oh, Mama," Aunt Pearlie almost shouted. "Something about a hole in the sky, for Pete's sake. Besides, if it was as dark as you say, how did you even know where the sky was?"

"Because I was *standing up*," Little Grandma said. "And as I stood there, the sky opened and opened . . ."

Aunt Pearlie rolled her eyes.

". . . and colors came pouring out of it," Little Grandma went on, "until there were colors where there'd only been darkness before."

"Then what?" I asked.

"Then I woke up."

"What?" Aunt Pearlie said. "What kind of a dream is that?"

Little Grandma smiled, and continued to stitch at her appliqué.

Down the hill, the cloud shadows drifted over the sugar fields. The shifting green and yellow of the cane, the red furrows of earth, and the blue curve of the water joined into a patchwork of shapes and colors. On the opposite shore of the bay, the skyline bristled with the metal and glass towers of the fast-spreading resort town, where there had been miles of empty beach and some of the best net fishing on the island just ten years before. I remembered accompanying my father when he'd gone there to sketch the Hawaiian fishermen, and how they'd taught us to identify the schools of fish, flashing beneath the surface of the water. Green for *manini*. Silver for *papio*.

Now, as I removed the cover from my box of oil crayons, I became aware of him watching me. He had wakened from his nap and was sitting up in his chair. His gaze shifted away from my face and moved out across the fields, then back to the box of colors on my lap. "That,"

he whispered, pointing to one of them. I held the box toward him, and he picked out black.

Later that afternoon, I left my grandmother and aunt disagreeing over what to cook for supper, and slipped off to my father's studio above the garage. "How many kinds of black can you see?" I remembered him asking as I learned to mix paints. His luminous, unfinished canvases gathered dust along the walls. In the sunny corner where he'd once worked, his easel still looked toward the window; a brush tipped with vermilion lay across the square of Plexiglas he'd used as a palette. Among the pencil drawings and color studies tacked to the wall were fliers for juried exhibits he'd planned to enter.

After my mother's death, when I was about a year old, Father and I had come to live with Little Grandma in Luhi, where he'd grown up. For the next seventeen years, he'd worked on the maintenance crew at the sugar mill and spent all his spare time painting. Then, just after I left for college in Honolulu, the "forgetting sickness," as Little Grandma called it, had begun creeping up on him. The first sign of anything seriously wrong occurred during a routine repair at the mill, when he took apart a piece of machinery and was not able to put it back together again. Soon afterward, my grandmother reported to me that he'd quit his job and had begun spending all his time in his studio. When I returned for the winter holidays, a few weeks later, I found him sitting at his easel, applying layer after layer of black to a single spot in the middle of the canvas. That was just before he'd stopped painting altogether.

Now, though he often seemed lucid, it was hard to tell what still had the power to reach him. He needed help dressing and feeding himself, and rarely spoke. As I wandered through his studio, I remembered the hours I had spent there as a child, coloring at the old table which we'd rescued from a neighbor's trash and which was now cluttered with dried-up tubes of pigment and dusty pages of yellowing newsprint. It was at that table that he'd given me my first "seeing lessons."

"Look, Hana," I could still hear him saying. "Everything is made of light."

"It's a pity, isn't it?" The sound of Aunt Pearlie's voice startled me.

I made an agreeing noise, then said, "The place sure could use a good going-over. Just look at this dust."

"If the dust was all we had to worry about, we wouldn't have a problem. We need to make plans," she said.

I knew that she wanted to discuss my father's future, a subject we'd been skirting ever since my return. I turned to face her. "What's that you

got there?" I asked, pointing to her bulging shopping bag. "Smells like fish with black bean sauce."

Aunt Pearlie snapped, "Your uncle Fred's got to eat, poor man. And don't think I don't know what you and your grandmother are up to—always changing the subject when we need to get some serious talking done."

I said, "If you mean about Father, that's up to Little Grandma, isn't it? In fact, she tells me that he's gotten much better these last few months, since she's begun taking him to the Prayer Lady." The Prayer Lady was famous in all the villages around Luhi for her healing touch.

"Your papa needs more than a good massage to fix what's wrong with him," Aunt Pearlie retorted. "And as for whose business it is, who do you suppose Mother turns to when you're not around?"

After she left, I went downstairs to help Little Grandma with Father's dinner, but she was already taking care of it. She murmured to him as she proffered spoonfuls of rice and fish, which he accepted passively, his eyes fixed blankly ahead. "Where are you now, Koshiro?" she said.

I couldn't help thinking that my aunt had been right. He was getting worse. I pushed the thought away and went to join Little Grandma at the kitchen table. "Here, let me do that," I said.

"We're nearly finished," she answered, without taking her eyes off my father. "But we'll be heading upstairs for a bath pretty soon. Would you mind bringing in the clean towels?"

"If the Laundry Burglar hasn't already gotten to them," I said.

Little Grandma looked at me then. "Ah, poor Pearlie," she said, but she was smiling.

That night I dreamed of the snow. The dream never changed. In it, I was crossing a vast, wintry field with no trees, or landmarks, or colors for as far as I could see in any direction. With each step, I sank further into the deep, white drifts—first to my ankles, then to my knees, and finally up to my hips. As I struggled to get free, it quietly began to snow.

I woke, as usual, with my heart racing. For a moment I imagined I was already in Alaska, until I began recognizing familiar objects in the room around me. The mahogany toy cabinet with the china tea set sitting on top, the red wooden child's rocker, and on the far wall the mural my father painted the year I turned six. Here and there in the moonlight, I could make out a tangerine-colored bear, a flying dog, a rabbit in top hat and tails.

The sound of Father's snoring came from his bedroom down the hall, and I thought of how he had been when he'd made those paintings. "Come Hana!" I could hear him calling, as I drifted back into sleep. "Oh, Hana, come see!" And once again, I was running toward his voice. When I arrived, he pointed to a crown flower hedge alive with monarch butterflies.

"*Akai tori, ko tori*," Little Grandma was singing upstairs in the attic. "Red bird, little red bird, why are you so red?" As she paused for breath, I could hear the crisp sound of her sewing shears, cutting patchwork.

"We'll all be in a nursing home before she finishes that thing," Aunt Pearlie said. "She's been working at that same quilt for the past hundred years, I'd swear."

It was the following afternoon, and she and I were sitting at the kitchen table looking out the window at Little Grandma and Father in their usual spot under the poinciana. Aunt Pearlie had appeared at the kitchen door before lunch, determined to corner me into a chat. For the past half hour she'd been trying to convince me that Father required professional care.

"I don't like it," I objected. "We can't just pass him on to a bunch of strangers. Besides, Little Grandma would never agree."

She said, "Look, Hana, nobody *likes* making this sort of a decision, but we don't have a choice. You've seen what a handful he can be—even when you're around to help."

The morning light flickered across the walls, and the contours of the room shifted, as the boundaries between shapes melted and colors slid away into shadow.

"If Mama were by herself," Aunt Pearlie went on, "she could sell this place and come stay with me. You know the Canadian investment company that built the new hotel across the bay? Well, one of their representatives dropped by about a week ago. He told me they wanted to buy some land around here to put up a time-sharing condominium."

As I was processing this information, the front gate squeaked open. It was Emi McAllister from down the road. She was carrying what looked like a dish or tray in a brown grocery bag.

"What's she got there?" Aunt Pearlie reached for the spectacles in her apron pocket and put them on. "Hmmm. Probably some of that brown fudge that sticks to the roof of your mouth. Or a bunch of those hard little puffed rice cakes."

Emi stopped to talk to Little Grandma, then came inside and handed her parcel to my aunt.

"Oh, rice cakes," Aunt Pearlie said, opening the bag and withdrawing a dish of the confections.

"Just a little welcome home for Hana." Emi smiled at me. "Your papa's looking fine."

"Well, he's not fine," Aunt Pearlie said and offered her the cakes.

Emi waved them aside. "Never touch the stuff, too hard on my old teeth." She patted my hand. "Things going badly, huh?"

Aunt Pearlie frowned. "So, Emi, how're you doing? What's the latest on the Laundry Burglar?"

"Mrs. Koyama says the Dancing School Teacher is missing her white satin nightcap," Emi answered. "Everyone knows that woman wears a wig."

Aunt Pearlie said, "It's disgraceful that this situation has been allowed to go on for so long."

"You have to admit, he hasn't done much of anything in the last four or five years," Emi said.

"Still, you never know what a twisted mind like that will think up next," my aunt pointed out. "Today he steals our laundry, tomorrow he murders us in our beds. I say it's about time the police began doing their jobs."

Emi said, "From what I hear, the sheriff doesn't have much to go on. The burglaries always stop before any real clues turn up."

"Meantime, you don't know how I worry," Aunt Pearlie said. "I can't be here with Mother twenty-four hours a day. And Hana will be leaving for Anchorage soon."

"That's odd," Emi said. She was looking out the window.

"It's more than odd," Aunt Pearlie replied.

Emi motioned toward the front yard. "I was just talking to your mother out there a minute ago."

The quilting mat was still spread out under the tree, but the wind had blown the cover off a box full of patchwork, leaving a trail of Bird Tracks across the yard. Neither Father nor Little Grandma was anywhere to be seen.

While Aunt Pearlie and Emi went to check with the neighbors, Little Grandma came limping up the road to the house. She had been concentrating on a tricky place in her sewing when Father took the opportunity to slip away.

After Aunt Pearlie returned and got on the phone to the police, I decided to go and check the beach. I remembered that, after the resort began going up across the bay, Father had confined his sketching excursions to the rocky coastline around Luhi. Every weekend in fine weather, he'd take his paintbox and portable easel out onto the lava jetty that enclosed our side of the water. Sometimes I'd go with him, especially in winter, when there were whales about, and he and I would compete to spot the beautiful plumes of spray rising above the waves.

"Father!" I called now, scanning the rocks and tidal pools along the shore. The sky and sea were the color of fire. A wave broke over the lava shelf and came swirling around my ankles. I had to hurry; the tide was rising.

Then I saw a speck of white out on the point. I picked my way across the jagged rocks, the waves crashing higher and higher, until I was wading

through knee-deep water. "You've scared us all to death," I scolded as I pulled myself up beside him.

He turned toward me, his face transfixed. He gestured toward the glittering path of red and gold, leading from where he stood, across the water, to the sun. "Look, Hana," he said.

"I just turned my back for one second," Little Grandma was explaining downstairs in the kitchen as I drew the water for my father's bath.

"That's all it takes," I heard Aunt Pearlie reply.

Father sat shivering on the edge of the tub, watching me.

"Just a minute and I'll help you out of those wet things," I said.

He had not spoken since I found him out on the point.

"Father, you've got to say something." I unbuttoned his shirt and helped him pull his arms through the sleeves. "If you don't say anything, people will think they can do anything they want to you." I got his undershirt over his head, then kneeled before him and began unlacing his shoes. I looked into his face. "Father, talk to me. I heard you out there."

The sound of quarreling came up the stairs. "Hardheaded old woman!" Aunt Pearlie shouted. There were heavy footsteps across the living room, and the front door slammed.

My father reached for the gold chain around my neck.

"Talk to me," I whispered.

The next morning I was wakened by the noise of my grandmother's antique washing machine rocking back and forth on the cement patio. The smell of burning french toast filled the room. I went downstairs to the kitchen and turned off the stove, then poured myself a cup of the tepid brown liquid from the aluminum coffeepot next to the sink.

As I took my first sip, Aunt Pearlie came in from hanging the wash. She said, "That's for the plants. Didn't you see the grounds at the bottom?"

I shook my head and pushed my cup away.

She came over and sat next to me, then began clasping and unclasping her hands as she stared out the window. Finally, she spoke again. "That was quite an adventure yesterday."

"Mmm. Do you know where Little Grandma is?" I asked.

"She and your father have gone off to the Prayer Lady's," Aunt Pearlie said.

I got up and went to fill the kettle. "Maybe I *will* have some of that bottled stuff."

Aunt Pearlie said, "Hana, we keep going around and around about this and not getting anywhere, but the Laniloa home isn't at all what you

think. It's brand new, and well run, and Clyde Sakamoto—you know, of Sakamoto Hardware—says that his mother-in-law gets the best of treatment there. The least you could do is drive over and take a look."

"That won't be necessary," I said, "because I'm not going to Anchorage. I've decided to stay here and help Little Grandma take care of Father."

She was silent. Her hands lay very still upon the table. Then she drew something silky and white from her apron pocket. I thought at first that it was a piece of fancy lingerie, and I wondered what my practical-minded aunt would be doing with such a thing. As she smoothed it flat on the table between us, I saw that it wasn't lingerie at all but some sort of hat, trimmed with lace.

Aunt Pearlie's mouth was set in a stubborn line. "And will you also take care of this?" she said. "I found it in one of your father's pockets."

I had no idea what she was getting at, until I looked out the screen door at the laundry hanging in the backyard, and it struck me.

"I believe this nightcap belongs to the Dancing School Teacher," she said.

Aunt Pearlie threatened to hand Father over to the law if Little Grandma and I didn't agree to put him into the home. "I'm only thinking about what's best for all of us," she said before going off to spend the rest of the afternoon at Emi McAllister's.

As we watched her striding away down the road, Little Grandma said, "Heaven spare us from Pearlie's worst."

We were sitting out under the poinciana. Overhead, the sunlight glimmered through the canopy of red flowers, casting a warm glow across the blank sketchpad lying open on my lap. "Maybe I'll be able to draw when I get to Alaska," I said, and felt the tears begin to come. "I can't go to Alaska."

Little Grandma put aside the square she'd been stitching and took my face in her hands. "Of course you must go," she said. "It won't make a bit of difference if you stay, but it will make all the difference in the world if you don't." A sly smile flickered across her lips. She woke my father, then gestured at me to follow them toward the house.

She led us up the stairs to her room on the second floor. Inside, it was nearly bare—except for a tiny cot with a hard loaf-shaped pillow, the family shrine on the cedar dresser, and a calendar from Rusty Chan's Automotive Repair. She directed us through the narrow door leading up the rickety flight of stairs to the attic.

The room was well lighted from windows covering the walls on two sides, and it had been cleared of all the clutter that one usually finds in attics. Instead, there were trunks spilling over with bolts of new fabric, and cardboard boxes stuffed with articles of clothing. I could make out one of

Father's old painting smocks, a floral shift of Aunt Pearlie's, and my first party dress. In the middle of the floor lay a mat surrounded by brown paper bags and shoe boxes filled with piecing in various stages of completion. Among the patterns I recognized were Ocean Waves, Hands All Around, Delectable Mountains, and Mongoose in the Pigeon Coop.

A rusty fan stood next to a quilting frame in a nearby corner. On the frame was a half-finished quilt of interlocking circles in seven colors, each standing for one of the jewels in Buddhist teaching. "I call that my Seven Treasures," Little Grandma said.

But it was to the far end of the room that my eyes were drawn. There hung an immense quilt, bordered by squares of bright-colored Bird Tracks. Though unfinished, the quilt covered nearly the entire wall. From where I stood, perhaps fifteen feet away, it seemed to contain every color in the entire world.

I moved closer, and the colors began to cohere into squares, the squares into scenes—each scene depicting places and people in the life of the village. There were the sugar fields sloping down to the water. The green and white company houses with a different-colored dog in every yard. The singing tree. The old head priest leading the procession of lights toward the sea. There was Henry Hanabusa performing his nightly calisthenics, and Emi McAllister in her garden. Every detail had been carefully chosen—down to the green and pink scarf on her tiny sun hat.

I looked closer. There was something familiar about the fabrics from which the pieces of appliqué had been cut. My heart quickened as I glanced at the last scene, of Aunt Pearlie hanging the wash. It was pinned but had not yet been stitched.

"I had to improvise on that one," Little Grandma said. "I was all set to do Minerva Sato's tap-dancing comeback, but Pearlie discovered the nightcap before I could make use of it. So I decided to do one of her instead. Pinned it just a little while ago."

"Were you and Father in this together?" I asked.

"It started by accident," Little Grandma explained. "He ran off one day, and when I brought him home, I found his pockets full of someone else's laundry. I was too embarrassed to return it, but I couldn't throw it away. Then I got the idea of making this quilt, and began going out with him." She watched to see how I was reacting, then added, "I made sure we took only very small items."

"As if that made any difference," I said. "It's because of your pilfering that we have to put Father away."

"No, Hana, it's Koshiro's illness that's stealing him from us," Little Grandma said.

Anchorage

I went to stand next to my father, who was looking out one of the windows. From where we were, we could see into the yards of all the houses around us. Across the road, the vacant lot where I had played as a child was up for sale, and it was rumored that a fried chicken operation from Texas was interested in setting up a franchise there. At the far end of the village, I could see the gleaming new structure of the Laniloa Geriatric Care Facility and, below it, the boats anchored in the harbor. Beyond the harbor stretched the open sea.

I looked at my father and his lips were moving. I leaned close to catch his words. He was saying, "To not forget."

Responding to the Selection

Questions for Discussion

1. What thoughts came to you as you finished reading this story?

2. How would you describe Hana's and Little Grandma's attitude toward Aunt Pearlie?

3. Do you agree with Aunt Pearlie that Hana's father belongs in a geriatric home? What seems to have motivated her decision?

4. Why might Watanabe have begun this story with Little Grandma's description of her dream?

5. Sylvia Watanabe once said about her writing, "I wanted to record a way of life which I loved and which seemed in danger of dying away." In this story, how does she connect the father's illness with changes that are affecting the entire community? What object in the story is a **symbol** of this desire to hold on to the past?

Activities

Writing about Setting

1. **Setting** is the time and place in which the events of a story occur. How does the setting of "Anchorage" help establish the mood of the story? How does it influence the way characters think and behave? Write a paragraph in response to one or both of these questions.

Writing a Letter

2. Hana got her first "seeing lessons" from her father. Write a letter in which she describes to him what she sees after arriving in Anchorage. Before you begin, read some travel guides to find vivid images that you can include in your letter.

Discussing Word Usage

3. Anchorage is the largest city in Alaska. But the word *anchorage* is also a noun. Look up the word in a dictionary. Then discuss with a partner some reasons why this word makes a good title for this story.

Before You Read

Waiting for Papa's Return

Cecilia Manguerra Brainard
Born 1947

"I like to give voice to Filipinos in America, to the women in particular, who are at a greater disadvantage."

About Brainard

Cecilia Manguerra Brainard grew up on the island of Cebu in the Philippines. She moved to the United States in 1969 to study filmmaking at the University of California at Los Angeles. As she attended writing classes there, she realized that she wanted to become a fiction writer instead of a filmmaker.

Brainard has published several collections of short stories and a novel called *When the Rainbow Goddess Wept*. Although her fiction is mainly based on personal experiences, she also makes use of Filipino folklore and epic songs. Brainard feels that her work as a newspaper columnist for *Philippine American News* aided her creative writing: "It kind of jogged my memory. An idea would come alive in my head, and I found myself batting it around and making fiction out of it."

Keeping a Diary

"Waiting for Papa's Return" is based on a traumatic experience in Brainard's life. When she was nine, her father died suddenly of a heart attack. What was once a peaceful and supportive household became very unsettled. Brainard comforted herself by reading books and by writing in her diary. She still keeps a journal, which she considers an important part of her writing process.

Waiting for Papa's Return

— *Cecilia Manguerra Brainard*

When Reverend Mother Superior tells Remedios her father died, all she can think is how ugly the nun looks. Remedios stares at the mustache fringing the nun's upper lip; Reverend Mother Superior stares back with pale watery eyes.

"This morning, child. Heart attack," the nun says.

In the distance the three o'clock bell rings as if repeating the nun's words. It is an October Thursday, warm and humid. The sound stays with Remedios as the nun takes her to the chapel. "Let us pray so your father will go straight to heaven," she whispers. They kneel in the front pew and Remedios closes her eyes. The ringing that echoes in her head fades and she hears her father's voice loud and clear: I'll be back in two weeks.

She clings to those words, mulling over them. I'll-be-back-in-two-weeks. That means next week because Mama and Papa have already been gone for a week. She pictures her father with his oval face, his gold-rimmed glasses, and his balding head. He was leaning on his cane when he asked, "What do you want me to bring?"

"Mama says she'll buy me shoes, clothes, candies, and chocolates."

"But what do you want?" his gentle voice prodded.

"A walking doll and a tea set like Mildred's. Not the plastic tea set, I want the kind that breaks."

"All right," he replied, tousling her dark hair. "I'll scour all of Hong Kong and I'll bring you your doll and tea set."

Her father said those words and he never lies. Remedios is confused. Reverend Mother Superior is the most important person in school and she doesn't lie either. She must have made a mistake. Papa and Mama will be back next week from their vacation.

Remedios thinks things over, trying to find a reason for this misunderstanding. Was it because she and Mildred giggled in church at the fat

Waiting for Papa's Return

woman singing with a warbling voice? Mildred elbowed her in the ribs and they had been bad, no doubt about it, snickering in the back row instead of paying attention to Father Ruis's novena.

The chapel smells of melted wax and when Remedios opens her eyes, she studies the bleeding Jesus nailed to the cross. "I'm sorry for having been bad," she prays over and over, until Reverend Mother Superior stands up and says, "Your aunt is picking you up, child."

They find Tiya Meding waiting in the office. She is wearing a brown dress; her face is pale, her eyes, pink-rimmed. "Poor, poor child," she mumbles. In the car she looks at Remedios in a way that makes Remedios think her aunt is trying to discover something in her—and Remedios does not know what.

Feeling awkward, Remedios rolls down her window and watches the hawkers selling lottery tickets, boiled bananas, and soft drinks. Her aunt delicately blows her nose and sniffles.

"Look, there's the woman in black dancing in front of the church," Remedios points out.

"Crazy woman," Tiya Meding answers.

"Papa says she's pathetic."

"Pathetic my foot. She's as loony as they come."

Remedios keeps quiet; pathetic is how her father describes the woman in black.

Her aunt's chauffeur—that is what Tiya Meding calls her driver—takes them to Vering the dressmaker. Remedios is surprised she will have a dress sewn, and she nods approvingly at the design: puffed sleeves, boat neck, and shirred skirt.

"And pockets, two square pockets," Remedios suggests.

Vering sketches in the pockets.

"And I don't want this black cloth. Yellow organdy would be nicer."

The two women eye each other.

"But the dress has to be black," Tiya Meding insists.

"I don't like black. Papa says I look prettiest in yellow."

"The dress will be black, Remedios." Her aunt sets her jaw and Remedios knows there is no use arguing.

Before leaving the dressmaker's shop, Tiya Meding asks for pieces of black cloth the size of postage stamps. She pins one on Remedios's blouse, right above her heart—a little bit of black cloth that flutters when the warm breeze blows.

At school she is the center of attention, like the actress Gloria Romero or the one-eyed freak with the Chinese Acrobatic Troupe, stared at by everybody. When she picks up her schoolbag, the children glance curiously at her. The visitors, streaming into Tiya Meding's house look at

Waiting for Papa's Return

her, and when she and her aunt go to the funeral parlor and church "to make arrangements," people study her. Remedios feels as if her nose were growing from her forehead. Pairs of glassy eyes follow her around and she does not know what they want, how to escape them.

At her aunt's house, she tries to amuse herself by inspecting the numerous porcelain figures in the living room—pretty dainty women with ducks beside them, little angels kneeling down in prayer, but her aunt snaps: "Don't touch those. They're breakable." She goes to the piano and plays "Chopsticks," but her aunt lifts a reprimanding finger. "The noise," she complains. Tiya Meding is on the phone and Remedios listens to her.

"Thank you," her aunt says. "Heart attack. Isn't that too bad? I warned my sister. An older man like that." Tiya Meding's diamond earrings dangle from her elongated ears and a huge diamond solitaire sparkles on her finger.

"Baubles," her father often says about Tiya Meding's jewelry. "She is a silly woman who likes baubles."

Remedios leaves the main house thinking to herself: Silly, silly woman. She goes to the kitchen and has a second lunch with the servants. Using her fingers, she makes a ball of rice and eats it with stewed fish. Later she helps the cook peel cassava and grate coconuts.

"Your father was a good man," the cook says. "He made my son foreman of the road construction."

"Yes," Remedios replies, "I can't wait until he comes home."

After speaking, she wonders why she said those words. She understands what Reverend Mother Superior said, what all the commotion is about, yet deep within herself she knows her papa will return.

The kitchen is sooty and smells of grease and bay leaves. The cook, who stands next to the huge wood-burning stove, looks at her. Remedios continues grating. She watches the curly slivers of white coconut meat fall into the basin. The kitchen smoke seems to engulf her and she feels warm. The pungent smell makes her temples throb. She begins to feel weak, just as she felt when her cousin told her she was adopted. He had lost in a game of checkers, and angrily, he told Remedios that her parents picked her up from a pile of trash, that she had been covered with fat flies. She did not cry; she crawled into bed to sleep off her tiredness. Her mother called the boy an idiotic pervert. Her father later placed her on his knee.

"See this bump on my nose?" he asked.

"Yes."

"Don't you have a bump on your nose like mine?" His warm forefinger traveled down her nose over the slight protrusion.

She nodded.

"That means that you are my very own little girl. We didn't adopt you."

Waiting for Papa's Return

The darkness lifted and the next time she saw her cousin she stuck her tongue out at him. But now the tiredness stays and she drags around until bedtime. It seems she has just tucked the mosquito net under the mattress when she falls asleep and begins dreaming.

It is Sunday, and she, Mama, and Papa are driving over bumpy, dusty roads to Talisay Beach. Remedios is happy because she enjoys clamming in the small inlet. But when they arrive, the sea is blood red and smells foul. Remedios cries and her papa asks why.

"Something terrible has happened," she says.

"It's all right," he answers. "I'm right beside you."

She dries her eyes, noticing that the water has turned blue and the air is clean once more. She laughs and hugs her papa.

"Don't cry. It makes me sad," her father says in the dream.

She wakes to Tiya Meding's voice telling her the plane is arriving in less than an hour. Trying to get excited, she bathes with her aunt's Maja soap and dabs Joy perfume behind her ears. Like a sleepwalker, she puts on her new black dress, white socks, and black patent leather shoes. Remedios ties yellow ribbons at the ends of her braids but Tiya Meding removes them. "Not for a year," she says.

Heavy-faced people wearing somber clothes crowd the airport. They stare at Remedios and she tries hard to figure out what they want from her. She laughs. "I can hardly wait to see them," she exclaims in a high thin voice. Pairs of eyes follow her, letting go only when the noisy plane arrives with a loud screech. The special cargo plane stops near the terminal, and some men open the side doors and struggle to bring down a casket. When Remedios spots her mother walking down the ramp, she runs shouting, "Ma!" The mourners around her pause. "Ma, where's my walking doll and tea set?" Her aunt tells her to be quiet. "She's just a child," someone else says. "Just a child."

Her mother appears dreary in her black dress—Remedios really hates that color—and she weeps constantly. She will not talk, nor will she tell Remedios that everything will be fine.

A hollow feeling grows inside Remedios. Sometimes she feels like the conch shell sitting on the writing desk. Other times it seems she is hanging on a thin thread, like the gray spider swinging back and forth from the ceiling. She feels odd, as if waiting for something to happen so all the staring will end, so the strangeness that has invaded her life will disappear.

The next day there is a mass. Then the men carry the coffin to the funeral car, so black and slick. When it starts raining, people scramble for umbrellas or newspapers and they mutter, "Ah, a good sign, heaven is weeping." She, Mama, and Tiya Meding walk behind the funeral car to the

Waiting for Papa's Return

old cemetery with gray crumbling crypts. Some women hold umbrellas over them to keep their heads dry. Remedios trudges along, splashing in puddles, watching the slum children playing in the rain.

At the cemetery, the men pick up the coffin, carry it to the family crypt and open it. The priest sprinkles holy water inside. Her mama, who emits wailing sounds and whose shoulders are shaking, bends over to kiss the man inside. Remedios has not looked but she knows that a man is in there. She heard people talking: "Looks like he's sleeping, doesn't he? They sure did a good job."

Her mama turns to her and Remedios walks toward the casket. She tiptoes and peers in. The man's face is a waxy mask. He doesn't wear glasses and his tight little smile is a grimace. There is a smell like moth-balls. Remedios feels faint. She wants to giggle, but stopping herself, she bends over and plants a kiss on the wax-man's cool cheek.

The men close the coffin and slide it into the crypt making a grating sound. There is a dull thud when the marble slab covers the niche, and briefly Remedios feels a lurching inside her stomach. She closes her eyes and hears that voice loud and clear: I'll be back in two weeks. I'll bring you your doll and tea set.

When she opens her eyes and sees the mourners crying, for just a moment she understands that they want her to weep, that they are waiting for her to cry. But soon she is thinking of dainty tea cups, the smooth feel of delicate china, the clinking sound as the cup hits the saucer. She is see-ing her father smiling broadly as she hands him his cup and they make a toast pretending to sip tea under the cool shade of the lush star apple trees.

Responding to the Selection

Questions for Discussion

1. What are the other characters in the story looking for when they stare at Remedios?

2. Which parent does Remedios feel closest to? What details lead you to this conclusion?

3. Do you think that Remedios doesn't understand the idea of death, or is she just unable to accept that her father is dead? Support your opinion with evidence from the story.

4. Does Remedios gain understanding over the course of the story? Why or why not?

5. This story is written in the present tense. Why might the author have decided to use this tense instead of the more common past tense?

Activities

Analyzing Characters

1. **Indirect characterization** requires readers to draw their own conclusions about a character based on the character's appearance, words, thoughts, and actions, as well as the comments and thoughts of other characters. Write a paragraph in which you analyze the indirect characterization of Remedios.

Writing a Journal Entry

2. What is the first death among your family members or acquaintances that you can recall? Freewrite in your journal about this experience.

Comparing and Contrasting Poetry

3. Assemble an anthology of ten or twelve poems on the subject of death and dying. Compare and contrast how the poems treat this theme.

Before You Read

The Mirror of Matsuyama

Sharon Hashimoto
Born 1953

for his wife. Soon afterward, the wife falls ill. Before dying, she tells Matsuyama to look for her in the mirror whenever she feels lonely. The father eventually remarries. His new wife is unkind to Matsuyama, but the girl comforts herself by gazing at her mother's face in the mirror. The new wife fears that Matsuyama is casting a spell on her. The father angrily questions Matsuyama. When he finds out the truth, he loves Matsuyama even more, and his wife begs for the girl's forgiveness. After that, they all live happily together.

About Hashimoto

Sharon Hashimoto is a third-generation Japanese American. She teaches literature and creative writing at Highline Community College in Seattle, Washington. The National Endowment for the Arts gave her a creative writing fellowship in 1989. Hashimoto has published a small book of poems called *Reparations*.

A Japanese Folktale

Hashimoto based "The Mirror of Matsuyama" on a Japanese folktale. In the tale, a man returns home with a present for his daughter, Matsuyama, and a mirror

The Mirror of Matsuyama

— *Sharon Hashimoto*

Daughter, this I give you before I die.
When you are lonely, take out this mirror.
I will be with you always.
> From a Japanese folktale

Mother, what trick of light
brings you back—your face rising to the surface?
Is it my need that imprisons you behind
the cold glass? When you lay still,
5   the flowered quilt no longer warm with your body,
I didn't believe your promise.
                Days passed,
and even the pauses between my breath
would remind me that you are not here.
But remembering your words, I held
10   your mirror before me.
              Amazed,
you looked back, your fingers stretched
to meet mine. Between us, I could feel
only the glass. The brown centers of your eyes
returned my stare.
           Mother, how do you see me?
15   Enclosed within your reflection, you can't answer
what I ask—how your teacup knows
the shape of my hands, the smooth rim
the bow of my lips. With every stroke
of my brush, why do I imagine the length
20   of your hair?
          Each time we meet, we press
closer together, as if you could make me whole.

Responding to the Selection ─────────

Questions for Discussion

1. Which images or lines help you feel the girl's longing for her absent mother?

2. Do you think that the mother is really appearing in the mirror? If not, what might be an explanation for what the girl sees?

3. How would you describe the theme of "The Mirror of Matsuyama"?

Activities

Writing a Monologue

1. How do you think the father, new wife, or dead mother would respond to Matsuyama's staring into the mirror? Write a monologue for one of these characters. Use details from the poem in your monologue.

Interpreting the Story

2. How do you feel about the way Matsuyama chooses to mourn her mother's death? Write a paragraph in response to this question.

Drawing a Book Cover

3. Draw a book cover for a published edition of the poem.

Mobility, 1994. Bharati Chaudhuri. Monotype, 18 × 24 in. SuperStock.

Theme Three

Places

Around us, there were mountains shaped like waves. I grew up yearning for the ocean.

—Yun Wang

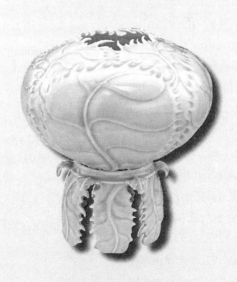

Before You Read

Eruption: Pu'u O'o

Garrett Hongo
Born 1951

"I believe that I'm in a conversation with society. Maybe society's not talking to me, but I'm talking to it."

About Hongo

Garrett Hongo was born in a small Hawaiian town called Volcano. His family moved to the Los Angeles area when he was a baby. As a high school student, he became convinced that his generation of Japanese Americans had the responsibility to speak up about the mistreatment of their parents and grandparents during World War II. At the time, he was interested in both photography and writing. Eventually he decided to focus on poetry because he felt that poets "were the truth-tellers, the passionate ones."

In addition to his two volumes of poetry and a memoir, Hongo has contributed to Asian American literature by editing important anthologies. His favorite place to work is Volcano. Hongo says that when he first returned to the beautiful town he was "astonished that a place like that existed and that I was from that place."

Volcanic Islands

The Hawaiian Islands were formed by a chain of volcanoes. Kilauea, one of three active volcanoes on the islands, has been erupting steadily since 1983 at a site called Pu'u O'o. Unlike the violent explosions released from volcanoes such as Mount St. Helens, Pu'u O'o sends forth fountains or streams of molten lava that run in channels like rivers. Pu'u O'o has added over 560 acres of new land to Hawaii. Unfortunately, the lava flows have destroyed many homes and other structures.

In line 9 of the poem, *ohi'a* is the Hawaiian name for the myrtle tree. The reference to fire in line 11 is to the descriptions of Hell in the works of the English poet William Blake (1757–1827). The Leviathan in line 26 is a monstrous sea creature, sometimes considered to be a whale, mentioned in the Bible.

Eruption: Pu'u O'o

— *Garrett Hongo*

We woke near midnight,
flicking on the coat closet's bulb,
the rainforest chilled with mist,
a yellow swirl of gas
5   in the spill of light outside.
Stars paling, tucked high
in the sky's blue jade,
we saw, through the back windows
and tops of *ohi'a* trees,
10   silhouettes and red showers
as if from Blake's fires,
magenta and billows of black volleying.
Then, a burbling underground,
like rice steaming in the pot,
15   shook through chandeliers of fern
and the A-frame's tambourine floor,
stirring the cats and chickens
from the crawl-space and their furled sleep.
The fountain rose to 900 feet that night,
20   without us near it, smoking white,
spitting from the cone 6 miles away,
a geyser of flame, pyramids and gyres of ash.
Novices, we dressed and drove out,
first to the crater rim, Uwekahuna
25   a canyon and sea of ash and moonstone,
the hardened, grey back of Leviathan
steaming and venting, dormant under cloud-cover.

Eruption: Pu'u O'o

    And then next down Volcano Road past the villages
    to Hirano Store on Kilauea's long plateau.
30   There, over canefield and the hardened lava land,
    all we saw was in each other's eyes—
    the mind's fear and the heart's delight,
    running us this way and that.

Responding to the Selection

Questions for Discussion

1. Which images in the poem did you find particularly striking or unusual?

2. At the end of the poem, the speaker refers to "the mind's fear and the heart's delight." How do you interpret this statement? Which of your own experiences has aroused this combination of emotions?

3. On the basis of the speaker's response to the eruption, how would you describe his attitude toward nature? How does this attitude compare to your own?

Activities

Giving an Oral Report

1. Do an Internet search to find out current information about the Pu'u O'o eruption and other volcanic activity in Hawaii. Present your findings to the class in an oral report.

Writing a Script

2. Imagine that you are a television news correspondent in Hawaii. Using details from Hongo's poem, write the script for a report on the Pu'u O'o eruption. You might wish to interview the poem's speaker in your report. Include suggestions for camera shots to accompany the report.

Discussing Poetry

3. Hongo has said that he became a poet to "explore the life of emotions." Discuss with a partner whether poetry is better suited to exploring the life of emotions than is prose. Use examples to justify your position.

Before You Read

I Remember Fermin 1930

Jeff Tagami
Born 1954

"In October Light, Tagami insistently invokes the passage of time, the revision of history, and the influence of place."

—Nerissa Balce-Cortes
and Jean Vengua Gier, critics

About Tagami

Jeff Tagami is a third-generation Filipino American. Born in Watsonville, California, he grew up working with his family in the agricultural fields of the Pajaro Valley. When he was in his twenties, he moved to San Francisco. However, rural California remained the focus of his writing. In his first poetry collection, *October Light,* Tagami portrays the conditions endured by migrant workers and their strong connection to the land. He based these poems on personal experiences as well as his knowledge of Filipino American history.

Tagami has also translated poetry and helped edit *Without Names,* a collection of poems by Bay Area Filipino American writers. After living in San Francisco for fourteen years, Tagami returned with his wife and children to Watsonville.

Fermin Tobera

The title of Tagami's poem refers to a tragic incident in California history. When Filipinos began arriving in the Watsonville area, they came into conflict with some European Americans who resented competition for jobs. This problem became even worse late in 1929 as the nation's economy deteriorated. In January 1930, a mob of four hundred people attacked a Filipino dance hall. Many Filipinos were terrorized or beaten over the next four days. During the riot, three local high school students shot and killed a Filipino worker named Fermin Tobera as he lay in his bunk at a labor camp. They were never convicted of his murder.

Okie in line 10 is a disparaging term used in the 1930s for a migrant farm worker from Oklahoma or other Midwestern states.

I Remember Fermin 1930

— *Jeff Tagami*

The old man remembered that year
Because it was the year they grew
Too many potatoes. "Dump 'em,"
The boss said, simply.

5 So all of September was spent
Lugging them on his back
In burlap sacks down the dirt road
To the Pajaro River.
Under a cotton wood
10 He met an Okie woman and her two sons
Who had been fishing. Loosening
His sack, he let them pick
A few good ones, then freed the rest
Into the calm mirror of water.
15 They floated, bobbing into one another.
He thought, then
Of his family in another country,
Of the small garden
Shaded by fronds of coconut palm
20 Where there grew the green tops
Of sweet potatoes called, camote.
As always,
He wondered if they had enough to eat.

Later, going back for another load,
25 He imagined the waterlogged potatoes
Beginning to sprout
And how, from a distance,

They resembled tiny islands
Before they drifted upriver, finally
30 Toward the hungry mouth
That was the sea.

❖

Responding to the Selection ——————

Questions for Discussion

1. What feelings did this poem stir up in you?

2. The old worker apparently responds to a question from the speaker by recalling his experiences in the year of Tobera's death. What is your impression of the worker? Which lines give you this impression?

3. How does Tagami use imagery to draw connections between the United States and the Philippines?

4. Fermin Tobera's murder was marked by a National Day of Humiliation in the Philippines. Which lines or passages in this poem might inspire Filipino pride? Explain.

Activities

Writing a Personal Essay

1. Write a brief essay in which you describe what you were doing at the time of an important event, such as a disaster or a national celebration. Explain how the event touched your life.

Reporting on the Great Depression

2. Do research to learn more about the conditions endured by migrant laborers during the Great Depression. Report your findings to the class.

Before You Read

Crossing

Richard E. Kim
Born 1932

> "The most important thing I learned [about writing] was cut, cut, cut."

About Kim

Richard E. Kim was eighteen when the Korean War broke out in 1950. After capturing the South Korean capital of Seoul, where Kim was living, the North Koreans forced him into an army training school. But Kim escaped by leaping from a second-story window. Later he became a South Korean army officer and served in an English-speaking unit as a liaison officer to the United Nations forces. His knowledge of English allowed him to win a scholarship to Middlebury College in Vermont after the war ended.

Kim settled in the United States and studied philosophy for years before he tried his hand at writing fiction. His first novel, *The Martyred,* became a bestseller in 1964. Critics praised his simple, straightforward writing style and his treatment of philosophical issues. Kim's third book, *Lost Names,* covers the first thirteen years of his life, when he and his parents lived in Japanese-occupied Korea and in Manchuria, a region in northeastern China occupied by the Japanese in 1931.

Japanese Occupation

"Crossing" is the first chapter of *Lost Names*. The book's title refers to a Japanese order that all Koreans replace their names with Japanese-style names. After Japan took over Korea in 1910, it imposed harsh laws in an attempt to wipe out Korean culture. Many Koreans left the country to look for jobs after the Japanese confiscated their land. The occupation ended in 1945 when Japan was defeated in World War II.

Crossing

— *Richard E. Kim*

". . . and the twilight, yes, the twilight," says my mother, closing her eyes for a moment. "The sun goes down quickly in the north, you know, especially in the winter." She pauses, remembering the twilight and the sunset in a small border town by Tuman River that separates northern Korea, Manchuria, and Siberia. 1933—I must have been only a year old. "Oh, but that twilight was glorious, almost awesome," says my mother. "It was windy that afternoon, and snow flurries were swirling and swishing around all over—over the shabby little town, the snow-covered railway station, the ice-capped mountains, the frozen river, the bridge, yes, the bridge which we had to cross but couldn't. Of course, I didn't see it all really until I was out of the train, until they took your father away from me, away from the train we were on." She stops again, as if to blot out that part of her remembrance—the Japanese Thought Policeman and the Japanese Military Policeman snatching away my father's papers and pushing him down the corridor and out of the train. She shakes her head slightly and smiles. "And it was so cold in the train. The steam heater wasn't working, not in our compartment anyway, and I had only thin socks on." Her thin cotton socks and her black patent leather shoes—and she is the only Korean woman in the compartment who wears Western-style clothes, has a baby, and has to watch, in tearful silence, her young husband being taken off the train by the Japanese.

And what was I doing? Asleep? Awake, wide awake—watching too. "And I almost wished you would start crying, and the Japanese would let your father alone so he could take care of me and you, but you didn't." She smiles. "We had been on the train almost all day, when it, at last, pulled into that railway station. The compartment was half-empty, cold, and there was a thick coat of ice on the windows, and you couldn't see out."

. . . the train gasps and puffs into the outer edge of the train yard, braking hard, slipping on the tracks. "Where are we?" my mother is asking, holding me up in her arms as the train jerks and lurches. "This is the last stop before the border," my father is saying, "this is the last Korean town before we get to Manchuria." Frozen windowpane crusted with sooty ice.

My father scratching the pane with his thumbnail, thawing it with his breath, and clearing a round patch with his fingers, so my mother and I can look outside, so his young wife can look at the last town on the Korean side of the border, before they take leave of their homeland that is no longer their homeland. She watches the snow flurries whipping and gyrating madly outside, subsiding suddenly once in a while, and she can see nothing for a while, as the train crawls into the station. Then, the train is slinking in between other trains and flatcars, and she is staring at the big guns of the Japanese artillery and the tanks on the flatcars and, then, the horses of the Japanese cavalry peering out of their open stalls next to the flatcars, the horses' white breath mixing with the steam from the train, and, then, the Japanese soldiers in their compartments, all look-ing out, some in their undershirts and some with their jackets open, eating and drinking. She turns to my father and says:

"Look."

My father looks out, turns to her, and nods.

It is then that a Japanese Thought Police detective and a Japanese Military Policeman come into the compartment. The detective is a middle-aged Korean who works for the Japanese; he is big and tall and wears a brown, dog-fur coat and a gray felt hat. The Japanese Military Policeman is not wearing an overcoat; he has on a brown leather belt with a big brass buckle, a pistol in a black leather holster, and a long saber that his white-gloved left hand clutches; he is young and short, with a flushed, boyish face; he is a corporal. "There were only about a dozen people in our compartment," says my mother, "and the detective took one look around and came straight to your father. He knew what he was up to. The Military Policeman followed right behind him, like a hunter following behind his hound, and all the Korean pas-sengers were looking at us, all very quiet. When the detective came to our seat, he turned around to look at the other passengers, and they all snapped their heads away from us, and the detective nodded to the Japanese Military Policeman." She stops. "As if to say to the corporal, 'Well, we got him.'"

. . . and she is looking down at the snow-covered toes of the corpo-ral's long, brown boots and the shiny toes of the detective's black shoes. The thin fingers of her young husband smoothing pieces of creased papers and holding them out, and the white-gloved hand of the corporal snatching them up. The papers crackle, and she thinks her husband's hand is trembling, not because he is afraid but because he is in poor health and weak; after all, he had been jailed by the Japanese for years for his resistance-movement activities, before she married him. . . . The corporal gives the papers to the detective and steps aside. His boots creak, and, as if on cue, the Korean detective says to her husband—my father—"So, you don't waste much time, do you? You could hardly wait to get out of the country."

My father is silent.

"Your parole was over only a week ago, and here you are sneaking out of the country."

"My papers are in order, as you can see," says my father, "and you must have had words about me from the police in my town."

"We know everything about you."

"Then you know I have official permission to travel."

"A piece of paper," says the detective.

"It is signed by the chief of police in my town and also by the Japanese judge of our district."

The detective folds the papers and stuffs them into his pocket. "What is the purpose of your travel?"

"It is stated in the papers."

"I am asking you a question."

"I have a job waiting for me."

"You couldn't get a job in the country?"

"I was a farmer," says my father. "I worked in my father's orchard."

"So—this high school is run by foreign missionaries. Do you have to work for foreigners?"

My mother thinks my father should say, "Look, you, too, are working for foreigners, as their hound." But my father says quietly, "It's a job."

"These missionaries—these foreign Christians—they feel sorry for you and give you a job and think they are protecting you from us?"

"It's a job; besides, I am a Christian," my father says and quickly glances at my mother. "And my wife is the daughter of a Christian minister, so it is natural that the foreign missionaries would want to hire me to teach."

"What do they want you to teach?"

"I am going to be teaching biology and chemistry."

The detective doesn't reply to that and looks at my mother.

My father says, "She will be teaching music at the school's kindergarten. It is all stated in the papers."

The detective says to my mother, "Is that a boy or a girl?"

I am all bundled up and wrapped in the wool blanket my grandmother made.

"A boy," says my mother. "He is only a year old."

My father says, "May I have the papers back?"

The detective says, "Do you understand Japanese?"

My father nods. "I don't speak it well."

Crossing

The detective whispers something to the Japanese corporal. He turns to my father. "You must come with us."

"Why?"

"The Military Police want to ask you a few questions."

"About what?"

"How would I know! I don't work for the Military Police!"

"But I can't leave the train. It will go out soon."

"No, it won't move for a while. The military trains will have to cross the bridge first, and that will take a while. Come!" He says to my mother, "You stay here. He will be back soon."

She tries to stand up, gathering me up in her arms. My father tells her not to worry. "Stay here," he says. Tears well up in her frightened eyes, and her husband shakes his head. She nods and sits down, clutching me close to her. He moves out of the seat, and she picks up his woolen gloves and hands them to him. Then, they are gone from the compartment. She presses her face to the window, trying to see if she can catch a glimpse of him, trying to find out where they are taking him. But all that she can see is the Japanese military train that is right alongside her train. The military train is now creaking out of the station and, through the frozen windowpane, she sees blurred images of the Japanese guns, tanks, soldiers, and the horses that are passing by. At last, she can see across the snow-covered tracks to the dingy station house, just as my father and his inquisitors disappear into it. Her breath is clouding the windowpane, and a thin coat of ice quickly blots out her view. Scratching at the windowpane, she is trying to be brave, but she is afraid for her young husband and for herself, alone with the baby; she weeps silently, all the time thinking that she must do something. It is quiet in the compartment; the other passengers try not to look at her. A little later, the conductor comes in and begins to collect the tickets. She doesn't have her ticket; her husband has it. She looks up at the conductor, who is a Korean, and tries to explain but words do not come out. A young Korean boy, a high school boy, comes over and quickly explains the situation to the conductor, who nods in sympathy and tells her not to worry. The high school boy bows to her and shyly asks her the name of her husband. She tells him. The boy smiles triumphantly, knowingly.

"I heard his name mentioned by the detective, but I wanted to make sure," he says, glancing at the conductor, who is standing by awkwardly. The boy says to her, "I go to the same high school he went to in Seoul. Everyone at the school knows his name and about his trial and going to prison and all." He tells the conductor that my father is a patriot who, as a college student, organized a resistance movement against the Japanese and was arrested by the Japanese and spent years in prison. He tells the conductor the name of the trial case. The conductor says he has heard about it and turns to her. "He will be all right. Don't worry too much. It probably is just a routine questioning. This is a border town, you know, and, what with the war and all the disturbances going on across the river—well, the Japanese have been pretty strict about security."

The high school boy whispers, "Is it true that the Chinese and Korean troops across the river demolished a whole Japanese regiment a while ago?"

The conductor hushes the young boy but nods. "In June," he says. "The regiment from Nanam." He cuts the cold air with his gloved hand. "All of them." He says to the boy, "I would be quiet about it, though, if I were you."

"Yes, sir," says the boy.

Suddenly, the train lurches forward and begins to move.

The conductor says, "What's going on? We aren't supposed to pull out for another hour!" He runs out of the compartment, saying, "I'll find out and let you know."

My mother, in panic, stands up, swaying. Quickly, she makes up her mind that she should get off the train. She gathers me up in her arms but doesn't know what to do with the two suitcases. The train slows down and stops. The boy says, "You can't get off the train! They wouldn't let the train go out without him. Trains can't go out without the Military Police's permission, you know."

But she is now determined. She should have followed her husband, she thinks, when they took him away. She is afraid, and she feels lost. She says to the boy, "I am going out."

The boy says, "The train is stopped now. Why don't you wait and see?"

The conductor runs into the compartment and shouts to everyone, "We'll be moving out in a minute!" He comes to her. "What are you going to do?"

"She wants to get off the train," says the boy.

"No, no! You mustn't!" says the conductor. "Look! I can tell the station clerk about your husband and have him tell your husband that you will be waiting for him across the river. He can join you there. There's another train coming in about two hours."

"That's a good idea," says the boy. "You can come with me and my mother and stay with us. We live right across the river. We can leave our address with the station clerk."

She doesn't answer. She quickly wraps me up tightly and is out of her seat.

The conductor says, "If you insist, then I'll take you to the station clerk who is a friend of mine. A Korean. It will be warm in his office, and you can wait there. Come."

She says to the boy, "Would you do me a favor? Would you mind taking these suitcases with you and leaving them at the station across the river?"

Crossing

The conductor says, "I'll help him. We can leave them with the Chinese station master there."

She thanks them all and starts down the corridor.

Someone says, "Take care of yourself."

Outside, icy wind and snow flurries lash at her. Her shoes are quickly buried under the snow on the tracks. She covers my face with the blanket, trudging across the tracks toward the station house. The conductor is carrying a small bag for her. Before they clear the tracks and climb up an embankment, the train they just left clanks and begins to move. The conductor, helping her up the embankment, swears under his breath. "I can't come with you. I must run back to the train. Be careful now and tell the station clerk I sent you. I may see you both on the other side of the river." He leaps over the tracks and runs back to the moving train. Her words of thanks are lost in the wind. She is now standing on the platform, which is deserted, except for a Japanese Military Policeman who is flagging the train out. She looks at the train chugging out of the yard, and she can see the old conductor and the young boy standing on the step of the compartment she was in. They are waving to her. Tears run down her frozen cheeks, and she silently watches the train move across the bridge, across the river, toward Manchuria. She hugs me close and wipes away her cold tears, rubbing her face against the blanket that keeps me warm. She looks up, aware that the Japanese Military Policeman is watching her, and it is then that she, standing forlorn on the barren platform, sees that it is twilight.

The sun, big and red in spite of the snow flurries, is setting, plummeting down toward the frozen expanse of the northern Manchurian plains. "Twilight"—she thinks—"it is twilight," and, somehow, she forgets everything for a moment, lost in the awesome sight of the giant, red sun, which, as though burning out, is swiftly sinking and being swallowed up by the darkening northern horizon. The silvery snow flurries are dancing in the air, whishing and roaring, as if cleansing the lingering rays of the bloody sun from the northern sky. . . . The air is cool and fresh, and she prays, "Lord, help me."

The sun has disappeared. It is now dark. The wind has died down. My mother is still standing there alone on the platform. I am asleep in her arms. She is facing toward the bridge. She can't see it clearly now. Only the red lights on both sides of its entrance and its dim silhouette against the starry northern sky are visible. Occasionally, she looks back at the main door of the station house. She can see a small room to the right of the station house; it is lighted inside by a green-shaded lamp that dangles from the ceiling. Someone inside the room, hunched over a little potbellied stove, gets up once in a while and looks out the window. My father is

Crossing

somewhere in town at the Japanese Military Police Detachment. "Too far to walk," said a Korean man, a ticket clerk at the station. "Why don't you and the baby come inside and keep warm?" My mother said no—she would wait for her husband outside; he might come any moment. She waits.

How long did she stand there alone waiting for my father? An hour? Two hours? She doesn't know. She only knows that it is getting darker and darker and, now, she can't see even the silhouette of the bridge. Her feet, protected only by the thin cotton socks, are numb, and, without realizing it, she is rocking back and forth. I am now awake and begin to whimper; I am thirsty and hungry. My mother begins to pace, rocking me; she is weeping quietly, swallowing a big lump of irrepressible terror. She says to herself she can't cry, she mustn't cry, and she must be brave. Her father has been in jail, too, on and off, many times because he would say in his sermons things that the Japanese Thought Police did not like; and, of course, her husband. . . .

All the men she knows—her father, husband, brothers-in-law, and many of her friends' relatives—they have all been to jail at least once. It was bad last year, she thinks, especially in May. A lot of Korean men were arrested and interrogated, and many have not yet returned home; all this began right after what happened in Shanghai—a Korean patriot threw bombs and killed the Japanese general who commanded all the Japanese forces in China, along with several other Japanese officials; the general and the officials were at a park in Shanghai, celebrating the birthday of their Sun-God Emperor. She remembers a Japanese Thought Police inspector who came to her father after that incident; the inspector told him that it would be in the best interest of everyone in his parish if, in his Sunday sermon, he would condemn the violent acts committed by a fellow Korean, a terrorist. Her father would not cooperate, and, the next day, they came for him and took him away; they released him two days later, just before Sunday. Her father had been beaten by the Police; all that he said in his sermon on Sunday was that God said vengeance was His. The Japanese are stupid, she thinks; they think the parishioners would believe their minister if he said what the police forced him to say, as if people are so stupid and naive, as if forcing a man to say what they want him to say would change his soul. . . .

The old ticket clerk opens the window and asks my mother to come into the room—the baby must be cold. She doesn't listen to him. Remembering her father and thinking about him have made her brave and proud. I come from a family . . . and I am married to a man . . . she lifts her face and looks at the star-studded night sky, proud; if her father and her husband can endure the torture and humiliation inflicted by the Japanese, she and the baby will endure the cold wind and the darkness. She lowers her gaze toward the plains of Manchuria across the river.

Crossing

Across the river—she thinks—across the river . . . she almost says to herself that life would be different across the river, that the family would be away from the Japanese, and that there would be quiet and peace. . . . Then, she remembers the Japanese guns, tanks, soldiers, horses. . . . The Japanese had conquered Manchuria and set up a puppet regime, just a year before, and they have already begun their invasion of the Chinese mainland itself. All those guns and tanks and soldiers, on their way to China. There are too many Japanese around; the Japanese are everywhere, toting guns and rattling sabers. Staring hard toward Manchuria, she feels neither despair nor sorrow but the outrage of a wounded soul. "Vengeance is Mine." "Lord," she prays, "free us from them and free us from this nightmare." The wind is quiet now, and there is a strange warmth in the air. Her tears flow freely now, but she does not mind. There is only her Lord to see her tears—and now her young husband, who is coming toward her, crossing the yellow patch of light on the snow outside the room.

She stands still and realizes she is crying. She quickly buries her face in the woolen blanket that is keeping me warm, as if to see whether I am awake or asleep, and rubs her tears dry. She suddenly feels that her throat is parched and that she is a little dizzy. She is afraid she may start crying again. She sways and I squirm and whimper, and that steadies her. My father is by her side now, without a word. She thinks he is trembling. He looks at her quietly, and she can see tears in his eyes. She feels her eyes welling up with tears and quickly she hands me to him as if saying, "Here, he is safe." My father takes me in his arms. My mother opens the blanket so that he can see my face. He touches her on the shoulder. She moves a little closer to him and sees that one of his nostrils is stuffed with tissue paper or cotton that is darkened. Then, she sees several welts on his left cheek. A sharp ache needles her heart. He raises one hand and brushes off snowflakes from her hair.

"We missed the train," he says.

"Another train was supposed to come in but it hasn't yet."

"You must be hungry," he says. "I have something for us to eat. Something for the baby, too."

"I am not hungry."

The ticket clerk opens the window and calls out to them. "Come inside! You'll freeze to death. Come!"

My father says, "Let's go inside. He is heating up some rice cakes I brought from the town. Come."

She nods and picks up her small bag. Snowflakes slide off the bag. "The baby can have some powdered milk. Some biscuits."

They walk into the station house. The ticket clerk opens the door to his room and beckons them in. The warm, steamy air makes her feel dizzy again.

Crossing

"Come in, come in," says the clerk. "Warm yourselves at the stove."

My father says to my mother, "Better sit down away from the stove. It is not good to get too hot all of a sudden, especially when you have been outside so long." He thanks the clerk for inviting them in.

"The least I can do for you young people," says the clerk. "I'll get you some tea. You must be starving. How is the baby doing?"

I am halfway out of the bundle of blankets, sitting up on my mother's lap.

My mother just looks at me, saying nothing.

The clerk says to my father, "Your wife is a strong-willed woman. She just wouldn't come in until you came back." He is heating the rice cakes on a grill placed on the top of the stove.

My father pours tea from an iron kettle into a small china cup and hands it to my mother, who says he should drink it first. He takes a sip and gives the cup to her. He picks me up from my mother and, bending down, notices that her shoes and socks are wet. "Better take your shoes off and dry them," he says.

The clerk, putting the cakes on a piece of cardboard, says, "Better dry your socks, too, and don't mind me at all."

She takes off her shoes and, turning away from the clerk, removes her wet socks. My father hands her his handkerchief so she can dry her feet. It is stained with blood. She looks up at him and sees the cotton in his nostril. She begins to sob.

"It is all right," he says. "Dry your feet."

The clerk puts a wooden chair between my parents' chairs and puts the cakes down on it. He quietly goes out of the room.

When the clerk returns to the room, my father thanks him and says that they are ready to leave.

The clerk says, "There is another train sometime tonight. Why don't you wait for it here?"

"It may not come," says my father. "It is already several hours late."

"If it doesn't come in, you can stay in town and leave in the morning."

"We'd better go now," says my father. "We can't stay in this town."

"With the baby, on a night like this?"

"We'll be all right."

"I want to go across the river," says my mother, wrapping me up with the blankets.

"We have someone waiting for us across the river," says my father. "Thank you for everything."

"I understand," says the clerk. "Do you know the way?"

My father nods. "I asked some people in town."

"You've got to go downstream a bit. There are always some people coming and going. You'll see them."

178 **Richard E. Kim**

Crossing

They are going to walk across the frozen river. People who can't afford the train have made a footpath across the river.

"There'll be a policeman out there, you know," says the clerk.

"I have my papers," says my father.

By now, my mother has put another pair of thin cotton socks on under the other pair. Her shoes are still damp. I am in my father's arms. She picks up the small bag, ready to go.

The old man says, "Take care of yourself. Raise the baby well." He wraps the leftover rice cakes in a piece of newspaper and puts them into my mother's small bag. He comes over to my father and pats me on the head before my father covers me up with the blanket. My mother unfolds the edge of the blanket carefully so that I will have a small opening to breathe through.

The old man opens the door for them, and my mother bows to him and bids him farewell. My father bows, too. The old man taps him on the shoulder. "Take care of your family," he says.

Half an hour later, they reach the bank of the river. There is a small hut, lighted inside. Smoke is curling up out of a stove pipe through the roof, and sparks fly off into the dark night air. A dozen people are lined up outside the hut to show their papers to a young Korean policeman. Another policeman is inside the hut. My father shows his papers. The policeman nods and waves my parents by. They are behind an elderly couple, and they follow the old people down the bank toward a path through the snow on the frozen river. They can see lights flickering at the other side of the river, on the Manchurian side. It doesn't seem too far. The old man looks back and says to my mother, "The baby must be cold."

She does not answer. I am warm and secure within the wool blankets. My father says to him, "Is the ice thick enough?"

"Nothing to worry about," he says, helping the old woman down the bank. "We've done this many times. Our son lives across the river, you know. You just follow us."

My father stretches out his hand, which my mother takes as she steps onto the ice. It is the first time they have touched hands since they left home, my grandparents' house. "Do you feel all right?" asks my father. She nods.

She goes behind him. Many people are behind her. No one is talking much. The path has been made by lots of footsteps that packed the snow hard. It is jagged and slippery, and my mother's leather shoes do not help her much. Other people are wearing straw shoes and heavy socks, thickly padded with cotton. "If I had a pair of socks like them," she thinks, "I would take off my shoes and walk on in my socks." Someone slips and falls down behind her. My mother stops.

Crossing*

My father stops, too, and asks her if she is all right. They both watch the people helping a young girl up. They look toward the south side of the river, the Korean side, but they can't see anything. With all the snow under the starry sky, the air is stangely white. People move on like ghosts, silently, except for their feet crunching on the ice. "People without a country"—my mother thinks—"people ousted and uprooted from their homeland. Forced out of their land and their homes by the Japanese, who are buying up land cheaply by threat and coercion. Displaced peasants driven out of their ancestral land to find new roots in an alien land." What fate is waiting for these people across the river? What destiny will unfold for her and her family across the river? She gazes at her husband's back. She can't see the baby. She slips on a large chunk of ice and almost falls. In that second, she lost sight of him and the baby and now she wants desperately to be at their side. She wants to touch him and the baby. She hurries over to them.

My father turns around. "Be careful," he whispers. "Here. Hold onto my hand." She is out of breath and clings to his outstretched hand. She opens the blanket a little to look at me. "He is all right. Asleep," says my father. "Poor thing," she says. "Come," he says, "it won't be long." They are halfway across the river.

Later, the old man ahead of them turns around and says, "You have to be careful now. The ice gets thin around here, and there are holes here and there. Last time I came by, I saw some Chinese fishing through holes." The old man squats down and unwraps a bundle he has been carrying on his back. He takes out a kerosene lantern and tries to light it. The wind blows out his match. The old woman tries to help him by crouching next to him and holding her skirt around the lantern, which the old man lights. "You people stay close behind us. Don't worry."

They can see lights and a few huts along the bank. My mother thinks they are now close to the bank, but there is still a long way to go. Then, she thinks of the holes and the thin ice. She clutches my father's hand. The old man's lantern bobs up and down, its yellowish light flickering. "There's a big crack on the left. Be careful," says the old man, holding the lantern high, waving it. Thin ice, holes, a big crack in the ice. She is afraid. "Be careful, dear," she says to her husband.

"We are almost there," he says. "Almost there now."

Almost there. Across the river. She looks toward the bank. There are people standing on the bank. She can see them dimly against the light from the huts. Almost there. Then, it strikes her that there hasn't been anyone going the other way across the river, toward the Korean side. She can hear voices coming from the bank. The sky is clear, and the stars in the northern plains seem larger and brighter than those in other directions.

Crossing

The snow all around her seems so white and almost shining. Her feet are cold and ache, but the crossing is almost over, and she is thinking only that, across the river, someone is waiting for them, someone from the missionary school. She hopes he has brought a buggy with two horses, which, she has heard, people ride in in Manchuria. "Taking a buggy ride in the snow would be nice," she thinks, "just as they do in Russia," or so she has read. Almost there. There will be quarters for them in the town where the school is. Two rooms and a kitchen. Her husband will be a teacher; students will visit them, and, of course, so will his fellow teachers and the missionary people. She, too, will be teaching, at the school's kindergarten. Twenty-five children—so they have written her. Mostly Korean children, but some Chinese and American and Canadian children, too. Almost there, across the river. "Oh—the suitcases," she thinks, "I hope the young boy and the train conductor made sure the suitcases were left with the Chinese station master. Some wool in one of the suitcases. I will knit a wool sweater for him so he can wear it under his coat when he goes to the school to teach, and the baby could use another wool jacket, and maybe another wool cap. Almost there now." "Is the baby still sleeping?" she asks her husband. "Yes," he says. "Just a little more and we'll be there."

The old man's lantern, the lights along the bank like haloes, and the voices calling to them. Almost there now. Then, she is suddenly seized with a violent fear of that strange alien land waiting for her. All those Chinese people there. "The town is almost a Korean town, really," her husband has said to her, "and the school, of course, is for Korean students. It really is like any other Korean town, except that there are lots of Chinese people around you." "A Korean ghetto, that's what it is," she thinks. She has heard from her father that, in many places in Europe, the Jewish people lived together among foreigners who did not welcome them, and the places where they lived were called ghettos. "Like our parish," he said; "We Christians in this country live close to each other around our churches, and that is not much different from the Jewish people living in their ghettos." "Will those Chinese people be friendly?" she wants to ask her husband, but it is not the time to ask a question like that. Almost there. And, suddenly, she again thinks of holes and thin ice and big cracks in the ice. Thin ice, holes, cracks. . . . The bank looms ahead of them, and it is as if, with one big leap over the ice, they can get onto it. But, now that they are so close to the other side of the river, she feels as if she is losing all her will and strength. "We have made it across," she says to herself. And again—holes, cracks, and thin ice frighten her. Thin ice especially. For one moment, she has a blinding vision of crashing through thin ice and being sucked into the cold water and pushed down under the ice . . . one of her hands is clinging to the edge of the ice, but her body is being pulled down and down . . . and the water freezes her instantly and she can't even scream for help but, then, her husband pulls her up out of the water onto the ice and she gets up . . . and asks, "Is the baby still asleep?"

He says, "Yes."

She says to him, squeezing his hand, "We've made it, haven't we?"

"We've made it across," he says, looking straight ahead.

"Good thing the baby slept through."

He turns to her. "Actually, he's been wide awake. All the way."

She smiles. "What a good little boy he is," she says. She is not thinking of thin ice, holes, and big cracks in the ice any longer. After this, she thinks, I can go with my family anywhere, anytime, to the end of the earth. . . .

And so, I, too, crossed that frozen river wide awake, and, years and years later, whenever I think of that crossing, I think of thin ice, holes and big cracks in the ice—especially the thin ice.

"But, I don't think I can do anything like that again," says my mother. "Not any more. I was young then. Lots of people never made it across that river, you know. Drowned or frozen to death when they were caught in a sudden snowstorm. No, I could not do anything like that again."

"But you can and you will," I say to her. "And you have, many times since, if not crossing a frozen river on foot."

She thinks it over. "Well, so I have, haven't I?" She thinks of the thirty some years since the night we crossed the frozen Tuman River. "And you have, too," she says, "on your own, by yourself."

"I have done it many times."

"Well, you've made it across," she says.

And I am still thinking of the thin ice of that frozen river in the north.

Responding to the Selection

Questions for Discussion

1. What feelings did you experience as you read this selection?

2. Why does the mother refuse to wait inside the station house while her husband is being questioned? What does this decision suggest about her character?

3. What concerns might have prompted the narrator's parents to make the crossing on foot instead of waiting for the train? Do you think that they made a good decision? Explain.

4. **Suspense** is the tension or excitement that a reader feels about what will happen next in a story. Which passage of "Crossing" did you find the most suspenseful? What techniques does Kim use to create suspense in this passage?

5. At the end of the selection, the narrator tells his mother that she has made crossings "many times" since her ordeal at the border. How do you interpret this statement? What kinds of events in your own life do you consider "crossings"? Why?

Activities

Writing a Paragraph

1. Which event in recent history reminds you of the Japanese occupation of Korea as it is described in "Crossing"? Write a paragraph in which you compare the two events.

Writing a Monologue

2. The narrator describes the crossing of the frozen river from the mother's perspective. Write a brief monologue in which you imagine the father's thoughts as he leads his family across the river.

Drawing a Picture

3. This is a story about one person's origins. How do you think this early experience helped shape Richard Kim's character? What early experiences in your own life do you feel helped make you who you are today? Draw a picture that represents one "crossing" in your own life.

Before You Read

Seoul, Korea

Jean Yoon
Born 1962

"A single tree in the wind can get knocked down in a very small storm. You need other trees to keep on standing."

About Yoon

Jean Yoon was born in Illinois, but she grew up in Toronto, Canada. As a high school student, she developed a strong interest in theater. Frustrated at the lack of roles available to her, she moved to China in the mid-1980s and taught English. When she returned to Toronto several years later, she found that Canadian arts organizations had become more open to working with people of Asian ancestry.

In 1995, Yoon started a theater company called Loud Mouth Asian Babes (her stage name, Seoul Babe, hints at her Korean background). She has written a group of plays called *The Kyopo Trilogy* and a multimedia performance work called *The Yoko Ono Project.* Yoon is also the author of a book of poems called *Under a Hostile Moon.* She enjoys collaborating with other artists on different kinds of projects.

Modern Seoul

Seoul, the capital of South Korea, has a population of over 11 million. Eighty percent of the city was destroyed during the Korean War, so most of its buildings are modern. In her poem about Seoul, Jean Yoon describes a skyline filled with neon crosses. About one-third of all South Koreans are Christian, a percentage much higher than in most other Asian countries. Christianity was introduced into Korea in the eighteenth century. The number of Protestant and Roman Catholic believers has risen dramatically during the past fifty years. One church in Seoul has half a million members!

Seoul, Korea

— *Jean Yoon*

Earth elbows against tight crowds
presses narrow
streets washed red with mud.

It is a cool dry evening, the dusk sky
5   spangled with a thousand neon crosses.

In the daytime, these churches are hard to find.
They look like offices
or vacant shops.

I am far from home.

10   The sun is heavy and perfect
a bloodied orange sinking into shadow.

Far away, sounds rattle together
like pebbles in a lazy hand.

Maybe if I believed in God and perfect heights
15   I would shy into one of these churches.

Instead I flick stones and bits of wood with my thumb.
There is a click, a blur of motion, the stone is gone.

Responding to the Selection

Questions for Discussion

1. What impression of Seoul do you get from reading this poem? Which images or lines give you this impression?

2. How do you interpret the last two lines of the poem?

3. What word would you use to describe the speaker's state of mind? Why might the speaker feel this way?

4. What do you think would happen if the speaker walked into one of the churches she describes? Explain your answer.

Activities

Writing Poetry

1. Write a poem about the city or town where you live. Use vivid imagery to suggest your feelings about this place.

Discussing Photographs

2. Bring in photos of a place where you used to live or a place that was home to your ancestors. Explain to classmates what you would like to see if you visited that place.

Listening to Music

3. Assemble a group of songs about home. Play the songs for the class and discuss what messages the songwriters are communicating about the idea of home and how they achieve their results.

Before You Read

The Carp

Yun Wang
Born 1964

> "During the years of the notorious 'Cultural Revolution,' I cultivated my own world of dreams, of the mysterious beauty of nature around me, of the ancient poets . . ."

About Wang

Yun Wang was born in a small town in southern China. Her father, a high school principal, used to recite ancient Chinese poetry to her when she was a little girl. She started writing her own poems in classical meters at age fourteen. While attending Tsinghua University in Beijing, she began to work in contemporary verse forms, which made it easier for her to get published.

In 1985, Wang came to the United States to study physics at Carnegie Mellon University. There she wrote her first poems in English. Encouraged by friends she met through her poetry, Wang continued to write while pursuing a Ph.D. in physics. She published a collection called *The Carp* in 1994. Now a professor of physics at the University of Oklahoma, Wang says that poetry remains an essential part of her life.

The Cultural Revolution

In her prose poem "The Carp," Wang addresses the horrors of the Cultural Revolution (see Background on page 320). During this violent upheaval, Chinese Communist leader Mao Zedong called upon students to rebel against school administrators. Wang's father was among those tortured and imprisoned. Fearful of the same fate happening to his daughter, he advised her to stay away from any career that involved politics or literature.

Although Wang was criticized by some university officials for her "non-positive poetry," she escaped more drastic sanctions. In the United States, she often hides her identity as a poet, but not because she worries about political persecution. According to Wang, many of her fellow physicists believe it is impossible to excel at both poetry and physics.

The Carp

— *Yun Wang*

My father was the school principal. The day I was born, he caught a twenty-pound carp. He gave it to the school kitchen. All the teachers and boarding students tasted it.

Around us, there were mountains shaped like waves. I grew up yearning for the ocean. Smoke arose from the ever green mountains to form clouds each morning. My father named me Cloud.

When a son was born to Confucius, the king of Lu sent over a carp as a present. Confucius named his son Carp.

The wise say a carp leaping over the dragon gate is a very lucky sign. My father says he named me Cloud because I was born in the year of the dragon, and there are always clouds following a dragon. Confucius' son died an early death. My father has only three daughters.

When I was three, I wandered all over the campus. A stray cat in a haunted town. My mother says I passed the room where my father was imprisoned. He whispered to me, hid a message in my little pocket. It was his will that I should grow up a strong woman, and find justice for him.

They caught me. My father was nearly beaten to death. Some of them were students, whose parents were peasants. Some of them were teachers, who used to be his best friends. They had tasted the carp.

It has been recorded that Confucius could not tell the difference between millet and wheat, and was thus mocked by a peasant. This peasant became a big hero, representing the wisdom of the people, thousands of years after Confucius' death.

My father still goes fishing, the only thing that seems to calm him. The mountains are still sleeping waves. My father catches very small fish. My mother eats them. My friends laugh at me when I tell them that once upon a time, my father caught a carp weighing twenty pounds.

Responding to the Selection

Questions for Discussion

1. What impression of the Cultural Revolution did you get from reading "The Carp"?

2. An **allusion** is a reference to a well-known person, place, or event from history, literature, or religion. How do the allusions to Confucius enrich Wang's poem?

3. What sort of theme, or message, do you find in "The Carp"? How might this theme be relevant to life in the United States?

Activity

Writing a Paragraph

Yun Wang has said that she took comfort in observing nature during the Cultural Revolution. How does she depict nature in "The Carp"? What effect does nature have on the people she describes in the poem? Write a paragraph in response to these questions.

Before You Read

Mango

Christian Langworthy
Born 1967

"We wanted to be soldiers. We wanted to march on the streets with the men in the green uniforms."

About Langworthy

Christian Langworthy is the son of a Vietnamese woman and a U.S. soldier. As a young boy in Vietnam, he spent his days playing with live ammunition and other military items that he found in the street. When he was six years old, he and his younger brother were given up for adoption to a family in upstate New York. His new parents discouraged him from discussing Vietnam. Only in college did he begin to examine his past.

After a brief period of military service, Langworthy decided to become a writer.

His first collection of poems is called *The Geography of War*. He has also published a novel, *Mango*, which is based on his childhood experiences. Langworthy says that writing has helped him realize "how much of an impact my past has had on me and what I need to do to transform myself."

Children of a War

Thousands of Amerasian children were born to Vietnamese women and U.S. servicemen during the Vietnam War. After the United States pulled out of Vietnam in the mid-1970s, these children often faced harsh discrimination in their home country. In 1982 and 1987, Congress relaxed immigration rules to make it easier for Amerasian children to enter the United States.

Mango

— *Christian Langworthy*

You put the mango in the clay jar,
bury it in rice. In the days that pass
you hope it will ripen. Your
mother has told you not to
5   lift the lid too soon, or
the mango will remain green.
You sweep away dust from the corner
where the jar sits like a shrine.
Now and then, you put your hand over
10   the clay lid and count the days gone by.

Monsoon season has passed. Men of war
had asked you questions and left with
their mysteries unsolved. You remember
your father in his pressed uniform,
15   the face of an American soldier,
followed by countless others who
handed you gum and patted your shoulder.

In the corner, the rice jar sits—the mango
deep inside. All the time, you wonder:
20   When will it be ripe? The sun bakes
the sidewalks. You learn to ignore
the pain of walking on hot cement.
From off the street, behind a screen door,
someone sees your face and spits at the dust.
25   They know who you are. They have a name for
your kind, you child of the dust.

In the one-room house, all you have left are
cloths and shelter, your mother and the mango.
The dust has settled. Day and night you wonder
30   how the mango will look after the days gone by.
You take the mango out of the jar
to see if it has ripened and wipe away
the rice dust that dulls the color
of a fruit once green and untouched.

Responding to the Selection ──────────

Questions for Discussion

1. The **speaker** of a poem is the voice that talks to the reader or to the person whom the poem addresses. How does the speaker's use of the second-person pronoun (*you*) influence your reading of "Mango"?

2. Why do you think the child pays so much attention to the mango? What might it symbolize for the speaker?

3. What attitude do strangers have toward the child? Why is he called a "child of dust"? What are some reasons that other Vietnamese might feel the way they do about the children of U.S. soldiers?

Activity
Preparing a Presentation
Research and prepare a class presentation on the history of Amerasian children. If possible, include photos and other visual aids in your presentation.

Before You Read

A Taste of Home

Nguyen Qui Duc
Born 1958

"Literature can have a role in reconciliation and healing."

About Nguyen

Nguyen Qui Duc comes from the former country of South Vietnam. (He pronounces his family name "Nwin" and his given name "Duke.") When Nguyen was nine, North Vietnamese soldiers captured his father, a high-ranking government official. His mother, a school principal, wound up selling noodles in the street to support her children. Nguyen fled Vietnam in 1975 and went to live with a brother in Ohio. Besides feeling guilty about leaving his parents behind, he had a hard time adjusting to life in the United States.

After graduating from college, Nguyen spent a year in Indonesia working with Vietnamese refugees. In 1984 his parents were allowed to leave Vietnam and join him in San Francisco. At around the same time, Nguyen began a career in journalism. He wrote about his family's ordeal in a memoir called *Where the Ashes Are.* The title refers to the cremated ashes of his sister, who had died in Vietnam. Nguyen carried the ashes from Vietnam to his family in San Francisco. The title also refers to his memories of life in his homeland.

Returning Home

Nguyen has made several trips to Vietnam. When he first decided to go back in 1989, his parents were afraid that he would get arrested. They also argued that the communists had destroyed everything of value in the country. National Public Radio sent a crew with Nguyen to document his return. Although he saw many problems there, he still considers Vietnam "a place where there is always time for friends and for friendship, for human contacts that deepen effortlessly and remain nurtured."

A Taste of
HOME

— Nguyen Qui Duc

Strange how the frozen heart of an exile is instantly thawed in the 95-degree heat of Saigon. Seven A.M. and it feels like high noon.

In America I can't even stand the smell of food this early, but here I suddenly want to go out and eat a whole bowl of fish ball noodle soup. And I want a tall glass of iced coffee. *Càfê sũa ãá*, with sweetened, condensed milk, which they only use for baking in America.

I get ready to go out. The shirt I'm putting on makes me feel unprotected. I never wear a short-sleeve shirt in San Francisco. I pull on my trousers, then I remember that I can't leave my hotel room. I don't have a visa.

Vietnam is the homeland, my homeland, and I needed a visa to come home. I should not have trusted the travel agent, who was sure a visa would be waiting for me at the Saigon airport. Last night Vietnamese custom officials seized my passport and sent me to this hotel.

It feels like I'm under house arrest. For a fleeting while, I relish the moment: there is something faintly romantic about being singled out and sequestered. I am a martyr; I feel important. But reality returns, and now I fear that I may indeed be truly arrested, and jailed.

Being holed up on the sixth floor of a government hotel is not my idea of being home. The ancient air conditioner hums loudly, but it only blows out warm air. I am thankful that the ceiling fan is still on the ceiling. It must be at least twenty-five or thirty years old, but it makes breathing in the room almost possible. All night I had kept it spinning as fast as it would go. This room is luxurious according to Saigon's standards, and it costs more than most places. The authorities have sent me here so they can make money off me. The Vietnamese have plenty of jails, but hotels like this one are more helpful to a country in need of foreign cash.

I'm hot, and I can't leave. I take off my shirt and walk out onto the balcony. The plastic sandals the hotel provides to its guests cut into my feet, and the heat feels like overactive and frustrated lust on my skin.

I've been up for an hour now and I have not had any coffee, but I feel awake, breathing in gulps of coarse and heavy air. After a few moments, my eyes are no longer blinded by the harsh sunlight, and I notice two construction workers on the roof of the hotel across the street. Their overalls are faded, and I can see that the back of their pants is almost white. The two men are leaning over a cement wall. I look down to the street and see two young girls pedaling around the corner. Construction workers are the same everywhere. Always on break, always shouting or whistling at women.

I go back inside and kick off the sandals. I want to unpack. I am compulsive about that. Whenever I travel, I unpack as soon as I get to a hotel room. When I go home, I am even more compulsive. I want to get things organized: what gifts to whom, which book I'll be reading first, as a means to later remember my first night home. But how can I unpack now? I don't even know how long I'll be here.

I call Cesais Tours, the representative of my travel agent in San Francisco, and I let the phone ring and ring. I'll try again at 7:30, I say to myself, and turn to organizing my cassette tapes. I've brought along several tapes of Middle Eastern music, I am obsessed by it. I even have an inexplicable attachment to the mullahs' passionate chanting of passages from the Koran. I've come to think of the Middle East as a spiritual home, even though I have never traveled there. It is the music of the region that has long seduced me: I hear in it the struggle of a people, and people who struggle move me. So now I have brought these tapes to Vietnam, as if I wanted to merge the two homes. I arrange the tapes on the nightstand, and remember that all the artists are in exile: a Turkish musician in Connecticut, a Syrian and a Tunisian in Paris, and an Iranian violinist in Los Angeles. I assume nostalgia is what adds to the way these artists play their instruments or sing their songs. I put on the tape of the Turkish singer Omar Faruk Tekbilek, and hear again how haunting his voice is. I can't tell what he is singing about, but the songs are mournful, and I imagine they are all about the sorrow of exile.

I want to get out of this hotel. I want to explore my home, even in the heat. I want to walk up and down the streets, smell the tropical fruits, hear the chatter of women going to the morning market. I imagine myself in all kinds of places, and I get all jittery. I call downstairs to order a cup of coffee. I think coffee will calm my nerves.

The receptionist answers in stiff but passable English: "May I help you?"

"Anh ơi, cho tôi xin một ly cà phê được không anh?"

"What room, sir?"

A Taste of **HOME**

"Three-oh-two," I say. Then in Vietnamese: *"Ba lé hai. Tôi là người Việt mà anh."* But I am Vietnamese, brother. I try to put a smile in my words, but I fear I sound angry all the same.

"Dạ, dạ," says the receptionist. Then he says, *"Xin lỗi anh, tại vì ... . em tưởng anh người Hồng Kông . . ."*

I interrupt him. I don't need his apologies, I don't want to hear what else he thinks about me, polite as he sounds. *"Cà fê sũa ăá nghe anh, cám ơn anh,"* I say. "Iced coffee, brother, thank you, brother."

I put down the phone. Why does he think I am from Hong Kong? But how does he know who I am, what I look like? Did he see me checking in last night? Then why did he ask for my room number? What else does he know? Is he just nosy, or does he work for the secret police?

Holed up in this hotel room, I have no answers to any of my questions about the people who live in my homeland. The differences between us become more pronounced. They live here. I am only visiting.

I turn to my suitcase and, unable to unpack, I decide to repack it. It takes half an hour, during which time I take two breaks to call the tour operator. No answer. The coffee comes, I have no Vietnamese money to tip the waiter. He smiles graciously and glances at the portable cassette player, pausing to listen for a quick second to the Turkish music before walking out of my room.

I take my coffee out to the balcony. The construction workers have gone. I sweat and feel sticky. I go in, take another shower. When I come out, I stand under the ceiling fan without drying myself. I try to tie the towel around my waist but it is too small. I am too fat.

I had been fat as a young boy, but after I arrived in America the year I turned sixteen, I became more rotund. For years, American food had seeped into me, and I've grown and grown, and it seemed Vietnam was slipping further and further away. But that homeland has stayed in the heart, and I have never stopped wanting to go home. I was allowed to go back once in 1989, and another time the next year. The third time I tried, I was denied a visa. I was in exile all over again, and it hurt.

I wasn't giving up on going home however. This time I left America with the blind belief that a visa would be available at the Saigon airport. From the luggage area, I walked to the customs desk, noticing a photographer taking instant head shots of people. When the customs officer sent me to him, I was relieved. I paid two dollars for the photographs and thought I didn't look too bad, considering that I had just spent nineteen hours on a crammed aircraft flying home from America, with a four-hour interval at the busy but lifeless airport in Seoul.

After I handed in my passport and photos, I waited for forty minutes. I slipped the customs and immigration officer at the desk five dollars but he gave them back to me. The man had gold teeth and spoke with a Hà Nội accent. "I'll get you a cab to the hotel, you'll stay there tonight. Don't go anywhere. Call your travel agency; otherwise I'll come by tomorrow to straighten out your visa problem."

"*Nó muôn kiêm chút tiên hôi lô rôi,*" someone whispered in my ears and disappeared. "He wants some bribe money."

"Can't you handle it for me right now? I'll pay whatever fees," I said to the customs and immigration officer.

"I don't want any money. Just go to the hotel."

He pulled me by the arm, and waved for a taxicab. Saigon now has a fleet of airport taxis, and I no longer had to fight and negotiate with whoever was operating whatever means of transportation was available. I stood in amazement, staring at the white-and-blue taxi for a long moment. It was then that I caught a glimpse of a friend from high school. His hair had gone white in many parts, his cheeks hollow, and he was darker-skinned, but I recognized him instantly. I called out to him. "Trung, Trung!"

Trung turned around, but the officer was pushing me into the taxi. Only after I had settled inside and looked out the window did I realize my friend wore the uniform of an airport porter. I shifted in my seat. The taxi was pulling away.

On the way to the hotel, I regretted not attempting to stop the taxi, to get out and talk to Trung. Not that I was confident our conversation would go well. After the excitement of finding one another, we would have had to acknowledge the differences in our lives. Home is a place of no escape.

The taxi driver told me he could take me to my relatives' in Saigon. In the morning, he would come back to pick me up to bring me to the hotel. "It'll cost you a lot of money to stay here tonight. I'll make sure you get here early tomorrow, before the officials arrive. They will take your money here and issue you a visa. There won't be any problems. Where do your relatives live?"

They're all in America, I almost said. I have no immediate family left in Vietnam. "The hotel will be fine," I said to the driver. "I'll work things out tomorrow."

The cassette tape comes to the end, the Turkish music dies. I sit down on my bed to turn the machine off. I pull out the drawer of the bedside table, and I'm surprised by the colorful cover of a thick book, the Saigon telephone directory—thick as the San Francisco one. Things seem normal somehow. This country has been isolated from the world for two decades, but a telephone book in the drawer of a hotel room makes things normal. And it helps take away my feelings of being locked up.

A Taste of HOME

I take a long while, ten, fifteen minutes, to flip through the book. All the names are in Vietnamese, all the Nguyens and Đoàns and Ngôs and Trâns and Hôs. I read the names with amazement: Saigon is full of people with private telephones now. But I know none of them. I have no one I can call.

Except Cesais Tour. Someone answers this time, and she recognizes my name. "Yes, yes, we know about you. We'll get you a visa this afternoon. Forty-five dollars," she says.

"This afternoon?" I ask.

"Rest your heart, brother," she says. "*Anh cữ yên tâm.* We take care of a lot of visiting overseas Vietnamese."

I am an overseas Vietnamese, a *Việt Kiều.* I have been in exile in America for twenty years. I've waited for a long time to come home. Each of the times before when I had been able to go home, I've stayed for four or five weeks. Each time I have rediscovered more of the things that once were familiar. This time I hope to confirm that I can actually stay for a longer while. That I can shed the outer layers American life had placed on my skin, to readjust to Vietnamese life with the deeper parts of me, the parts I know have remained Vietnamese. I want to confirm that I can again live in my estranged homeland. So far I've only had a glimpse of it, and the names in the phone book, the construction workers, the girls on their bicycles, all still seem distant.

I say none of this to the woman from the tour company. "It's all right, sister," I say, and thank her before putting the phone down. I put in another tape, and with my suitcase packed and ready, I have nothing left to do but to sit back and begin to wait. The music is soothing, but after a while I can't sit still. I pace my room. I call Cesais Tour every hour. And then I dial a number outside the country. It is now possible to dial direct from Vietnam to the United States. A communications link, cut off for twenty years after a war that has lasted just as long, has been reestablished between the former enemies. I dial the number to our apartment in San Francisco and lie to my wife. "I'm all right," I say. "It's great to be back."

In between hasty words of love, and mundane news about the weather, our landlord and our cat, she tells me there is a demonstration by the *Việt Kiêus* in San Francisco. Over a thousand people have converged outside a hotel in the city's financial district. They are refugees, boat people, former political prisoners who have made their home in America. On this day, they have come to the hotel to protest the presence of a delegation from Hô Chí Minh City, which, like all of its residents, I still call Saigon. The delegation is in San Francisco for a conference, sponsored by *The Wall Street Journal*, to discuss investment opportunities in Vietnam. President Clinton had lifted the nineteen-year-old trade sanctions against Vietnam, and business with a former enemy is the priority of the day. America is try-ing to catch up with Japan and Taiwan and Singapore and the European nations who have been signing all kinds of deals with Hà Nội.

For many of the *Việt Kĩềus*, this is travesty. They oppose the communist government in Vietnam, and they oppose all contacts with Vietnamese offi-cials. Their banners contain harsh words about communism and human rights conditions in Vietnam. Some of the *Việt Kĩềus* become violent, some are always vocal, some more reasonable. Others speak loudly against trading with Vietnam, but they quietly carry on with visits to their relatives or busi-ness trips to Vietnam.

The more violent *Việt Kĩềus* have driven some of us into silence. As they complain about the tyranny of a communist system, they create terror within the Vietnamese community in the United States: one can easily be labeled a communist sympathizer. Houses have been set afire, and people have been shot. But writers can't keep quiet. I write about all tyrannies, and so I have made enemies within the Vietnamese community in America. The Vietnam War ended in 1975, but for many Vietnamese who had been driven from their homes, the war continues.

In the late 1970s and early 1980s, I received complaints about the apolitical tone of my Vietnamese radio broadcasts. I moved away from San Jose, which has the second-largest concentration of Vietnamese popu-lation in the United States, and avoided large gatherings of Vietnamese. There had been times in those days when I feared the noises outside the door to my apartment, and I hesitated before picking up my ringing phone. I became an exile within a community of exiles.

For twelve years my father was jailed by the communists in Vietnam. Still, there were those who considered what I wrote about Vietnam in the late 1980s to be propaganda for the regime in Hà Nội. On the other hand, the Hà Nội authorities denied me a visa because I've helped expose the terrible conditions in communist Vietnam. My inability to go home then enhanced my status with the Vietnamese in America, but all the same, I felt the humiliation and frustration of not being accepted by either side, of not belonging. The demonstrators in San Francisco would hate to find out I'm in Vietnam now, and perhaps they would have a good laugh that I am put away in this hotel room.

"I wish these people wouldn't drag this war out anymore," I say to my wife.

"Just take care, and come home soon."

"I am home," I say.

Home. Twenty years in America has not been enough for me to call it home. I know I should appreciate the open doors I found when I first came to America at the end of the war, but I have trouble loving America: the

A Taste of **HOME**

images of American soldiers charging through Vietnamese villages are lodged too deeply in my mind. Political and historical considerations aside, I simply don't feel I belong in America. Underneath the initial mat of welcome America gave an exile, I keep finding things that bother me about life in the West. I function well enough in a culture that values individual achievements, and there is something admirable about the American spirit of moving on in search of wider horizons, of facing the challenges of a new world. But making yourself anew in America also means abandoning friends and family: I miss the sense of community, the traditional bonds that get thrown away in the pursuit of the American Dream.

I find the work-dominated life in America dehumanizing, I detest the racism hidden behind politically correct attitudes. I struggle with the moral corruption, the materialistic bent, and the pretense of offering freedom to the people. I am sad that many Vietnamese can't stop taking the advice of TV commercials and resist the urge to be a consumer. Like the majority of people in America, we go about our lives rushing from office to home, working from year to year only to go from one mortgage and credit card payment to the next. We are slaves, but pleased to have an income, and we continue to work at jobs we don't like. Sacrificing for the next generation is the Asian excuse we use for no longer dreaming about a different future, no longer pursuing hobbies and work that can bring satisfaction. When I think of a life in America, I think of a life locked inside a house or an office, without time and patience.

Ever since I was a child, going to school in the morning, as normal as any children in the world, but going to bed at night fearing rockets, I have been living in a world of contradictions. As a grown man, I have not become used to the black-and-white simplicity of Americans and their righteous ways. Ensconced in San Francisco, I hide from Southern California's conservatism, the East Coast's superiority complex, Washington's self-absorption, and the blind flag-waving patriotism in the rest of the country. Still, San Francisco is in America, and America doesn't question itself all that incisively. I think of America as an adolescent without a soul.

And so I keep trying to come home. To a place I call home. But Vietnam is having trouble welcoming me back. In a Saigon hotel room, I am forced to lie to my wife, to say that I feel safe. I am physically in Vietnam. But I must wait for the approval from Customs and Immigration to get out of this hotel. Then I must wait for the people of Vietnam to let me reach them and their souls.

"I thought you were Korean," the pedicab driver says to me.

I am in downtown Saigon. My visa had finally been approved, no explanation had been offered for its delay. I have moved to one of the hundreds of mini-hotels that have surfaced all over the city: brand-new cinder-block buildings, with square rooms still smelling of cement and paint, cooled by air conditioners newly imported from Thailand and Taiwan. The buildings have simply gone up, charmless next to the French villas with faded façades and crumbling columns. They seem characterless even when compared to the ugly angular three-story structures inspired by the pragmatic architecture from the days of warfare.

It had taken over half an hour to fill out all the proper registration forms at my mini-hotel, and as soon as I unpacked and showered, I went out in the streets, with no particular destination. I simply wanted to be out.

I have a load of Vietnamese piasters in my money belt, and I wander from street to street, overwhelmed by the heat and the noises, at times self-conscious because some people stare at me, the giant Asian man with a crisp white shirt in their midst. After a while, I get used to smiling at those who stare at me, and I am happy that most people are too busy with their chores to pay attention to me.

My mini-hotel is five minutes from the business and tourist center of Saigon. The late-afternoon breeze coming from the riverfront cools me and dries my sweat-drenched shirt. I approach the pedicab just behind the building that used to be the South Vietnamese House of Congress. Now it is the city's performance hall. It keeps changing colors every time I've visited, yet the coats of whitewash never look new. There is something in me that is attracted to what's old, however, and I find the bright streets and clean buildings of American cities sterile and without character in contrast.

The pedicab driver at first speaks to me in English. He keeps repeating that he thinks I am Korean. It takes a few moments for him to believe that I am a native speaker of Vietnamese. "But you're so fat," he says in the end.

I no longer look like people in Vietnam. I am fatter than most people here, and my skin has turned pale after the years away from the tropical sun. My baggy khaki pants look awfully out of place in a city where most men wear tight-fitting dress slacks. I want to convince the pedicab driver and others that a Vietnamese soul has remained intact within me, but they only notice that I prefer shoes and socks rather than the plastic sandals everyone here wears. My hair is short, while the men here are still hanging on to the long-haired fashion of the 1970s. In its isolation since the end of the war, Vietnam has remained unglued from 1975. At least this is true of the southern half of the country, even though the garish signs from war-related wealth of the 1970s have been replaced with the somber poverty of the years of communism.

I tell the pedicab the address of a friend's house. We circle the central boulevards, heading toward the main thoroughfare out of the city. This evening, a few lampposts and building fronts in the blocks around the performance hall are decorated with red banners. It's Hồ Chí Minh's birthday. I'd expected this to be a holiday with huge government-sponsored ceremonies, especially in this city that bears his name, but nothing has happened. Cars and motorcycles circle the kiosks, everyone rushes along the wide boulevards, coming, going, carrying on with their chores in a normal business day. I can't tell whether anyone is thinking of Hồ Chí Minh. In the North, more people remember Hồ Chí Minh as the leader who brought independence to Vietnam. In Hồ Chí Minh City, he is often thought of as the traitor who brought communism to the country. But people don't even tell acerbic jokes about him anymore. All I hear now are the noises of the marketplace. There are no tributes to a revered leader or the interminable communist propaganda on a public-address system.

The pedicab driver leans over close to my head and laughs at his own earlier mistake. "You really look Korean," he says. "I hate driving the Koreans. They're real cheap. And they always look down on us. They say to me our people are stupid, and they're more advanced than us. But I bet without the wars and communism, we'd be far ahead of them," he says.

I can't think of anything to say to the driver. I keep thinking of Hồ Chí Minh, of how he spent his adult life fighting foreigners, leading the wars that took the lives of thousands of people. Independence has been regained, but along with independence came the unworkable policies of a communist system. Now that that system is all but bankrupt, the foreigners are all over Vietnam, with arrogant and imperialistic attitudes barely disguised. Meanwhile, Hồ Chí Minh's former comrades-in-arms and devoted followers are marching away from his socialist dreams. They are all smiles and open arms with the foreigners with whom they fought bitter wars. Chinese, French, Japanese, all are welcome now. The foreigners do not attack the Vietnamese with guns and helicopters anymore. They are not forcing their way into Vietnam to be lords of the land, or to secure a market. Today, they are welcomed back by the communists, who allow them limitless access to Vietnam, turning the country into a consumer market and the people into cheap laborers. Like a moth flying toward a flame, I keep wanting to go home, believing that, along with Westerners, I can play a role in bringing about political openness. But a sadness overcomes me, for I realize it is much too easy to import the worst traits of capitalism. Democratic ideals are harder to achieve.

I shudder in the hot evening in thinking of the millions that have died in all those years to keep the foreigners out. I think of the destruction of the country by bombs and rockets and defoliants. My pedicab ride takes me past monstrous glass-and-steel and stucco structures springing up over the Saigon skyline, and I feel angry. The anger gets worse when I see all around me now the destruction of the soft-mannered and gracious ways of the Vietnamese. Capitalism is the game now, at least in Saigon, and it is ruthless.

A Taste of **HOME**

"But aren't the Koreans and other foreigners creating lots of opportunities for the people here?" I ask my driver.

"Yeah, many of us are benefiting from them, but mainly in Saigon," the driver says. "It's gonna take a long time before we can all breathe better."

I stop talking to the driver, but I carry on a debate with myself. A long time, but how many will breathe better? How many will die in construction accidents, how many will lose a home to make way for skyscrapers? How many will succumb to modern diseases, to pollution and environmental damages? And how many will have to sell their Vietnamese soul? I want to recognize that the prices for development, modernization, and prosperity are high. Capitalism is corrupting, and it shows signs that it can turn those fierce and dedicated communists in the Vietnamese leadership into greedy people. I even believe that out of this mess may come a degree of democracy. But how do I explain to a hungry pedicab driver any of this?

He pedals hard to move his pedicab with my weight in it. When he slows down to regain his breath, he asks about my stay in Vietnam. "You should come back here," he advises me. "You can make a lot of money. Make sure you earn a foreigner's salary, though. And then you can buy anything you want, live like a king." He points to a vintage French car parked on the side of the street, a meticulously restored Citroën in burgundy and beige, with a glinting chrome grill. White linen covers the back seats. "See that car?" asks the pedicab driver. "You can buy that. All the foreigners are buying those cars now. When can a Vietnamese here afford one like that? Nobody here can buy them, but you can. Bring your dollars here, buy anything you want."

"That would be nice," I say. "But I don't think I can afford it."

"You live now in America. What's a few thousand dollars to you?"

My friend Vĩnh is more realistic about my financial powers. "Are you on assignment or did you pay your own way back here?"

"Doesn't matter. I'm just glad I can be back home. How are you?"

"Breathing in, breathing out, surviving."

Vĩnh had been a classmate from elementary school. I found him in my first return trip, a man who has retained his boyish looks but whose eyes wear the dull expression of a seasoned man. Vĩnh had been smuggling and selling all sorts of things on the black market to feed his parents and four siblings.

"Your eyes are looking worse," I say to him. "Why don't you stop drinking?"

"You'd be drinking too. In fact, do you want a beer? It's only to help me sleep."

A Taste of HOME

I wonder how many Vietnamese need help sleeping. On the way to Vĩnh's, I have gone past countless beer halls packed with men sitting on stools barely off the ground. And I've noticed that in some restaurants, the waiters simply bring out cans of beer for you as soon as you sit down. Vietnam has turned into a drinking nation, and Vĩnh is, I think, an alcoholic. His eyes are ocher where they should be white. Vĩnh pours me a beer, and I accept it. Refusing it would be an act too transparent: a feeble, judgmental, and improper demonstration that I am worried about him drinking so much. I needed the beer as a way to strengthen our friendship. I wanted a way to make me feel closer to my friend and his misery. I'll need help sleeping tonight in any case. In a couple of weeks, I'll leave, go back to America. Vĩnh's yellowed eyes might appear in my dreams then, but for now, I desperately need to break down the barriers between two former classmates with different adult lives.

Vĩnh says he no longer wants to leave the country. Years before, he had made three attempts to escape by boat. He had been unsuccessful and jailed. Now he says he has too much work. "Services. This is a poor country, we haven't got anything to offer people. To make money, we can only offer our services. Labor services, hotel services, food, do it all for people."

Vĩnh is now helping a sister run an auto-repair shop. I keep thinking of the way the workers there used to switch the steering wheels in the cars—smuggled in from Thailand—from the right side to the left. The workers changed the floorboards, the pedals, the dashboard, the electrical wiring, etc., all that for seventy dollars. The garage has now expanded, and more services have been added. The last time I saw Vĩnh, he was talking about struggling to bring a meal to the table each day. Tonight, he is letting the beer flow, and he actually encourages me to come back. "Just make sure you're here to provide some type of service," Vĩnh says as he pours me another beer. "Otherwise, what are you going to do here?"

I ask Vĩnh about fitting back in, living and working in Vietnam. "Write, but you can't get published here. That'll be like asking for a jail sentence. Besides, how much do you think words and meanings can earn for you here? Sell something else."

"Do you think I can live here, though?"

"Why not? But remember that black hair and yellow skin doesn't mean you're a local person. You're a foreigner. Can you afford the houses people rent out to foreigners?"

"How expensive is that?"

"If you can't afford it, you live like me. Out here in the outskirts of town, dusty and dark. People and rats and dogs and motorcycles packed on top of each other . . . And your wife . . ."

"Well . . ."

A Taste of HOME

"And what about your parents in America? Can you leave them there by themselves? Who's going to take care of them? They won't come back here, will they?"

"No," I say, but give up on saying anything further. Vĩnh is full of questions, and he knows some of the answers. I hide from them, and I hide from Vĩnh, much as I want to confront everything about coming home and again living in Vietnam.

I leave Vĩnh in a haze. As my pedicab turns into the downtown area, I feel the terror of my youth, when Viet Cong soldiers threw hand grenades into the early-morning markets of our town, or tore up our nights with rockets from surrounding hills. For years after the Tet offensive of 1968, when Viet Cong soldiers invaded our hometown, captured my father and marched him away to prison, these men in olive-green uniforms had haunted my sleep.

Tonight, I can recognize the same uniforms and pith helmets that had driven so much fear into my stomach. A dozen soldiers are running in formation just ahead of me. For a few moments, their mechanical footsteps pound my heart. Seeing them in numbers is to come face to face with the men that had once intruded on my sleep, turning my nighttime images into nightmares. The pedicab pulls to a stop. The soldiers run across our path, at arm's length from me. I sit still—as if waiting for them to surround me in the darkness. I become hostage to them for a second, and then I can see their faces. I recognize that these are boys who would not have been born in 1968. They could not have known much about the war that has been so much a part of my life. Gradually my fears disappear; the soldiers continue on with their formation, away from me.

"That'll be the parade for Uncle Hồ's birthday," the pedicab driver says. I laugh, unable to think of anything to say. The driver explains that he is serious. "They have to do something for the birthday. But they know nobody cares. So they take a midnight run, a parade for themselves, really." A parade without an audience, without a crowd.

I ask the driver to take me for another tour of Saigon, promising him a sum of money that would barely buy me a meal in a run-down restaurant in San Francisco's Chinatown, but he accepts my proposal with gratitude, and with grace, considering how tired he seems from pedaling an overweight *Việt Kĩều.* From my pedicab seat, I stare out into the darkness. Houses set behind walls and the overhanging trees blend themselves into a continuous shadow, punctuated by a few lightbulbs too infrequent to let me have a real look at Saigon at rest. The insane activities of the day are gone. It is quiet now but I can't see clear enough to imagine myself in a room, a house in this city. I regret the alcohol in me that is preventing me from answering the questions in my head.

We ride around for half an hour, my mind clears a little, and I think of a room. A writer's place, late at night, with an old bench, a rustic table, open windows. A breeze, cricket calls, and petals from a dying chrysanthemum falling over a golden mango. A lone lightbulb casting just enough clarity over a page. For now, the page is still blank, but at least I can see the questions. I'll have to question my ability to leave my parents without a son to care for them, my obligations to friends in America. I'll question how I can live in a society still not free from communism, the return of the Westerners and the traders. I'll have to question again and again how I can leave the freedom I've discovered in America. But in the quietness of this Saigon night, the questions don't seem so daunting anymore. I know that without them coming home is impossible. Time and patience have been rare all these years in America. In Vietnam, I will have time, I will learn to be patient again. After that, the answers will come.

"I'll run into you again soon," I say to the pedicab driver outside my mini-hotel. He smiles and thanks me. I wave goodbye, not explaining that I suddenly feel sure that I will come home to live. And when I need a late-night ride to clear my mind and help with my writing, I am sure I will look for him again.

Responding to the Selection

Questions for Discussion

1. What impression of Vietnam did you get from reading "A Taste of Home"?

2. What does Nguyen hope to accomplish on this trip? Do you think that he reaches his goal? Explain.

3. How did you react to Nguyen's description of life in the United States?

4. **Irony** is a conflict between reality and what seems to be real. Identify an irony involving Vietnam's present condition or Nguyen's return to his homeland.

5. Nguyen says that he has always lived in "a world of contradictions." Why might an exile be especially likely to feel this way?

Activities

Writing a Letter

1. Suppose that Nguyen told you that he was considering a move back to Vietnam. Write a letter to him offering your advice. Consider the questions that his friend Vinh raised in their meeting.

Discussing a Title

2. The title of a famous novel by U.S. writer Thomas Wolfe is *You Can't Go Home Again.* Discuss this idea with a partner, both as it applies to Nguyen Qui Duc's life and to your own.

MEDIA connection

Newspaper Article

This newspaper article excerpt describes how the Hmong people of Laos have turned an ancient art form into a modern-day commentary on their recent past.

The fabric of their lives: Beauty, tragedy captured in Hmong needlework

by Carol Guensburg—*Journal Sentinel*, Milwaukee, Wisconsin, June 16, 1996

Black-clothed men and women grinding corn with a crude machine in a mountain village in northern Laos. A baby strapped to its mother's back as she feeds chickens. A warplane strafing a row of huts. More peasants, with green bamboo poles tucked under their arms to float to safety across the silvery Mekong River. Guards wielding bats at a Thai refugee camp. People filing onto a big jet bound for the United States.

These scenes—embroidered with bright thread on so-called "storycloths"—recount the traumatic exodus of Hmong people from their tribal homelands in southeast Asia during the last two decades. American allies during the Vietnam War, they faced persecution and death at the hands of Viet Cong when U.S. armed forces pulled out in '75. Thousands of Hmong hid in the jungles and fled to Thailand before eventually resettling in America—primarily in Wisconsin, California and Minnesota.

Storycloths and more traditional Hmong needlework or *paj ntaub* are considered decorative works of art, finding their way into more and more homes. . . .

Paj ntaub—a phrase that means "flower cloth" and is pronounced "pandoa"—dates back 2,000 years. It encompasses embroidery and applique, often featuring geometric designs and sometimes depicting animals or other creatures.

The storycloths came much later. Evolving in Thai refugee camps, these picture cloths grew out of an earlier effort to teach written language to the hill people, Tim Pfaff writes in "Hmong in America: Journey from a Secret War" (1995, Chippewa Valley Museum Press).

"Missionaries had collected Hmong folk tales in Laos in the 1960s to use in school primers. They taught Hmong men to draw characters to illustrate the

books. Years later, faced with the unwelcome idleness of refugee camp life, men continued to draw and Hmong women experimented with transferring the illustration to cloth."

"I'm not sure who came up with the particular suggestion of the storycloth," adds James Leary, a consultant on the book and a member of the University of Wisconsin-Madison's folklore program. "There were various social workers among them who were trying to look ahead to (the Hmongs') transition to the United States and had the notion that they could translate their needlework skills into a larger American market."

Xao Yang Lee . . . is one such entre-preneur. She began selling storycloths and other needlework after reaching a Thai refugee camp in 1976.

"My husband got kill. I move the (five) children to Thailand. I was very poor, so I start to sew these," says Lee, unfold-ing a storycloth in the Sheboygan apart-ment she shares with her second husband and assorted children and grandchildren. The 49-year-old woman has eight chil-dren, ranging in age from 7 to 28.

Lee continues to sew to help support her children. She spent the past eight years making socks at Wigwam Mills,

where she was laid off in April. All along, she has supplemented that income with her exquisite storycloths and *paj ntaub*.

"Every weekend during summer, my mother is off to a craft fair selling," teases 18-year-old Tong Lee, who just finished his freshman year at the University of Wisconsin-Milwaukee. He hopes to become a physician one day.

"My children make me not tired because my children do well in school," Lee says, shrugging off her long hours.

The elaborate stitching of *paj ntaub*, which she learned as a young girl in northern Laos, requires patience and deftness. A 9- or 10-inch square of reverse applique—which layers cloth sewn in strips that expose the bottom or background fabric—takes several hours. . . .

The abstract applique patterns some-times contain symbolism.

"This is the pattern for elephant's paw," Tong Lee says, indicating a pur-ple and black square. Speaking on behalf of his mother after a brief con-sultation in Hmong, he says: In Laos, "we didn't go to school, we didn't learn to write. Since we didn't have any camera, we would just leave our footprints behind."

Questions for Discussion

1. Why do you think the Hmong refugees started creating storycloths?

2. What are some other art forms used by groups of people to remember and celebrate their history?

Focus on . . .
Vietnam War
Refugees

When the United States became involved in the war between North and South Vietnam in the early-1960s, only a few hundred Vietnamese lived in the United States. They are now estimated to be the third largest Asian American group, with a population of nearly one million. The first big wave of refugees arrived in 1975 as Communist troops descended upon Saigon, South Vietnam's capital. The United States accepted about 130,000 people who were in danger because of their ties to the South Vietnamese government or military. Refugee agencies scattered them throughout the country, but soon they began concentrating in a few communities.

In the late 1970s and early 1980s, a second wave of refugees fled Vietnam in poorly equipped and overcrowded boats. They faced not only storms but also brutal attacks from Thai pirates. More than thirty percent of these "boat people" died. The survivors reached Thailand and other Asian countries, where they were placed in squalid refugee camps. Many refugees were allowed into Western nations only after waiting

months or years. Alarmed at the plight of the boat people, the United Nations negotiated an agreement with Vietnam to allow some of its citizens to emigrate. This group included political prisoners and the children of U.S. soldiers and Vietnamese women.

Additional refugees came from Laos and Cambodia, which had been drawn into the Vietnam conflict. The Cambodians were traumatized by the genocidal policies of their government, the Khmer Rouge. The Hmong of Laos had fought against communism on behalf of the United States in the 1950s and 1960s in the so-called "Secret War." Because written language was first introduced into Hmong culture only in the 1950s, most of them were illiterate in their own language, making it difficult for them to learn English. The Vietnamese refugees who were political prisoners also have special problems. Many of them suffer from depression and physical ailments resulting from their harsh treatment in prison camps.

According to historian Ronald Takaki, Southeast Asian refugees are more uprooted than other Asian American groups: "They did not think and dream about coming; in fact, most of them had no time to plan and prepare for their movement to a new land." Under these circumstances, the refugees have generally adjusted well to life in the United States. Perhaps the biggest symbol of their success is Little Saigon in southern California's Orange County, which elected the nation's first Vietnamese public official. The thriving community has hundreds of businesses that cater to the needs of Vietnamese Americans.

Linking to . . .
• Think about this background information as you read the selections in this book that have to do with refugee life.

Before You Read
The Tonle Sap Lake Massacre

Ronnie Yimsut
Born 1962

"Cambodia will always be home to me despite the fact that I have nothing left there anymore."

About Yimsut

Ranachith "Ronnie" Yimsut grew up in Siem Reap, a Cambodian city near the famous ruins of Angkor. He was thirteen when the Khmer Rouge, a radical Communist movement, came to power in 1975. Over the next two years, soldiers drove Yimsut's family from one labor camp to another. He survived a massacre in which most of his relatives perished. After spending eight months in a Thai prison and refugee camp, Yimsut immigrated to the United States.

Yimsut completed high school and earned a degree from the University of Oregon. He now works as a landscape architect for the USDA Forest Service. In 1984, he learned that a sister and a brother were still alive in Cambodia. Eventually he managed to bring them to the United States. Since the downfall of the Khmer Rouge, Yimsut has made several trips to Cambodia, helping to rebuild his devastated homeland.

Brutal Regime

The Khmer Rouge led one of the most brutal regimes in history. Between 1975 and 1979, more than one and a half million Cambodians died from starvation, overwork, torture, and execution. Vietnamese troops invaded Cambodia in 1979 and overthrew the Khmer Rouge. The selection you will read describes an event that began on the last day of 1977. At the time, Yimsut had been working on a huge canal project with a group of relatives and neighbors.

The Tonle Sap Lake Massacre

— *Ronnie Yimsut*

A pointy object poked at me very hard and woke me up from the muddy bottom of the canal. I slowly opened my eyes to look at a soldier, who continued to poke me with his oversized AK-47 rifle. He was no older than twelve, just a few years younger than I was, but much, much fatter. He was yelling angrily for me to get up from the mud. "Go ahead and shoot me," I said to myself. I was ready to die. It was hopeless. I finally pushed my weak, skinny body up from the mud and wearily walked toward where my group was congregated. It was our time to go, at last. I began to have mixed feelings about the sudden relocation plan. Normally we would stay in one place for weeks or even months at a time before they shipped us out again.

They ordered us to file in rows of four. A small group of soldiers who were to escort us was made up of all ages. Some were as young as ten. There were only five of them to escort what was left of my original group of people. By then there were only seventy-nine of us together. During five awful days at this place, eight of us had died, including six children and two elderly men. I wondered why there were so few of them if they were going to kill all seventy-nine of us.

The oldest soldier came over in front of us and spoke loudly so that everyone could hear him. He told us that we were being moved to Tonle Sap, which meant "Great Lake," to catch fish for the government. He also said that there would be food to eat there. Suddenly people were talking among themselves about the news. We were all very skeptical about this miraculous news, but it made sense, since most of us were once commercial fisherman at Tonle Sap. They told us just what we wanted to hear. The food, the chance to catch and eat fresh fish from the lake and to get away from the misery. It all sounded too good to be true. I was completely fooled by the news. And so were the rest of the people.

They took us south over a familiar muddy road toward Tonle Sap, which was about six or seven miles away. The longer we were on that road the more relaxed we became. Perhaps they were telling us the truth? We seemed to be headed in the right direction. There were only five of them and they can't possibly kill all seventy-nine of us . . . could they?

The Tonle Sap Lake Massacre

After about three miles of walking they asked us to stop and wait for the rest of the group. People were very weak, and the three-mile hike took its toll. Another child died on the way. The soldiers allowed the mother to bury her child. It was another twenty or thirty minutes before the rest caught up.

They wanted us to move on quickly with the setting of the sun. They first asked all the able men, both young and old, to come and gather in front of the group. The men were then told to bring all kinds of tools, especially knives and axes, with them. They said the men needed to go ahead of the group to build a camp for the rest of us. The men soon lined up in single file with their tools in hand. I watched my brother, Sarey, as he walked reluctantly to join the line after saying good-bye to his pregnant wife. I told him that I would take good care of Oum, my sister-in-law. The group disappeared shortly as the sky darkened. That was the last time I saw Sarey and the rest of the men again.

The sky was getting darker and it grew chillier. The notorious Tonle Sap mosquitoes began to rule the night sky. After about thirty minutes or so, the two soldiers that had led the men away returned. They quickly conferred with their fellow comrades about something not far away. One or two of the people from my group overheard something quite unbelievable, and the shocking news quickly spread among the people within the group. I learned that they said something like, "a few got away." It only meant one thing: the men were all dead except for a few who managed to escape.

It was about seven or eight o'clock at night when we were ordered to move on again. By this time the children who still had enough energy to cry were crying and screaming as loud as they could. It was mainly from hunger and exhaustion, but also from the attack by the swarming mosquitoes. Above the cry of the children I could hear the sobbing and weeping of the people who had lost their loved ones. The odds were stacked against us. If we didn't die of starvation, exhaustion, or mosquito bites, there was a good chance that we would be killed by the soldiers.

The thought of coming face to face with death terrified me for the first time. I thought about escaping right then but after long consideration couldn't do it. I didn't have the heart to leave my family, especially my pregnant sister-in-law, who was already a week overdue. Besides, where would I go from here? I would eventually be recaptured and killed. If I was to die, I preferred to die among my loved ones. There were plenty of opportunities for me to escape, but I just couldn't do it.

I reluctantly trekked with the rest of the group, with my sister-in-law Oum holding onto my right shoulder and a small bag of belongings on my left. It was ironic that night. We knowingly walked toward our death, just like cattle that were being herded to the slaughterhouse. Even the children

The Tonle Sap Lake Massacre

seemed to know it. But I still had a little hope despite everything I had seen and heard.

A few miles before we were to reach Tonle Sap they ordered us to turn off to the west instead of continuing down south as planned. It was a very muddy, sticky road. My feet seemed to get stuck in the mud every single time I put them down. Progress was slow and cumbersome. A few people got stuck in the mud, which was just like quicksand, and the soldiers came over to kick and beat them. I never knew if they made it. I was busy helping Oum and myself move forward and didn't really care anymore.

All that time I was trying to calm myself down and keep a clear mind. Oum was beyond help. Her quiet weep had now became a full-blown scream. She was in bad shape physically and emotionally. She said that she had a stomach cramp or was in labor, she wasn't sure. It was to be her first child. She didn't know much about childbirth or contractions, and neither did I. All I could do was to drag her across the muddy flat so that the soldiers wouldn't come and beat us to death. It was pathetic.

We were no more than 300 yards off the main road when they asked us to sit down on the edge of a small shallow canal that ran east to west. Both of our legs were stretched forward, and we had to shut up or they would beat us up. In a matter of minutes a large group of soldiers numbering more than fifty suddenly emerged from a hidden place in the nearby forest. It was really dark by then, but from their silhouettes I could tell that they were soldiers with AK-47 rifles, carbines, and large clubs in their hands. One began to shout loudly to us as the rest surrounded the group, their rifles aimed directly at us. People began to plead for their lives.

The soldiers screamed for all of us to shut up. They said they wished only to ask a few questions. They said they suspected that there were enemies among our group. They claimed there were Vietnamese agents in our group, which was a bogus claim since we had known each other for many years. It was a tactic, their dirty trick to keep us calm, weak, and under control. It was very effective because all the strong men who could have risen against them were the first to go. What was left of the people in my group were women, children, the sick, and the weak. They had us right where they wanted us. It was a premeditated plan.

A soldier walked toward me and yanked a cotton towel from me and shredded it into small strips. I was the first one to be tied up tightly by the soldiers with one of the cotton strips. I was stunned and terrified. I began to resist a little. After a few blows to the head with rifle butts, I let them do as they pleased with me. My head began to bleed from the cuts. I was still semiconscious. I could feel the pain and the blood flowing down my face. They were using me as an example of what one would get if they got any kind of resistance.

The Tonle Sap Lake Massacre

They quickly tied the rest of the people without any problems. By this time it was totally chaotic, and people continued to plead for their lives. I was getting more and more dizzy as blood continued to drip across my face and into my right eye. It was the first time that I had tears in my eyes, not from the blood or the pain, but from the reality that was setting in. I became numb with fear.

I was beyond horrified when I heard the clobbering begin. Oum's elderly father was next to me, and his upper torso contracted several times before it fell on me. At that moment I noticed a small boy whom I knew well get up and start to call for his mother. And then there was a warm splash on my face and body. I knew that it was definitely not mud. It was the little boy's blood and perhaps brain tissue that got splattered from the impact.

The rest let out only a short but terrifying sound, and I could hear their breathing stop. Everything seemed to happen in slow motion, and it was so unreal. I closed my eyes but the terrifying sounds continued to penetrate my ear canals and pierce my eardrums. The first blow to hit me came when I was lying face down on the ground. It hit me just below my right shoulder blade. The next one hit me just above the neck on the right side of my head. I heard fifteen more blows, and the victims landed everywhere on my skinny body.

Fortunately, I didn't feel them until much later. I didn't remember anything after that, and I slept very well that night. I woke up to the sound of mosquitoes, which were still buzzing like bees over my body. Only this time there were tons of them feasting on my and the other people's blood. I was unable to move a muscle. My eyes were open, but my sight was blurry. I thought I was blind. I was disoriented. I couldn't remember where I was. I thought I was sleeping at home in my bed. I was wondering why there were so many mosquitoes. Where was I? Why couldn't I move? I was still tied up with the cloth rope. After a few minutes I was able to see a little, but everything else was still blurry. I saw a bare foot in the line of my sight, but I didn't know whose it was.

Suddenly reality set in at full blast and I broke into a heavy sweat. The memories of the event came rushing back and smacked me right in the head. I realized what the sharp dull pain was all over my body and head. I was very cold. I have never been so cold in my entire life. Fear ran rampant in my mind. I suddenly realized where I was and what had happened. Am I already dead? If I am, why do I still suffer like this? I kept asking myself those questions over and over, but could only come to the same conclusion. I am still alive. I am alive! Why? I couldn't understand why I was still alive and suffering. I should have been dead.

The faint light of dawn broke through, revealing my shivering, blood-soaked body in the mud. It must have been about four or five o'clock in

The Tonle Sap Lake Massacre

the morning on January 1, 1978. "Not a happy New Year today," I thought. It was still dark and cold. My motor skills came back little by little and I was able to move with great difficulty. I pushed myself to sit up by hanging onto the pile of dead bodies. I began to work to untie myself from the cloth rope.

I broke the rope after a few painful tries. My eyesight came back, but after seeing the scattered bodies lying in every direction, I wished that I was blind. Some were beyond recognition. Some were stripped completely naked. Bloodstains that had already turned a dark color gave the area a new dimension. It definitely was not a sight for sore eyes.

I wanted to look for my relatives but was unable to turn around. My neck was stiff with pain. My head hurt, oh, it hurt so bad. I could only feel around me with my hands. Everywhere I touched was cold flesh. My hands were both trembling and I couldn't keep them from shaking. I cried my heart out when I recognized a few dead bodies next to me. One of them was Oum and her unborn child. I suddenly remembered the bare foot I saw when I woke up. It was hers. Her elderly father and two sisters were all part way on top of each other and side by side as though they were embracing just before they lost their lives.

I couldn't go on. My cry turned to a sob, and it was the only sound around besides the mosquitoes, which continued to torment my almost bloodless body. I began to fade and feel as though my life was slipping away. I passed out again on top of the dead bodies.

I woke up to the sound of people coming toward the killing field. I sat up and listened closely. I began to panic. "They are back to finish me off," I told myself. "They are going to bury me alive!" They might as well, I thought. I've nothing to live for. Technically I was already dead. I was ready to give up as the voices were getting closer and louder when my survival instinct finally took control. I pushed myself, inching my way toward nearby bushes. I was no more than twenty feet away from where I was earlier and commanded a good view of the area. The people soon arrived at the site. I was right. They were back with a new batch of victims. Most of the people were men, but a few were women. Their hands were all tightly bound together with rope.

One of the soldiers gave a command. In broad morning light, I was again witnessing the slaughter of humans. In just seconds they were all clobbered to death just like the rest of my family and friends, whose bodies were still scattered on the muddy ground. My heart just stopped. My entire body shook convulsively and I wanted to throw up. My left hand squeezed tightly over my mouth so that I wouldn't accidentally cry out and give myself away. I felt as though I had gone through the same ordeal all over again. My mind just couldn't take it anymore. I went blank and passed out again.

The Tonle Sap Lake Massacre

It was not until the next night that I was really awake. More people were coming toward me again. I assumed that they were more victims to be killed. I didn't wait to find out. I decided then that I wanted to be alive. I began to slip away from the area by crawling on my elbows and knees. I was no longer bleeding, but I knew that I was in bad shape. I was hungry and very thirsty. My lips cracked like mud in the hot sun. I had to find water soon or I would die of thirst. I worked my way west along the shallow dried-up canal and then turned north. By this time it was really dark and chilly again. I found myself in the middle of impenetrable brush and forest. I went back and forth trying to find a way through the thick forest and ended up back where I started, near the killing area.

For the next seventeen days, I hid out in the forest. I slept only at day time, spending my night raiding one village after another for whatever I could find to eat. My injuries healed quickly and I began to put on some weight thanks to the food that I stole from the surrounding villages. I never stayed in one place long. I was on the move and always watching out for any sign of danger. I knew that they were searching for me, and I was able to keep a step or two ahead of them. They always counted bodies, and if one was missing, they searched and usually recaptured the escapees. For seventeen days I was the king of the jungle.

I stumbled accidentally onto a group of escapees who were also hiding in the forest. I almost got killed because they thought I was a Khmer Rouge spy. The only thing that saved me from certain death was my recent injuries.

We headed for Thailand. After fifteen days of hiking the 150 miles we found ourselves in a Thai jail and then in prison. The Thai authorities considered us political prisoners because we arrived after they closed the border.

Over 600 others like us were kept in a 75-by-75-meter cell. The living conditions were bad and the treatment we got from the Thais was even worse, but I'd rather be in a Thai prison than in the forced labor camps with the Khmer Rouge anytime. At least we were fed and clothed like human beings. Because I was the youngest of the prisoners, I got better treatment. I got to know some of the guards really well, and within four weeks at the Thai border I gained over twenty pounds. I was under eighty pounds when I arrived there.

We all spent five months in the Thai prison before we were moved to a refugee camp near the Thai-Cambodian border. I waited for a recruitment drive for freedom fighters to fight the Khmer Rouge while I was in the refugee camp, but they didn't accept me because I was "too young and too skinny." I even told them that I was almost eighteen, but it was no use. I couldn't go back to fight, and staying in the camp would only lead me to suicide. I had nothing to live for. I thought that I should end my life just

The Tonle Sap Lake Massacre

like my fellow refugees who had already killed themselves. But that was too easy! I was a survivor.

My life began to turn around when a CBS news producer named Brian T. Ellis showed up at the camp one day. I was interviewed for a documentary film called *What Happened To Cambodia*, which was later broadcast in the United States. Mr. Ellis took me outside of the camp for the very first time in months. I tasted freedom and I liked it a lot. That day with Mr. Ellis was special and I have never forgotten it. My life began to change for the better after Mr. Ellis left. I now had a reason to go on living. It was a chance for a new life.

I still have nightmares about the massacre on that dark December night. It has never completely gone away from my mind, and I am still horrified just thinking about it. Time does not heal such emotional trauma, at least not for me. I have long since learned to live with it. My life must go on.

Responding to the Selection

Questions for Discussion

1. **Imagery** is language that appeals to the senses. Which images from this selection did you find the most powerful? What feelings did they create in you?

2. Yimsut says that he and the other members of his group "knowingly walked toward our death, just like cattle that were being herded to the slaughterhouse." Why do you think these people made no effort to escape during the march or to fight the soldiers? Could such efforts have been successful? Explain.

3. Some refugees committed suicide in the Thai camp where Yimsut was held. Why might they have chosen to end their lives after struggling so hard to survive?

4. What lesson can you draw from Yimsut's experiences in Cambodia? How would you apply this lesson to your own life?

Activities

Writing a Paragraph

1. How would you explain Yimsut's escape from the massacre? Was he more resourceful than the others? What role did luck play in his survival? Write a paragraph in response to these questions.

Writing a Letter

2. Write a letter to a politician or some other public figure offering suggestions on how we should help refugees. Try to draw upon Yimsut's memoir to bolster your argument.

Listening to Music

3. Choose a piece of music to accompany a reading of this essay. Play the music for your class. Explain why you chose the particular piece and why you feel it is especially appropriate.

Before You Read

The Diameter of the Bomb

Yehuda Amichai
Born 1924

*"My personal history
has always coincided with
a larger personal history. For
me it's always been one and
the same."*

About Amichai

Yehuda Amichai often writes about the history, natural beauty, and political concerns of Israel, a nation for which he fought during the 1940s. Born in Germany to Orthodox Jewish parents, Amichai moved to Palestine with his parents when he was eleven years old. During World War II, he served with the British army (Palestine was under British rule at that time). He then joined underground forces fighting for the creation of a Jewish state. This goal was achieved in 1948, when Israel proclaimed its independence. Considered to be Israel's leading poet, Amichai has published a novel, short stories, and several collections of verse, all of which are available in English translation.

Terrorist Acts

Terrorism, as we use the term today, means the use of violence against nonmilitary targets with no advance warning. As such, terrorism dates back to the late 1800s, when dissident groups, especially in Tsarist Russia, were denied any peaceful means of working toward their goals. These terrorists directed their attacks at government representatives. More recently terrorists have regarded any unarmed civilians as fair game. It is doubtful that terrorist activities have ever caused a significant or lasting change in any government's policies.

Although terrorist acts have been committed all over the world, including in the United States, terrorism has played an especially prominent role in the politics of southwest Asia. Besides such acts as airplane hijackings, terrorism includes the random bombing of nonmilitary targets. Such acts, as Amichai shows in this poem, often result in emotional and physical devastation.

The Diameter of the Bomb

— *Yehuda Amichai*
Translated by Chana Bloch
and Stephen Mitchell

The diameter of the bomb was thirty centimeters
and the diameter of its effective range about seven meters,
with four dead and eleven wounded.
And around these, in a larger circle
5   of pain and time, two hospitals are scattered
and one graveyard. But the young woman
who was buried in the city she came from,
at a distance of more than a hundred kilometers,
enlarges the circle considerably,
10   and the solitary man mourning her death
at the distant shores of a country far across the sea
includes the entire world in the circle.
And I won't even mention the crying of orphans
that reaches up to the throne of God and
15   beyond, making
a circle with no end and no God.

Responding to the Selection

Questions for Discussion

1. How would you describe the attitudes of Ronnie Yimsut and Yehuda Amichai toward the experiences that led to the writing of "The Tonle Sap Lake Massacre" and "The Diameter of the Bomb"?

2. One of these works is a poem, while the other is a nonfictional narrative. Which form do you feel is more effective in communicating the kinds of horrible experiences these works describe? Why?

3. The victims in Amichai's poem are never named; they remain anonymous. Some of the victims in Yimsut's narrative are named. What do you feel is the effect on the reader of naming the victims? Of allowing them to remain anonymous?

Activities

Writing a Dialogue

1. Yehuda Amichai and Ronnie Yimsut have probably never met. What do you think they would talk about if they did? Write a dialogue between the two men. Base your writing on what you know about their lives and their works of literature.

Discussing Art

2. Look through an illustrated history of art. Find paintings, sculptures, drawings, or other works of art that address war and violence. Create a gallery of such works to display in your classroom. Lead a discussion that compares how visual artists deal with war and violence to how writers address the subject.

Rewriting

3. Rewrite "The Tonle Sap Lake Massacre" as a poem or rewrite "The Diameter of the Bomb" as a nonfiction narrative.

Before You Read

Near-Sightedness

Edmond Yi-Teh Chang
Born 1965

About Chang

Edmond Yi-Teh Chang was born in Taiwan. He lived in Libya for a while before moving to the United States in 1980. After graduating from Tufts University, he spent a year as poet-in-residence at St. Andrew's School in Delaware. Chang received his Master of Fine Arts degree from the Iowa Writer's Workshop in 1991. He is especially interested in studying classical Chinese poetry.

Childhood in Malta

In Chang's poem "Near-Sightedness," the speaker recalls attending school in Malta, a country composed of a group of Mediterranean islands. Located between Italy and Africa, the islands have been occupied for at least six thousand years. Some ancient Maltese temples are older than the Egyptian pyramids. Before gaining full independence in 1964, Malta was ruled by a series of outside powers, including the Roman and British empires. Officially a Roman Catholic country, Malta has a number of splendid churches.

Near-Sightedness

— Edmond Yi-Teh Chang

In fall, when afternoons begin
to melt quickly into night,
when billboards and street signs
blur in the distance, I'm reminded
5   again of my failing eyes,
of the gradual obscuring of things.
I've tried eating more carrots
as my mother suggests. Lately,
I sit by the window watching
10   grackles perched on power lines.
They're the only birds on my block.
An acupuncturist told me once
it weakens the eyes to stare at birds.
Look for green meadows, he said.

15   Where I live now there are no meadows,
only rows of gray live-oaks
with profuse and dense leaves.
Without my glasses, they're dark,
monolithic shapes, looming mysteries.

20   Eight years old, I squinted
through two entire terms in Malta.
After Brother Martin turned off the lights,
what I saw outside the window each night
must have really been white doves
25   circling the steeples of San Giuseppi,
not the angels I believed they were.
I couldn't see the stars
that must have been out there.

Where I live now there are no stars,
30   the night yellow with city lights,
a sulphur dome separating this place
and that clarity we long for.

Near-Sightedness

Is vision a kind of desire,
the need to see things we want
35   and places we'd rather be?
I used to think near-sightedness
was every child's natural affliction,
inevitable like leaving home.

Still each night I prayed
40   for the angels over San Giuseppi
to fly closer to my window,
and offer to take me home.

Responding to the Selection

Questions for Discussion

1. How did you interpret the poem's ending?

2. A **symbol** is a person, place, or thing that stands for something in addition to itself. What might near-sightedness symbolize in Chang's poem?

3. Is the speaker's poor vision entirely a handicap, or does it also benefit him in some way? Explain.

4. Have you ever longed to be in another place? How did you cope with this feeling?

Activities

Analyzing Poetry

1. Write a paragraph in which you analyze "Near-Sightedness." You might discuss literary elements such as theme, imagery, tone, or style.

Describing Illusions

2. Have you ever experienced an optical illusion? Write a description of the illusion and discuss its effect on you.

Discussing Poetry

3. Draw an illustration to accompany "Near-Sightedness." Try to give a sense of the speaker's blurred vision in your drawing.

Before You Read

The Man with the Saxophone

Ai
Born 1947

"I wanted to be someone else, live some other life, and then return to my own when I was done with the poem."

About Ai

Ai, which means "love" in Japanese, is the pen name of Florence Anthony. Part Japanese, African American, Native American, and Irish, she is often confronted with questions about her ethnic identity. Ai doesn't want either herself or her work to be forced into neat categories. "If a poet's work isn't universal," she asks, "then what good is it?" Yet she has long been fascinated with Japanese culture, even before she found out that her biological father was Japanese.

Poetic Voice

Almost all of Ai's poems are dramatic monologues, speeches given by one person. "People just assume that you're writing about yourself," she says, "but I really don't." Sometimes, as in "The Man with the Saxophone," she assumes the voice of an anonymous character. In other poems, she speaks through a famous person, such as John F. Kennedy or Marilyn Monroe.

The Man with the Saxophone

— *Ai*

New York. Five A.M.
The sidewalks empty.
Only the steam
pouring from the manhole covers seems alive,
5   as I amble from shop window to shop window,
sometimes stopping to stare, sometimes not.
Last week's snow is brittle now
and unrecognizable as the soft, white hair
that bearded the face of the city.
10   I head farther down Fifth Avenue
toward the thirties,
my mind empty
like the Buddhists tell you is possible
if only you don't try.
15   If only I could
turn myself into a bird
like the shaman I was meant to be,
but I can't,
I'm earthbound
20   and solitude is my companion,
the only one you can count on.
Don't, don't try to tell me otherwise.
I've had it all and lost it
and I never want it back,

The Man with the Saxophone

25   only give me this morning to keep,
the city asleep
and there on the corner of Thirty-fourth and Fifth,
the man with the saxophone,
his fingerless gloves caked with grime,
30   his face also,
the layers of clothes welded to his skin.
I set down my case,
he steps backward
to let me know I'm welcome,
35   and we stand a few minutes
in the silence so complete
I think I must be somewhere else, not here,
not in this city, this heartland of pure noise.
Then he puts the sax to his lips again
40   and I raise mine.
I suck the air up from my diaphragm
and bend over into the cold, golden reed,
waiting for the notes to come,
and when they do,
45   for that one moment,
I'm the unencumbered bird of my imagination,
rising only to fall back
toward concrete,
each note a black flower,
50   opening, mercifully opening
into the unforgiving new day.

Responding to the Selection

Questions for Discussion

1. A poet's **style** is reflected in word choice, figurative language, and other qualities that distinguish his or her work. What adjectives would you use to describe Ai's style?

2. What impression of New York City do you get from reading this poem?

3. Compare the speaker's feelings before and after the music begins.

4. The speaker of the poem says that "solitude is my companion, / the only one you can count on." What do you think he or she means by this statement? Do you agree?

Activities

Writing Poetry

1. Write a brief poem in which the speaker is someone other than yourself. You could invent a character or assume the voice of a real person. Before you begin, think carefully about the speaker's personality.

Writing about Music

2. In this poem, music is able to transport the listener out of her everyday world. What piece of music that you know is able to do the same thing? Write in your journal about the effects of the piece of music on you.

Homage to Mehandi III. Bharati Chaudhuri (b. 1951). Acrylic on canvas, 50 x 25 in. SuperStock.

Theme Four

Challenges

You give me your lips with no smile
You give me your arms without tenderness

— *Tran Mong Tu*

Before You Read

Coming Home Again

Chang-Rae Lee
Born 1965

> "[My ideal reader] is attuned, really attuned, to how language can create a great part of the story."

About Lee

Chang-Rae Lee was three years old when his family moved to the United States from South Korea. His father soon learned to speak English well enough to become a psychiatrist. Lee says he was inspired by this achievement: "My father could have been a surgeon, where language isn't as important. But instead he chose a profession where talking is everything."

Lee took a job with a Wall Street firm after graduating from Yale University. He resigned a year later to write a novel. Although his first effort ended in failure, he immediately began work on a new novel, *Native Speaker,* which won major awards when it was published in 1995. In his fiction, Lee is especially concerned with the problems that minority characters face when they try to assimilate into society.

Exeter

In "Coming Home Again," Lee describes feeling overwhelmed when he arrives at Phillips Exeter Academy. One of the oldest and most prestigious boarding schools in the United States, Exeter is known for its competitive atmosphere. The school has produced a number of distinguished writers, including Gore Vidal, James Agee, and John Knowles.

Coming Home Again

— Chang-Rae Lee

When my mother began using the electronic pump that fed her liquids and medication, we moved her to the family room. The bedroom she shared with my father was upstairs, and it was impossible to carry the machine up and down all day and night. The pump itself was attached to a metal stand on casters, and she pulled it along wherever she went. From anywhere in the house, you could hear the sound of the wheels clicking out a steady time over the grout lines of the slate-tiled foyer, her main thoroughfare to the bathroom and the kitchen. Sometimes you would hear her halt after only a few steps, to catch her breath or steady her balance, and whatever you were doing was instantly suspended by a pall of silence.

I was usually in the kitchen, preparing lunch or dinner, poised over the butcher block with her favorite chef's knife in my hand and her old yellow apron slung around my neck. I'd be breathless in the sudden quiet, and, having ceased my mincing and chopping, would stare blankly at the brushed sheen of the blade. Eventually, she would clear her throat or call out to say she was fine, then begin to move again, starting her rhythmic *ka-jug;* and only then could I go on with my cooking, the world of our house turning once more, wheeling through the black.

I wasn't cooking for my mother but for the rest of us. When she first moved downstairs she was still eating, though scantily, more just to taste what we were having than from any genuine desire for food. The point was simply to sit together at the kitchen table and array ourselves like a family again. My mother would gently set herself down in her customary chair near the stove. I sat across from her, my father and sister to my left and right, and crammed in the center was all the food I had made—a spicy codfish stew, say, or a casserole of gingery beef, dishes that in my youth she had prepared for us a hundred times.

It had been ten years since we'd all lived together in the house, which at fifteen I had left to attend boarding school in New Hampshire. My

Coming Home Again

mother would sometimes point this out, by speaking of our present time as being "just like before Exeter," which surprised me, given how proud she always was that I was a graduate of the school.

My going to such a place was part of my mother's not so secret plan to change my character, which she worried was becoming too much like hers. I was clever and able enough, but without outside pressure I was readily given to sloth and vanity. The famous school—which none of us knew the first thing about—would prove my mettle. She was right, of course, and while I was there I would falter more than a few times, academically and otherwise. But I never thought that my leaving home then would ever be a problem for her, a private quarrel she would have even as her life waned.

Now her house was full again. My sister had just resigned from her job in New York City, and my father, who typically saw his psychiatric patients until eight or nine in the evening, was appearing in the driveway at four-thirty. I had been living at home for nearly a year and was in the final push of work on what would prove a dismal failure of a novel. When I wasn't struggling over my prose, I kept occupied with the things she usually did—the daily errands, the grocery shopping, the vacuuming and the cleaning, and, of course, all the cooking.

When I was six or seven years old, I used to watch my mother as she prepared our favorite meals. It was one of my daily pleasures. She shooed me away in the beginning, telling me that the kitchen wasn't my place, and adding, in her half-proud, half-deprecating way, that her kind of work would only serve to weaken me. "Go out and play with your friends," she'd snap in Korean, "or better yet, do your reading and homework." She knew that I had already done both, and that as the evening approached there was no place to go save her small and tidy kitchen, from which the clatter of her mixing bowls and pans would ring through the house.

I would enter the kitchen quietly and stand beside her, my chin lodging upon the point of her hip. Peering through the crook of her arm, I beheld the movements of her hands. For *kalbi*, she would take up a butchered short rib in her narrow hand, the flinty bone shaped like a section of an airplane wing and deeply embedded in gristle and flesh, and with the point of her knife cut so that the bone fell away, though not completely, leaving it connected to the meat by the barest opaque layer of tendon. Then she methodically butterflied the flesh, cutting and unfolding, repeating the action until the meat lay out on her board, glistening and ready for seasoning. She scored it diagonally, then sifted sugar into the crevices with her pinched fingers, gently rubbing in the crystals. The sugar would tenderize as well as sweeten the meat. She did this with each rib, and then set them all aside in a large shallow bowl. She minced a half-dozen cloves of garlic, a stub of ginger-root, sliced up a few scallions, and

Coming Home Again

spread it all over the meat. She wiped her hands and took out a bottle of sesame oil, and, after pausing for a moment, streamed the dark oil in two swift circles around the bowl. After adding a few splashes of soy sauce, she thrust her hands in and kneaded the flesh, careful not to dislodge the bones. I asked her why it mattered that they remain connected. "The meat needs the bone nearby," she said, "to borrow its richness." She wiped her hands clean of the marinade, except for her little finger, which she would flick with her tongue from time to time, because she knew that the flavor of a good dish developed not at once but in stages.

Whenever I cook, I find myself working just as she would, readying the ingredients—a mash of garlic, a julienne of red peppers, fantails of shrimp—and piling them in little mounds about the cutting surface. My mother never left me any recipes, but this is how I learned to make her food, each dish coming not from a list or a card but from the aromatic spread of a board.

I've always thought it was particularly cruel that the cancer was in her stomach, and that for a long time at the end she couldn't eat. The last meal I made for her was on New Year's Eve, 1990. My sister suggested that instead of a rib roast or a bird, or the usual overflow of Korean food, we make all sorts of finger dishes that our mother might fancy and pick at.

We set the meal out on the glass coffee table in the family room. I prepared a tray of smoked-salmon canapés, fried some Korean bean cakes, and made a few other dishes I thought she might enjoy. My sister supervised me, arranging the platters, and then with some pomp carried each dish in to our parents. Finally, I brought out a bottle of champagne in a bucket of ice. My mother had moved to the sofa and was sitting up, surveying the low table. "It looks pretty nice," she said. "I think I'm feeling hungry."

This made us all feel good, especially me, for I couldn't remember the last time she had felt any hunger or had eaten something I cooked. We began to eat. My mother picked up a piece of salmon toast and took a tiny corner in her mouth. She rolled it around for a moment and then pushed it out with the tip of her tongue, letting it fall back onto her plate. She swallowed hard, as if to quell a gag, then glanced up to see if we had noticed. Of course we all had. She attempted a bean cake, some cheese, and then a slice of fruit, but nothing was any use.

She nodded at me anyway, and said, "Oh, it's very good." But I was already feeling lost and I put down my plate abruptly, nearly shattering it on the thick glass. There was an ugly pause before my father asked me in a weary, gentle voice if anything was wrong, and I answered that it was nothing, it was the last night of a long year, and we were together, and I was simply relieved. At midnight, I poured out glasses of champagne, even one for my mother, who took a deep sip. Her manner grew playful and

Coming Home Again

light, and I helped her shuffle to her mattress, and she lay down in the place where in a brief week she was dead.

My mother could whip up most anything, but during our first years of living in this country we ate only Korean foods. At my harangue-like behest, my mother set herself to learning how to cook exotic American dishes. Luckily, a kind neighbor, Mrs. Churchill, a tall, florid young woman with flaxen hair, taught my mother her most trusted recipes. Mrs. Churchill's two young sons, palish, weepy boys with identical crew cuts, always accompanied her, and though I liked them well enough, I would slip away from them after a few minutes, for I knew that the real action would be in the kitchen, where their mother was playing guide. Mrs. Churchill hailed from the state of Maine, where the finest Swedish meatballs and tuna casserole and angel food cake in America are made. She readily demonstrated certain techniques—how to layer wet sheets of pasta for a lasagna or whisk up a simple roux, for example. She often brought gift shoeboxes containing curious ingredients like dried oregano, instant yeast, and cream of mushroom soup. The two women, though at ease and jolly with each other, had difficulty communicating, and this was made worse by the often confusing terminology of Western cuisine ("corned beef," "deviled eggs"). Although I was just learning the language myself, I'd gladly play the interlocutor, jumping back and forth between their places at the counter, dipping my fingers into whatever sauce lay about.

I was an insistent child, and, being my mother's firstborn, much too prized. My mother could say no to me, and did often enough, but anyone who knew us—particularly my father and sister—could tell how much the denying pained her. And if I was overconscious of her indulgence even then, and suffered the rushing pangs of guilt that she could inflict upon me with the slightest wounded turn of her lip, I was too happily obtuse and venal to let her cease. She reminded me daily that I was her sole son, her reason for living, and that if she were to lose me, in either body or spirit, she wished that God would mercifully smite her, strike her down like a weak branch.

In the traditional fashion, she was the house accountant, the maid, the launderer, the disciplinarian, the driver, the secretary, and, of course, the cook. She was also my first basketball coach. In South Korea, where girls' high school basketball is a popular spectator sport, she had been a star, the point guard for the national high school team that once won the all-Asia championships. I learned this one Saturday during the summer, when I asked my father if he would go down to the schoolyard and shoot some baskets with me. I had just finished the fifth grade, and wanted desperately to make the middle school team the coming fall. He called for my mother and sister to

Coming Home Again

come along. When we arrived, my sister immediately ran off to the swings, and I recall being annoyed that my mother wasn't following her. I dribbled clumsily around the key, on the verge of losing control of the ball, and flung a flat shot that caromed wildly off the rim. The ball bounced to my father, who took a few not so graceful dribbles and made an easy layup. He dribbled out and then drove to the hoop for a layup on the other side. He rebounded his shot and passed the ball to my mother, who had been watching us from the foul line. She turned from the basket and began heading the other way.

"*Um-mah*," I cried at her, my exasperation already bubbling over, "the basket's over *here!*"

After a few steps she turned around, and from where the professional three-point line must be now, she effortlessly flipped the ball up in a two-handed set shot, its flight truer and higher than I'd witnessed from any boy or man. The ball arced cleanly into the hoop, stiffly popping the chain-link net. All afternoon, she rained in shot after shot, as my father and I scrambled after her.

When we got home from the playground, my mother showed me the photograph album of her team's championship run. For years I kept it in my room, on the same shelf that housed the scrapbooks I made of basketball stars, with magazine clippings of slick players like Bubbles Hawkins and Pistol Pete and George (the Iceman) Gervin.

It puzzled me how much she considered her own history to be immaterial, and if she never patently diminished herself, she was able to finesse a kind of self-removal by speaking of my father whenever she could. She zealously recounted his excellence as a student in medical school and reminded me, each night before I started my homework, of how hard he drove himself in his work to make a life for us. She said that because of his Asian face and imperfect English, he was "working two times the American doctors." I knew that she was building him up, buttressing him with both genuine admiration and her own brand of anxious braggadocio, and that her overarching concern was that I might fail to see him as she wished me to—in the most dawning light, his pose steadfast and solitary.

In the year before I left for Exeter, I became weary of her oft-repeated accounts of my father's success. I was a teenager, and so ever inclined to be dismissive and bitter toward anything that had to do with family and home. Often enough, my mother was the object of my derision. Suddenly, her life seemed so small to me. She was there, and sometimes, I thought, *always* there, as if she were confined to the four walls of our house. I would even complain about her cooking. Mostly, though, I was getting more and more impatient with the difficulty she encountered in doing everyday things. I was afraid for her. One day, we got into a terrible argument when she asked me to call the bank, to question a discrepancy she

Coming Home Again

had discovered in the monthly statement. I asked her why she couldn't call herself. I was stupid and brutal, and I knew exactly how to wound her.

"Whom do I talk to?" she said. She would mostly speak to me in Korean, and I would answer in English.

"The bank manager, who else?"

"What do I say?"

"Whatever you want to say."

"Don't speak to me like that!" she cried.

"It's just that you should be able to do it yourself," I said.

"You know how I feel about this!"

"Well, maybe then you should consider it *practice*," I answered lightly, using the Korean word to make sure she understood.

Her face blanched, and her neck suddenly became rigid, as if I were throttling her. She nearly struck me right then, but instead she bit her lip and ran upstairs. I followed her, pleading for forgiveness at her door. But it was the one time in our life that I couldn't convince her, melt her resolve with the blandishments of a spoiled son.

When my mother was feeling strong enough, or was in particularly good spirits, she would roll her machine into the kitchen and sit at the table and watch me work. She wore pajamas day and night, mostly old pairs of mine.

She said, "I can't tell, what are you making?"

"*Mahn-doo* filling."

"You didn't salt the cabbage and squash."

"Was I supposed to?"

"Of course. Look, it's too wet. Now the skins will get soggy before you can fry them."

"What should I do?"

"It's too late. Maybe it'll be ok if you work quickly. Why didn't you ask me?"

"You were finally sleeping."

"You should have woken me."

"No way."

She sighed, as deeply as her weary lungs would allow.

"I don't know how you were going to make it without me."

"I don't know, either. I'll remember the salt next time."

"You better. And not too much."

We often talked like this, our tone decidedly matter-of-fact, chin up, just this side of being able to bear it. Once, while inspecting a potato fritter batter I was making, she asked me if she had ever done anything that I wished she hadn't done. I thought for a moment, and told her no. In the next breath, she wondered aloud if it was right of her to have let me go to

Coming Home Again

Exeter, to live away from the house while I was so young. She tested the batter's thickness with her finger and called for more flour. Then she asked if, given a choice, I would go to Exeter again.

I wasn't sure what she was getting at, and I told her that I couldn't be certain, but probably yes, I would. She snorted at this and said it was my leaving home that had once so troubled our relationship. "Remember how I had so much difficulty talking to you? Remember?"

She believed back then that I had found her more and more ignorant each time I came home. She said she never blamed me, for this was the way she knew it would be with my wonderful new education. Nothing I could say seemed to quell the notion. But I knew that the problem wasn't simply the *education;* the first time I saw her again after starting school, barely six weeks later, when she and my father visited me on Parents Day, she had already grown nervous and distant. After the usual campus events, we had gone to the motel where they were staying in a nearby town and sat on the beds in our room. She seemed to sneak looks at me, as though I might discover a horrible new truth if our eyes should meet.

My own secret feeling was that I had missed my parents greatly, my mother especially, and much more than I had anticipated. I couldn't tell them that these first weeks were a mere blur to me, that I felt completely overwhelmed by all the studies and my much brighter friends and the thousand irritating details of living alone, and that I had really learned nothing, save perhaps how to put on a necktie while sprinting to class. I felt as if I had plunged too deep into the world, which, to my great horror, was much larger than I had ever imagined.

I welcomed the lull of the motel room. My father and I had nearly dozed off when my mother jumped up excitedly, murmured how stupid she was, and hurried to the closet by the door. She pulled out our old metal cooler and dragged it between the beds. She lifted the top and began unpacking plastic containers, and I thought she would never stop. One after the other they came out, each with a dish that traveled well—a salted stewed meat, rolls of Korean-style sushi. I opened a container of radish kimchi and suddenly the room bloomed with its odor, and I reveled in the very peculiar sensation (which perhaps only true kimchi lovers know) of simultaneously drooling and gagging as I breathed it all in. For the next few minutes, they watched me eat. I'm not certain that I was even hungry. But after weeks of pork parmigiana and chicken patties and wax beans, I suddenly realized that I had lost all the savor in my life. And it seemed I couldn't get enough of it back. I ate and I ate, so much and so fast that I actually went to the bathroom and vomited. I came out dizzy and sated with the phantom warmth of my binge.

And beneath the face of her worry, I thought, my mother was smiling. From that day, my mother prepared a certain meal to welcome me home. It was always the same. Even as I rode the school's shuttle bus from Exeter to Logan airport, I could already see the exact arrangement of my mother's table.

I knew that we would eat in the kitchen, the table brimming with plates. There was the *kalbi*, of course, broiled or grilled depending on the season. Leaf lettuce, to wrap the meat with. Bowls of garlicky clam broth with miso and tofu and fresh spinach. Shavings of cod dusted in flour and then dipped in egg wash and fried. Glass noodles with onions and shiitake. Scallion-and-hot-pepper pancakes. Chilled steamed shrimp. Seasoned salads of bean sprouts, spinach, and white radish. Crispy squares of seaweed. Steamed rice with barley and red beans. Homemade kimchi. It was all there—the old flavors I knew, the beautiful salt, the sweet, the excellent taste.

After the meal, my father and I talked about school, but I could never say enough for it to make any sense. My father would often recall his high school principal, who had gone to England to study the methods and traditions of the public schools, and regaled students with stories of the great Eton man. My mother sat with us, paring fruit, not saying a word but taking everything in. When it was time to go to bed, my father said good night first. I usually watched television until the early morning. My mother would sit with me for an hour or two, perhaps until she was accustomed to me again, and only then would she kiss me and head upstairs to sleep.

During the following days, it was always the cooking that started our conversations. She'd hold an inquest over the cold leftovers we ate at lunch, discussing each dish in terms of its balance of flavors or what might have been prepared differently. But mostly I begged her to leave the dishes alone. I wish I had paid more attention. After her death, when my father and I were the only ones left in the house, drifting through the rooms like ghosts, I sometimes tried to make that meal for him. Though it was too much for two, I made each dish anyway, taking as much care as I could. But nothing turned out quite right—not the color, not the smell. At the table, neither of us said much of anything. And we had to eat the food for days.

I remember washing rice in the kitchen one day and my mother's saying in English, from her usual seat, "I made a big mistake."

"About Exeter?"

"Yes. I made a big mistake. You should be with us for that time. I should never let you go there."

"So why did you?" I said.

"Because I didn't know I was going to die."

I let her words pass. For the first time in her life, she was letting herself speak her full mind, so what else could I do?

"But you know what?" she spoke up. "It was better for you. If you stayed home, you would not like me so much now."

Coming Home Again

I suggested that maybe I would like her even more.

She shook her head. "Impossible."

Sometimes I still think about what she said, about having made a mistake. I would have left home for college, that was never in doubt, but those years I was away at boarding school grew more precious to her as her illness progressed. After many months of exhaustion and pain and the haze of the drugs, I thought that her mind was beginning to fade, for more and more it seemed that she was seeing me again as her fifteen-year-old boy, the one she had dropped off in New Hampshire on a cloudy September afternoon.

I remember the first person I met, another new student, named Zack, who walked to the welcome picnic with me. I had planned to eat with my parents—my mother had brought a coolerful of food even that first day—but I learned of the cookout and told her that I should probably go. I wanted to go, of course. I was excited, and no doubt fearful and nervous, and I must have thought I was only thinking ahead. She agreed whole-heartedly, saying I certainly should. I walked them to the car, and perhaps I hugged them, before saying goodbye. One day, after she died, my father told me what happened on the long drive home to Syracuse.

He was driving the car, looking straight ahead. Traffic was light on the Massachusetts Turnpike, and the sky was nearly dark. They had driven for more than two hours and had not yet spoken a word. He then heard a strange sound from her, a kind of muffled chewing noise, as if something inside her were grinding its way out.

"So, what's the matter?" he said, trying to keep an edge to his voice.

She looked at him with her ashen face and she burst into tears. He began to cry himself, and pulled the car over onto the narrow shoulder of the turnpike, where they stayed for the next half hour or so, the blank-faced cars droning by them in the cold, onrushing night.

Every once in a while, when I think of her, I'm driving alone some-where on the highway. In the twilight, I see their car off to the side, a blue Olds coupe with a landau top, and as I pass them by I look back in the mirror and I see them again, the two figures huddling together in the front seat. Are they sleeping? Or kissing? Are they all right?

Responding to the Selection

Questions for Discussion

1. What is your impression of the relationship between Lee and his mother?

2. What role does cooking play in the interactions of the family members?

3. **Irony** is a conflict between reality and expectations. Identify an example of irony in "Coming Home Again." What expectation or appearance conflicts with reality in your example?

4. What attitude did Lee's mother have toward her own talents and abilities? Do you think she would have had the same attitude had she been raised in the United States? Explain your answer.

5. Toward the end of the essay, Lee's mother says that if he had stayed home instead of going to Exeter, he would not like her as much as he does now. Do you think she was right? Why or why not?

Activities

Writing Poetry

1. Which parent, relative, or guardian do you feel has had the greatest influence on your life? Write a poem about your relationship with this person.

Comparing Characters

2. Write a paragraph in which you compare the efforts that Lee, his mother, and his father each made to adapt to American society.

Creating an Annotated Bibliography

3. Love between parents and their children is one of the great themes of literature. Make a list of some of your favorite poems, songs, and stories about this theme. Then work in a small group to compile an annotated bibliography of literary works on this theme.

Before You Read

Hybrid

Persis M. Karim

"When I finally learned the Persian word for people like me, do-rageh ("two veined"), with two bloods running through me, I began to embrace my complex heritage."

About Karim

Persis Karim was raised in the San Francisco Bay area. The daughter of an Iranian father and a French mother, she had a hard time figuring out which culture she fit into. Eventually she grew to appreciate her mixed ethnic background. She gained a clearer sense of Iranian American identity in the 1980s, when there was a sudden influx of immigrants from Iran.

Karim teaches comparative and ethnic American literature at San Jose State University in California. In addition to writing poetry and fiction, she has written essays about literary works that deal with exile, migration, and displacement. Karim also co-edited the anthology *A World Between: Poems, Short Stories, and Essays by Iranian-Americans*.

Iranians in the United States

Only about 40,000 Iranians lived in the United States before the 1979 Iranian Revolution. According to some estimates, that number has grown to nearly one million. Many came for political or religious reasons or because they wanted to escape the bloodshed of the Iran-Iraq War. Iranian Americans tend to be affluent and highly educated. However, they often face negative stereotypes. These stereotypes developed in the 1980s, when relations between Iran and the United States were at a low point. Today, Iranian Americans are working to build closer ties between the two countries.

Hybrid

— *Persis M. Karim*

By the time I figured out
what made an Iranian girl
good
it was too late.
5   I had already been corrupted by America,
her loose hips and ungracious manner
had watered me down further.
I couldn't even be called "Iranian-American"
I lacked the sensibility, the language,
10   the distaste for body hair
and the desire for a small nose.
It was too late . . . I'd already
become something else
and couldn't read the codes
15   one needs
to function
as an Iranian.
It was bad enough that I had four brothers
and a mother who wasn't glamorous,
20   I had learned to curse and cared more
about grades than boys.
Occasionally, when I didn't do what he wanted
my father reminded me
that I was *too* American . . .
25   a phrase that cut like a dagger
against the skin,
separated me out
and drove a wedge
between us.

30   I could never quite figure out how much
        was too American.
        Did he mean, don't disrespect your parents,
        tell them everything,
        don't sleep with a boy
35   before marriage,
        don't give yourself too easily?
        Did he mean that my American part
        should not disobey *his* law?
        It was too late.
40   Like all immigrant parents, he wants me to succeed,
        to get an education, to be smart and beautiful
        but not to forget
        that I had to find a man.
        "Women are like fruit trees," he said, "they have to bear children
           or they'll wither."
45   When he put it like that,
        all I wanted was to be
        one of those hybrid
        ornamental plums
        whose blossoms are sweet and glorious
50   but fall to the ground
        without ever bearing fruit.

Responding to the Selection

Questions for Discussion

1. Explain the **metaphor** in lines 45–51. How do you interpret this metaphor?

2. An **internal conflict** occurs within the mind of a character who is torn between opposing goals or feelings. What internal conflict does the speaker observe in her father? Do you think she shares this conflict? Explain.

3. Do you think that the speaker has a generally positive or negative image of herself? Use evidence from the poem to support your opinion.

Activities

Writing a Paragraph

1. How serious is the speaker's disagreement with her father? Is her problem unique to the children of immigrants, or could any teenager experience it? Write a paragraph in response to these questions.

Writing Poetry

2. Write a poem about how you are affected by the values of a parent or guardian.

Discussing Gender in Society

3. Do research to learn more about Iranian attitudes toward women and their place in society. How have these attitudes changed in recent decades? Are there diverse opinions about what makes "an Iranian girl good"? Discuss your findings with the class.

Before You Read

The Bread of Salt

N. V. M. Gonzalez
1915–1999

"Writers create their own nation, even if they've never set foot in it."

About Gonzalez

N. V. M. Gonzalez was one of the most important modern Filipino writers. He wrote mainly in English rather than Tagalog, the traditional literary language of the Philippines. Of English, his adopted tongue, he said, "An alien language does not fail if it is employed in honest service to the scene, in evocation of the landscape, and in celebration of the people one has known from birth."

Gonzalez published his first collection of stories in 1947. This led to a fellowship at Stanford University, where he refined his understated yet lyrical prose style.

Gonzalez said that coming to the United States enhanced his personal as well as his professional development: "It was in America that I began to recognize my involvement in the process of becoming a new person . . . of trying to shed my skin as a colonial." Gonzalez taught at universities in the United States and in the Philippines.

Colonial Culture

"The Bread of Salt" is set in a rural community in the Philippines, where the leading family is of Spanish descent. For centuries, the Philippine Islands were ruled by Spain; the colony was named after King Philip II. Colonists introduced the Spanish language and Roman Catholicism to the islands. English became widely spoken there after Spain handed the colony over to the United States in 1898. Filipino culture has also been influenced by immigrants from other parts of Asia. The Philippines gained full independence in 1946.

The story contains several Spanish words. An *asalto* is a party or reception. A *panuelo* is a scarf. A *sala* is a large room. A middy is a girl's blouse, resembling a sailor's, or midshipman's, outfit.

The Bread of Salt

— N. V. M. Gonzalez

Usually I was in bed by ten and up by five and thus was ready for one more day of my fourteenth year. Unless Grandmother had forgotten, the fifteen centavos for the baker down Progreso Street—and how I enjoyed jingling those coins in my pocket!—would be in the empty fruit jar in the cupboard. I would remember then that rolls were what Grandmother wanted because recently she had lost three molars. For young people like my cousins and myself, she had always said that the kind called *pan de sal* ought to be quite all right.

The bread of salt! How did it get that name? From where did its flavor come, through what secret action of flour and yeast? At the risk of being jostled from the counter by early buyers, I would push my way into the shop so that I might watch the men who, stripped to the waist, worked their long flat wooden spades in and out of the glowing maw of the oven. Why did the bread come nut-brown and the size of my little fist? And why did it have a pair of lips convulsed into a painful frown? In the half light of the street, and hurrying, the paper bag pressed to my chest, I felt my curiosity a little gratified by the oven-fresh warmth of the bread I was proudly bringing home for breakfast.

Well I knew how Grandmother would not mind if I nibbled away at one piece; perhaps, I might even eat two, to be charged later against my share at the table. But that would be betraying a trust; and so, indeed, I kept my purchase intact. To guard it from harm, I watched my steps and avoided the dark street corners.

For my reward, I had only to look in the direction of the sea wall and the fifty yards or so of riverbed beyond it, where an old Spaniard's house stood. At low tide, when the bed was dry and the rocks glinted with broken bottles, the stone fence of the Spaniard's compound set off the house as if it were a castle. Sunrise brought a wash of silver upon the roofs of the laundry and garden sheds which had been built low and close to the fence. On dull mornings the light dripped from the bamboo screen which covered the veranda and hung some four or five yards from the ground. Unless it was August, when the damp, northeast monsoon had to be kept away from the rooms, three servants raised the screen promptly at six-thirty until it was completely hidden under the veranda eaves. From the sound of the pulleys, I knew it was time to set out for school.

It was in his service, as a coconut plantation overseer, that Grandfather had spent the last thirty years of his life. Grandmother had been widowed three years now. I often wondered whether I was being depended upon to spend the years ahead in the service of this great house. One day I learned that Aida, a classmate in high school, was the old Spaniard's niece. All my doubts disappeared. It was as if, before his death, Grandfather had spoken to me about her, concealing the seriousness of the matter by putting it over as a joke. If now I kept true to the virtues, she would step out of her bedroom ostensibly to say Good Morning to her uncle. Her real purpose, I knew, was to reveal thus her assent to my desire.

On quiet mornings I imagined the patter of her shoes upon the wooden veranda floor as a further sign, and I would hurry off to school, taking the route she had fixed for me past the post office, the town plaza and the church, the health center east of the plaza, and at last the school grounds. I asked myself whether I would try to walk with her and decided it would be the height of rudeness. Enough that in her blue skirt and white middy she would be half a block ahead and, from that distance, perhaps throw a glance in my direction, to bestow upon my heart a deserved and abundant blessing. I believed it was but right that, in some such way as this, her mission in my life was disguised.

Her name, I was to learn many years later, was a convenient mnemonic for the qualities to which argument might aspire. But in those days it was a living voice. "Oh that you might be worthy of uttering me," it said. And how I endeavored to build my body so that I might live long to honor her. With every victory at singles at the handball court—the game was then the craze at school—I could feel my body glow in the sun as though it had instantly been cast in bronze. I guarded my mind and did not let my wits go astray. In class I would not allow a lesson to pass unmastered. Our English teacher could put no question before us that did not have a ready answer in my head. One day he read Robert Louis Stevenson's *The Sire de Maletroit's Door*, and we were so enthralled that our breaths trembled. I knew then that somewhere, sometime in the not too

The Bread of Salt

improbable future, a benign old man with a lantern in his hand would also detain me in a secret room, and there daybreak would find me thrilled by the sudden certainty that I had won Aida's hand.

It was perhaps on my violin that her name wrought such a tender spell. Maestro Antonino remarked the dexterity of my stubby fingers. Quickly I raced through Alard—until I had all but committed two thirds of the book to memory. My short, brown arm learned at last to draw the bow with grace. Sometimes, when practising my scales in the early evening, I wondered if the sea wind carrying the straggling notes across the pebbled river did not transform them into Schubert's "Serenade."

At last Mr. Custodio, who was in charge of our school orchestra, became aware of my progress. He moved me from second to first violin. During the Thanksgiving Day program he bade me render a number, complete with pizzicati and harmonics.

"Another Vallejo! Our own Albert Spalding!" I heard from the front row.

Aida, I thought, would be in the audience. I looked around quickly but could not see her. As I retired to my place in the orchestra I heard Pete Saez, the trombone player, call my name.

"You must join *my* band," he said. "Look, we'll have many engagements soon. It'll be vacation time."

Pete pressed my arm. He had for some time now been asking me to join the Minviluz Orchestra, his private band. All I had been able to tell him was that I had my schoolwork to mind. He was twenty-two. I was perhaps too young to be going around with him. He earned his school fees and supported his mother hiring out his band at least three or four times a month. He now said:

"Tomorrow we play at the funeral of a Chinese—four to six in the afternoon; in the evening, Judge Roldan's silver wedding anniversary; Sunday, the municipal dance."

My head began to whirl. On the stage, in front of us, the principal had begun a speech about America. Nothing he could say seemed interesting. I thought of the money I would earn. For several days now I had but one wish, to buy a box of linen stationery. At night when the house was quiet I would fill the sheets with words that would tell Aida how much I adored her. One of these mornings, perhaps before school closed for the holidays, I would borrow her algebra book and there, upon a good pageful of equations, there I would slip my message, tenderly pressing the leaves of the book. She would perhaps never write back. Neither by post nor by hand would a reply reach me. But no matter; it would be a silence full of voices.

That night I dreamed I had returned from a tour of the world's music centers; the newspapers of Manila had been generous with praise. I saw my

The Bread of Salt

picture on the cover of a magazine. A writer had described how, many years ago, I used to trudge the streets of Buenavista with my violin in a battered black cardboard case. In New York, he reported, a millionaire had offered me a Stradivarius violin, with a card that bore the inscription: "In admiration of a genius your own people must surely be proud of." I dreamed I spent a weekend at the millionaire's country house by the Hudson. A young girl in a blue skirt and white middy clapped her lily-white hands and, her voice trembling, cried "Bravo!"

What people now observed at home was the diligence with which I attended to my violin lessons. My aunt, who had come from the farm to join her children for the holidays, brought with her a maidservant, and to the poor girl was given the chore of taking the money to the baker's for rolls and pan de sal. I realized at once that it would be no longer becoming on my part to make these morning trips to the baker's. I could not thank my aunt enough.

I began to chafe on being given other errands. Suspecting my violin to be the excuse, my aunt remarked:

"What do you want to be a musician for? At parties, musicians always eat last."

Perhaps, I said to myself, she was thinking of a pack of dogs scrambling for scraps tossed over the fence by some careless kitchen maid. She was the sort you could depend on to say such vulgar things. For that reason, I thought, she ought not to be taken seriously at all.

But the remark hurt me. Although Grandmother had counseled me kindly to mind my work at school, I went again and again to Pete Saez's house for rehearsals.

She had demanded that I deposit with her my earnings; I had felt too weak to refuse. Secretly, I counted the money and decided not to ask for it until I had enough with which to buy a brooch. Why this time I wanted to give Aida a brooch, I didn't know. But I had set my heart on it. I searched the downtown shops. The Chinese clerks, seeing me so young, were annoyed when I inquired about prices.

At last the Christmas season began. I had not counted on Aida's leaving home, and remembering that her parents lived in Badajoz, my torment was almost unbearable. Not once had I tried to tell her of my love. My letters had remained unwritten, and the algebra book unborrowed. There was still the brooch to find, but I could not decide on the sort of brooch I really wanted. And the money, in any case, was in Grandmother's purse, which smelled of "Tiger Balm." I grew somewhat feverish as our class Christmas program drew near. Finally it came; it was a warm December afternoon. I decided to leave the room when our English teacher

The Bread of Salt

announced that members of the class might exchange gifts. I felt fortunate; Pete was at the door, beckoning to me. We walked out to the porch where, Pete said, he would tell me a secret.

It was about an *asalto* the next Sunday which the Buenavista Women's Club wished to give Don Esteban's daughters, Josefina and Alicia, who were arriving on the morning steamer from Manila. The spinsters were much loved by the ladies. Years ago, when they were younger, these ladies studied solfeggio with Josefina and the piano and harp with Alicia. As Pete told me all this, his lips ash-gray from practising all morning on his trombone, I saw in my mind the sisters in their silk dresses, shuffling off to church for the evening benediction. They were very devout, and the Buenavista ladies admired that. I had almost forgotten that they were twins and, despite their age, often dressed alike. In low-bosomed voile bodices and white summer hats, I remembered, the pair had attended Grandfather's funeral, at old Don Esteban's behest. I wondered how successful they had been in Manila during the past three years in the matter of finding suitable husbands.

"This party will be a complete surprise," Pete said, looking around the porch as if to swear me to secrecy. "They've hired our band."

I joined my classmates in the room, greeting everyone with a Merry Christmas jollier than that of the others. When I saw Aida in one corner unwrapping something two girls had given her, I found the boldness to greet her also.

"Merry Christmas," I said in English, as a hairbrush and a powder case emerged from the fancy wrapping. It seemed to me rather apt that such gifts went to her. Already several girls were gathered around Aida. Their eyes glowed with envy, it seemed to me, for those fair cheeks and the bobbed dark-brown hair which lineage had denied them.

I was too dumbstruck by my own meanness to hear exactly what Aida said in answer to my greeting. But I recovered shortly and asked:

"Will you be away during the vacation?"

"No, I'll be staying here," she said. When she added that her cousins were arriving and that a big party in their honor was being planned, I remarked:

"So you know all about it?" I felt I had to explain that the party was meant to be a surprise, an asalto.

And now it would be nothing of the kind, really. The women's club matrons would hustle about, disguising their scurrying around for cakes and candies as for some baptismal party or other. In the end, the Rivas sisters would outdo them. Boxes of meringues, bonbons, ladyfingers, and cinnamon buns that only the Swiss bakers in Manila could make were perhaps coming on the boat with them. I imagined a table glimmering

The Bread of Salt

with long-stemmed punch glasses; enthroned in that array would be a huge brick-red bowl of gleaming china with golden flowers around the brim. The local matrons, however hard they tried, however sincere their efforts, were bound to fail in their aspiration to rise to the level of Don Esteban's daughters. Perhaps, I thought, Aida knew all this. And that I should share in a foreknowledge of the matrons' hopes was a matter beyond love. Aida and I could laugh together with the gods.

At seven, on the appointed evening, our small band gathered quietly at the gate of Don Esteban's house, and when the ladies arrived in their heavy shawls and trim *panuelos*, twittering with excitement, we were commanded to play the *Poet and Peasant* overture. As Pete directed the band, his eyes glowed with pride for his having been part of the big event. The multicolored lights that the old Spaniard's gardeners had strung along the vine-covered fence were switched on, and the women remarked that Don Esteban's daughters might have made some preparations after all. Pete hid his face from the glare. If the women felt let down, they did not show it.

The overture shuffled along to its climax while five men in white shirts bore huge boxes of goods into the house. I recognized one of the bakers in spite of the uniform. A chorus of confused greetings, and the women trooped into the house; and before we had settled in the *sala* to play "A Basket of Roses," the heavy damask curtains at the far end of the room were drawn and a long table richly spread was revealed under the chandeliers. I remembered that, in our haste to be on hand for the asalto, Pete and I had discouraged the members of the band from taking their suppers.

"You've done us a great honor!" Josefina, the more buxom of the twins, greeted the ladies.

"Oh, but you have not allowed us to take you by surprise!" the ladies demurred in a chorus.

There were sighs and further protestations amid a rustle of skirts and the glitter of earrings. I saw Aida in a long, flowing white gown and wearing an arch of *sampaguita* flowers on her hair. At her command, two servants brought out a gleaming harp from the music room. Only the slightest scraping could be heard because the servants were barefoot. As Aida directed them to place the instrument near the seats we occupied, my heart leaped to my throat. Soon she was lost among the guests, and we played "The Dance of the Glowworms." I kept my eyes closed and held for as long as I could her radiant figure before me.

Alicia played on the harp and then, in answer to the deafening applause, she offered an encore. Josefina sang afterward. Her voice, though a little husky, fetched enormous sighs. For her encore, she gave "The Last

The Bread of Salt

Rose of Summer"; and the song brought back snatches of the years gone by. Memories of solfeggio lessons eddied about us, as if there were rustling leaves scattered all over the hall. Don Esteban appeared. Earlier, he had greeted the crowd handsomely, twisting his mustache to hide a natural shyness before talkative women. He stayed long enough to listen to the harp again, whispering in his rapture: "Heavenly. Heavenly . . ."

By midnight, the merrymaking lagged. We played while the party gathered around the great table at the end of the sala. My mind traveled across the seas to the distant cities I had dreamed about. The sisters sailed among the ladies like two great white liners amid a fleet of tugboats in a bay. Someone had thoughtfully remembered—and at last Pete Saez signaled to us to put our instruments away. We walked in single file across the hall, led by one of the barefoot servants.

Behind us a couple of hoarse sopranos sang "La Paloma" to the accompaniment of the harp, but I did not care to find out who they were. The sight of so much silver and china confused me. There was more food before us than I had ever imagined. I searched in my mind for the names of the dishes; but my ignorance appalled me. I wondered what had happened to the boxes of food that the Buenavista ladies had sent up earlier. In a silver bowl was something, I discovered, that appeared like whole egg yolks that had been dipped in honey and peppermint. The seven of us in the orchestra were all of one mind about the feast; and so, confident that I was with friends, I allowed my covetousness to have its sway and not only stuffed my mouth with this and that confection but also wrapped up a quantity of those egg-yolk things in several sheets of napkin paper. None of my companions had thought of doing the same, and it was with some pride that I slipped the packet under my shirt, There, I knew, it would not bulge.

"Have you eaten?"

I turned around. It was Aida. My bow tie seemed to tighten around my collar. I mumbled something, I did not know what.

"If you wait a little while till they've gone, I'll wrap up a big package for you," she added.

I brought a handkerchief to my mouth. I might have honored her solicitude adequately and even relieved myself of any embarrassment; I could not quite believe that she had seen me, and yet I was sure that she knew what I had done, and I felt all ardor for her gone from me entirely.

I walked away to the nearest door, praying that the damask curtains might hide me in my shame. The door gave on to the veranda, where once my love had trod on sunbeams. Outside it was dark, and a faint wind was singing in the harbor.

With the napkin balled up in my hand, I flung out my arm to scatter the egg-yolk things in the dark. I waited for the soft sound of their fall on

The Bread of Salt

the garden-shed roof. Instead, I heard a spatter in the rising night-ride beyond the stone fence. Farther away glimmered the light from Grandmother's window, calling me home.

But the party broke up at one or thereabouts. We walked away with our instruments after the matrons were done with their interminable good-byes. Then, to the tune of "Joy to the World," we pulled the Progreso Street shopkeepers out of their beds. The Chinese merchants were especially generous. When Pete divided our collection under a street lamp, there was already a little glow of daybreak.

He walked with me part of the way home. We stopped at the baker's when I told him that I wanted to buy with my own money some bread to eat on the way to Grandmother's house at the edge of the sea wall. He laughed, thinking it strange that I should be hungry. We found ourselves alone at the counter; and we watched the bakery assistants at work until our bodies grew warm from the oven across the door. It was not quite five, and the bread was not yet ready.

Responding to the Selection

Questions for Discussion

1. Do you admire the narrator of this story? Why or why not?

2. In your opinion, why does the narrator fall in love with Aida?

3. Why does the narrator become ashamed when Aida offers to wrap up a package of food for him after the party? Why does he lose his infatuation for her at this point?

4. Do you think that the narrator will continue to play the violin after his feelings for Aida change? What leads you to make this prediction?

5. Which aspects of the narrator's life do you associate with the bread of salt? Why might Gonzalez have chosen this bread's name as the title of his story?

Activities

Charting the Plot

1. The **plot** of a story is the sequence of related events, each event causing or leading to the next. Draw a graph or chart of the plot of "The Bread of Salt," indicating which events fall into the following categories: *exposition* (introduction to the characters, setting, and situation), *rising action* (part of the plot that adds complications and increases the reader's interest), *climax* (the point of greatest emotional intensity, interest, or suspense), *falling action* (part of the story that follows the climax), and *resolution* (part of the story that reveals the outcome).

Writing a Letter

2. Write a letter from the narrator to an advice columnist in which he discusses his love for Aida. Include details from the story. Then write a response from the columnist.

Discussing Filipinos

3. A critic said of Gonzalez that the Filipinos in his stories are "a truly submerged people" because of the effects of colonialization. In a small group, discuss the meaning of this phrase. Then list other works of literature that you feel describe other "submerged" peoples. How is their condition similar to that of the Filipinos in this story? How is it different?

Before You Read

Assimilation and Milkfish

Eugene Gloria
Born 1957

About Gloria

Eugene Gloria spent his early childhood in Manila, the capital of the Philippines. In 1966, he moved with his family to San Francisco. After earning his Master of Fine Arts degree from the University of Oregon, Gloria received a Fulbright scholarship that allowed him to live in Manila for a year and a half. In 1999, he won a prize from the National Poetry Series for his first collection of poems, *Drivers at the Short-Time Motel*.

Japan and the Philippines

Gloria's poem "Milkfish" refers to the period of Japanese occupation of the Philippines during World War II. Japan invaded the Philippines, a self-governing commonwealth of the United States, in December 1941. Although resistance from United States and Filipino troops was fierce, Japan conquered the islands within six months. Many civilians suffered from food shortages and acts of brutality under the occupation, which lasted until 1945.

Assimilation

— *Eugene Gloria*

On board the Victory Line Bus
boring down Kennon Road
from a weekend in Baguio
is the bus driver's sideline:
5   a Coleman chest full of cold Cokes and Sprites,
a loaf sack of sandwiches
wrapped in pink napkin and cellophane.
My hunger sated by thin white
bread thick with mayonnaise,
10   diced pickles and slim slice of ham.
What's mere snack
for my gaunt Filipino seatmate,
was my American lunch, a habit
of eating, shaped by boyhood shame.
15   You see, there was a time when I believed
that a meal meant at least a plate of rice
with a sauced dish like *kare kare*,
or *pinakbet* pungent with *bagoong*.
But homeboys like us are marked
20   by experience of not being part of the whole
in a playground full of white kids lined
on red-painted benches in the fall chill of noon,
lunchpails bright with their favorite cartoons,
and a thermos of milk, or brown paper sacks
25   with Glad bags of chips, peeled Sunkist,
Mom's special sandwich with crisp leaf of lettuce,
and pressed turkey thick in between—
crumbed with the breakfast table bread.
I remember that first day of school, my mother, with the purest
30   intention,
took two sheets of foil hollowed
with a cup of steamed rice
and a helping of last night's
caldereta: chunks of potatoes, sliced

35 red peppers, and a redder sauce with beef;
    and I, with hunger, could not
    bring myself to eat.
    Ashamed to be more different
    than what my face had already betrayed,
40 the rice, I hid from my schoolmates.
    Next morning, my mother grasped
    the appropriate combination: fruit,
    sandwich cut in two triangles,
    handful of chips, my best broken English.
45 And weeks passed while the scattered rice—
    beneath the length of that red-painted bench—
    blackened with the schoolyard's dirt.

Milkfish

— *Eugene Gloria*

You feed us milkfish stew
and long grain rice, make us eat
blood soup with chili peppers,
and frown at us when we lose our appetite.
5   I remember when I was young and you
told me of that monsoon: the Japanese occupation—
stories of a time before you met my father,
when you learned the language
of an occupied city in order to feed your family.
10   You were the pretty one at seventeen,
your skin, white as milkfish.
The pretty ones, you said,
were always given more food—
the Japanese soldiers, sentried above
15   the loft where you worked dropped
sweet yams and you caught them
by the billow of your skirt.
I remember you in sepia-brown photographs
of a *mestiza* who equated liberation
20   with Hershey bars and beige nylons
from American GIs—and the season of the monsoon,
as dark as hunger, was not about suffering
but what you knew of beauty.

❖

Responding to the Selection

Questions for Discussion

1. Which images from these poems linger in your mind?

2. In "Milkfish," the speaker tells how his mother obtained food from Japanese and U.S. soldiers during World War II. Does the speaker seem to approve or disapprove of her actions? Explain.

3. The title "Assimilation" refers to the process by which immigrants are absorbed into the dominant culture of their new countries. What is the attitude of the poem's speaker toward assimilation? How does it compare with your own?

4. What kinds of meals do you generally eat at home? Is your taste in food similar to that of your family? Did you ever refuse to eat something prepared for you? How might the refusal of an immigrant child to eat the traditional food affect the parents?

Activities

Writing a Paragraph

1. How have your friends and classmates influenced your eating habits? Do you think that this influence has been good or bad? Write a paragraph in response to these questions.

Discussing Traditional Foods

2. Track the food that is served in your school cafeteria over a period of one week. Which meals do you consider to be traditionally American? Which meals are borrowed from other cultures? Discuss your findings with the class.

Writing Poetry

3. In the poem, the speaker says "homeboys like us are marked / by experience of not being part of the whole." How do you interpret this statement? Write a poem about the idea of not being part of the whole.

In this excerpt from an interview, Wayne Wang talks about the making of *The Joy Luck Club*, the film adaptation of Amy Tan's best-selling novel.

A Delicate Balance: An Interview with Wayne Wang about *The Joy Luck Club*

by John C. Tibbetts—*Literature and Film Quarterly* volume 22, number 1, 1994

Question: *This isn't your first film to deal with several generations of Chinese and Chinese Americans, is it?*

Wang: *Dim Sum*, obviously, comes to mind, because that one's also about a mother-daughter relationship. There's one other film that I completed in 1989 called *Eat a Bowl of Tea*, which is about a father-son relationship, set after the war in 1949. That one is in some ways also very much related to *The Joy Luck Club*, because it's about a generation gap, the Chinese American culture, the particular period when actually the Chinese were not allowed to bring their wives over. It wasn't until after the war that the GIs could use the GI Bill to bring their wives over. And that was the introduction to the Chinese American families. In that sense it's related to the roots of *The Joy Luck Club*.

Question: *Do you see recent Asian American films, like* Joy Luck *and Ang Lee's* The Wedding Banquet, *especially, becoming as popular as the martial arts and ghost-story genres?*

Wang: It's true the family genre seems to be very popular now. I guess the American audience is becoming interested in seeing movies about Chinese Americans—although elsewhere in the world the ghost stories, the action films, and the kung fu films seem to be more popular. . . . I think we're still pretty much a country of immigrants, some older and some newer than others. Stories about immigrants and the different generations and how the parents may be closer to their roots in their own history, and the kids are not. Those things concern all of us and are very strong, universal themes that way.

Question: *Tell me how you came to [the] project in the first place.*

Wang: I was given Amy Tan's book, read it, and found it very moving. It was familiar in the sense that the stories reminded me of stories I heard while growing up. And yet at the same time it

was very universal. Not just about Chinese, but about all immigrants. . . .

Question: *. . . There's such a delicate balance you maintain between the tragic and the comic elements. Everybody talks about it as an "eight-handkerchief movie," but it really is quite funny in places.*

Wang: I especially like the scene where Andrew McCarthy goes to have dinner with the parents of his girl friend [Rosalind Chao as Rose]. He doesn't understand anything about their customs and the affair is a disaster! Ms. Tan told me that scene grew out of experiences she had had. And when I read it I remembered different things in my own background where a Caucasian had to cope with the Chinese "Emily Post" kind of things. It's funny how such small details of table etiquette can create such serious problems!

Question: *The problems of the daughters don't seem particularly serious, after all, when they are compared to what their mothers had to go through.*

Wang: I'm forty-four years old and my generation has been very lucky. We haven't been through major wars or major tragedies, so to speak, in terms of having been bombed by another country, having to escape from our own country, having lost family members, giving up babies—all that kind of stuff. And we live in a way a very self-centered life, our generation. And our problems are quite minor compared to what my parents in China have gone through. And I feel like sometimes I forget about that. And through this film I feel there's a lot we can learn from the dramas, tragedies, and sufferings that our parents have gone through. And what they've gone through to get us to this country and bring us up and all that. On the one hand, it's a burden, their expectations on us; on the other hand, we need to learn from their history and past, because that's where our roots are.

Question: *Do you feel sometimes like your characters, poised between generations, between the Old and New World? Is that a potentially tragic dilemma?*

Wang: I think my parents definitely fit that description. My dad has always wanted to become an American. And he finally became an American just a couple of years ago. And now he's kinda—he doesn't feel like he belongs here, either. He's a big baseball fan, football fan, all that good American stuff; but he feels there's something that's not his home here. He wants to move back to China, now that it's opened up. It's very strange to be caught between those two poles.

Questions for Discussion

1. According to Wayne Wang, what is the basis for the appeal of a film like *The Joy Luck Club*?

2. Would you recommend this movie to a friend based on seeing it or reading the interview with Wayne Wang? Why or why not?

Before You Read

Two Kinds

Amy Tan
Born 1952

> **"Fiction is the way to come to a truth."**

About Tan

As a high school student in California, Amy Tan scored much higher in math than in English. One of her bosses later said that writing was her worst skill. Fortunately, she enjoys "the challenge of disproving assumptions made about me." Tan built up a successful career as a business writer. When she began to feel overwhelmed by her heavy workload, she tried writing fiction. She is now one of the most prominent novelists in the United States.

Tan found her writing voice by imagining an ideal reader. The person she chose was her mother. Tan's first novel, *The Joy Luck Club,* explores the memories of three older Chinese American women. "I knew I had succeeded where it counted," Tan says, "when my mother finished reading my book and gave me her verdict: 'So easy to read.'" Tan based her second novel, *The Kitchen God's Wife,* on her mother's bitter experiences in China.

Chinatown

The story "Two Kinds" takes place in Chinatown in San Francisco, probably during the early 1960s. Chinatown in downtown San Francisco is one of the largest Chinese communities located outside of Asia. The neighborhood—with its fascinating mix of restaurants, shops, bazaars, businesses, and religious and cultural institutions—is a crowded and bustling place. Chinatown has long been a favorite destination of tourists. The area was settled by Chinese immigrants who arrived during the Gold Rush of 1849. Chinatown continues to grow, as Chinese immigrants arrive in San Francisco to begin a new life—just as the mother in "Two Kinds" had done in 1949.

Two Kinds

— *Amy Tan*

My mother believed you could be anything you wanted to be in America. You could open a restaurant. You could work for the government and get good retirement. You could buy a house with almost no money down. You could become rich. You could become instantly famous.

"Of course, you can be prodigy, too," my mother told me when I was nine. "You can be best anything. What does Auntie Lindo know? Her daughter, she is only best tricky."

America was where all my mother's hopes lay. She had come to San Francisco in 1949 after losing everything in China: her mother and father, her family home, her first husband, and two daughters, twin baby girls. But she never looked back with regret. Things could get better in so many ways.

We didn't immediately pick the right kind of prodigy. At first my mother thought I could be a Chinese Shirley Temple. We'd watch Shirley's old movies on TV as though they were training films. My mother would poke my arm and say, "*Ni kan.* You watch." And I would see Shirley tapping her feet, or singing a sailor song, or pursing her lips into a very round O while saying "Oh, my goodness."

"*Ni kan,*" my mother said, as Shirley's eyes flooded with tears. "You already know how. Don't need talent for crying!"

Soon after my mother got this idea about Shirley Temple, she took me to the beauty training school in the Mission District and put me in the hands of a student who could barely hold the scissors without shaking. Instead of getting big fat curls, I emerged with an uneven mass of crinkly black fuzz. My mother dragged me off to the bathroom and tried to wet down my hair.

"You look like Negro Chinese," she lamented, as if I had done this on purpose.

The instructor of the beauty training school had to lop off these soggy clumps to make my hair even again. "Peter Pan is very popular these days," the instructor assured my mother. I now had hair the length of a boy's, with curly bangs that hung at a slant two inches above my eyebrows. I liked the haircut, and it made me actually look forward to my future fame.

Two Kinds

In fact, in the beginning I was just as excited as my mother, maybe even more so. I pictured this prodigy part of me as many different images, and I tried each one on for size. I was a dainty ballerina girl standing by the curtain, waiting to hear the music that would send me floating on my tiptoes. I was like the Christ child lifted out of the straw manger, crying with holy indignity. I was Cinderella stepping from her pumpkin carriage with sparkly cartoon music filling the air.

In all of my imaginings I was filled with a sense that I would soon become perfect. My mother and father would adore me. I would be beyond reproach. I would never feel the need to sulk, or to clamor for anything.

But sometimes the prodigy in me became impatient. "If you don't hurry up and get me out of here, I'm disappearing for good," it warned. "And then you'll always be nothing."

Every night after dinner my mother and I would sit at the Formica-topped kitchen table. She would present new tests, taking her examples from stories of amazing children that she had read in *Ripley's Believe It or Not* or *Good Housekeeping, Reader's Digest*, or any of a dozen other magazines she kept in a pile in our bathroom. My mother got these magazines from people whose houses she cleaned. And since she cleaned many houses each week, we had a great assortment. She would look through them all, searching for stories about remarkable children.

The first night she brought out a story about a three-year-old boy who knew the capitals of all the states and even of most of the European countries. A teacher was quoted as saying that the little boy could also pronounce the names of the foreign cities correctly. "What's the capital of Finland?" my mother asked me, looking at the story.

All I knew was the capital of California, because Sacramento was the name of the street we lived on in Chinatown. "Nairobi!" I guessed, saying the most foreign word I could think of. She checked to see if that might be one way to pronounce *Helsinki* before showing me the answer.

The tests got harder—multiplying numbers in my head, finding the queen of hearts in a deck of cards, trying to stand on my head without using my hands, predicting the daily temperatures in Los Angeles, New York, and London. One night I had to look at a page from the Bible for three minutes and then report everything I could remember. "Now Jehoshaphat had riches and honor in abundance and . . . that's all I remember, Ma," I said.

And after seeing, once again, my mother's disappointed face, something inside me began to die. I hated the tests, the raised hopes and failed expectations. Before going to bed that night I looked in the mirror above the bathroom sink, and when I saw only my face staring back—and

Two Kinds

understood that it would always be this ordinary face—I began to cry. Such a sad, ugly girl! I made high-pitched noises like a crazed animal, trying to scratch out the face in the mirror.

And then I saw what seemed to be the prodigy side of me—a face I had never seen before. I looked at my reflection, blinking so that I could see more clearly. The girl staring back at me was angry, powerful. She and I were the same. I had new thoughts, willful thoughts—or, rather, thoughts filled with lots of won'ts. I won't let her change me, I promised myself. I won't be what I'm not.

So now when my mother presented her tests, I performed listlessly, my head propped on one arm. I pretended to be bored. And I was. I got so bored that I started counting the bellows of the foghorns out on the bay while my mother drilled me in other areas. The sound was comforting and reminded me of the cow jumping over the moon. And the next day I played a game with myself, seeing if my mother would give up on me before eight bellows. After a while I usually counted only one bellow, maybe two at most. At last she was beginning to give up hope.

Two or three months went by without any mention of my being a prodigy. And then one day my mother was watching the *Ed Sullivan Show* on TV. The TV was old and the sound kept shorting out. Every time my mother got halfway up from the sofa to adjust the set, the sound would come back on and Sullivan would be talking. As soon as she sat down, Sullivan would go silent again. She got up—the TV broke into loud piano music. She sat down—silence. Up and down, back and forth, quiet and loud. It was like a stiff, embraceless dance between her and the TV set. Finally, she stood by the set with her hand on the sound dial.

She seemed entranced by the music, a frenzied little piano piece with a mesmerizing quality, which alternated between quick, playful passages and teasing, lilting ones.

"*Ni kan,*" my mother said, calling me over with hurried hand gestures. "Look here."

I could see why my mother was fascinated by the music. It was being pounded out by a little Chinese girl, about nine years old, with a Peter Pan haircut. The girl had the sauciness of a Shirley Temple. She was proudly modest, like a proper Chinese child. And she also did a fancy sweep of a curtsy, so that the fluffy skirt of her white dress cascaded to the floor like the petals of a large carnation.

In spite of these warning signs, I wasn't worried. Our family had no piano and we couldn't afford to buy one, let alone reams of sheet music and piano lessons. So I could be generous in my comments when my mother bad-mouthed the little girl on TV.

Two Kinds

"Play note right, but doesn't sound good!" my mother complained. "No singing sound." "What are you picking on her for?" I said carelessly. "She's pretty good. Maybe she's not the best, but she's trying hard." I knew almost immediately that I would be sorry I had said that.

"Just like you," she said. "Not the best. Because you not trying." She gave a little huff as she let go of the sound dial and sat down on the sofa.

The little Chinese girl sat down also, to play an encore of "Anitra's Tanz," by Grieg. I remember the song, because later on I had to learn how to play it.

Three days after watching the *Ed Sullivan Show* my mother told me what my schedule would be for piano lessons and piano practice. She had talked to Mr. Chong, who lived on the first floor of our apartment building. Mr. Chong was a retired piano teacher, and my mother had traded house-cleaning services for weekly lessons and a piano for me to practice on every day, two hours a day, from four until six.

When my mother told me this, I felt as though I had been sent to hell. I whined, and then kicked my foot a little when I couldn't stand it anymore.

"Why don't you like me the way I am?" I cried, "I'm *not* a genius! I can't play the piano. And even if I could, I wouldn't go on TV if you paid me a million dollars!"

My mother slapped me. "Who ask you to be genius?" she shouted. "Only ask you be your best. For you sake. You think I want you to be genius! Hnnh! What for! Who ask you!"

"So ungrateful," I heard her mutter in Chinese. "If she had as much talent as she has temper, she'd be famous now."

Mr. Chong, whom I secretly nicknamed Old Chong, was very strange, always tapping his fingers to the silent music of an invisible orchestra. He looked ancient in my eyes. He had lost most of the hair on the top of his head, and he wore thick glasses and had eyes that always looked tired. But he must have been younger than I thought, since he lived with his mother and was not yet married.

I met Old Lady Chong once, and that was enough. She had a peculiar smell, like a baby that had done something in its pants, and her fingers felt like a dead person's, like an old peach I once found in the back of the refrigerator; its skin just slid off the flesh when I picked it up.

I soon found out why Old Chong had retired from teaching piano. He was deaf. "Like Beethoven!" he shouted to me. "We're both listening only in our head!" And he would start to conduct his frantic silent sonatas.

Our lessons went like this. He would open the book and point to different things, explaining their purpose: "Key! Treble! Bass! No sharps or flats! So this is C major! Listen now and play after me!"

Two Kinds

And then he would play the C scale a few times, a simple chord, and then, as if inspired by an old unreachable itch, he would gradually add more notes and running trills and a pounding bass until the music was really something quite grand.

I would play after him, the simple scale, the simple chord, and then just play some nonsense that sounded like a cat running up and down on top of garbage cans. Old Chong would smile and applaud and say, "Very good! But now you must learn to keep time!"

So that's how I discovered that Old Chong's eyes were too slow to keep up with the wrong notes I was playing. He went through the motions in half time. To help me keep rhythm, he stood behind me and pushed down on my right shoulder for every beat. He balanced pennies on top of my wrists so that I would keep them still as I slowly played scales and arpeggios. He had me curve my hand around an apple and keep that shape when playing chords. He marched stiffly to show me how to make each finger dance up and down, staccato, like an obedient little soldier.

He taught me all these things, and that was how I also learned I could be lazy and get away with mistakes, lots of mistakes. If I hit the wrong notes because I hadn't practiced enough, I never corrected myself. I just kept playing in rhythm. And Old Chong kept conducting his own private reverie.

So maybe I never really gave myself a fair chance. I did pick up the basics pretty quickly, and I might have become a good pianist at that young age. But I was so determined not to try, not to be anybody different, that I learned to play only the most ear-splitting preludes, the most discordant hymns.

Over the next year I practiced like this, dutifully in my own way. And then one day I heard my mother and her friend Lindo Jong both talking in a loud, bragging tone of voice so that others could hear. It was after church, and I was leaning against a brick wall, wearing a dress with stiff white petticoats. Auntie Lindo's daughter, Waverly, who was my age, was standing farther down the wall, about five feet away. We had grown up together and shared all the closeness of two sisters, squabbling over crayons and dolls. In other words, for the most part, we hated each other. I thought she was snotty. Waverly Jong had gained a certain amount of fame as "Chinatown's Littlest Chinese Chess Champion."

"She bring home too many trophy," Auntie Lindo lamented that Sunday. "All day she play chess. All day I have no time do nothing but dust off her winnings." She threw a scolding look at Waverly, who pretended not to see her.

"You lucky you don't have this problem," Auntie Lindo said with a sigh to my mother.

Two Kinds

And my mother squared her shoulders and bragged: "Our problem worser than yours. If we ask Jing-mei wash dish, she hear nothing but music. It's like you can't stop this natural talent."

And right then I was determined to put a stop to her foolish pride.

A few weeks later Old Chong and my mother conspired to have me play in a talent show that was to be held in the church hall. By then my parents had saved up enough to buy me a secondhand piano, a black Wurlitzer spinet with a scarred bench. It was the showpiece of our living room.

For the talent show I was to play a piece called "Pleading Child," from Schumann's *Scenes From Childhood*. It was a simple, moody piece that sounded more difficult than it was. I was supposed to memorize the whole thing. But I dawdled over it, playing a few bars and then cheating, looking up to see what notes followed. I never really listened to what I was playing. I daydreamed about being somewhere else, about being someone else.

The part I liked to practice best was the fancy curtsy: right foot out, touch the rose on the carpet with a pointed foot, sweep to the side, bend left leg, look up, and smile.

My parents invited all the couples from their social club to witness my debut. Auntie Lindo and Uncle Tin were there. Waverly and her two older brothers had also come. The first two rows were filled with children either younger or older than I was. The littlest ones got to go first. They recited simple nursery rhymes, squawked out tunes on miniature violins, and twirled hula hoops in pink ballet tutus, and when they bowed or curtsied, the audience would sigh in unison, "Awww," and then clap enthusiastically.

When my turn came, I was very confident. I remember my childish excitement. It was as if I knew, without a doubt, that the prodigy side of me really did exist. I had no fear whatsoever, no nervousness. I remember thinking, This is it! This is it! I looked out over the audience, at my mother's blank face, my father's yawn, Auntie Lindo's stiff-lipped smile, Waverly's sulky expression. I had on a white dress, layered with sheets of lace, and a pink bow in my Peter Pan haircut. As I sat down, I envisioned people jumping to their feet and Ed Sullivan rushing up to introduce me to everyone on TV.

And I started to play. Everything was so beautiful. I was so caught up in how lovely I looked that I wasn't worried about how I would sound. So I was surprised when I hit the first wrong note. And then I hit another, and another. A chill started at the top of my head and began to trickle down. Yet I couldn't stop playing, as though my hands were bewitched. I kept thinking my fingers would adjust themselves back, like a train switching to the right track. I played this strange jumble through to the end, the sour notes staying with me all the way.

When I stood up, I discovered my legs were shaking. Maybe I had just been nervous, and the audience, like Old Chong, had seen me go through the right motions and had not heard anything wrong at all. I swept my right foot out, went down on my knee, looked up, and smiled. The room was quiet, except for Old Chong, who was beaming and shouting, "Bravo! Bravo! Well done!" But then I saw my mother's face, her stricken face. The audience clapped weakly, and as I walked back to my chair, with my whole face quivering as I tried not to cry, I heard a little boy whisper loudly to his mother, "That was awful," and the mother whispered back, "Well, she certainly tried."

And now I realized how many people were in the audience—the whole world, it seemed. I was aware of eyes burning into my back. I felt the shame of my mother and father as they sat stiffly through the rest of the show.

We could have escaped during intermission. Pride and some strange sense of honor must have anchored my parents to their chairs. And so we watched it all: The eighteen-year-old boy with a fake moustache who did a magic show and juggled flaming hoops while riding a unicycle. The breasted girl with white makeup who sang an aria from *Madame Butterfly* and got an honorable mention. And the eleven-year-old boy who won first prize playing a tricky violin song that sounded like a busy bee.

After the show the Hsus, the Jongs, and the St. Clairs, from the Joy Luck Club, came up to my mother and father.

"Lots of talented kids," Auntie Lindo said vaguely, smiling broadly.

"That was somethin' else," my father said, and I wondered if he was referring to me in a humorous way, or whether he even remembered what I had done.

Waverly looked at me and shrugged her shoulders. "You aren't a genius like me," she said matter-of-factly. And if I hadn't felt so bad, I would have pulled her braids and punched her stomach.

But my mother's expression was what devastated me: a quiet, blank look that said she had lost everything. I felt the same way, and everybody seemed now to be coming up, like gawkers at the scene of an accident, to see what parts were actually missing.

When we got on the bus to go home, my father was humming the busy-bee tune and my mother was silent. I kept thinking she wanted to wait until we got home before shouting at me. But when my father unlocked the door to our apartment, my mother walked in and went straight to the back, into the bedroom. No accusations. No blame. And in a way, I felt disappointed. I had been waiting for her to start shouting, so that I could shout back and cry and blame her for all my misery.

I had assumed that my talent-show fiasco meant that I would never have

Two Kinds

to play the piano again. But two days later, after school, my mother came out of the kitchen and saw me watching TV.

"Four clock," she reminded me, as if it were any other day. I was stunned, as though she were asking me to go through the talent-show torture again. I planted myself more squarely in front of the TV.

"Turn off TV," she called from the kitchen five minutes later.

I didn't budge. And then I decided. I didn't have to do what my mother said anymore. I wasn't her slave. This wasn't China. I had listened to her before, and look what happened. She was the stupid one.

She came out from the kitchen and stood in the arched entryway of the living room. "Four clock," she said once again, louder.

"I'm not going to play anymore," I said nonchalantly. "Why should I? I'm not a genius."

She stood in front of the TV. I saw that her chest was heaving up and down in an angry way.

"No!" I said, and I now felt stronger, as if my true self had finally emerged. So this was what had been inside me all along.

"No! I won't!" I screamed.

She snapped off the TV, yanked me by the arm and pulled me off the floor. She was frighteningly strong, half pulling, half carrying me toward the piano as I kicked the throw rugs under my feet. She lifted me up and onto the hard bench. I was sobbing by now, looking at her bitterly. Her chest was heaving even more and her mouth was open, smiling crazily as if she were pleased that I was crying.

"You want me to be someone that I'm not!" I sobbed. "I'll never be the kind of daughter you want me to be!"

"Only two kinds of daughters," she shouted in Chinese. "Those who are obedient and those who follow their own mind! Only one kind of daughter can live in this house. Obedient daughter!"

"Then I wish I weren't your daughter. I wish you weren't my mother," I shouted. As I said these things I got scared. It felt like worms and toads and slimy things crawling out of my chest, but it also felt good, that this awful side of me had surfaced, at last.

"Too late change this," my mother said shrilly.

And I could sense her anger rising to its breaking point. I wanted to see it spill over. And that's when I remembered the babies she had lost in China, the ones we never talked about. "Then I wish I'd never been born!" I shouted. "I wish I were dead! Like them."

It was as if I had said magic words. Alakazam!—her face went blank, her mouth closed, her arms went slack, and she backed out of the room, stunned, as if she were blowing away like a small brown leaf, thin, brittle, lifeless.

It was not the only disappointment my mother felt in me. In the years that

Two Kinds

followed, I failed her many times, each time asserting my will, my right to fall short of expectations. I didn't get straight As. I didn't become class president. I didn't get into Stanford. I dropped out of college.

Unlike my mother, I did not believe I could be anything I wanted to be. I could only be me.

And for all those years we never talked about the disaster at the recital or my terrible declarations afterward at the piano bench. Neither of us talked about it again, as if it were a betrayal that was now unspeakable. So I never found a way to ask her why she had hoped for something so large that failure was inevitable.

And even worse, I never asked her about what frightened me the most: Why had she given up hope? For after our struggle at the piano, she never mentioned my playing again. The lessons stopped. The lid to the piano was closed, shutting out the dust, my misery, and her dreams.

So she surprised me. A few years ago she offered to give me the piano, for my thirtieth birthday. I had not played in all those years. I saw the offer as a sign of forgiveness, a tremendous burden removed.

"Are you sure?" I asked shyly. "I mean, won't you and Dad miss it?"

"No, this your piano," she said firmly. "Always your piano. You only one can play."

"Well, I probably can't play anymore," I said. "It's been years."

"You pick up fast," my mother said, as if she knew this was certain. "You have natural talent. You could be genius if you want to."

"No, I couldn't."

"You just not trying," my mother said. And she was neither angry nor sad. She said it as if announcing a fact that could never be disproved. "Take it," she said.

But I didn't, at first. It was enough that she had offered it to me. And after that, every time I saw it in my parents' living room, standing in front of the bay window, it made me feel proud, as if it were a shiny trophy that I had won back.

Last week I sent a tuner over to my parents' apartment and had the piano reconditioned, for purely sentimental reasons. My mother had died a few months before, and I had been getting things in order for my father, a little bit at a time. I put the jewelry in special silk pouches. The sweaters she had knitted in yellow, pink, bright orange—all the colors I hated—I put in mothproof boxes. I found some old Chinese silk dresses, the kind with little slits up the sides. I rubbed the old silk against my skin, and then wrapped them in tissue and decided to take them home with me.

After I had the piano tuned, I opened the lid and touched the keys. It sounded even richer than I remembered. Really, it was a very good piano.

Two Kinds

Inside the bench were the same exercise notes with handwritten scales, the same secondhand music books with their covers held together with yellow tape.

I opened up the Schumann book to the dark little piece I had played at the recital. It was on the left-hand page, "Pleading Child." It looked more difficult than I remembered. I played a few bars, surprised at how easily the notes came back to me.

And for the first time, or so it seemed, I noticed the piece on the right-hand side. It was called "Perfectly Contented." I tried to play this one as well. It had a lighter melody but with the same flowing rhythm and turned out to be quite easy. "Pleading Child" was shorter but slower; "Perfectly Contented" was longer but faster. And after I had played them both a few times, I realized they were two halves of the same song.

Responding to the Selection ———————

Questions for Discussion

1. What two faces does Jing-mei see when she looks in the mirror after another failed prodigy training session?

2. Explain what provokes the nasty argument between Jing-mei and her mother.

3. Why do you think Jing-mei decides to stop trying to become a prodigy?

4. Why do Jing-mei and her parents feel so humiliated by her performance at the recital?

5. Jing-mei and her mother seem to be fighting about the piano. In your opinion, what are they really fighting about?

6. To what does the title of this story refer? Do you think it's a good title for the story? Give a reason for your answer.

Activities

Personal Writing

1. Imagine some of the possible drawbacks of success—for example, the pressure to achieve, the fear of failure, the loss of privacy, the time demands of your career. Write a journal entry in which you describe what you like least about your success.

Debating Issues

2. Should parents ever require their children to take music lessons, as Jing-mei's mother did, or to play a sport or participate in any particular activity? First, list reasons for and against mandatory after-school activities for children. Debate whether it does more harm or more good to require a child to participate in an activity in which he or she has little or no interest.

Before You Read

The Chessmen

Toshio Mori
1910–1980

"...the reader is allowed to experience the people and situations directly, immediately. In effect, Toshio [Mori] allows each reader to be a Japanese American and to experience that life, from the inside out."
—Lawson Fusao Inada

About Mori

Toshio Mori was the first Japanese American to publish a book of fiction. *Yokohama, California* is a collection of stories set in Oakland. Mori wrote most of them in the 1930s. He would work about fourteen hours each day in his family's flower nursery, then go home to write for at least four hours. A publisher accepted his manuscript in 1941, but the book didn't appear in print for eight years. Mori continued to write even while he was held in an internment camp during World War II.

Influenced by writers such as Sherwood Anderson and Anton Chekhov, Mori focused on the lives of ordinary people. He hoped that his realistic and gently humorous portraits of Japanese Americans would overcome stereotypes in popular fiction of the time. Although critics praised his book, it sold poorly. Mori was unable to publish another collection of stories until the year before his death.

Japanese American Farmers

"The Chessmen" is set in a flower nursery in northern California. During the early twentieth century, Japanese immigrants played an important role in California's agricultural economy. They started out as field laborers working long hours for little pay. After saving up wages, many were able to lease plots of land. Their farms often flourished because they worked hard, cooperated, and used unpaid family labor. However, many Japanese never managed to become independent farmers, especially after California passed laws making it difficult for Japanese immigrants to lease land.

The Chessmen

— *Toshio Mori*

Perhaps I would have heard the news in time, but if I hadn't met the third party of the three principals at the beginning it wouldn't have been the same to me. By luck that day, while I was leaning on the fence resting after a hot day's work, a young Japanese came up to me. "Hello. Where's Hatayama's nursery?" he asked me. "I was told the place was somewhere around here."

"It's half a mile farther down," I said. I pointed out the road and told him to go until he reached the greenhouses. That was Hatayama Nursery. The young Japanese thanked me and went away.

At Hatayama Nursery I knew two men, Hatayama-san and Nakagawa-san. They were the only men there the year around. The boss and his help. The two managed the three greenhouses of carnations quite capably. Only in the summer months when the carnation boxes must be lined up and filled with new soil and the plants for the next year planted, Hatayama-san hired additional men. Hatayama-Nakagawa combination worked beautifully. For seven years the two men never quarreled and seldom argued with each other. While Hatayama-san was at the flower market selling flowers to the florists Nakagawa-san carried on at the nursery. He was wise on everything. He attended the boiler, watered the plants, made cuttings, cut flowers and tackled the rest of the nursery work.

Every once in awhile I used to visit the place and talk to these middle-aged men. Perhaps Nakagawa-san was older than his boss. I don't know. "Listen to him, Takeo," Hatayama-san used to tell me. "If you want to become a good carnation grower listen to this man. He's got something. He has many years of experience and a young man like you will learn plenty by listening to him."

Nakagawa-san used to smile with these words. He talked very little. "I don't know much," he would say. "I know very little."

One of the strange things about Nakagawa-san was his family life. I used to visit him only on the weekdays. On Saturday nights and Sundays he was in Oakland to see his family. I used to wonder how he could stand it. His wife and three grown children lived in the city while he worked alone in the nursery. He made his bed, washed his work clothes, swept and

The Chessmen

mopped his bunkhouse after work hours. The only domestic work he didn't do was cook. He ate with the Hatayamas.

When I'd sit and talk with him he'd talk about his family and his week-end visits.

"My youngest boy is now out of high school," he would tell me. "He's a smart boy but I can't send him to college."

"That's too bad for him," I would say. "But you're sending Tom to Cal. That's plenty."

"Yes," he would proudly say. "I hope he'll amount to something."

Nakagawa-san's only daughter worked as a domestic in an American home and helped with the upkeep of her parents' home. Often he would tell me of his children and his eyes would shine with a far-away look.

"Why don't you stay with the family all the time, Nakagawa-san?" I'd ask him. "Why can't you get a job in Oakland and live with your family?"

He would smile. "Ah, I wish I could," he'd say. "But what could an old nursery worker do in a city? I'm too old to find other jobs. No, I must remain here."

"It's a shame," I'd tell him.

"I guess we can't have everything," he'd say and smile. "I'm lucky to have this job so long."

Several weeks after the young man had asked about Hatayama Nursery he came to see me one night. He said his name was George Murai. "I get very lonely here," he explained to me. "I never knew a nursery could be so lonely."

"You're from the city, aren't you?" I asked.

"Oakland," he said.

He was a pleasant fellow. He talked a lot and was eager. "Whenever I have the time I'm going to drop in and see you. That's if you don't mind," he said. "Over at Hatayama's I don't see any young people. I'll go crazy if I don't see somebody. In Oakland I have lots of friends."

I brought out beer and shredded shrimp. George could take beer.

"How do you like the work?" I asked him.

"Fine," he said. "I like it. Someday I'd like to have a nursery of my own. Only I hope I get over being lonely."

"You'll be all right after you get used to it," I said.

"If I don't give up at the start I'll be all right," George said. "I don't think I'll quit. I have a girl, you see."

He pulled out of his wallet a candid shot of a young girl. "That's Lorraine Sakoda of Berkeley," he said. "Do you know her?"

I shook my head.

"We're crazy about each other," George said. "As soon as I find a steady job we're going to get married."

The Chessmen

Before the evening was over I knew George pretty well. Several times when we mentioned friends we found them mutual. That made us feel pretty good.

After the first visit George Murai came often. He would tell me how the work progressed at Hatayama Nursery. It was getting busy. The carnation boxes had to be laid out evenly on the tracks. The soil had to be worked and shoveled in. The little carnation plants must be transplanted from the ground to the boxes. It was interesting to George.

"I'm learning everything, Takeo," he said. "Some day I'll get a nursery for myself and Lorraine."

When I went over to Hatayamas to see the boss as well as Nakagawa-san and George Murai, I would catch a glimpse of a new liveliness on the place. The eagerness of George Murai was something of a charm to watch. He would trot from one work to another as if he were eagerly playing a game. His shouts and laughter filled the nursery and the two men whose capering days were over would look at each other and smile. George's singing ability pleased Hatayama-san. After supper he'd ask George to sing. George knew only the modern popular songs.

Sometimes Nakagawa-san, George and I got together in the little house. Nakagawa-san shared the place with George. At such times George would ask question after question about carnation growing. He would ask how to get rid of red spiders; how such things as rust and spots, the menaces of the plants, could be controlled. He would press for an answer on how to take the crops at a specific period, how to avoid stem rot and root rot, what fertilizers to mix, how to take care of the cuttings. I would sit aside and listen to Nakagawa-san answer each problem patiently and thoroughly.

Sometimes the talk swung to Oakland. The three of us were attached to Oakland one way or another.

"I know your son Tom pretty well," George Murai told Nakagawa-san one night.

"Do you? Do you know Tom?" Nakagawa-san asked eagerly.

"Sure. Tom and I used to go to Tech High together," George said. "He's going to college now."

"Sure! Sure!" Nakagawa-san said.

"I know your daughter Haruyo," George said. "But I don't know Tetsuo so well."

Nakagawa-san nodded his head vigorously. "He's a smart boy but I can't send him to college like Tom."

It wasn't until I was alone with Hatayama-san one day that I began to see a change on the place. In the latter part of August Hatayama-san was usually busy hunting around for two husky men to work on the boxes. It was the time when the old plants in the greenhouses were rooted out and the boxes

The Chessmen

filled with the old soil hauled away. Then the boxes with the new carnation plants were to be hauled in. It was the beginning of heavy work in a nursery.

This year Hatayama-san said, "I can't afford to hire more men. Flower business has been bad. We'll have no flowers to sell until November. That's a long way off. After the new boxes are in I'll have to lay off Murai boy."

"Who's going to work the boxes this year?" I asked.

"Murai and Nakagawa," Hatayama-san said. "They'll have to do it."

When the heavy work at Hatayama Nursery actually started George Murai stopped coming to see me. One afternoon when I got off early and went over there they were still out on the field. It was then I saw the struggle that knew no friendship, the deep stamp of self-preservation in human nature. Here was no flowery gesture; here were no words.

I stood and watched Nakagawa-san and George Murai push the truck-loads of carnation boxes one after another without resting. In the late afternoon their sweat dried and the cool wind made the going easier. It was obvious that George being young and strong could hold a stiff pace; and that he was aware that he would be laid off when the heavy work was finished. With the last opportunity to impress the boss George did his stuff.

I was certain that Nakagawa-san sensed the young man's purpose. He stuck grimly to the pace. All this was old stuff to him. He had been through it many times. Two men were needed to lift the boxes with the old soil and toss it deftly onto the pile so that no clump of dirt would be left sticking to the boxes. Two men were needed to carefully lift the boxes with the new plants and haul them into the greenhouses. The pace which one of the men worked up could show up the weaker and the slower partner. A man could break another man with a burst of speed maintained for several days. One would be certain to break down first. When a young man set up a fast pace and held it day after day it was something for a middle-aged man to think about.

Nakagawa-san straightened as if his back ached, but he was trying to conceal it. His forearms must have been shot with needle-like pains but he worked silently.

As I watched Nakagawa-san and George Murai heaving and pushing with all their might I lost sight of the fact that they were the friends I knew. They were like strangers on a lonely road coming face to face with fear. They looked like men with no personal lives; no interests in family life, in Oakland, in Lorraine Sakoda, in the art of plant-growing, in friendship. But there it was in front of my eyes.

I turned back and went home. I wondered how they could share the little shack after what was happening on the field.

I went over several times but each night they were so worn out with the strain of their pace they slept early. I saw them less and less. Their

The Chessmen

house was often dark and I knew they were asleep. I would then go over to see Hatayama-san.

"Come in, come in," he would greet me.

By the manner in which he talked about Nakagawa-san and George it was plain that he too had seen the struggle on the field. He would tell me how strong and fast George was. At the rate they were going they would be finished a week ahead of the last year's schedule.

"Nakagawa is getting old," he would tell me of his friend. "He's getting too old for a worker."

"He's experienced," I would reply.

"Yes," he'd say, "but George is learning fast. Already he knows very much. He's been reading about the modern method of plant growing. I've already put in an electric hotbed through George's suggestion."

Then I knew George Murai was not so close to being fired. "Are you going to keep both of them this winter?" I asked.

Hatayama-san shook his head. "No. Can't afford it. I've got to let one of them go."

Several nights later I saw lights in their little shack and went over. George was up. He was at the sink filling the kettle with water. Nakagawa-san was in bed.

"What's happened, George?" I said. "Is Nakagawa-san sick?"

"No," George said. "He's just tired. His back aches so I'm warming it with hot water and mustard."

"I'll be all right tomorrow," Nakagawa-san said.

"You're working too hard these days, Nakagawa-san," I said. "You're straining yourself."

Nakagawa-san and George were silent. They looked at me as if I had accused them in one way or another.

Soon Nakagawa-san was back on the field. However, when I went to see how he was getting along I saw Hatayama-san out on the field with George. By the time I reached them they had pushed the truckloads of carnation boxes in and out of the greenhouses several times. George whistled when he saw me. Hatayama-san nodded his head and grinned. Something had happened to Nakagawa-san.

"I knew it was going to happen," Hatayama-san told me. "Nakagawa's getting too old for nursery work. His back troubles him again."

In the morning Nakagawa-san had stuck grimly to the work. At noon when he sat down for lunch he couldn't get up afterwards. He had to be carried to the little shack. Mrs. Hatayama applied a new plaster to his back.

"I've been on the job for two days. We'll finish on time," Hatayama-san said. "George's been a big help to me."

George looked at me and grinned.

The Chessmen

When the pair resumed carting the boxes I went to see Nakagawa-san. As I entered the room he opened his eyes and smiled at me. He looked very tired. His repeated attempts to smile reminded me of his family and his pride for his sons.

"I'll be all right in a few days," he said eagerly. "When my back's healed I'll be like new again."

"Sure," I said. "You'll be all right."

He read to me a letter from his wife. It was filled with domestic details and his boys' activities at school. They wanted to see him soon. They missed him over the week end. They reasoned it was due to the work at the place. They missed the money too. They wanted him to be sure and bring the money for the house rent and the gas bill.

When I came away in the late afternoon Hatayama-san and George were washing their faces and hands back of the woodshed.

"How's he getting along?" Hatayama-san asked me.

"He says he's all right," I said.

"I'll go and see if he wants anything before I eat," George said.

George trotted off to the little shack. Hatayama-san motioned me toward the house. "At the end of this month I'm going to drop Nakagawa. I hate to to see him go but I must do it," he said. "Nursery is too much for him now. I hate to see him go."

"Are you really going to let him go?" I asked.

"I'm serious. He goes." He took my arm and we went inside the house. I stayed for dinner. During the courses George talked. "Someday I want to bring my girl here and introduce her," he told Hatayama-san and me. "You'll both like her."

Hatayama-san chuckled. "When will you get married, my boy?"

George smiled. "I think I can get married right away," he said.

Afterwards we listened to a few Japanese records. George got out Guy Lombardo's records and we listened to them. Mrs. Hatayama brought hot tea and Japanese teacakes. When I left George accompanied me to the road. He was in a merry mood. He whistled "I Can't Give You Anything But Love."

We said, "So long."

"Be sure to come again," he said. As I walked down the road I heard his whistling for quite a distance. When the whistling stopped the chants of the crickets in the fields became loud. Across the lot from the greenhouses I saw the little shack lit by a single light, and I knew that Nakagawa-san was not yet asleep.

Responding to the Selection ────────────

Questions for Discussion

1. How do you feel about what happens to Nakagawa-san? Compare your response with the attitude of the story's narrator.

2. Do George and Nakagawa-san dislike each other, or are they merely competing for the same job? Support your response with evidence from the story.

3. Could Nakagawa-san have avoided his fate? What, if anything, would he have done differently?

4. Why do you think Mori decided to call this story "The Chessmen"?

5. Does this story portray a situation that is unique to Japanese Americans or Asian Americans of the period? Could the characters have belonged to any ethnic group? Explain your response.

Activities

Writing a Paragraph

1. What do you think will happen to Nakagawa-san after he is fired? Write a paragraph in response to this question.

Writing a Letter

2. Write a letter from Nakagawa-san to his eldest son in which he explains what happened at the nursery. In the letter, have Nakagawa-san express his feelings about Hatayama-san and George.

Before You Read

Connecting to Poland: Encounter

Czesław Miłosz
Born 1911

> *"A poet carries his land within him. I never left Poland."*

About Miłosz

Czesław Miłosz was born in an ethnically mixed area of Europe that became part of Poland after World War I and the destruction of the Russian Tsarist empire. He published his first volume of poetry at the age of twenty-one. During the Nazi occupation of Poland, he remained in the country, participating in the resistance movement as a writer calling for freedom. After World War II, the Polish government appointed him to a position in the foreign service. However, by 1951 he could no longer ignore the abuses of the Communist regime. He defected to the West and eventually settled in the United States, where he became a professor of Slavic literature. In 1980 he won the Nobel Prize for Literature. Miłosz's writing is generally restrained, even when he addresses tragic events. He is often described as a philosophical poet because of his fascination with moral issues and the nature of existence and identity. In addition to poetry, he has also written critical essays, novels, and an autobiography.

The Polish Landscape

Miłosz has written many superb descriptions of landscapes. As a boy, he wanted to become a naturalist, and this interest carried over into his poetry: "The forests, the valleys and the rivers which I saw in my childhood possess for me a strong evocative force." In his writings, Miłosz draws a sharp distinction between an attachment to one's homeland and extreme forms of nationalism that encourage ethnic hatred. He also refuses to idealize nature.

Encounter

— *Czesław Miłosz*
Translated by the author and Lillian Vallee

We were riding through frozen fields in a wagon at dawn.
A red wing rose in the darkness.

And suddenly a hare ran across the road.
One of us pointed to it with his hand.

That was long ago. Today neither of them is alive,
Not the hare, nor the man who made the gesture.

O my love, where are they, where are they going
The flash of a hand, streak of movement, rustle of pebbles.
I ask not out of sorrow, but in wonder.

Responding to the Selections

1. Compare and contrast the narrator in "The Chessmen" with the speaker in "Encounter." How would you describe their attitudes towards the events they describe?

2. In what way do both of these works describe a process that could be called natural and ordinary?

3. Do you think people should accept the workings of the natural order, or should they try to change them? Explain your answer.

Activities

Writing an Essay

1. Write an essay on the role of nature in these two works.

Discussing Story Titles

2. Work with a partner to make a list of alternate titles for each of these works. Discuss why each suggested new title is appropriate for the story.

Communicating Nonverbally

3. Choose an episode from "The Chessmen." Without revealing which episode you have chosen, try to represent it without using words for a partner. You may choose dance, pantomime, body gestures and motions, or any other way to get across the episode's meaning nonverbally. Ask your partner to identify the episode you represented. Then work with your partner to act out the events described in "Encounter."

Before You Read

Talk to Me, Milagros

M. Evelina Galang
Born 1961

> *"I texture my stories with the details that have been with me all my life."*

About Galang

M. Evelina Galang was born in Harrisburg, Pennsylvania. The eldest of six children, she grew up in a household where the holidays were "loud and full of laughter and much teasing." In high school, Galang worked on the school paper and the literary magazine. "I was a geek who liked to read—not very athletic but long and skinny as if I were," she says.

After graduating from college, Galang worked for a television station and several film production companies. Then she went back to school to earn a master's degree in creative writing. She published a collection of short stories, *Her Wild American Self,* in 1996. Reviewers praised her fresh insights into issues such as immigration and prejudice, as well as her "elegant, mesmerizing style."

Fitting In

As a high-school student, Galang belonged to the only family of color in her suburb. She worked hard to fit in, maintaining what she calls an "All-American teenage look." She went through a similar period in her writing career when she avoided subjects related to her ethnic background. Eventually she realized that her experiences as a Filipino American woman help set her apart from other writers. "I would not say I'm writing about Filipinos; rather, I write about families who happen to be American Filipino," Galang says. "My culture enters into it, because I finally understand that to reach the universal, I must be specific, detailed, particular."

Talk to Me, Milagros

— M. Evelina Galang

On the day Milagros Bustos and her family arrived from the Philippines, my mother ran around the house with a dish towel, shooing us into action. Vacuum this, she ordered, dust that, sweep here, pick-up, pick-up, pick-up! It was Saturday, our day of rest, our cartoon morning, and Mom refused to give us any peace. Dad was at the hospital making rounds, which meant we had dibs on the television at least until lunch. My twin brothers hung upside down from the leather loveseat, punching and tickling each other at once, while my baby sister lay flat on her tummy with her favorite blanket smashed up into her face. She was still sucking her thumb then. This would not do for Mom, and when she came through the TV room waving that rag, we scattered like chicks across a barnyard.

"Your Uncle Victor and Auntie Nita will be here tonight," Mom told us. "There are nine of them in all. We need to get organized."

"What's the name of the girl my age?" I asked.

"Milagros."

Victor and Nita Bustos were not blood relatives, but they came from Dad's town, so that made them as good as family. People from Dad's province often made Peoria their first American experience, stopping in for months at a time until they could settle into homes of their own. The families were usually small in number and young. We never had this many people come over at once and I was glad to hear that there was a girl my age. I had always wanted a sister to play with. Len, my own sister, was too young to be anything but a pest. To my annoyance she followed me around, slow like a shadow turtle, repeating my words like a parrot. I liked the idea of having someone who was mature like me, who knew how to get along in the company of fifth and sixth graders.

We would talk about clothes and rock stars—I liked David Cassidy from the Partridge Family. We would talk about how to get along with our mothers and how to boss our younger siblings. I had great plans for me and Milagros.

At six that evening, my father arrived and brought with him the sounds of many feet shuffling through our kitchen door, foreign tongues speaking voice over voice, mixing orders with salutations. The Bustos clan carried leather suitcases and brown carton boxes wrapped with hemp and marked in big black letters: USA.

Auntie Nita was a short woman with a round and generous face. She kissed each of my brothers, my sister, and me, zealously, leaving heavy lipstick prints on our cheeks. She squeezed the breath out of us and rolled us in the cavity of her bosom. She smelled of fading perfume—islands and salt water drifting from her along with the musty scent of travel. She placed her seven girls before us naming them as she did.

"This is Milagros," she told us. "She is like you, Nelda," she said, pushing her slightly towards me. Milagros was small. Her skin was dark brown and her elbows stuck out at her sides like stick-figure arms. Her bald knees were dry and white. Her hair was long, a shiny blue-black midnight that covered her back like a satin curtain. I could tell that luck lived with Milagros, for above her right eye was a giant black dot. My mother had once told me that moles were a sign of good fortune. Special people with special gifts were marked by moles, and Milagros' mole was big, flashing "Lucky" like a neon sign.

"Hi," I said, but she only stared at me. Her mother told us she was shy and went on rattling off introductions. Besides Milagros there was Myette, Melina, Malu, Maritess, Maya and Monette.

"Look, Nelda," my mother said. "You and Milagros will have your hands full, babysitting all these girls as well as your own brothers and sister."

That night I brought her to my room and introduced her to my things. "Do you have your own room in the Philippines," I asked her, "or do you have to share?" Milagros sat in my rocking chair, legs drawn to her chest, head up. Her long hair shifted from her shoulders to her face as she rocked, never looking at me, never saying one word. When she didn't answer me, I went on. "You probably don't know any English, so that's okay. You'll figure it out." I walked about my room, picking up objects and explaining them to her. "These are my favorite stories," I told her, pointing to my collection of Beverly Cleary books. "Henry's a boy and Ribsy's a dog—they're friends with Ellen Tibits and Ramona the pest." I showed her my favorite pair of platform shoes, a paper flower from last summer's fair, my painted stones from the beach. Milagros sat in my chair and rocked past my show-and-tell, never looking up to see my treasures.

Talk to Me, Milagros

She walked over to her little brown suitcase and pulled something out. She stretched out her hand and offered me a photograph. The picture was black and white. It had white scalloped edges that were rough and uneven like waves in the ocean. "Who are these girls?" I asked her. The photo was taken in front of a white clay building. On the edge of the picture you could see the trunks of palm trees and huge ferns. In the middle of the picture were three rows of girls dressed in white cotton sailor dresses. They were all small like Milagros and they all had long hair tied up or brushed back in some neat fashion. "These your friends?" I asked her. She nodded.

"Here are my dolls," I said. "Crissy's my favorite 'cause you can make her hair short or long by pressing a button in back." I fingered Crissy's blond hair, which felt dry like straw. "I wish I could make my hair long or short that fast—don't you?" I pulled Milagros from the rocking chair and brought her to my vanity mirror.

In the mirror I could see that I was much taller than she, and while my skin had always been milk chocolate, I seemed pale and yellow next to Milagros. "Is that your natural skin color, or are you tan?" I asked her. I told Milagros that in the summertime all the kids on the block would lay out on the Ozowski's porch and sunbathe. I told her how my mother never let me join them, saying I was already too brown. Milagros stood perfectly still, staring at our reflection. "I think you're pretty," I said. I touched the ends of her hair which were even coarser than the doll's. "Mom keeps cutting mine." There was a gold glimmer, a sparkle, buried underneath her mane of hair, near the nape of her brown neck. I remember thinking she was a lucky girl, for she had pierced ears with two tiny pearls set in gold.

I played my Partridge Family records for her and showed her how to dance to them. I moved about my room and utilized all the floor space, weaving around the bed and rocking chair, flailing my arms like a giant bird. "Want to dance?" I asked her, but she sat back down and rocked in the chair.

During the next few weeks, she grew to like my records too. Sometimes Milagros would pull me through the house by the wrist, leading me to the bedroom. She'd point at the records underneath my turntable and I would put on the Partridge Family. Then she would sit on that chair by the window and rock. She'd rock a little faster when the needle got to songs like "I Think I Love You" and "Point Me in the Direction of Albuquerque." Sometimes I danced around the room or I stretched my body across the bed. Milagros always sat in my chair, sometimes staring out the window or down at the floor, sometimes pulling out that picture of the girls. Every now and then, I'd catch her looking at me and we'd lock eyes. I'd smile at her. She'd smile back. We always listened to the same side of the album. We listened long and hard and even though Milagros never spoke, she learned to mouth the lyrics on that record. We'd sit there until we were called to set the table or get the younger children ready for bed.

Once I asked my mother why Milagros was always so quiet.

"She never talks," I complained. "She's kind of boring."

My mother told me to be patient. "It's not easy," she said as she ran her fingers through my hair. "Milagros has just left her home and all her friends. Be patient, Nelda."

My mother distributed the Bustos family into different parts of the house: Uncle Victor and Auntie Nita and the two babies slept in the extra bedroom below the kitchen. The three older Bustos girls, Milagros, Myette and Melina, stayed on the floor in my bedroom. Malu and Maritess shared the bed in Len's room.

I liked the way things were set up. At night my floors were covered with blankets, pillows, and sleeping bags. It was always a slumber party, what with bodies on the floor and giggling in the dark and secrets between Myette and Melina. Every night the ritual was the same. We bathed the children, two at a time, dried them thoroughly with mother's heavy white towels, and then dusted each one in talcum powder. My brothers and sister and the rest of the Bustos girls would meet in my bedroom where Milagros and I would lead the nightly prayers. After the prayers, just when we all should have been quieting down for sleep, came a serious round of tickling fits and pillow fights—Bustos girls against the Carreros kids.

Sometimes, after the little ones were in bed, Milagros and I sat on the stairs and watched the grown-ups. Since Uncle Victor and Auntie Nita had come over, my parents had been acting like teenagers. The four of them would sit up late at night, talking and laughing as they played many rounds of mah-jongg. They would sit at a card table, rolling the marble tiles about, building them into walls and telling jokes in *Taglish*—their own brand of *Tagalog* mixed with English.

Uncle Victor was excited to be in America. "Nita and I will build a house soon, and the girls will go to a nice Catholic school. Next year, we'll vacation in Florida."

"With what money?" Auntie Nita always wanted to know. She called her husband *ma ya bang*, which meant he was a talker, a showoff, a Mr. Big Shot. Dreamer.

My father let Uncle Victor talk, but sometimes warned him, "It's true, if you save, you can have a much better life here, Victor, but first you have to find work."

"No problem," Uncle Victor said, laughing. "This is America."

Every morning, Uncle Victor woke up at five. He showered, shaved, and slapped his face with pine-smelling aftershave. He slicked his hair back with a dab of pomade. I can still see him sitting at the edge of the sofa, dressed in his fancy gray suit, buffing the tops of his black oxford shoes as he read the morning paper. When Auntie Nita and my mother would wake up, he'd serve them coffee and eggs, with onions and fried rice. Then, waving the paper at them, he'd set off to find a job.

In the Philippines, Uncle Victor was an attorney in the city of Pitogo. His practice was strong and he had the respect of the whole community. Auntie Nita said he was famous for grand speeches in the court house and that he had won many cases solely on his wit.

"Is he looking for a job in the court house?" I asked her. But she said that he couldn't be an attorney here, not yet, since the laws back home were different from those in America. When I told Auntie Nita that I didn't understand why he left such a great job, she told me that he had done it for the girls. "They will have better opportunity here, Nelda," she assured me. "They'll have the chance to be more than wives," she told me.

Milagros looked up from her basket of laundry, tossed a cloth diaper down and shaking her head, she grumbled something in *Tagalog*. I couldn't catch all the words.

"Ay *anak*," Auntie Nita sighed. "Child, I've told you before, it's for your own good. We know what we're doing, trust, *anak*."

So Uncle Victor interviewed for jobs at department stores and restaurants. He called on small businesses.

Whenever he came home at the end of the day, he would be whistling and smiling, bearing chocolate candy bars for all the children. His baby girls would climb up his torso and my brothers would leap on to his back and chant, "Uncle Victor, Uncle Victor!" We'd cover him like ants on sugar and he would tickle us all.

"Did you find work?" I'd ask him and he would shake his head and say, "Not yet, *hija*, not yet, but soon."

Milagros was the only one who never came running. She would stand at the end of the hall and wait for the children to climb off him. Then she'd approach him, kiss him on the cheek, and hand him his slippers.

Every night when my dad got home from the hospital, he and Uncle Victor had the same conversation. They sat under the lamp in our living room, my father sinking back into the leather of his reclining chair and Uncle Victor leaning forward on the edge of the sofa. They always initiated these talks with idle banter and as the conversation took a solemn turn, the men's voices grew softer and each man perched himself closer to the end of his seat, resting his weight forward, nearly whispering into the other's ear. My dad would always get around to Uncle Victor's job hunt and Uncle Victor would lighten the conversation again. "I think that any day now, I will find something. I think that soon I will have a great job." My father always assured Uncle Victor that it was still early and that he shouldn't be discouraged if he didn't find work right away, but Uncle Victor interrupted him every time, saying, "Don't worry, this is America, I'll be working soon." Uncle Victor would not listen to negative talk, would not hear of discrimination.

Once everyone went to sleep and all you could hear was the slow methodical tumble of the washer-dryer, the whir of the dishwasher, and the occasional hum of our refrigerator, Uncle Victor would pull out his law books and spread them carefully underneath the lamp that hung over the kitchen table. While we rested, Uncle Victor murmured American laws and rules and cases to himself. Once I got up to get a glass of water and I saw him at the table, reverently whispering the Constitution out loud. Like a child memorizing prayers during Mass, he uttered every syllable. Then, checking himself for accuracy, he peered over the bridge of his glasses, into stacks of white-papered books.

After three weeks, things were still not clicking for me and Milagros. Sometimes I thought it was because we were too busy executing chores or watching over our siblings. It seemed we never had time to talk or get to know each other as friends were supposed to do. Every night after we rinsed the dishes and swept the kitchen floor, after we wiped the counters and before we gave the children their baths, we went to my room where I would write out my homework or read a book. Milagros had a pen pal. She wrote a letter every night. Then every day she'd check the mailbox for letters and slip the one she wrote into the silver box.

"Who are you writing to?" I asked her once. "One of your friends?" She covered up the note with her free hand and pressed her face close to the desk, scribbling her perfect tiny letters fast. Maybe she thought if she wrote small enough and fast enough, I wouldn't be able to see who she was writing to. She kept a stack of letters written on light blue paper in her purse. The handwriting was angular and jagged so that the L's looked like right triangles and the capital G's were rectangles with wings. I was jealous of the way she poured words onto the letters she wrote, of how she hoarded the ones from the Philippines as though she were all alone in America.

Her eyes, two big black dots glaring, seemed masked and disguised from me and my understanding. I often found her looking at me and it seemed she didn't care. She never looked away. She never seemed embarrassed or awkward like me.

Sometimes when Milagros and I babysat, she spoke to her sisters in *Tagalog*. She must have been telling them stories, for they would settle around her, hanging onto her sleeve or her leg. They'd braid the long black strands of her hair, responding to her words in sighs and gasps and brittle bits of laughter. Even Len, who couldn't understand a word Milagros said, fell victim to the rhythm of her voice, a voice that rose and fell like water running along the rocks of a river.

The funny thing was, I often heard Auntie Nita speak to Milagros in English—"Change Monette's diaper" or "Make some rice" or "Tell your *tita* I'm here." Milagros always obeyed her, never speaking back, never asking her mother to repeat the words. Once when we were sitting on the steps, watching the children play a game of tag, I asked her why she wouldn't speak back in English.

She turned to look at me through strands of hair that fell into her brown face. She looked like an island girl to me, someone pretty and exotic. She pushed her hair away from her face and revealed her beautiful pearl earring. Shrugging, she said, "Ay *wong ko.*" She didn't know. Then one of the little ones fell and she was off, reprimanding them for playing so rough. "*Tama na!*" she told them, pulling one sister off of another. "Enough!"

One Sunday, we had a barbecue in our backyard. My father invited people from his hometown who might know the Bustos family, as well as those he thought should know them. Many of these people had stayed with us at one time or another when they first got to the States. These events were practically a circus with many voices speaking at once, and bodies small and large moving about in circles.

We roasted a pig on a spit in the backyard. The men took turns spinning the pig while the women kept bringing food out to a long table in the shade. We had two card tables set up for poker or mah-jongg. The Reyes brothers brought an acoustic guitar and a set of bongo drums and sang Philippine love songs to our families. My parents had a way of encouraging talk from everyone, talk that happened at once, talk that often went unheard. For us, noise was a sign of happiness and *fiesta*.

Milagros and I wandered about the party, weaving in and out of people in silence. We went from table to table, watching the women rapidly flipping mah-jongg tiles to the center of the table, taking long drags from their unfiltered cigarettes, and blowing smoke from the corners of their painted mouths.

For a while we sat in front of the Reyes brothers and listened to them—their voices were soft, sliding from one note to the next like lounge singers crooning in an Elvis bar. Tony Reyes stood in front of us wearing a pair of bell-bottom denims and a flowered shirt that he left unbuttoned. His crucifix swung as he strummed and sometimes you could hear Jesus banging across the instrument's wood, echoing into the hollow of the guitar.

Sitting cross-legged in front of the Reyes brothers, I leaned into Milagros' ear and whispered, "Are they cute?"

She giggled back and said, "*Hindi naman!*" which meant, no way.

Talk to Me, Milagros

We watched the older men roasting the *baboy* on the spit. In the center of the circle, Uncle Joe, an old timer who first came to the U.S. in 1920, sat on an old tree stump. His legs were thrown apart and he leaned his elbows on the top of his thighs, shaking his pipe and nudging the brim of his straw cap.

"When I first came to this country," he told them, "I lived in San Francisco. There were restaurants that had signs on the doors: Absolutely No Filipinos. Back then they called us *Pinoys*, monkeys, you know. Work was hard to come by. *Ay naku*, it was really something."

"I don't believe it," Uncle Victor said.

"You see, I thought that too because that is what they tell us back home—America land of opportunity." He shook his head, clicking his tongue, and confessed, "I was so homesick, I almost gave up twice—once in 1937 and then again in forty-two. I just wanted to get back home."

When we had enough of the hoopla, Milagros and I wandered back into the house, me, to sit at the edge of my bed paging through my latest copy of *Teen Beat*, and Milagros to rock my chair.

I looked at her and thought of times in the middle of the night when I had heard her sniffling to herself. "Milagros," I'd call. "Are you okay?"

"*Hindi na bali*," she'd say. Never mind.

"Why?" I'd ask her. *Bakit?* She never had an answer.

I ran my hands along the pages of my magazine, pretending that the photo of David Cassidy was real. I held the picture up to her.

"Do you think he's handsome?" I asked her. "Do you think that he might like me, I mean if he met me?" She looked at me with that heart-shaped faced, framed by her neatly parted hair, and smiled. "You don't think so?" I asked. I went to the mirror and examined myself. My pixie-cut hair stood up on its ends—down by my neck trailed little wisps of hair frayed and loose like David's own shag hairdo. My big teeth stuck out from under my lip, dressed in silver bands—braces that promised to mold my mouth into something pretty and petite. On the bridge of my nose, a pair of psychedelic plastic glasses helped me see far away. My body was stick straight, thin like a boy's, so thin that when I turned sideways, people said they couldn't see me. I was cloaked in cotton—a pair of pants with colorful prints like bright yellow pineapples and purple bananas, blue apples and orange watermelons. My shirt was a ribbed sleeveless turtleneck with blue piping around the armpit. Mom had bought it from the summer rack in the Ladies' department at Gimbel's. I was wearing a bra that my mother had bought—it was padded and much too big for my eleven year old body, but I wore it anyway. I turned to Milagros and told her I thought maybe David Cassidy would think she was the pretty one.

Talk to Me, Milagros

When she didn't answer me, I began to get annoyed. I walked over to the rocking chair and asked her, "Why won't you speak? Why won't you ever answer me?" I pushed the back of the chair, rocking her faster as I spoke. "Say something. Tell me to shut up. You're in America now, you know: we speak English here. What's the matter with you?"

Milagros drew her lips into a straight line and wrapped her fingers around the handles of the rocking chair. "Your mother speaks to you in English—she told me they teach English at your little convent school in the Philippines—why won't you talk it?" I shoved the chair harder, trying my best to make her answer me. I pushed again and again. But she stayed there, sitting, sturdy as ever.

Then I went to the closet where she hung her purse and I pulled out the stack of air-mail letters. She jumped up then, scratching at me, prying the letters from my hands. I threw them up and they sailed across the room like a flurry of giant snowflakes.

Milagros bit her lip, grabbed my hands, and leaned her weight against mine. We stood for a moment, pressing up against our invisible walls, tummy to tummy, palm against palm. I was tired of being the nice hostess. I was sick of having this girl in my house. Even though this was my house, she was the one who got all the attention now— "See how Milagros can cook? See how Milagros can bathe all her sisters? Isn't Milagros beautiful?" Milagros and her lucky mole or not, this was my house, not hers, the least she could do was talk to me. I locked my hands with hers and dug my nails into her cocoa-brown skin. Her hair tumbled into her face, strayed into the corners of her mouth, and stuck.

Milagros growled at me, tightened the muscles in her face. *"Bastus Americana!"* she said.

"What do you know about Americans," I asked. "You're the stupid one. You can't even talk English. You know what? I don't want to be your friend. Go back to your little group of girlfriends!"

Tears pooled in her black eyes, rolled down her face, and streaked across the slope of her cheek. "You cry baby," I said, "go back to the Philippines. Go back to where you belong!"

Just as Milagros began to fall, Len came toddling into the room. "Your mommy wants you," Len told Milagros. "She wants you to dance."

Down in the backyard, Auntie Nita lined up five of her seven girls (Maya and Monette were still babies). They stood in a straight line, waiting for the music, and as the drone of the ukelele began, the Bustos girls twirled their hips and rotated their wrists. They shuffled their feet right then left and swayed to the strains of Don Ho's song, "Tiny Bubbles."

Talk to Me, Milagros

Milagros led her sisters in the dance, swaying up ahead of them to encourage them, remind them, show them how to do it. She curled her fingertips, then stretched them out, allowing a wash of ukelele mixed with Don Ho's croon to move through her hand, then forearm and elbow and shoulder. The sisters moved together and stirred the air like gentle waves rippling onto sandy beaches. Milagros moved her hips in a circle.

"That's called around the island!" Auntie Nita told everyone.

Then Milagros' movements grew big and her arms stretched through space, rearranged the atmosphere, popped the tiny bubbles. The other sisters followed Milagros as they seemed to float among our guests and turn our Midwest garden into a tropical paradise.

I watched the eyes of our friends and neighbors. Everyone at the party had stopped to watch the Bustos girls. Conversations were traded for sighs and exclamations. "*Ganda!*" they gasped. And they were right, the five little island girls were beautiful. They told a story about Don Ho's tiny bubbles that made him feel happy, made him feel fine. Who cares? I thought. What a dumb song.

A few of the women tried coaxing me to join the sisters, but I had never taken a dance lesson in my life, much less hula lessons. There was no way I was going to dance up there next to Milagros and there was no way that I could ever forgive her for standing up in the middle of my backyard and dancing.

That night, after everyone had gone, Milagros and her mother sat in the corner of the living room, talking quietly. Milagros fingered the photo of her friends and occasionally held it out to her mother. I watched their bodies cast giant silhouettes against our white walls, their shadows melting in and out of each other. Milagros cried, placed her head onto her mother's lap, while Auntie Nita clicked her tongue and sighed. "*Ay naku,*" she whispered. "You'll see, *hija,* things will get better. Don't worry, *naman.*" She kissed the top of Milagros' head and told her, "Enough now, daughter, *Tama na.*" And Milagros nodded, Okay.

Whenever we were given a chore to do together, she would lead the work and I would follow. She knew how to do more than I did. Her mother let her fold the laundry and iron. She was allowed to use the stove. These were things my mother had always taken care of and so I let Milagros take the lead, since she seemed to know what she was doing.

I know these were only chores to Milagros, but for me it was like playing house. I was always amazed when the rice that we put in the pan and covered with water turned out fluffy and light. I loved that an article of clothing covered with mud from the garden could be whitened with bleach and come out new. Sometimes we stitched old pieces of fabric together and stuffed them with holey socks and nylons to make throw pillows. Before Milagros, I took all this for granted.

Sitting at the kitchen counter while my mother washed chicken parts, I asked her how come Milagros knew so much.

"It's different in the Philippines," she said. "Because life's harder back there, girls learn early how to do housework, how to help."

"I thought everyone had maids," I said.

"A lot of people do," my mother said. "But still, the Philippines is old-fashioned that way, you know. Girls learn how to do women's work and boys learn to do men's work."

"Why don't you want me to help?" I asked her as I doodled on the corner of my homework.

"Maybe I've spoiled you, ha, *hija?*"

"Maybe," I said. I thought about the way Milagros was always so serious, how she never seemed to want to play. Maybe, I thought, it's because they never gave her time to play in the Philippines. She was too busy working.

Tuesday Uncle Victor came home, while Mom and Auntie Nita were at the grocery store. He came into the house whistling as he always did, giving us chocolate too. We went through the rituals we had established with him, the children crawling all over him, the slipper thing with Milagros, everything. It had been two months since they had arrived.

"Where did you go today?" I asked.

"I went to the shopping mall," he told us. "I talked to the man at the shoe store, the lady at the dress shop, the book store. I spoke to somebody at a place where they sold little silver and gold trinkets with engravings."

"Did you go to the jewelry store?" I wanted to know.

Uncle Victor nodded his head. "I did."

"Did they need a lawyer?" my brother asked.

"Well, children," Uncle Victor announced. "It looks like someone needed a lawyer!"

Myette, Melina and Maritess danced around their father, pulling on his pants leg and kissing his hands.

"Really, Uncle Victor?" asked one of my brothers.

"Yes, *hijo*, really! Elroy's Easy Diner."

I looked at Milagros and smiled at her. "This is good, huh? Aren't you glad?" She smiled stiffly at me.

"Okay, *na*," she said.

Uncle Victor swooped down to cradle Milagros in his thick arms. "*Hija*," he said. "Aren't you gonna kiss me congratulations?" Milagros nodded her head, leaned into his cheek and kissed.

"Congratulations, Papa," she told him.

Talk to Me, Milagros

"Soon," Uncle Victor told her, "I will pass the law review and I can start my own practice. You and the girls will go to a nice school and have lots of pretty clothes. You'll see, *hija*, you'll see." He put his face against hers, and spun her around the room.

"Okay, Papa," she said. "Okay."

A week later, Milagros and I decided to visit her father at Elroy's Easy Diner. We walked along the boulevard in silence. The sun was out, warming my face, and a spring breeze blew secrets past my ear. I was not in the mood to talk, so I kept my eyes fixed on the path in front of me. I dragged my toe, marking the dirt behind me, scuffing my new red tennis shoe. I hummed under my breath, rattled lyrics to myself.

"Aren't you excited?" I asked her. "Aren't you excited to see your dad at work? They don't let kids in hospitals, so I've never seen my dad at work. Plus, your dad'll give us treats."

"It's okay," she said.

"Hey, Nelda!" called a voice. "Hey, you stuffer!"

There in the hollow of the creek stood Trent Collins, a neighborhood boy, and with him were Carrie Shamanski, Mark Checkolinski, Amy Owlrick, and Stanley Martin, the boy I had a crush on. Trent ran up to me and snapped my bra. "So you still stuffing?"

"I do not stuff!" I yelled. It wasn't my fault that this bra my mother bought didn't fit me, it had been on sale.

"What?" Stanley asked.

"Yeah," Trent said as he danced around me, "Nelda the Nerd, stuffs— look, can't you see?" He lurched forward, thrust the palm of his hand onto my chest.

The sun was glaring into the lens of my glasses, and so I had to squint. The children stood frozen like shadows in a game of statues, staring at me. I swung my arm, which was as thin as a sapling, at Trent. I heard them laugh at my attempt. Someone said something about my clothes. Someone said something about my nerdy little Chinky glasses that went with my nerdy little Chinky face—I don't know who because the sun had blurred their horrid little mouths—maybe they all said it. Maybe they said it at once, together, several times. I looked down at my chest and I could see the crinkled little cup-cakes of my padded bra smashed across my chest, my cotton pants ballooning out into the afternoon wind. I swung again. I missed.

Milagros leapt from behind me, tossed a stone at the group of children, broke the spell.

"Leave Nelda alone," she said as she rubbed her hands. "You are *bastus* for teasing my friend." She held up her fist, ready to fight, but I grabbed her sleeve, pulling her close to me.

"What?" Trent said laughing. The rest of the gang scattered, leaving him alone in the ditch.

One of the kids called to him, warning him, "Let's go, Collins. Let 'em alone all ready."

Milagros turned to me and smiled, "You know *bastus?*" she asked, steering me in the direction of the diner.

"Stupid?"

"Yes, he is stupid," she said.

We fell back into silent step, me with Milagros, or Milagros with me. I looked at her and for the first time, I felt I understood.

"You went to an all-girl school in the Philippines?" I asked her.

She nodded.

"You were kind of lucky," I told her. "At least girls don't snap each other's bras."

"Oh, yes," Milagros said, smiling. "Sometimes."

At the diner, Uncle Victor welcomed us, calling out our names as he wiped his hands off onto his apron. Uncle Victor was busy, but he brought us both a brownie and milk. I told Uncle Victor what had happened at the creek.

"Don't worry," he said. "Don't pay attention to those kids. They just don't understand."

"Do you know what they call me?" I asked him. "Nerdy Nelda."

"What is nerdy?" he wanted to know.

Milagros explained it to him in *Tagalog*: To be a nerd is to be a geek, a hang-around-with-the-book-crowd kind of individual.

"Oh," he said as he rubbed my shoulder with the palm of his hand. "You know, Nelda, nerds do very important things—they invent gadgets and machinery, they discover great cures and write beautiful poems."

Looking into his face, the roundness of his cheeks and the soft and easy comfort of his dark eyes, I thought Milagros resembled her father. She had his eyes, his manner. "I know," I told him. "That's what my mother always says."

"Hey," someone called from the other side of the diner. "Could I get some coffee here, or what?" Uncle Victor looked around but the waiter was in back—he must have been in the bathroom. Two men sat on the other side of the diner. One was huge—two hundred-some pounds. He wore a checkered shirt underneath a black windbreaker with the word "Goodyear" painted in yellow-gold letters. His jeans were baggy and worn to almost white with splotches of dirt woven into its threads. The other man was smaller, older and full of wrinkles. He had on a pair of black plastic glasses.

Talk to Me, Milagros

Uncle Victor waved at the man and smiled. He got up to get the waiter at the back of the restaurant. "One minute, sir," Uncle Victor said.

Milagros grabbed onto my wrist, squeezed. She was holding her breath. I turned to the man, as if ready to say something, but Milagros pinched me and shook her head no.

The waiter came out from back, carrying a pot of coffee. "I got it, Victor," he said. "I'll take care of it."

Uncle Victor smiled weakly at the waiter and after that he went back to bussing tables.

Later that night, Milagros and I stood on stools in my mother's kitchen, peeling potatoes. After a while I heard a heavy thumping sound that was constant and loud. It seemed to shake the walls and echo within the framework of our house.

"Where's your father?" Auntie Nita asked Milagros. "Is that him?" Without looking up from her work, Milagros nodded her head. "Ay *naku*," whispered Auntie Nita. "Not again." Then she calmly went to Uncle Victor. "Watch the kids, ha, Milagros?"

Soon I could also hear an occasional moan, like a wolf that had been trapped. I looked at Milagros who was intent on peeling her potatoes.

"Don't you hear that?" I whispered. "What is that?"

She picked up another potato and rinsed it. Taking the peeler in her right hand she began to shave its skin off.

I shook her shoulder. "What's the matter with you?" I yelled. I put my work down and ran to the extra bedroom.

The drumming against the wall felt heavy and full of pain. I could hear my uncle crying, sobbing, sometimes quietly and at other times howling. Auntie Nita's voice sang in a dialect I could not comprehend. Her lullaby was low and soothing. Soon she hushed his muttering.

I stood at the door, wanting to peek, wanting to know what was the matter, but I couldn't move. I'd never heard a man cry like that. I thought everything was going well now. Hadn't he found what he had been looking for? A job? In America?

My mother hissed at me to get away from the door. "Leave them alone," she warned. "That is none of your business."

But the door cracked open just then and light shed onto the walls outside of their room. I stepped up to the door and peeked in.

Auntie Nita was rubbing Uncle Victor's shoulder, pulling him gently towards her, but he wouldn't let her hold him. Instead he was cracking his head against the wall, again and again and again. His face was red, swollen and washed with tears. Uncle Victor wailed and I heard a sound rising from some deep, dark place.

Talk to Me, Milagros

Milagros pushed passed me, opened the door. She helped her mother pull Uncle Victor from the wall, helped Auntie Nita place his head on her mother's lap, ran her small hand up and down the curve of his spine, kissed him, and pressed her cheek to his shoulder. Then Milagros stood and pulled me out the door. She wiped her eyes with the back of her hand, dragging tears across her face. "He will be okay," she said.

I studied the black at the center of her eye, how the color seemed to swirl deep into forever. I wanted to stay, so when she leaned her slight body against the heavy wooden door I reached out and tried to hold it open. I pushed. The door rocked between us, was suspended in mid-air for a few seconds, but she was stronger than I. "Don't worry, Nelda," she said. "Never mind." Then she closed the door and I stood there and stared at the knots, at the faces that ran from the wood's swirling grain, at the eyes and teeth and giant sized moles, and I waited.

Responding to the Selection

Questions for Discussion

1. Who is your favorite character in this story? What did you find appealing about this character?

2. Why is Milagros so reluctant to speak in English? Which details in the story support your response?

3. Do Nelda and Milagros ever develop a close friendship? Why or why not? If you feel that they become close to each other, when does this occur?

4. Why does Uncle Victor cry in his bedroom at the end of the story? Do you think that he is reacting to a specific incident or to circumstances in general? How do you think you would feel if you were in his position?

5. **Setting** is the time and place in which the events of a story occur. Which details in "Talk to Me, Milagros" help establish when the story's events occur?

6. Galang has said that "to reach the universal, I must be specific, detailed, particular." How does this story reach beyond the experiences of the two families?

Activities

Writing a Letter

1. Write a letter from Milagros to her pen pal back home. Have her describe her feelings about something that happens in the story.

Interpreting the Story

2. Victor gives up a successful career in the Philippines so that his daughters can have greater opportunities in the United States. Do you think that he made the right decision? Write a paragraph in response to this question.

Illustrating a Scene

3. Draw an illustration to accompany one of the scenes in "Talk to Me, Milagros." Before you start working on the illustration, reread Galang's descriptions of her characters' appearances.

Conducting an Interview

4. All immigrants to this country face some of the problems that Uncle Victor and his family face in this story. Interview a recent immigrant to this country to learn about the challenges he or she faced. Share the results of your interview with the class.

Focus on . . .
The Philippines and Filipino Immigration

Spain had ruled the Philippines for three centuries by the time of the Spanish-American War. When U.S. warships steamed into Manila's harbor in 1898 and destroyed the Spanish fleet, Filipino nationalists believed that independence was at hand. However, the United States decided to seize the colony. Hundreds of thousands died over the next three years as Filipino rebels fought against their new occupiers.

The takeover sparked a wave of Filipino immigration to Hawaii and the United States. Filipinos were not subject to laws designed to exclude Asians. As "American nationals," they could enter the United States freely, although they were ineligible for citizenship. Between 1910 and 1930, the number of Filipinos on the mainland soared from 406 to 45,208. The majority of these immigrants settled in California, where they performed backbreaking agricultural labor or held low-paying service jobs. Many Filipinos also went to Alaska and found work in the fisheries.

Like other Asian immigrants, Filipinos clashed with white laborers who feared competition and lowered wages. Sometimes this antagonism led to violent attacks on Filipinos. The immigrants also experienced racism off the job. Since they could not become citizens, Filipinos were barred from owning property, and landlords often refused to rent to them. Hotels and restaurants put up signs announcing that they would not serve Filipinos. "I feel like a criminal running away from a crime I did not commit," Carlos Bulosan wrote. "And the crime is that I am a Filipino in America."

Immigrants began to feel more welcome during World War II, when Filipino troops fought alongside other U.S. soldiers in the Philippines. Filipino Americans could now become citizens by enlisting in the U.S. armed forces. Congress passed a law in 1946 that made all Filipino immigrants eligible for citizenship. After the Philippines gained independence in 1949, Filipinos continued to move here in large numbers. Many recent immigrants are highly educated professionals. According to estimates, Filipinos have become the largest Asian group in the United States.

Linking to . . .
• Think about this information as you read the selections about Filipinos in this theme.

Before You Read

Dance of the Letters and *Beetle on a String*

Vince Gotera
Born 1952

About Gotera

Vince Gotera was born in San Francisco. He spent part of his early childhood in the Philippines. Gotera currently teaches creative writing and poetry at the University of Northern Iowa. His first book of poetry, *Dragonfly,* came out in 1994. Gotera has also published a study of poetry written by Vietnam War veterans. In his spare time, he plays guitar in blues, rock, and jazz bands.

The Land of Opportunity

In his poem "Dance of the Letters," Gotera addresses a fairly common problem among Filipino immigrants. Most Filipinos who have come to the United States in recent decades are professionals or technical workers. Although their home country's government and educational system are modeled after those of the United States, Filipino professionals still must apply for state licenses to practice here. They often find it difficult to prepare for licensing exams while holding down full-time jobs to support their families. Many Filipino lawyers, doctors, engineers, and teachers manage to overcome this hurdle, but some find themselves locked out of their profession and are forced to work at jobs for which they may be overqualified.

Dance of the
Letters

— Vince Gotera

My father, in a 1956 gray suit,
had the jungle in his tie,
a macaw on Kelly green.
But today is Saturday, no briefs
5   to prepare, and he's in a T-shirt.

I sit on his lap with my *ABC*
Golden Book, and he orders the letters
to dance. The *A* prancing red
as an apple, the *E* a lumbering elephant,
10   the *C* chased by the *D* while the sly *F*

is snickering in his russet fur coat.
My mother says my breakthrough
was the *M* somersaulting into a *W*.
Not a mouse transformed into a wallaby
15   at all, but sounds that we can see.

Later, my father trots me out
to the living room like a trained *Z*.
Not yet four, I read newspaper headlines
out loud for Tito Juanito and Tita Naty
20   or for anyone who drops in.

Six years later, I am that boy
in a black Giants cap, intertwining orange
letters *S* and *F*, carrying my father's
forgotten lunch to the catacombs
25   of the UCSF Medical Center,
and I love the hallway cool before the swirling,

heat from the Print Shop door.
In his inky apron, my father smiles,
but his eyes are tired. The night before,
30   I pulled the pillow over my head, while he
argued with my mother
till two a.m. about that old double bind:
a rule to keep American citizens from
practicing law in the Philippines.
35   His University of Manila

law degree made useless.
But California's just as bad.
"You can't work in your goddamn
profession stateside either!" he shouts.
40   "Some land of opportunity."

There in the shimmer of the Print Shop, I can't
understand his bitterness. I savor
the staccato sounds. He leans
into the noise of huge machines, putting
45   vowels and consonants into neat stacks.

Beetle on a String

— *Vince Gotera*

When I was a kid, I walked bugs on a leash.
This was in the Philippines, where my parents
and I moved when I was a toddler, trading
foggy San Francisco for Manila's typhoons.

5   Actually, it was an idyllic place for a child—
warm evenings drenched in the sweet scent
of sampaguita flowers, but most of all,
a huge universe of enthralling insects

filling the night with buzzing and clicks, strobe
10   flashes of their glow-in-the-dark wingflicks.
It was my father who showed me how to catch
a scarab beetle in the cup of your hand, wait

for the wings to subside and close, then loop a thread
between thorax and carapace, tying it off—
15   not too tight—to allow the insect to fly
on a two-foot-long lasso. I remember

how I would smile and laugh, maybe five
or six years old, as a beetle would circle my head
like a whirring kite, iridescent green in the sun,
20   the thread stretched almost to the breaking point.

At night, I would tie my beetles to the round knobs
on my dresser drawers and be soothed to sleep
by a lullaby of buzzing. By morning, the beetles
were always dead, weights hung on string.

Beetle on a String

25   Those long nights must have been horrible.
Straining your body to shift an immovable weight,
unable to evade the swooping flight
of predators, banging again and again hard

against the dead wood, brought up short
30   by that unforgiving tether, cutting off
your pulsing blood every time, the long tube
of your heart quivering. It makes me shiver now

to wonder what thoughtless boy holds my string?

Responding to the Selection

Questions for Discussion

1. Which of these two poems made a stronger impression on you? Explain.

2. "Dance of the Letters" contains many images of clothing. What clues do these images provide about the people portrayed in the poem?

3. In the last stanza of "Dance of the Letters," the boy can't understand his father's bitterness. Why would this bitterness be difficult for him to understand?

4. How do you interpret the question at the end of "Beetle on a String"?

5. A **theme** is an important idea or message in a literary work. What theme, if any, do "Dance of the Letters" and "Beetle on a String" have in common? If you don't think they share any themes, state a theme for each poem.

6. Do you think that immigration is generally easier for adults or for children? Explain your response.

Activities

Writing Poetry

1. In "Dance of the Letters," Gotera includes an interesting "letter" simile ("trots me out to the living room like a trained Z"). Write a brief poem in which you use the alphabet to create figurative language.

Writing an Essay

2. The father in "Dance of the Letters" speaks ironically of the United States as a "land of opportunity." Do you think that this country treats its immigrants fairly? Write a brief essay on this topic.

Giving a Report

3. People may have very different views about the extent to which they control their own lives. Come up with two or three questions that address this topic. Get responses from a group of friends and report your findings to the class.

Before You Read

The Gift in Wartime

Tran Mong Tu
Born 1943

About Tran

"War is a terrible thing," says Tran Mong Tu, who has firsthand experience. Tran Mong Tu was born in Hai Dong, North Vietnam. She and her family were forced to relocate to South Vietnam in 1954, she says, "due to the French-Indochina war," in which communist forces battled and eventually drove out the French. Yet South Vietnam did not remain safe for long; a civil war soon raged between communist and non-communist sympathizers.

By the time the United States became heavily involved in the Vietnam War in the 1960s, Tran worked for the Associated Press (a large U.S. news service) in Saigon, the capital of South Vietnam. When the United States pulled its troops out of Vietnam in 1975, the Associated Press evacuated its Vietnamese employees because it feared communist reprisal against those working for American companies. Tran's immediate family and thousands of other Vietnamese also fled to the United States at that time.

Although Tran had wanted to be a writer since elementary school, her poetry was not published until she reached the United States. Today Tran frequently contributes poems and short stories to Vietnamese literary publications in the United States and overseas.

Vietnamese Poetry

Vietnam has a tradition of poetry that goes back more than a thousand years. Poetry helped the Vietnamese develop and sustain a strong sense of national identity. For much of Vietnam's history, anyone who hoped to obtain an official position had to master the craft of poetry. Even Ho Chi Minh, leader of the Vietnamese Communist movement, was an accomplished poet. This strong association between poetry and patriotism has its negative side, however. During the United States–Vietnam conflict, poets were expected to produce uplifting verse. North Vietnamese and South Vietnamese poets who wrote critically of the war were often censored or persecuted by their governments.

The Gift in Wartime

— *Tran Mong Tu*
Translated by Vann Phan

I offer you roses
Buried in your new grave
I offer you my wedding gown
To cover your tomb still green with grass

5   You give me medals
Together with silver stars
And the yellow pips on your badge
Unused and still shining

I offer you my youth
10   The days we were still in love
My youth died away
When they told me the bad news

You give me the smell of blood
From your war dress
15   Your blood and your enemy's
So that I may be moved

I offer you clouds
That linger on my eyes on summer days
I offer you cold winters
20   Amid my springtime of life

You give me your lips with no smile
You give me your arms without tenderness
You give me your eyes with no sight
And your motionless body

The Gift in Wartime

25   Seriously, I apologize to you
       I promise to meet you in our next life
       I will hold this shrapnel as a token
       By which we will recognize each other

Responding to the Selection

Questions for Discussion

1. Which images in "The Gift in Wartime" did you find especially interesting or memorable? What sort of poem would you expect to find them in? Explain.

2. A **theme** is an important message or idea in a literary work. How would you state the theme of this poem?

3. What attitude does the speaker have toward war? How might a poem such as this one have influenced readers during the Vietnam War?

Activities

Writing a Letter

1. Write a letter from the dead soldier in response to the speaker's promise and offers.

Illustrating the Poem

2. Draw an illustration to accompany "The Gift in Wartime." Use one or more of the striking visual images from the poem in your illustration.

Hmong Tapestry, artist unknown. Found in the museum's collection, 1990. 19 × 19 in. Collection of The Wing Luke Asian Museum, Seattle, WA.

Theme Five

Dreams

He stood before us and in his beautiful sad way, tried to make us understand as he understood.

—Toshio Mori

Before You Read

Lipstick

Wang Ping
Born 1957

"The more I write, the more I realize how alive and violent language can be."

About Ping

Wang Ping was born in Shanghai, China. She studied English and American literature at Beijing University. Before she could enroll in college, she worked in the countryside for three years. She moved to the United States in 1985 to attend graduate school.

Wang Ping's publications include a novel, a collection of stories, and a book of poetry. When she started writing poetry, she would switch between Chinese and English. Eventually she found that she could write more freely in her second language. She says that her need to look up words in English is actually an advantage:

"I find a lot of things that a native speaker might not notice. I like this, because I like the feeling of getting at the roots of language, the origins of language."

The Cultural Revolution

"Lipstick" is set in China during the Cultural Revolution. Communist leader Mao Zedong started this upheaval in 1966 to strengthen his hold on power and to reinvigorate the Chinese revolutionary spirit. Mobilizing the country's youths into groups known as the Red Guards, Mao attacked all traditional values and anything he considered "bourgeois," or middle class. The Red Guards vandalized museums, libraries, religious buildings, and bookstores. They also confiscated items from the private homes of intellectuals and of those who had had contacts with the West. Many people were beaten or killed. The Cultural Revolution lost momentum with Mao's death in 1976.

Lipstick

— *Wang Ping*

In some deep corner of the dinner table, I found an old lipstick.

The cover was gone, its green plastic body coated with dark greasy dirt. I wiped it with a tablecloth and held it under my nose. I smelled the fragrance of wild roses. Slowly I turned the tube as far as it could go. About an inch of scarlet red appeared between my fingers. The print of someone's lips on the top, its angle so tender that I dare not touch it. Whose lipstick could it be? Who still had the guts to keep a lipstick in 1971, the prime time of the Cultural Revolution? Anything which was related to beauty, whether Western or Oriental, had been banned. Gray *zhongshanzhuang*—Mao's suit—became the uniform for the middle-aged and old people, and the green and navy blue uniforms became young people's most desirable objects. All the women had short hair cut just below their ears. Some girls tied their hair with rubber bands into two brushlike pigtails. They were called revolutionary brushes because they resembled the brushes people used to write critical big-character posters.

Whose lipstick could it be? My sister Sea Cloud's or my mother's? Sea Cloud's power seemed limitless. Although she was only twelve, and was two years younger than me, she was three inches taller—five foot, five inches—and looked like my older sister. In fact she had me completely under her thumb. She made me do her share of the housework, which was only one-third of the work I had to do. Her excuse was that I had no friends to see and no places to go to anyway. She made me tell her a story every evening. If I refused, she pinched and cursed me as my mother did: *dead ghost, wooden-head, abacus.* Sometimes when the pinch was too painful and I grabbed her wrists, she would holler for my mother. My mother always punished me with the bamboo stick behind the door. She said that since I was the oldest daughter, I should love and take care of my younger sisters and brother. I had two sisters and one brother. Fortunately, my youngest sister stayed with my grandma in Shanghai, and my brother was not as wily as Sea Cloud. Everyone said Sea Cloud looked exactly like my mother: big double-lidded eyes, long clean eyebrows, straight delicate nose, and clear white skin. She looked like a foreigner, people also said, with admiration in their voices.

Lipstick

I couldn't understand why Western books and ideas were poisonous but to look foreign was desirable. Whenever I couldn't bring any food from the food market or broke a bowl or burnt rice, my mother would sigh: If only you were half as smart as Sea Cloud. I talked back in my heart: If only she could do her own homework.

Every Chinese New Year, my mother killed one of the chickens I raised and made chicken broth. She asked me to bring a bowl of chicken soup to Sea Cloud, who was always sick in bed with a stomach ache or a bad sore throat just when every hand was needed for the holiday preparations. I hated Chinese New Year. It meant endless washing of dishes and vegetables in cold water and listening with an empty stomach to guests feasting and laughing. I slowly dried my swollen frost-bitten hands on my apron, staring at the hot chicken soup with hatred. I'd been washing dishes piled up to my chest from nine to three o'clock. My mother said, "Don't pull a long face. You should love your sister and take care of her. She's sick." As soon as my mother turned her back, I spat into the soup and stirred it with my greasy finger. Then I brought it to Sea Cloud with a big smile.

The lipstick. My sister wouldn't have hidden it inside the table. She had her own steel box with a lock on it. If it had been hers, she would have shown it off long ago.

Then it must be one of Mother's old belongings. Somehow it had escaped the Red Guards' confiscations in the fall of 1967 and had been lying in the table since then. The dinner table was the only piece of furniture that survived the confiscation. All other pieces were taken away or burnt, together with books. It was an eight-fairy table made of *nanmu* wood, square, with heavily decorated legs and edges, and a drawer on each side. The drawers were no longer there. The vacated space was perfect for hiding my books. As long as I kept them in the center, no one could reach them. Only my thin arm could get through the six-inch-wide and two-and-a-half-inch-high drawer space.

Today was my lucky day. At fourteen and a half, I had my first lipstick.

There was some dust on top of the lipstick. I wiped it on the ball of my left thumb, the only spot on my hands not covered with frostbite scars. The bright red mark startled me and the slightly sticky lipstick on my skin sent an unspeakable sensation along my arm to my scalp. I trembled as I rubbed the lipstick mark on my hand. I was remembering a scene in my childhood.

I was five years old, a senior in the Navy Boarding Kindergarten. That night we were going to give a performance in the Navy Auditorium. My parents would come to the show. I hadn't seen them for two weeks. The

Lipstick

weekend before, my father's ship was on duty in the East China Sea, and my mother was too sick to take me home. I was too excited to nap, so I stole into the playroom. The teacher forgot to lock the closet where the costumes for the performance were stored. I picked up the general's hat with its shiny beads and two long striped whips sticking out on each side. Since I'd be singing behind the curtain with the chorus, the teacher said I didn't need to wear any costume. I tried on the hat. As I was looking for a mirror, I found a basket with some lovely round boxes and tubes in it. I opened one of them. Rouge. How beautiful the pink color was! The teacher said she'd put the makeup on for us after dinner. This must be it. I lifted the pad and rubbed it on my cheeks. I wished my parents could see me. I wished I had a mirror. Someone grabbed my pigtail and pulled me out of the closet. It was the teacher. She yelled and shook me like a madwoman. "You smelly beauty, you little bourgeoisie! Just like your mother." Her screaming was so loud and piercing that soon I couldn't hear anything, although her mouth was still opening and closing like a stranded fish on the beach. She dragged me into the room where twenty other children were napping and walked me around. I must have looked strange with that general's hat on and rouge all over my face. The children laughed and called in chorus: *smelly beauty, smelly beauty*.

I was taken out of the performance and delivered to my parents that night.

I rubbed some lipstick from the ball of my thumb onto the back of my hand, its scarlet red thinned and faded into pink, like the color that always glowed so splendidly on my sister's cheeks. Whenever I saw her, I'd pray with an aching heart: Oh God, please give me beauty like Sea Cloud! But I remained the ugliest in the family. My eyes were small and my eyelids were single-layered; my eyebrows short and thick; my nose bony and too big on my small face. Whenever we had a fight, my sister would call me "small-eyed devil." I was pathetically thin and pale. My mother sometimes ground her teeth in anger and told me that I deliberately made myself skinny so that I could make the neighbors pity me and accuse her of maltreatment.

I looked at my rosy hand, hoping for a miracle.

It was nine o'clock. I had three hours to perform this experiment, find my book, and cook before mother came back for lunch. Little by little I lifted the table from the floor. I was actually looking for a book that I'd hidden in the table the night before. I'd pushed it inside in a hurry and pretended to study English when I heard Mother's footsteps. Its title was *Deep Is the Night*, written in semi-ancient Chinese about a woman warrior disguised as a man who somehow remained pure among the lustful and

Lipstick

corrupt men. After the five-year ban, books were very hard to get. The bookstores had only Mao's books on their shelves. I'd secretly been trading books at school through a well-organized underground book network. Everyone obeyed its strict rules: Never betray the person you got the book from; never delay returning books; never re-lend without the owner's permission; pay back with three books if you lose a book. I owned some very good books: *Grimm's Fairy Tales*, *The Blossom of Bitter Herb*, and some Russian spy novels. I had torn off the covers and wrapped them with the red plastic covers for Mao's works. I traded for books about herbs, medicine, stars and constellations, and of course, I cherished novels. Once I got a porno book about monks and nuns digging tunnels between their temples to meet at night. Something called *Burning the Red Lotus Temple*. My sister caught me reading it in the public bathroom and threatened to tell on me unless I let her read it. I had no other choice but to give it to her. She wasn't as skillful as me in terms of keeping books away from my parents. Maybe she just thought they wouldn't punish her. My father caught her and hit her for the first time. He hit her so hard that he broke the handle of the broom. The book was thrown into the stove; my sister had to write three self-criticism papers and read them in the family training class my father organized. To my surprise, my sister, who had told on me and gotten me in trouble with my mother many times in the past, took the punishment alone with heroic silence. I really admired her for being such a good sport, and I willingly gave up three of my best books to my friend as a compensation for the lousy porno book.

I straightened the table, locked the door, and stood in front of the mirror on the wardrobe door in my parents' room. I looked at myself in despair. My features were still as bad as they were a month ago—white patches of fungus and strips of peeling skin on my dark face, the result of the strong liniment my father had applied to my face to cure the fungus. He had believed that my face was infected with athlete's foot. My jacket—passed down from my grandma to my mother, then from my mother to me—was splotched with dirt on its shredded sleeves, patched elbows, and front. I looked pathetic. I was pathetic. I'd graduated from high school two months ago, the youngest graduate, with straight As in every subject. Still I couldn't go to college. Universities were open only to peasants, workers, soldiers, and the students who had received reeducation for more than two years in the countryside, factories, or army. Nor could I get a job in town. Factories and other businesses had stopped hiring people since the Cultural Revolution started; they could hardly give the salaries to their old employees. No one worked, no one was allowed to work. Making revolution was more important than production. My only choice was to go to

Lipstick

the countryside to receive reeducation from the poor and middle-class peasants. I was willing to go. After two or three years, I might have a chance to be recommended to college. But Mother said I was too young. She wanted me to stay home to grow fat and learn some English. The truth was she wanted a free maid. Since graduating in February, I had taken over all the housework, cleaning, washing, shopping for daily food, and cooking. My mother didn't have to do anything except sit down for meals and take naps at noon. It was my mother who grew fat. I got thinner and paler.

The lipstick was the only bright color in the room. Everything else was gray or brown—my face, the walls, the furniture, the sheets. I held it up to my mouth. It brightened my face.

I applied it to my lips. The first touch was frightening. I practically jumped as the lipstick left the first red mark on my lips. It was like being kissed. I laughed at the idea. How much did I know about kissing? I'd never been kissed on the lips or anywhere else. My mother never touched me except when she knocked on my head with her knuckles. Not that I wanted her to touch me anyway. I put some lipstick on the ball of my thumb and rubbed it on my cheekbones. Then I turned to the mirror.

The figure in the mirror was grotesque, with her scarlet lips and uneven red rouge over white patches of fungus on dirty cheeks, the tube of lipstick between her chapped, stained fingers. The effect was like a rose in cow dung. I pushed the mirror away. There was no miracle. Was I destined to be a housemaid all my life?

I poured some hot water into my mother's basin and washed my face. No one must see any trace of lipstick on me. As I rubbed my cheeks, rolls of dirt came off. I hadn't been to the public bathhouse the whole winter. I took off my clothes and soaked my mother's washcloth in the water, breathing in the warm comforting steam. Little by little I cleaned myself, from my face to my legs, until the water in the basin turned black. Then I picked the coal out of my nails and the folds of my knuckles with my mother's toothbrush. Yesterday I made coal balls from coal powder for the stove. It was cheaper than buying them. Mother said we must be more economical since we had an idler at home, meaning me of course. I opened mother's bottle of vaseline on the dresser and applied some to my face and hands.

Finally I took hold of my braids. They were the only thing on which the neighbors ever complimented me. Thick and glowing with bluish darkness, they hung loosely down to my waist and swayed as I walked. It was almost a miracle that I still had them. Long braids, together with curly hair and colorful clothing, were considered the tails of capitalism at the

Lipstick

beginning of the Cultural Revolution. I still remembered how the Red
Guards patrolled the streets with scissors in hand and jumped at passersby
who were wearing tight pants or had long hair. After they cut open the
legs of the pants or cut off the braids, the victims had to recite Mao's
words and express their sincere gratitude to the Red Guards for saving
them from the horrors of capitalism. Although things had quieted down a
lot, my long hair could still bring me trouble. My parents also hated my
hair. My father thought it was dirty. Whenever he picked out a long hair
from the food I cooked, he'd stare at me and roar, "Cut it off tonight!" My
mother kept telling me my hair sucked all the nutrition out of my body.
"You look like a ghost with long untidy hair," she screamed with her beautiful voice. Slowly I unbraided my hair and brushed it with my mother's
hairbrush. It worked much better than my little plastic comb. My hair was
so thick even my mother's brush couldn't get through it.

When I turned back to the mirror, I saw a different person. She was
clean, had shapely lips, a slender neck, long legs, and breasts that were
firm like pigeons' bellies. I turned to see my back. Once my mother measured my hips to make me a pair of shorts. After the measuring, she
pinched me and said, "You have a big behind." My big behind looked fine
in the mirror. It traced a smooth curve below my waist. I raised my arms,
holding two handfuls of hair. It looked like the wings of some powerful
black bird in the sunshine. Tears filled my eyes. I wasn't going to be ugly
all my life.

I wrapped the lipstick in a piece of white paper and put it back into
the dinner table. No one else except me could reach into that two-and-a-
half-inch-high, six-inch-wide drawer. I had an hour to clean my mother's
towel, hairbrush, and toothbrush, and to cook lunch. Today's menu was
fish, pickles with sliced pork, sprouts, and seaweed soup.

Responding to the Selection

Questions to Discuss

1. How did you respond to the story's ending?

2. Do you consider the narrator to be a rebellious child? Why or why not?

3. A **symbol** is a person, place, or thing that stands for something in addition to itself. What does the tube of lipstick symbolize for those who believe in the Cultural Revolution? What does it symbolize for the narrator?

4. The narrator thinks that the lipstick makes her look grotesque, yet she carefully hides it at the end of the story. In your opinion, why does she continue to value the lipstick?

5. The narrator says, "I looked at my rosy hand, hoping for a miracle." What do you think she was hoping for? Explain your answer.

Activities

Interpreting the Story

1. Do you think that the narrator is troubled more by the political turmoil of the Cultural Revolution or by her poor relations with family members? Write a paragraph in response to this question, supporting your position with evidence from the story.

Writing a Journal Entry

2. Think of a time when you discovered something new about yourself. Write a journal entry about this discovery.

Giving a Presentation

3. Research the Cultural Revolution in China. Prepare a multimedia presentation for the class. Include readings, photos and illustrations, music, videotapes, and other media that will explain and describe this period.

Before You Read

The Elephants Are in the Yard

Indran Amirthanayagam
Born 1960

*"Stay away from delusion.
Welcome illusion."*

About Amirthanayagam

Indran Amirthanayagam is a Tamil from Sri Lanka. When he was eight years old, his family moved to London; later they settled in the United States. He says that his poetry was inspired by his longing for Sri Lanka and his concerns about the country's civil war: "When I began to write poetry I found a solace for something in me. I found in poetry a salvation."

Amirthanayagam published his first book, *The Elephants of Reckoning,* in 1993. "Elephants," he explains, "are a symbol for many things in my book, including the best of ourselves–the best of human potential. That, too, is the role of the poet: to enter the hearts and minds of the people and ask them to realize their own potentials." Shortly after the book came out, Amirthanayagam entered the U.S. Foreign Service. He feels that it is important for poets to be involved in politics: "I like the freedoms I've been enjoying in America and recognize that these do come at a cost."

Sri Lanka

Sri Lanka is an island located in the Indian Ocean, near the southern tip of India. The country (formerly known as Ceylon) achieved independence from Great Britain in 1948. Since then, there has been increasing friction between the mostly Buddhist, majority Sinhalese and the mostly Hindu, minority Tamils. Throughout much of the 1980s, Sri Lanka was in a state of civil war. Ethnic conflict continues to plague the country.

The Elephants Are in the Yard

— Indran Amirthanayagam

I see the elephants in the yard
Pappa, the white snake too
peering out of the neem tree's trunk
hissing poisons

5   Pappa, I see the wild boar
in the thicket, the branches
burning with his smell, Pappa
bring out your gun,

I want to eat the boar's meat
10   and stare at his head
on my wall, Pappa I see
the elephants in the yard

The partridge and jungle fowl
you shot from the air and bush
15   to conquer alone
the harvest of the jungle

You were always a sport
took on bird in flight, boar
in fierce charge, your life or his
20   I see the elephants in the yard

The Elephants Are in the Yard

and poachers cock-eyed
devouring their tusks in dreams
building grand compounds
massing riches in stainless steel

25 Pappa, the sport is finished
the elephants are in the yard
and there is no forest
and there are lots of knives

and forks and tractors
30 and babies to feed
and guerrillas hiding
in the shade of neem and mango

right there beyond the verandah,
in the center of the garden
35 where your dowry will build
your last daughter's house

the elephants spread their heavy bodies
tired from the journey up country
and down country, the long herding
40 to some safe peaceful house.

Responding to the Selection

Questions for Discussion

1. How do you interpret the last stanza of the poem?

2. A **symbol** is a person, place, or thing that stands for something in addition to itself. Amirthanayagam has said that he uses elephants to symbolize many things in his poems. What do you think they symbolize in "The Elephants Are in the Yard"?

3. What do stanzas 6–8 suggest about the current state of the speaker's homeland?

4. Describe the speaker's attitude toward his father. Is the attitude consistent throughout the poem? Explain.

5. Do you feel this poem expresses hope? What elements in the poem lead you to your conclusion?

Activities

Writing a Paragraph

1. What did this poem remind you about in your own childhood? Write a paragraph in response to this question.

Discussing Human Conflict

2. One theme in this poem is the destruction of natural habitats to make way for human civilization. Arrange a class discussion on this worldwide conflict. Focus on how the needs of animals and plants for habitat and the demands of people for farming and living areas can be balanced.

Illustrating the Poem

3. This poem contains many striking images. Choose an art medium (such as watercolors, print, sculpture, or computerized graphics) and create a work that represents one of the images from the poem.

Before You Read

Seventeen Syllables

Hisaye Yamamoto
Born 1921

"I write when something sticks in my craw."

About Yamamoto

Hisaye Yamamoto was born in Redondo Beach, California. Her parents, immigrant farmers, had to move frequently because state law at that time prohibited noncitizens from owning property. Despite her unsettled existence, she managed to attend college, studying French, Spanish, German, and Latin. Then World War II broke out. Like thousands of other Japanese Americans, Yamamoto was sent with her family to an internment camp. They remained at the camp, near Poston, Arizona, for three years.

Yamamoto started writing stories at age fourteen. While in the internment camp, she wrote fiction and also reported for the camp newspaper. She became one of the first Asian American writers to gain national attention following World War II. Her stories are often reprinted in anthologies.

Getting Published

Like the mother in "Seventeen Syllables," Hisaye Yamamoto first published her work in Japanese American newspapers. Long before she received acceptance letters from prestigious literary journals, these newspapers nurtured her talent: "On weekends they would have a feature page, where people would send in all kinds of things. They'd print anything, so that's how I started, and I haven't stopped yet! I'm still writing for those newspapers."

Seventeen Syllables

— *Hisaye Yamamoto*

The first Rosie knew that her mother had taken to writing poems was one evening when she finished one and read it aloud for her daughter's approval. It was about cats, and Rosie pretended to understand it thoroughly and appreciate it no end, partly because she hesitated to disillusion her mother about the quantity and quality of Japanese she had learned in all the years now that she had been going to Japanese school every Saturday (and Wednesday, too, in the summer). Even so, her mother must have been skeptical about the depth of Rosie's understanding, because she explained afterwards about the kind of poem she was trying to write.

See, Rosie, she said, it was a *haiku*, a poem in which she must pack all her meaning into seventeen syllables only, which were divided into three lines of five, seven, and five syllables. In the one she had just read, she had tried to capture the charm of a kitten, as well as comment on the superstition that owning a cat of three colors meant good luck.

"Yes, yes, I understand. How utterly lovely," Rosie said, and her mother, either satisfied or seeing through the deception and resigned, went back to composing.

The truth was that Rosie was lazy; English lay ready on the tongue but Japanese had to be searched for and examined, and even then put forth tentatively (probably to meet with laughter). It was so much easier to say yes, yes, even when one meant no, no. Besides, this was what was in her mind to say: I was looking through one of your magazines from Japan last night, Mother, and towards the back I found some *haiku* in English that delighted me. There was one that made me giggle off and on until I fell asleep—

> It is morning, and lo!
> I lie awake, comme il faut,
> sighing for some dough.

Now, how to reach her mother, how to communicate the melancholy song? Rosie knew formal Japanese by fits and starts, her mother had even less English, no French. It was much more possible to say yes, yes.

Seventeen Syllables

It developed that her mother was writing the *haiku* for a daily newspaper, the *Mainichi Shimbun*, that was published in San Francisco. Los Angeles, to be sure, was closer to the farming community in which the Hayashi family lived and several Japanese vernaculars were printed there, but Rosie's parents said they preferred the tone of the northern paper. Once a week, the *Mainichi* would have a section devoted to *haiku*, and her mother became an extravagant contributor, taking for herself the blossoming pen name, Ume Hanazono.

So Rosie and her father lived for awhile with two women, her mother and Ume Hanazono. Her mother (Tome Hayashi by name) kept house, cooked, washed, and, along with her husband and the Carrascos, the Mexican family hired for the harvest, did her ample share of picking tomatoes out in the sweltering fields and boxing them in tidy strata in the cool packing shed. Ume Hanazono, who came to life after the dinner dishes were done, was an earnest, muttering stranger who often neglected speaking when spoken to and stayed busy at the parlor table as late as midnight scribbling with pencil on scratch paper or carefully copying characters on good paper with her fat, pale green Parker.

The new interest had some repercussions on the household routine. Before, Rosie had been accustomed to her parents and herself taking their hot baths early and going to bed almost immediately afterwards, unless her parents challenged each other to a game of flower cards or unless company dropped in. Now if her father wanted to play cards, he had to resort to solitaire (at which he always cheated fearlessly), and if a group of friends came over, it was bound to contain someone who was also writing *haiku*, and the small assemblage would be split in two, her father entertaining the non-literary members and her mother comparing ecstatic notes with the visiting poet.

If they went out, it was more of the same thing. But Ume Hanazono's life span, even for a poet's, was very brief—perhaps three months at most.

One night they went over to see the Hayano family in the neighboring town to the west, an adventure both painful and attractive to Rosie. It was attractive because there were four Hayano girls, all lovely and each one named after a season of the year (Haru, Natsu, Aki, Fuyu), painful because something had been wrong with Mrs. Hayano ever since the birth of her first child. Rosie would sometimes watch Mrs. Hayano, reputed to have been the belle of her native village, making her way about a room, stooped, slowly shuffling, violently trembling (*always* trembling), and she would be reminded that this woman, in this same condition, had carried and given issue to three babies. She would look wonderingly at Mr. Hayano, handsome, tall, and strong, and she would look at her four pretty friends. But it was not a matter she could come to any decision about.

On this visit, however, Mrs. Hayano sat all evening in the rocker, as motionless and unobtrusive as it was possible for her to be, and Rosie found the greater part of the evening practically anaesthetic. Too, Rosie spent most of it in the girls' room, because Haru, the garrulous one, said almost as soon as the bows and other greetings were over, "Oh, you must see my new coat!"

It was a pale plaid of gray, sand, and blue, with an enormous collar, and Rosie, seeing nothing special in it, said, "Gee, how nice."

"Nice?" said Haru, indignantly. "Is that all you can say about it? It's gorgeous! And so cheap, too. Only seventeen-ninety-eight, because it was a sale. The saleslady said it was twenty-five dollars regular."

"Gee," said Rosie. Natsu, who never said much and when she said anything said it shyly, fingered the coat covetously and Haru pulled it away.

"Mine," she said, putting it on. She minced in the aisle between the two large beds and smiled happily. "Let's see how your mother likes it."

She broke into the front room and the adult conversation and went to stand in front of Rosie's mother, while the rest watched from the door. Rosie's mother was properly envious. "May I inherit it when you're through with it?"

Haru, pleased, giggled and said yes, she could, but Natsu reminded gravely from the door, "You promised me, Haru."

Everyone laughed but Natsu, who shamefacedly retreated into the bedroom. Haru came in laughing, taking off the coat. "We were only kidding, Natsu," she said. "Here, you try it on now."

After Natsu buttoned herself into the coat, inspected herself solemnly in the bureau mirror, and reluctantly shed it, Rosie, Aki, and Fuyu got their turns, and Fuyu, who was eight, drowned in it while her sisters and Rosie doubled up in amusement. They all went into the front room later, because Haru's mother quaveringly called to her to fix the tea and rice cakes and open a can of sliced peaches for everybody. Rosie noticed that her mother and Mr. Hayano were talking together at the little table—they were discussing a *haiku* that Mr. Hayano was planning to send to the *Mainichi*, while her father was sitting at one end of the sofa looking through a copy of *Life*, the new picture magazine. Occasionally, her father would comment on a photograph, holding it toward Mrs. Hayano and speaking to her as he always did—loudly, as though he thought someone such as she must surely be at least a trifle deaf also.

The five girls had their refreshments at the kitchen table, and it was while Rosie was showing the sisters her trick of swallowing peach slices without chewing (she chased each slippery crescent down with a swig of tea) that her father brought his empty teacup and untouched saucer to the sink and said, "Come on, Rosie, we're going home now."

"Already?" asked Rosie.

"Work tomorrow," he said.

He sounded irritated, and Rosie, puzzled, gulped one last yellow slice and stood up to go, while the sisters began protesting, as was their wont.

"We have to get up at five-thirty," he told them, going into the front room quickly, so that they did not have their usual chance to hang onto his hands and plead for an extension of time.

Rosie, following, saw that her mother and Mr. Hayano were sipping tea and still talking together, while Mrs. Hayano concentrated, quivering, on raising the handleless Japanese cup to her lips with both her hands and lowering it back to her lap. Her father, saying nothing, went out the door, onto the bright porch, and down the steps. Her mother looked up and asked, "Where is he going?"

"Where is he going?" Rosie said. "He said we were going home now."

"Going home?" Her mother looked with embarrassment at Mr. Hayano and his absorbed wife and then forced a smile. "He must be tired," she said.

Haru was not giving up yet. "May Rosie stay overnight?" she asked, and Natsu, Aki, and Fuyu came to reinforce their sister's plea by helping her make a circle around Rosie's mother. Rosie, for once having no desire to stay, was relieved when her mother, apologizing to the perturbed Mr. and Mrs. Hayano for her father's abruptness at the same time, managed to shake her head no at the quartet, kindly but adamant, so that they broke their circle and let her go.

Rosie's father looked ahead into the windshield as the two joined him. "I'm sorry," her mother said. "You must be tired." Her father, stepping on the starter, said nothing. "You know how I get when it's *haiku*," she continued, "I forget what time it is." He only grunted.

As they rode homeward silently, Rosie, sitting between, felt a rush of hate for both—for her mother for begging, for her father for denying her mother. I wish this old Ford would crash, right now, she thought, then immediately, no, no, I wish my father would laugh, but it was too late: already the vision had passed through her mind of the green pick-up crumpled in the dark against one of the mighty eucalyptus trees they were just riding past, of the three contorted, bleeding bodies, one of them hers.

Rosie ran between two patches of tomatoes, her heart working more rambunctiously than she had ever known it to. How lucky it was that Aunt Taka and Uncle Gimpachi had come tonight, though, how very lucky. Otherwise she might not have really kept her half-promise to meet

Seventeen Syllables

Jesus Carrasco. Jesus was going to be a senior in September at the same school she went to, and his parents were the ones helping with the tomatoes this year. She and Jesus, who hardly remembered seeing each other at Cleveland High where there were so many other people and two whole grades between them, had become great friends this summer—he always had a joke for her when he periodically drove the loaded pick-up up from the fields to the shed where she was usually sorting while her mother and father did the packing, and they laughed a great deal together over infinitesimal repartee during the afternoon break for chilled watermelon or ice cream in the shade of the shed.

What she enjoyed most was racing him to see which could finish picking a double row first. He, who could work faster, would tease her by slowing down until she thought she would surely pass him this time, then speeding up furiously to leave her several sprawling vines behind. Once he had made her screech hideously by crossing over, while her back was turned, to place atop the tomatoes in her green-stained bucket a truly monstrous, pale green worm (it had looked more like an infant snake). And it was when they had finished a contest this morning, after she had pantingly pointed a green finger at the immature tomatoes evident in the lugs at the end of his row and he had returned the accusation (with justice), that he had startlingly brought up the matter of their possibly meeting outside the range of both their parents' dubious eyes.

"What for?" she had asked.

"I've got a secret I want to tell you," he said.

"Tell me now," she demanded.

"It won't be ready till tonight," he said.

She laughed. "Tell me tomorrow then."

"It'll be gone tomorrow," he threatened.

"Well, for seven hakes, what is it?" she had asked, more than twice, and when he had suggested that the packing shed would be an appropriate place to find out, she had cautiously answered maybe. She had not been certain she was going to keep the appointment until the arrival of mother's sister and her husband. Their coming seemed a sort of signal of permission, of grace, and she had definitely made up her mind to lie and leave as she was bowing them welcome.

So as soon as everyone appeared settled back for the evening, she announced loudly that she was going to the privy outside, "I'm going to the *benjo!*" and slipped out the door. And now that she was actually on her way, her heart pumped in such an undisciplined way that she could hear it with her ears. It's because I'm running, she told herself, slowing to a walk. The shed was up ahead, one more patch away, in the middle of the fields. Its bulk, looming in the dimness, took on a sinisterness that was funny when Rosie reminded herself that it was only a wooden frame with a canvas roof and three canvas walls that made a slapping noise on breezy days.

Jesus was sitting on the narrow plank that was the sorting platform and she went around to the other side and jumped backwards to seat herself on the rim of a packing stand. "Well, tell me," she said without greeting, thinking her voice sounded reassuringly familiar.

"I saw you coming out the door," Jesus said. "I heard you running part of the way, too."

"Uh-huh," Rosie said. "Now tell me the secret."

"I was afraid you wouldn't come," he said.

Rosie delved around on the chicken-wire bottom of the stall for number two tomatoes, ripe, which she was sitting beside, and came up with a left-over that felt edible. She bit into it and began sucking out the pulp and seeds. "I'm here," she pointed out.

"Rosie, are you sorry you came?"

"Sorry? What for?" she said. "You said you were going to tell me something."

"I will, I will," Jesus said, but his voice contained disappointment, and Rosie fleetingly felt the older of the two, realizing a brand-new power which vanished without category under her recognition.

"I have to go back in a minute," she said. "My aunt and uncle are here from Wintersburg. I told them I was going to the privy."

Jesus laughed. "You funny thing," he said. "You slay me!"

"Just because you have a bathroom *inside,*" Rosie said. "Come on, tell me."

Chuckling, Jesus came around to lean on the stand facing her. They still could not see each other very clearly, but Rosie noticed that Jesus became very sober again as he took the hollow tomato from her hand and dropped it back into the stall. When he took hold of her empty hand, she could find no words to protest; her vocabulary had become distressingly constricted and she thought desperately that all that remained intact now was yes and no and oh, and even these few sounds would not easily out. Thus, kissed by Jesus, Rosie fell for the first time entirely victim to a helplessness delectable beyond speech. But the terrible, beautiful sensation lasted no more than a second, and the reality of Jesus' lips and tongue and teeth and hands made her pull away with such strength that she nearly tumbled.

Rosie stopped running as she approached the lights from the windows of home. How long since she had left? She could not guess, but gasping yet, she went to the privy in back and locked herself in. Her own breathing deafened her in the dark, close space, and she sat and waited until she could hear at last the nightly calling of the frogs and crickets. Even then, all she could think to say was oh, my, and the pressure of Jesus' face against her face would not leave.

No one had missed her in the parlor, however, and Rosie walked in and through quickly, announcing that she was next going to take a bath. "Your father's in the bathhouse," her mother said, and Rosie, in her room, recalled that she had not seen him when she entered. There had been only Aunt Taka and Uncle Gimpachi with her mother at the table, drinking tea. She got her robe and straw sandals and crossed the parlor again to go outside. Her mother was telling them about the *haiku* competition in the *Mainichi* and the poem she had entered.

Rosie met her father coming out of the bathhouse. "Are you through, Father?" she asked. "I was going to ask you to scrub my back."

"Scrub your own back," he said shortly, going toward the main house.

"What have I done now?" she yelled after him. She suddenly felt like doing a lot of yelling. But he did not answer, and she went into the bathhouse. Turning on the dangling light, she removed her denims and T-shirt and threw them in the big carton for dirty clothes standing next to the washing machine. Her other things she took with her into the bath compartment to wash after her bath. After she had scooped a basin of hot water from the square wooden tub, she sat on the gray cement of the floor and soaped herself at exaggerated leisure, singing "Red Sails in the Sunset" at the top of her voice and using da-da-da where she suspected her words. Then, standing up, still singing, for she was possessed by the notion that any attempt now to analyze would result in spoilage and she believed that the larger her volume the less she would be able to hear herself think, she obtained more hot water and poured it on until she was free of lather. Only then did she allow herself to step into the steaming vat, one leg first, then the remainder of her body inch by inch until the water no longer stung and she could move around at will.

She took a long time soaking, afterwards remembering to go around outside to stoke the embers of the tin-lined fireplace beneath the tub and to throw on a few more sticks so that the water might keep its heat for her mother, and when she finally returned to the parlor, she found her mother still talking *haiku* with her aunt and uncle, the three of them on another round of tea. Her father was nowhere in sight.

At Japanese school the next day (Wednesday, it was), Rosie was grave and giddy by turns. Preoccupied at her desk in the row for students on Book Eight, she made up for it at recess by performing wild mimicry for the benefit of her friend Chizuko. She held her nose and whined a witticism or two in what she considered was the manner of Fred Allen; she assumed intoxication and a British accent to go over the climax of the Rudy Vallee recording of the pub conversation about William Ewart Gladstone; she was the child Shirley Temple piping, "On the Good Ship Lollipop"; she was the gentleman soprano of the Four Inkspots trilling, "If I Didn't Care." And she felt reasonably satisfied when Chizuko wept and gasped, "Oh, Rosie, you ought to be in the movies!"

Her father came after her at noon, bringing her sandwiches of minced ham and two nectarines to eat while she rode, so that she could pitch right into the sorting when they got home. The lugs were piling up, he said, and the ripe tomatoes in them would probably have to be taken to the cannery tomorrow if they were not ready for the produce haulers tonight. "This heat's not doing them any good. And we've got no time for a break today."

It *was* hot, probably the hottest day of the year, and Rosie's blouse stuck damply to her back even under the protection of the canvas. But she worked as efficiently as a flawless machine and kept the stalls heaped, with one part of her mind listening in to the parental murmuring about the heat and the tomatoes and with another part planning the exact words she would say to Jesus when he drove up with the first load of the afternoon. But when at last she saw that the pick-up was coming, her hands went berserk and the tomatoes started falling in the wrong stalls, and her father said, "Hey, hey! Rosie, watch what you're doing!"

"Well, I have to go to the *benjo*," she said, hiding panic.

"Go in the weeds over there," he said, only half-joking.

"Oh, Father!" she protested.

"Oh, go on home," her mother said. "We'll make out for awhile."

In the privy Rosie peered through a knothole toward the fields, watching as much as she could of Jesus. Happily she thought she saw him look in the direction of the house from time to time before he finished unloading and went back toward the patch where his mother and father worked. As she was heading for the shed, a very presentable black car purred up the dirt driveway to the house and its driver motioned to her. Was this the Hayashi home, he wanted to know. She nodded. Was she a Hayashi? Yes, she said, thinking that he was a good-looking man. He got out of the car with a huge, flat package and she saw that he warmly wore a business suit. "I have something here for your mother then," he said, in a more elegant Japanese than she was used to.

She told him where her mother was and he came along with her, patting his face with an immaculate white handkerchief and saying something about the coolness of San Francisco. To her surprised mother and father, he bowed and introduced himself as, among other things, the *haiku* editor of the *Mainichi Shimbun*, saying that since he had been coming as far as Los Angeles anyway, he had decided to bring her the first prize she had won in the recent contest.

"First prize?" her mother echoed, believing and not believing, pleased and overwhelmed. Handed the package with a bow, she bobbed her head up and down numerous times to express her utter gratitude.

"It is nothing much," he added, "but I hope it will serve as a token of our great appreciation for your contributions and our great admiration of your considerable talent."

"I am not worthy," she said, falling easily into his style. "It is I who should make some sign of my humble thanks for being permitted to contribute."

"No, no, to the contrary," he said, bowing again.

But Rosie's mother insisted, and then saying that she knew she was being unorthodox, she asked if she might open the package because her curiosity was so great. Certainly she might. In fact, he would like her reaction to it, for personally, it was one of his favorite *Hiroshiges*.

Rosie thought it was a pleasant picture, which looked to have been sketched with delicate quickness. There were pink clouds, containing some graceful calligraphy, and a sea that was a pale blue except at the edges, containing four sampans with indications of people in them. Pines edged the water and on the far-off beach there was a cluster of thatched huts towered over by pine-dotted mountains of gray and blue. The frame was scalloped and gilt.

After Rosie's mother pronounced it without peer and somewhat prodded her father into nodding agreement, she said Mr. Kuroda must at least have a cup of tea after coming all this way, and although Mr. Kuroda did not want to impose, he soon agreed that a cup of tea would be refreshing and went along with her to the house, carrying the picture for her.

"Ha, your mother's crazy!" Rosie's father said, and Rosie laughed uneasily as she resumed judgment on the tomatoes. She had emptied six lugs when he broke into an imaginary conversation with Jesus to tell her to go and remind her mother of the tomatoes, and she went slowly.

Mr. Kuroda was in his shirtsleeves expounding some *haiku* theory as he munched a rice cake, and her mother was rapt. Abashed in the great man's presence, Rosie stood next to her mother's chair until her mother looked up inquiringly, and then she started to whisper the message, but her mother pushed her gently away and reproached, "You are not being very polite to our guest."

"Father says the tomatoes . . ." Rosie said aloud, smiling foolishly.

"Tell him I shall only be a minute," her mother said, speaking the language of Mr. Kuroda.

Seventeen Syllables

When Rosie carried the reply to her father, he did not seem to hear and she said again, "Mother says she'll be back in a minute."

"All right, all right," he nodded, and they worked again in silence. But suddenly, her father uttered an incredible noise, exactly like the cork of a bottle popping, and the next Rosie knew, he was stalking angrily toward the house, almost running in fact, and she chased after him crying, "Father! Father! What are you going to do?"

He stopped long enough to order her back to the shed. "Never mind!" he shouted. "Get on with the sorting!"

And from the place in the fields where she stood, frightened and vacillating, Rosie saw her father enter the house. Soon Mr. Kuroda came out alone, putting on his coat. Mr. Kuroda got into his car and backed out down the driveway onto the highway. Next her father emerged, also alone, something in his arms (it was the picture, she realized), and, going over to the bathhouse woodpile, he threw the picture on the ground and picked up the axe. Smashing the picture, glass and all (she heard the explosion faintly), he reached over for the kerosene that was used to encourage the bath fire and poured it over the wreckage. I am dreaming, Rosie said to herself, I am dreaming, but her father, having made sure that his act of cremation was irrevocable, was even then returning to the fields.

Rosie ran past him and toward the house. What had become of her mother? She burst into the parlor and found her mother at the back window watching the dying fire. They watched together until there remained only a feeble smoke under the blazing sun. Her mother was very calm.

"Do you know why I married your father?" she said without turning.

"No," said Rosie. It was the most frightening question she had ever been called upon to answer. Don't tell me now, she wanted to say, tell me tomorrow, tell me next week, don't tell me today. But she knew she would be told now, that the telling would combine with the other violence of the hot afternoon to level her life, her world to the very ground.

It was like a story out of the magazines illustrated in sepia, which she had consumed so greedily for a period until the information had somehow reached her that those wretchedly unhappy autobiographies, offered to her as the testimonials of living men and women, were largely inventions: Her mother, at nineteen, had come to America and married her father as an alternative to suicide.

At eighteen she had been in love with the first son of one of the well-to-do families in her village. The two had met whenever and wherever they could, secretly, because it would not have done for his family to see him favor her—her father had no money; he was a drunkard and a gambler besides. She had learned she was with child; an excellent match had already been arranged for her lover. Despised by her family, she had given premature birth to a stillborn son, who would be seventeen now. Her family did not turn her out, but she could no longer project herself in any direction without refreshing in them the memory of her indiscretion. She wrote to Aunt Taka, her favorite sister in America, threatening to kill herself if Aunt Taka would not send for her. Aunt Taka hastily arranged a marriage with a young man of whom she knew, but lately arrived from Japan, a young man of simple mind, it was said, but of kindly heart. The young man was never told why his unseen betrothed was so eager to hasten the day of meeting.

The story was told perfectly, with neither groping for words nor untoward passion. It was as though her mother had memorized it by heart, reciting it to herself so many times over that its nagging vileness had long since gone.

"I had a brother then?" Rosie asked, for this was what seemed to matter now; she would think about the other later, she assured herself, pushing back the illumination which threatened all that darkness that had hitherto been merely mysterious or even glamorous. "A half-brother?"

"Yes."

"I would have liked a brother," she said.

Suddenly, her mother knelt on the floor and took her by the wrists. "Rosie," she said urgently, "Promise me you will never marry!" Shocked more by the request than the revelation, Rosie stared at her mother's face. Jesus, Jesus, she called silently, not certain whether she was invoking the help of the son of the Carrascos or of God, until there returned sweetly the memory of Jesus' hand, how it had touched her and where. Still her mother waited for an answer, holding her wrists so tightly that her hands were going numb. She tried to pull free. Promise, her mother whispered fiercely, promise. Yes, yes, I promise, Rosie said. But for an instant she turned away, and her mother, hearing the familiar glib agreement, released her. Oh, you, you, you, her eyes and twisted mouth said, you fool. Rosie, covering her face, began at last to cry, and the embrace and consoling hand came much later than she expected.

Responding to the Selection

Questions for Discussion

1. After reading this story, which character did you feel closest to? Why?

2. How would you characterize the relationship between Rosie and her mother?

3. **Foreshadowing** is the use of clues by the author to prepare readers for events that will happen in a story. How is Mr. Hayashi's destructive rage at the end foreshadowed earlier in the story?

4. Describe Rosie's feelings toward Jesus before and after he kisses her. What impact does Jesus have on Rosie's dealings with her parents?

5. Why does Mrs. Hayashi become upset with Rosie at the end of the story? Do you feel that she is being fair to her daughter? Why or why not?

Activities

Writing a Review

1. Write a brief review of "Seventeen Syllables." In your review, discuss at least one of the following literary elements: characterization, setting, theme, or plot.

Writing Haiku

2. Write a haiku that describes a character in the story or addresses one of its themes.

Presenting a Multimedia Report

3. Research the internment of Japanese Americans during World War II. Present a multimedia report to the class, using text; visuals such as photos, videos, maps, and charts; music; and other media.

Before You Read

Easter: Wahiawa, 1959

Cathy Song
Born 1955

"Young poets and writers should remember that ethnic background doesn't make your voice any less American."

About Song

Cathy Song was born and raised in Hawaii. Her father used to buy surplus army targets to supply her with paper because she was such a prolific writer. (Many of her early manuscripts have a bull's-eye on the back of the sheets.) Song earned a master's degree in creative writing from Boston University in 1981. The next year she won the prestigious Yale Series of Younger Poets Award for her first book, *Picture Bride*. The title poem refers to arranged marriages of Asian immigrant men who found brides from their homelands by looking at photos.

Song often writes about her experiences as a mother and about her Korean and Chinese heritage. "Being a woman and an Asian American has only helped my work as an artist," Song says. "You have to be on the periphery, on the outside looking in, marginalized in some way, to gain a different perspective."

Harvesting Sugarcane

Cathy Song spent part of her childhood in Wahiawa, a former plantation town on the island of Oahu. Her paternal grandfather had moved there from Korea to work in the sugarcane fields. His wife had been a picture bride who came to Hawaii to marry a stranger thirteen years older than her. In "Easter: Wahiawa, 1959," Song refers to the difficult work of harvesting sugarcane, which has sharp leaves and grows to a height of twelve feet. Many of the plantation laborers in Hawaii were Chinese, Japanese, Filipino, and Korean. They would spend at least ten hours each day in the fields, breathing in red dust and enduring the discomfort of cuts, blisters, and aching backs.

Easter: Wahiawa, 1959

— *Cathy Song*

1

The rain stopped for one afternoon.
Father brought out
his movie camera and for a few hours
we were all together
5   under a thin film
that separated the rain showers
from that part of the earth
like a hammock
held loosely by clothespins.

10   Grandmother took the opportunity
to hang the laundry
and Mother and my aunts
filed out of the house
in pedal pushers and poodle cuts,
15   carrying the blue washed eggs.

Grandfather kept the children
penned in on the porch,
clucking at us in his broken English
whenever we tried to peek
20   around him. There were bread crumbs
stuck to his blue gray whiskers.

I looked from him to the sky,
a membrane of egg whites
straining under the weight

25   of the storm that threatened
to break.

We burst loose from Grandfather
when the mothers returned
from planting the eggs
30   around the soggy yard.
He followed us,
walking with stiff but sturdy legs.
We dashed and disappeared
into bushes,
35   searching for the treasures;
the hard-boiled eggs
which Grandmother had been simmering
in vinegar and blue color all morning.

2

When Grandfather was a young boy
40   in Korea,
it was a long walk
to the riverbank,
where, if he were lucky,
a quail egg or two
45   would gleam from the mud
like gigantic pearls.
He could never eat enough
of them.

It was another long walk
50   through the sugarcane fields
of Hawaii,
where he worked for eighteen years,
cutting the sweet stalks
with a machete. His right arm

Easter: Wahiawa, 1959

55   grew disproportionately large
        to the rest of his body.
        He could hold three
        grandchildren in that arm.

        I want to think
60   that each stalk that fell
        brought him closer
        to a clearing,
        to that palpable field
        where from the porch
65   to the gardenia hedge
        that day he was enclosed
        by his grandchildren,
        scrambling around him,
        for whom he could at last buy
70   cratefuls of oranges,
        basketfuls of sky blue eggs.

        I found three that afternoon.
        By evening, it was raining hard.
        Grandfather and I skipped supper.
75   Instead, we sat on the porch
        and I ate what he peeled
        and cleaned for me.
        The scattering of the delicate
        marine-colored shells across his lap
80   was something like what the ocean gives
        the beach after a rain.

Responding to the Selection

Questions for Discussion

1. What do the last four lines of the poem suggest to you about this encounter between the speaker and her grandfather?

2. Why might Song have chosen to repeat images of eggs and the grandfather's walking?

3. What is the poem's **theme,** or central message?

4. Compare the speaker's current feelings and thoughts about her grandfather with her feelings and thoughts in 1959, when the Easter egg hunt took place.

5. A **symbol** is a person, place, or thing that stands for something in addition to itself. What are some reasons an egg is an appropriate symbol in this poem?

Activities

Writing an Essay

1. Write an essay about someone whose sacrifices have increased your opportunities.

Illustrating the Poem

2. Draw an illustration to accompany "Easter: Wahiawa, 1959." You may illustrate a scene described in the poem or create an abstract drawing inspired by its theme or images.

Discussing Traditions

3. Describe a family tradition or ritual that is meaningful to you. Explain to a partner why this tradition is important to you.

Focus on . . .
Asian Americans in Hawaii

Hawaii's first inhabitants were Polynesians who had journeyed to the islands by canoe more than fifteen hundred years ago. In the mid-nineteenth century, these original inhabitants began to lose control of the islands to sugar-plantation owners from the United States. Unable to hire enough native Hawaiians, the owners imported Chinese laborers. After the first big wave of Chinese immigrants, the owners brought immigrants from Japan and the Philippines. Although the policy of importing Asian workers from a variety of countries created a highly diverse society, the policy had not been motivated by a spirit of tolerance. The plantation owners had believed that they could keep workers in line by pitting one ethnic group against another.

The workers spent about ten hours in the fields, six days a week. They weren't allowed to talk to each other or even to stretch their backs. At the end of the day, they returned to camps that were often crowded and filthy. However, Asian immigrants in Hawaii had some advantages over Asian immigrants on the mainland United States. Because the plantation owners had wanted a stable work force, they had encouraged immigrants to bring over wives and children. Asians in Hawaii did not have to compete against large groups of European Americans for jobs. Some work camps were integrated, allowing immigrants from various nations to exchange foods and learn more about each other. In time the Asians developed a common language called "pidgin English," which helped create a new Hawaiian identity.

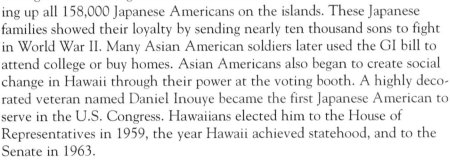

When Japan bombed Pearl Harbor, Hawaiian officials and business leaders discouraged the federal government from rounding up all 158,000 Japanese Americans on the islands. These Japanese families showed their loyalty by sending nearly ten thousand sons to fight in World War II. Many Asian American soldiers later used the GI bill to attend college or buy homes. Asian Americans also began to create social change in Hawaii through their power at the voting booth. A highly decorated veteran named Daniel Inouye became the first Japanese American to serve in the U.S. Congress. Hawaiians elected him to the House of Representatives in 1959, the year Hawaii achieved statehood, and to the Senate in 1963.

Over 60 percent of Hawaii's residents are Asian American. Once relegated to the bottom of society, Asian Americans now hold prominent positions in business, government, science, and education. Most groups in the state have benefited from the rapid growth of tourism and other industries. However, most native Hawaiians of Polynesian descent were left behind by the economic boom. In recent decades, they have formed movements to promote their rights and to preserve their ancient culture.

Linking to . . .
• Think about this information about Hawaii as you read the selections in this theme.

Before You Read

The Water Faucet Vision

Gish Jen
Born 1955

> *"I have sometimes struggled to make my work less funny. My natural facility is to find the laugh."*

About Jen

Lillian Jen began calling herself "Gish" (after the American silent-screen actress Lillian Gish) in high school. Taking on a new name was "part of becoming a writer . . . not becoming the person I was supposed to be." Yet Jen was reluctant to pursue her dream of being a writer. Her parents had experienced turmoil as Chinese immigrants, and they wanted her to have a financially and psychologically secure life. Jen tried out various career paths, considering both medicine and business, before she realized that writing was her destiny.

Much of Jen's fiction is set in Scarsdale, New York, an affluent suburb of New York City where she grew up. She feels her work has been strongly influenced by Jewish writers, in part because of Scarsdale's large Jewish population. "I think that all the groups in America have rubbed off on each other," she says. "There is really no such thing as one who is purely Chinese American or anything else."

Recipe for Writing

In an interview, Jen once compared the writing process to making soup: "Some of the ingredients come from your life; some come from things you've read, or from other people's lives: many, many things you've just made up. . . . Mostly, when you're writing, you're not thinking about the ingredients—just the soup." When she wrote "The Water Faucet Vision," Jen had recently moved into an old house with her husband. She feels that her frustration with the renovation work is one of the story's ingredients.

The Water Faucet Vision

— *Gish Jen*

To protect my sister, Mona, and me from the pains—or, as they pronounced it, the *pens*—of life, my parents did their fighting in Shanghai dialect, which we didn't understand; and when my father one day pitched a brass vase through the kitchen window, my mother told us he had done it by accident.

"By accident?" said Mona.

My mother chopped the foot off a mushroom.

"By accident?" said Mona. "By *accident?*"

Later, I tried to explain to her that she shouldn't have persisted like that, but it was hopeless.

"What's the matter with throwing things?" she shrugged. "He was *mad*."

That was the difference between Mona and me: fighting was just fighting to her. If she worried about anything, it was only that she might turn out too short to become a ballerina, in which case she was going to be a piano player.

I, on the other hand, was going to be a martyr. I was in fifth grade then, and the hyperimaginative sort—the kind of girl who grows morbid in Catholic school, who longs to be chopped or frozen to death but then has nightmares about it from which she wakes up screaming and clutching a stuffed bear. It was not a bear that I clutched, though, but a string of three malachite beads that I had found in the marsh by the old aqueduct one day. Apparently once part of a necklace, they were each wonderfully striated and swirled, and slightly humped toward the center, like a jellyfish; so that if I squeezed one, it would slip smoothly away, with a grace that altogether enthralled and—on those dream-harrowed nights—soothed me, soothed me as nothing had before or has since. Not that I've lacked occasion for soothing: Though it's been four months since my mother died, there are still nights when sleep stands away from me, stiff as a well-paid sentry. But that is

The Water Faucet Vision

another story. Back then, I had my malachite beads, and if I worried them long and patiently enough, I was sure to start feeling better, more awake, even a little special—imagining, as I like to, that my nightmares were communications from the Almighty Himself, preparation for my painful destiny. Discussing them with Patty Creamer, who had also promised her life to God, I called them "almost visions"; and Patty, her mouth wadded with the three or four sticks of Doublemint she always seemed to have going at once, said, "I bet you'll be doin' miracleth by seventh grade."

Miracles. Today Patty laughs to think she ever spent good time stewing on such matters, her attention having long turned to rugs, and artwork, and antique Japanese bureaus—things she believes in.

"A good bureau's more than just a bureau," she explained last time we had lunch. "It's a hedge against life. I tell you, if there's one thing I believe, it's that cheap stuff's just money out the window. Nice stuff, on the other hand—now *that* you can always cash out, if life gets rough. *That* you can count on."

In fifth grade, though, she counted on different things.

"You'll be doing miracles, too," I told her, but she shook her shaggy head and looked doleful.

"Na' me," she chomped. "Buzzit's okay. The kin' things I like, prayers work okay on."

"Like?"

"Like you 'member that dreth I liked?"

She meant the yellow one, with the crisscross straps.

"Well gueth what."

"Your mom got it for you."

She smiled. "And I only jutht prayed for it for a week," she said.

As for myself, though, I definitely wanted to be able to perform a wonder or two. Miracle working! It was the carrot of carrots. It kept me doing my homework, taking the sacraments; it kept me mournfully on key in music hour, while my classmates hiccuped and squealed their carefree hearts away. Yet I couldn't have said what I wanted such powers for, exactly. That is, I thought of them the way one might think of, say, an ornamental sword—as a kind of collectible, which also happened to be a means of defense.

But then Patty's father walked out on her mother, and for the first time, there was a miracle I wanted to do. I wanted it so much, I could see it: Mr. Creamer made into a spitball. Mr. Creamer shot through a straw into the sky. Mr. Creamer unrolled and replumped, plop back on Patty's doorstep. I would've cleaned out his mind and given him a shave en route. I would've given him a box of peanut fudge, tied up with a ribbon, to present to Patty with a kiss.

But instead, all I could do was try to tell her he'd come back.

The Water Faucet Vision

"He will not, he will not!" she sobbed. "He went on a boat to Rio Deniro. To Rio Deniro!"

I tried to offer her a stick of gum, but she wouldn't take it.

"He said he would rather look at water than at my mom's fat face. He said he would rather look at water than at me." Now she was really wailing, and holding her ribs so tightly that she almost seemed to be hurting herself—so tightly that just looking at her arms wound around her like snakes made my heart feel squeezed.

I patted her on the arm. A one-winged pigeon waddled by.

"He said I wasn't even his kid, he said I came from Uncle Johnny. He said I was garbage, just like my mom and Uncle Johnny. He said I wasn't even his kid, he said I wasn't his Patty, he said I came from Uncle Johnny!"

"From your Uncle Johnny?" I said stupidly.

"From Uncle Johnny," she cried. "From Uncle Johnny!"

"He said that?"

She kept crying.

I tried again. "Oh Patty, don't cry," I said. Then I said, "Your dad was a jerk anyway."

The pigeon produced a large runny dropping.

It was a good twenty minutes before Patty was calm enough for me to run to the girls' room to get her some toilet paper; and by the time I came back she was sobbing again, saying "to Rio Deniro, to Rio Deniro" over and over, as though the words had stuck in her and couldn't be gotten out. Seeing as how we had missed the regular bus home and the late bus, too, I had to leave her a second time to go call my mother, who was only mad until she heard what had happened. Then she came and picked us up, and bought us each a Fudgsicle.

Some days later, Patty and I started a program to work on getting her father home. It was a serious business. We said extra prayers, and lit votive candles. I tied my malachite beads to my uniform belt, fondling them as though they were a rosary, and I a nun. We even took to walking about the school halls with our hands folded—a sight so ludicrous that our wheeze of a principal personally took us aside one day.

"I must tell you," she said, using her nose as a speaking tube, "that there is really no need for such peee-ity."

But we persisted, promising to marry God and praying to every saint we could think of. We gave up gum, then gum and Slim Jims both, then gum and Slim Jims and ice cream; and when even that didn't work, we started on more innovative things. The first was looking at flowers. We held our hands beside our eyes like blinders as we hurried past the violets by the flagpole. Next it was looking at boys: Patty gave up angel-eyed

The Water Faucet Vision

Jamie Halloran, and I, gymnastic Anthony Rossi. It was hard, but in the end our efforts paid off. Mr. Creamer came back a month later, and though he brought with him nothing but dysentery, he was at least too sick to have all that much to say.

Then, in the course of a fight with my father, my mother somehow fell out of their bedroom window.

Recently—thinking a mountain vacation might cheer me—I sublet my apartment to a handsome but somber newlywed couple, who turned out to be every bit as responsible as I'd hoped. They cleaned out even the eggshell chips I'd sprinkled around the base of my plants as fertilizer, leaving behind only a shiny silver-plate cake server and a list of their hopes and goals for the summer. The list, tacked precariously to the back of the kitchen door, began with a fervent appeal to God to help them get their wedding thank-yous written in three weeks or less. (You could see they had originally written "two weeks" but scratched it out—no miracles being demanded here.) It went on:

> *Please help us, Almighty Father in Heaven Above, to get Ann a teaching job within a half-hour drive of here in a nice neighborhood.*
>
> *Please help us, Almighty Father in Heaven Above, to get John a job doing anything where he won't strain his back and that is within a half-hour drive of here.*
>
> *Please help us, Almighty Father in Heaven Above, to get us a car.*
>
> *Please help us, A. F. in H. A., to learn French.*
>
> *Please help us, A. F. in H. A., to find seven dinner recipes that cost less than 60 cents a serving and can be made in a half hour. And that don't have tomatoes, since You in Your Heavenly Wisdom made John allergic.*
>
> *Please help us, A. F. in H. A., to avoid books in this apartment such as You in Your Heavenly Wisdom allowed John, for Your Heavenly Reasons, to find three nights ago (June 2nd).*

Et cetera. In the left-hand margin they had kept score of how they had fared with their requests, and it was heartening to see that nearly all of them were marked "Yes! Praise the Lord" (sometimes shortened to "PTL"), with the sole exception of learning French, which was mysteriously marked "No! PTL to the Highest."

That note touched me. Strange and familiar both, it seemed as though it had been written by some cousin of mine—some cousin who had stayed home to grow up, say, while I went abroad and learned painful things. This, of course, is just a manner of speaking. In fact, I did my growing up at home, like anybody else.

The Water Faucet Vision

But the learning was painful. I never knew exactly how it happened that my mother went hurtling through the air that night years ago, only that the wind had been chopping at the house, and that the argument had started about the state of the roof. Someone had been up to fix it the year before, but it wasn't a roofer, only a man my father had insisted could do just as good a job for a quarter of the price. And maybe he could have, had he not somehow managed to step through a knot in the wood under the shingles and break his uninsured ankle. Now the shingles were coming loose again, and the attic insulation was mildewing besides, and my father was wanting to sell the house altogether, which he said my mother had wanted to buy so she could send pictures of it home to her family in China.

"The Americans have a saying," he said. "They saying, 'You have to keep up with Jones family.' I'm saying if Jones family in Shanghai, you can send any picture you want, *an-y* picture. Go take picture of those rich guys' house. You want to act like rich guys, right? Go take pictures of those rich guys' house."

At that point, my mother sent Mona and me to wash up, and started speaking Shanghainese. They argued for some time in the kitchen, while we listened from the top of the stairs, our faces wedged between the bumpy Spanish scrolls of the wrought-iron railing. First my mother ranted, then my father, and then they both ranted at once, until finally there was a thump, followed by a long quiet.

"Do you think they're kissing now?" said Mona. "I bet they're kissing, like this." She pursed her lips like a fish, and was about to put them to the railing when we heard my mother locking the back door. We high-tailed it into bed; my parents creaked up the stairs. Everything at that point seemed fine. Once in their bedroom, though, they started up again, first softly, then more and more loudly, until my mother turned on a radio to try to disguise the noise. A door slammed; they began shouting at each other; another door slammed; a shoe or something banged the wall behind Mona's bed.

"How're we supposed to *sleep?*" said Mona, sitting up.

There was another thud; more yelling in Shanghainese; and then my mother's voice pierced the wall, in English. "So what you want I should do? Go to work like Theresa Lee?"

My father rumbled something back.

"You think you are big shot, but you never get promotion, you never get raise. All I do is spend money, right? So what do you do, you tell me. So what do you do!"

Something hit the floor so hard, our room shook.

"So kill me," screamed my mother. "You know what you are? You are failure. Failure! You are failure!"

The Water Faucet Vision

Then there was a sudden, terrific, bursting crash—and after it, as if on a bungled cue, the serene blare of an a capella soprano picking her way down a scale.

By the time Mona and I knew to look out the window, a neighbor's pet beagle was already on the scene, sniffing and barking at my mother's body, his tail crazy with excitement. Then he was barking at my stunned and trembling father, at the shrieking ambulance, at the police, at crying Mona in her bunny-footed pajamas, and at me, barefoot in the cold grass, squeezing my sister's shoulder with one hand and clutching my malachite beads with the other.

My mother wasn't dead, only unconscious—the paramedics figured that out right away—but there was blood everywhere, and though they were reassuring about her head wounds as they strapped her to the stretcher—commenting also on how small she was, how delicate, how light—my father kept saying, *I killed her, I killed her* as the ambulance screeched and screeched headlong, forever, to the hospital. I was afraid to touch her, and glad of the metal rail between us, even though its sturdiness made her seem even frailer than she was. I wished she were bigger, somehow, and noticed, with a pang, that the new red slippers we had given her for Mother's Day had been lost somewhere along the way. How much she seemed to be leaving behind, as we careened along—still not there, still not there—Mona and Dad and the medic and I taking up the whole ambulance, all the room, so that there was no room for anything else; no room even for my mother's real self, the one who should have been pinching the color back to my father's gray face, the one who should have been calming Mona's cowlick—the one who should have been bending over us, to help us be strong, to help us get through, even as we bent over her.

Then suddenly we were there, the glowing square of the emergency room entrance opening like the gates of heaven; and immediately the talk of miracles began. Alive, a miracle. No bones broken, a miracle. A miracle that the hemlocks had cushioned her fall, a miracle that they hadn't been trimmed in a year and a half. It was a miracle that all that blood, the blood that had seemed that night to be everywhere, was from one shard of glass, a single shard, can you imagine, and as for the gash in her head, the scar would be covered by hair. The next day, my mother cheerfully described just how she would part it so that nothing would show at all.

"You're a lucky duck-duck," agreed Mona, helping herself, with a little pirouette, to the cherry atop my mother's chocolate pudding.

That wasn't enough for me, though. I was relieved, yes, but what I wanted by then was a real miracle. Not for my mother simply to have survived, but for the whole thing never to have happened—for my mother's head never to have been shaved and bandaged like that, for her high,

The Water Faucet Vision

proud forehead never to have been swollen down over her eyes, for her face and neck and hands never to have been painted so many shades of blue-black, and violet, and chartreuse. I still want those things—for my parents not to have had to live with this affair like a prickle bush between them, for my father to have been able to look my mother in her swollen eyes and curse the madman, the monster who had dared do this to the woman he loved. I wanted to be able to touch my mother without shuddering, to be able to console my father, to be able to get that crash out of my head, the sound of that soprano—so many things that I didn't know how to pray for them, that I wouldn't have known where to start even if I had had the power to work miracles, right there, right then.

A week later, when my mother's head was beginning to bristle with new hairs, I lost my malachite beads. I had been carrying them in a white cloth pouch that Patty had given me, and was swinging the pouch on my pinkie on my way home from school, when I swung just a bit too hard; the pouch went sailing in a long arc through the air, *whooshing* like a perfectly thrown basketball through one of the holes of a nearby sewer. There was no chance of fishing it out. I looked and looked, crouching on the sticky pavement until the asphalt had crazed the skin of my hands and knees, but all I could discern was an evil-smelling murk, glassy and smug and impenetrable.

My loss didn't quite hit me until I was home, but then it produced an agony all out of proportion to my string of pretty beads. I hadn't cried at all during my mother's accident, but now I was crying all afternoon, all through dinner, and then after dinner, too—crying past the point where I knew what I was crying for, wishing dimly that I had my beads to hold, wishing dimly that I could pray, but refusing, refusing, I didn't know why, until I finally fell into an exhausted sleep on the couch. There my parents left me for the night—glad, no doubt, that one of the more tedious of my childhood crises seemed to be winding off the reel of life, onto the reel of memory. They covered me, and somehow grew a pillow under my head, and, with uncharacteristic disregard for the living room rug, left some milk and Pecan Sandies on the coffee table, in case I woke up hungry. Their thoughtfulness was prescient. I did wake up in the early part of the night; and it was then, amid the unfamiliar sounds and shadows of the living room, that I had what I was sure was a true vision.

Even now, what I saw retains an odd clarity: the requisite strange light flooding the room, first orange, and then a bright yellow-green. A crackling bright burst like a Roman candle going off near the piano. There was a distinct smell of coffee, and a long silence. The room seemed to be getting colder. Nothing. A creak; the light starting to wane, then waxing again, brilliant pink now. Still nothing. Then, as the pink started to go a

The Water Faucet Vision

little purple, a perfectly normal, middle-aged man's voice, speaking something very like pig latin, told me not to despair, not to despair, my beads would be returned to me.

That was all. I sat a moment in the dark, then turned on the light, gobbled down the cookies—and in a happy flash understood that I was so good, really, so near to being a saint that my malachite beads would come back through the town water system. All I had to do was turn on all the faucets in the house. This I did, stealing quietly into the bathroom and kitchen and basement. The old spigot by the washing machine was too gunked up to be coaxed very far open, but that didn't matter. The water didn't have to be full blast, I understood that. Then I gathered together my pillow and blanket and trundled up to my bed to sleep.

By the time I woke up in the morning, I knew that my beads hadn't shown up; but when I knew it for certain, I was still disappointed. And as if that weren't enough, I had to face my parents and sister, who were all abuzz with the mystery of the faucets. Not knowing what else to do, I, like a puddlebrain, told them the truth. The results were predictably painful.

"Callie had a *vision*," Mona told everyone at the bus stop. "A vision with lights, and sinks in it!"

Sinks, visions. I got it all day, from my parents, from my classmates, even from some sixth and seventh graders. Someone drew a cartoon of me with a halo over my head in one of the girls' room stalls; Anthony Rossi made gurgling noises as he walked on his hands at recess. Only Patty tried not to laugh, though even she was something less than unalloyed understanding.

"I don' think miracles are thupposed to happen in *thewers*," she said.

Such was the end of my saintly ambitions. It wasn't the end of all holiness. The ideas of purity and goodness still tippled my brain, and over the years I came slowly to grasp of what grit true faith is made. Last night, though, when my father called to say that he couldn't go on living in our old house, that he was going to move to a smaller place, another place, maybe a condo—he didn't know how, or where—I found myself still wistful for the time religion seemed all I wanted it to be. Back then, the world was a place that could be set right. One had only to direct the hand of the Almighty and say, Just here, Lord, we hurt here—and here, and here, and here.

Responding to the Selection

1. Which incident in this story made the biggest impression on you? Why do you find the incident so memorable?

2. A **dynamic character** changes in the course of a story, while a **static character** remains the same. Would you classify Callie, the narrator, as dynamic or static? Explain.

3. How far removed in time is Callie from the events she narrates? What clues lead you to this conclusion?

4. Why might Gish Jen have chosen to devote a whole paragraph to the beagle's barking in the scene where Callie's mother falls out of the window?

5. Why is Callie unsatisfied with the "miracle" that her mother survived the fall with no serious injuries?

Activities

Interpreting the Story

1. In the last paragraph, the narrator says that she "came slowly to grasp of what grit true faith is made." Write an interpretation of this statement. Explain what the statement suggests about the narrator's present view of religion and how this view contrasts with her beliefs when she was in the fifth grade.

Discussing Parenting

2. In the story's first sentence, the narrator says her parents tried to protect their children from the "pains of life." In a small group, discuss whether it is possible, or even beneficial, for parents to protect their children from life's pains. In what ways can negative moments be important learning experiences?

Before You Read

Mother's Pearls

Bao-Long Chu

About Chu

Bao-Long Chu is a teacher in a Houston elementary school. He holds a master of fine arts degree in poetry.

Vietnam Veterans Memorial

The black wall mentioned in "Mother's Pearls" is the Vietnam Veterans Memorial. The memorial consists of two granite walls that meet at an angle. Inscribed on the polished black surface are the names of all U.S. veterans killed or missing in Vietnam. Maya Ying Lin, a twenty-one-year-old architecture student from Ohio, came up with this unconventional design in 1980. At first her design aroused con- troversy, but the memorial was embraced by the public when it opened in 1982. No other monument in Washington, D.C., attracts so many visitors. Many have left behind war memorabilia and personal items associated with loved ones who died in the war. The National Park Service has collected these items and exhibits a selection of them at the Smithsonian Institution.

The "ebony seeds" of line 4 are dark gray, or "black," pearls. The *ao dai* is the Vietnamese national costume for women; white is traditionally worn by mourners in many parts of Asia. Napalm, mentioned in line 27, is a jelly-like material used in flame-throwers and bombs.

Mother's Pearls

— *Bao-Long Chu*

Broken shadow gestured winter
trees in Maine, black on white
I thought of my mother's pearls,
ebony seeds, old as the sea
5   They lie
suspended from her white ao dai
      The color of mourning
      or of mornings in 1975
      unbroken, silent
10   after a rain of bombs
      except for the tears of women
      crying for broken temples against green
      sky; fallen idols
      with carved breasts,
15   jade, I think, in the black earth,
      in the twisted vines

Last summer, in Washington
I saw the black wall
My shadow reflected
20   the names of faceless men.
I traced the ruins
carved in stone but did not find
Mother's name
or the names of other women
25   who stood against the wall of a temple
garden, parting leaves, weeping
napalm tears
      Sandalwood incense
      sweet crooked smoke
30   they drove all things
out of mind.

Mother's Pearls

And the pearls
forty seeds, black and unruly,
I thought they were beautiful against
35   my mother's carved breasts.

They lie now,
I think, on a sloping knoll
farther than Maine
or Washington.

Responding to the Selection

Questions for Discussion

1. What feelings does this poem stir up in you?

2. **Setting** is the time and place of a literary work. Which places are described in "Mother's Pearls"? How are the places connected in the poem?

3. What does the speaker feel is missing at the Vietnam Veterans Memorial? What is he searching for in his life?

Activities

Writing Poetry

1. Write a poem about mourning. You might treat this theme in a general way, or you might discuss a particular person that you have mourned.

Researching the Vietnam Veterans Memorial

2. Research the Vietnam Veterans Memorial in Washington, D.C. A good source of information about the memorial is the Web site of the U.S. National Park Service (www.nps.gov). Share your findings with the class.

Designing a Memorial

3. Design a memorial for the women who suffered in the Vietnam War or in another conflict. Write a brief proposal for the memorial and draw a sketch of it.

Before You Read

The Real Inada

Lawson Fusao Inada
Born 1938

> *"Inada's ear for the musicality of English is unsurpassed."*
> —Leslie Marmon Silko

About Inada

As a high school student, Lawson Inada developed a love for jazz and blues. Listening to performers such as Little Walter and Charlie Parker made him "want to 'say' something." Later on, Inada found a way to use the rhythms and language of jazz to express himself in verse. Some of his poems are about the musical heroes who inspired him. In others, as in this nonfiction remembrance, he explores his family and personal history, including his experiences in internment camps during World War II.

Inada has published three volumes of poetry. His book *Legends from Camp* won the American Book Award. Inada is also one of the editors of *Aiiieeeee!*, a groundbreaking anthology of Asian American literature. Since 1966 he has taught literature and creative writing at Southern Oregon State College.

Troubled History

Lawson Inada was a small boy when the U.S. government began to round up all Japanese Americans living on the West Coast. At first he and his family were held in the fairgrounds near their home in Fresno, California, but they spent much of the war in internment camps in Arkansas and Colorado. Recently Inada visited some camps while collaborating with his son on a video project. "It still bothers you to go to these places, to see the remnants, to realize what actually happened there," Inada says. "It makes you realize that history doesn't just go away."

The Real Inada

— Lawson Fusao Inada

If I had to choose one person of my greater clan to include in some listing of remarkable Americans, it would have to be my uncle Yoshitaro Inada. I was thinking about him the other day when I drove the old river road through the Sacramento delta, where my cousin Lily lives with her family on a farm below the levee. Many of our people settled there at the turn of the century, creating tiny, still-existing villages and orchards and farms. Although my uncle never lived there, I'm sure he approved and was proud of his daughter's choice of a husband.

He was that kind of guy—proud, supportive, traditional, and a man of the land. And his history was such that he could remain that way, maintain that way—relying on the integrity of his mind, his knowledge, his wits, his senses, and calling upon the resources of his body and community. As the saying goes, they don't make them like that anymore.

Yoshitaro, Uncle Y, was born in a southern Japanese village in 1890. Times were tough, life was hard; thus, his father left for America in 1896, followed by his mother in 1901, and it took them years of laboring on a Hawaii plantation to earn passage to California in 1905.

In the meantime, Yoshitaro and his sister (who eventually made her way to Brazil) were entrusted to the village for raising (Yoshitaro's grandfather, my great-grandfather, was a highly respected village healer and spiritual leader, who happened to be blind); thus, when Yoshitaro was finally sent for, in 1910, he was a fully formed individual. (My father was born that same year, on the Pajaro River in Watsonville.)

Which is to say that, unlike my father, who went on to become a dentist, Uncle Y never had to become "Americanized"—he never had to attend American schools, and he only had to learn enough English to get by (I would guess he acquired a driver's license, but perhaps not; I would also guess he knew some Spanish); in other words, Uncle Y could stay himself, which was considerable. This is not to say that an American education is not valuable, but what it often consists of, and how it is imparted, can have a negating effect on some; nor do I mean to imply that Yoshitaro

The Real Inada

was not an American; on the contrary, he was *very* American—an exemplary American, an embodiment of American ideals—but he just didn't speak much English.

He was about as American as, say, a Navajo. (And with his dark, handsome features, it is easy to picture him at home among their nation.) He considered this his home, even homeland, never wanting to return to Japan, and during World War II he sent his only son off to join the U.S. military, to serve with honor. But what truly exemplified his "Americanness" was his love of the *land*—the land itself (whatever it was labeled) and all that came with it—and this sense ran deeper than labels or lip service.

Because he truly loved and knew and appreciated the land—which included the creatures and vegetation. He lived with the land, on the land, and was *of* the land; he knew it as he knew his hands, and they went together, like harvest and rain, like sunsets and song.

Now by the time I came along and got to know the man, we were in a concentration camp in Arkansas, hard by the Mississippi. Uncle Y, not being one to take such things lightly, had brought a bunch of seeds with him and, in short order, with handmade implements, started not just a garden but a small farm. The camp was a standard, makeshift installation of fenced barracks and scraped ground, good for dust and mud; but that's not the way he saw it. And since he served on the work crew that went out into the swamp each day to chop firewood, he was able to smuggle in his various found-treasures: plants, more plants, some wild creatures, and special chunks of wood.

Burls too good to be burned. Burls with swirling grains and curved, angular shapes suitable for polishing and displaying, either as is or with tiny plants planted in orifices, becoming miniature landscapes, and one served to display his son's cards and letters from throughout Europe. So with handmade scrap-lumber furnishings to augment government cots, he and my aunt were rather comfortable, especially since, for the first time, they had indoor plumbing and running water—albeit a block away in the public laundry and communal toilet.

The one thing lacking, however, was a furo, a Japanese bath; thus, since Uncle Y had never taken a shower in his life and wasn't about to start, he quickly fashioned a furo out of, once again, scraps and ingenuity—and there it was, in the corner of the open shower stalls. It included a wooden-slatted area for soaping and rinsing, with a wooden bucket (handmade, I'm sure, along with the wooden stool). And the tub, of course, heated by a fire beneath, was strictly for soaking, steaming, sighing, singing—and the warm scent of wet wood served to negate the smell of industrial disinfectant. Eventually, Uncle Y might have invited his fellow laborers on the outside to come in and partake, to ease their aches from plantation cottonfields.

The Real Inada

And while the rest of the camp proceeded in the prescribed, concentration-camp manner—grim, grimy, like a grainy black-and-white newsreel—my uncle transformed his barrack-grounds into a technicolor nature documentary. Everything from outside had made its way into the barrens to flourish, including fish and frogs and crawdads in the pond; the effect was not artsy either, but more like an extension of the swamp; as a result, many birds and insects gathered in the foliage, perhaps causing neighbors to complain of the noise (prisoners are supposed to be quiet); it was even rumored that, somewhere, ol' Yoshitaro kept a pet water moccasin.

Ah, yes, he could have stayed there forever, loving the land, being creative, productive, useful, extending himself to the greater community, but, alas, we were re-moved to a camp in the Colorado desert, where the land wasn't as fecund, but he managed to make do with a grand rock garden of cacti and sage, sandy, craggy home of scorpions, tarantulas, lizards, snakes, one old tortoise, and many birds. Then came recruiters for farm workers to combat the labor shortage, and Uncle Y was gone in a flash.

And didn't return. For he had managed to work his way clear up to northern Colorado, to an apparently beautiful place not far from Denver— a sugar beet farm on the high plains with the big sky and the grand landscape, looking out on the Rockies. "Rockies," he could say that all right. He had arranged for his wife to come and cook, on the same "work-release program," and even his elderly father, born in the 1860s, would serve as some sort of caretaker. The way they figured it, the bunkhouse beat the barracks—for the duration.

And then some. Because although the war went and ended, and we all reimmigrated to California, Yoshitaro and family stayed in Colorado! They enjoyed the sugar beet life, loved the grainy soil, the clear water, and, like the old days, had acquired some horses. And they'd write poetic letters praising the wonderfully extravagant thunderstorms, the luxurious snow, and the sparkling, gem-like hail.

Finally, however, in July 1947, after repeated requests, they consented to return to somewhat humdrum California and resume farming in the Santa Clara valley. Starting from scratch never bothered him; that entire region bore his "scratch marks," where he had helped build houses, roads, creating farms and sharecropping communities where there weren't any. It was his territory; time after time, remote, hidden places in the rocky, forbidding foothills had sprung forth with production, each furrow shaped into a Y.

After the war, though, he rented various preexisting farms, near Gilroy, and settled down as a respected elder of the community. He had certain admirable qualities that are talked about to this day: he knew

The Real Inada

everything there was to know about farming, of course, including weather patterns, which he could feel in his bones; he could repair any kind of machinery, including his vintage utility vehicle, a Crosley; he could be trusted to work—and work without complaining. Times had always been tough, but so was he; he was a man's man, a devoted father and son, and as a brother he supported my father through college. He never had much, but he had a lot.

And one thing he possessed was not his to own: respect. This was conferred by the community; thus, he was called upon to attend and participate in many significant events—weddings, funerals, anniversaries—in our greater San Jose region community because, well, just because he was a cultured, distinguished, sophisticated gentleman of presence, one to be entrusted with responsibility.

He could drink with the best, and tell the best jokes; he could give the best toasts—toasts that spoke like prophecy, for the whole community. And best of all, he could sing like no one else. And his singing, naturally, was not conventionally "American"; rather, it was older, and ran deeper, than the very concept of the nation itself. Some of the lyrics, for instance, contained ancient terms no longer in everyday usage; and his singing style demonstrated such mastery, range, and nuance that it was not to be taught, and certainly not learned, in conventional courses.

It had to be lived; and he had to partake of it, from infancy on, from his blind grandfather, at that old healer's knee. And in Uncle Y's singing, I could envision my great-grandfather, could hear the old one's voice saying, "Yoshitaro, Yoshitaro . . ." And the child would sing, displaying his comprehension of each word, each historical or mythological reference, and the breathing would have to be just so, each pause in place. And for any blessing or healing to occur, the intonation had to be perfect, each rise, each fall, each guttural quaver emanating not so much from the throat and mouth but from the pit of the stomach, the bottom of the heart.

To my young ears, it all sounded rather strange, mysterious, but it was effective enough to silence us children without our being asked, to stop us in our tracks no matter what we were doing. We'd peer out from under banquet tablecloths to watch, and listen; and we'd look around the room at familiar faces and see glazed, unfamiliar expressions, eyes staring off into space as Yoshitaro sang, slowly intoning each syllable with such power and passion.

And when he was finished, the atmosphere was different—we could hear better, clearer, we would feel calmer, more at peace. And I imagine that, for the elders, it took quite some time to return from their journeys, and late that night, falling asleep, they'd still be departing misty villages, embarking on ships, arriving in challenging lands, laboring to

The Real Inada

raise families, and then those families, entire communities, would be embarking on trucks and trains to camp, eventually returning to this room in San Jose, where even the kitchen staff would be transfixed, lost in their journeys, at the kitchen door. And all I could do was whisper to another child: "*That's* my Uncle Y."

He wasn't a happy man; he was *contented*. And in his final years, he and family members finally managed to buy a farm, which they mostly tended to, enabling Yoshitaro to embark on his major project, the transformation of his *own American land*.

Surely, a vision came to him, looking out the kitchen window, seeing all that space, and the space was his. There was that old tree over there, and that other old tree over there, close enough for their branches to touch, but with enough space in between to set a barrack. He had to chuckle about that, smile his famous smile—and then he set immediately to work.

And since his was a world of cisterns and shovels, of bent nails sorted and stored in old fruit jars, and since he never knowingly wasted anything, he had all he needed to accomplish his vision. And what he created was Japan. California. Arkansas. Colorado. Plus.

Whatever grew anywhere, it was there. Whatever was not supposed to grow there, it was there. Tropics, desert, tundra—it was there. Things that needed delicate treatment, they were there, flourishing in his personal atmosphere. And when the public got word of what he was doing, friends and strangers alike would drop off plants in his care—rejects, diseased, whatever . . .

Even my wife, a certified "master gardener," would bring him sick exotic plants she had given up on, little spotted, droopy things on their last legs—and when we'd come by several months later, she couldn't recognize them! They probably didn't recognize themselves—because these little decorative houseplants would be well on their way to becoming big bushes, even trees! And there was this one tiny cactus that, even using an eyedropper just once a week, she had somehow overwatered, causing it to curl up and melt down to nothing. Well, when she saw it again, she thought Yoshitaro was lying or had replaced it with another, because he claimed he had talked to it, hosed it off a lot, and there it stood—like a blooming child! And it wasn't supposed to bloom until the 21st century . . .

He had so many plants that they created their own climate. Some were in the ground, others were at various levels, in tiers. Among the many bonsai trees were some that were not supposed to be—for instance, who ever heard of a miniature sequoia? But there it was, next to the tiny redwood, thriving on lyrics and mist . . .

So, as with the rest of the community, we had to take him at his word—for he was known as a man of his word—and if he said he was

The Real Inada

doing some talking, we figured he was doing some tall talking. And listening. Because that's exactly what he did with the fish and frogs in the pond, the lizards on the moss, and all the birds in the foliage: talked and listened. But he didn't necessarily feed those creatures to alter or tame their nature; rather, they fed themselves in his organic environment. And although he built the pond and received the fish from friends, and although he built and hung some miniature barracks for the birds, the birds and other creatures relocated there on their own.

And every morning, he'd call them, and they'd come—some birds even perching on his shoulders. And several of these creatures had come to him for healing—desperate, wounded birds, maimed dogs, stray cats with broken legs; there was even a healed raccoon under the barn . . . then Uncle Y would be off among the plants, humming, talking, listening, singing . . .

He was just one man, one Inada in this country, and what he left behind wasn't much. And what could have become his legacy is pretty much decimated now, but not by choice: what the family realized, as soon as he died, was that it would take a whole crew of professional caretakers to maintain his space, to take his place, because each tree, each plant, had to be nurtured in an individual manner—and rather than have everything die, the family called upon the community to help assume the responsibility. So the people came, and came, and came, carting off some specimens that could be worth good money on the market.

So Yoshitaro's remarkable legacy lives on, endures in his home community. And as his nephew, I aspire to carry on his legacy of song, through my efforts in poetry—but I'm an ignorant upstart compared to him. And in the meantime, I sometimes stand outside and call the birds.

And sometimes they come.

Responding to the Selection

Questions for Discussion

1. What thoughts did you have as you finished reading this essay?

2. According to Inada, an American education can have "a negating effect" on some people. Support or oppose this statement, giving reasons for your position.

3. Inada says that Uncle Yoshitaro was an embodiment of American ideals. Which ideals did he embody? Name at least two.

4. A **theme** is a central message or idea that a literary work conveys. State the theme of this essay in your own words.

5. How might you have reacted if you were one of the Japanese Americans sent to internment camps? Would you have adjusted as well as Yoshitaro did? Why or why not?

Activities

Writing an Essay

1. If you had to choose a relative or a friend to include in a listing of remarkable Americans, whom would you name? Describe this person in an essay.

Writing a Proposal

2. Suppose that the community where Yoshitaro spent his last years wanted to honor his memory in some way. Write a proposal explaining your ideas for a memorial. Include a sketch of your proposed memorial.

Discussing in Class

3. When Japanese Americans were interned during World War II, almost none of the internees refused to go to the camps. Like Yoshitaro, they agreed to relocate and make the best of the situation. Discuss in your class whether Japanese Americans should have resisted the move to the camps. Give examples from history of how Japanese Americans might have resisted their internment. Do you think these methods would have succeeded?

Before You Read ——————————

Freedom to Breathe

Aleksandr Solzhenitsyn
Born 1918

"Lies can prevail against much in this world, but never against art."

About Solzhenitsyn

Aleksandr Solzhenitsyn grew up in poverty. After earning degrees in various sciences, he became a teacher. During World War II, he served in the artillery, rising to the rank of captain. Late in the war, however, he wrote some letters in which he criticized Communist leader Joseph Stalin. For this he was arrested and sent to a prison camp in Siberia, the vast and forbidding eastern part of Russia. He wrote of his experiences there in his first novel, *One Day in the Life of Ivan Denisovich,* published in 1962.

The authorities soon clamped down on Solzhenitsyn again. But in 1970 his powerful writings won him the Nobel Prize for Literature. Four years later, the Soviet government deported him, and he took refuge in the United States. He continued to write novels and nonfiction. In 1994 he returned to Russia, having outlasted the Communist regime.

The Gulag

In 1919, two years following the Russian Revolution, the Communist Party established a system of forced-labor camps known as the Gulag. The system expanded rapidly during the dictatorship of Joseph Stalin. Between 1934 and 1947, at least ten million people were sent to the Gulag. Besides ordinary criminals, political dissidents, peasants who resisted the government's seizure of their farms, and people merely suspected of opposing the government were confined. Many were executed, and many more died from disease, malnutrition, and overwork. Solzhenitsyn's greatest nonfiction work, *The Gulag Archipelago*—for which he was expelled from Russia—is based on his own experiences and the testimony of other inmates.

Freedom to Breathe

— *Aleksandr Solzhenitsyn*
Translated by Michael Glenny

A shower fell in the night and now dark clouds drift across the sky, occasionally sprinkling a fine film of rain.

I stand under an apple tree in blossom and I breathe. Not only the apple tree but the grass round it glistens with moisture; words cannot describe the sweet fragrance that pervades the air. I inhale as deeply as I can, and the aroma invades my whole being; I breathe with my eyes open, I breathe with my eyes closed—I cannot say which gives me the greater pleasure.

This, I believe, is the single most precious freedom that prison takes away from us: the freedom to breathe freely, as I now can. No food on earth, no wine, not even a woman's kiss is sweeter to me than this air steeped in the fragrance of flowers, of moisture and freshness.

No matter that this is only a tiny garden, hemmed in by five-story houses like cages in a zoo. I cease to hear the motorcycles backfiring, radios whining, the burble of loudspeakers. As long as there is fresh air to breathe under an apple tree after a shower, we may survive a little longer.

Responding to the Selection

Questions for Discussion

1. What experiences in his life might have led Aleksandr Solzhenitsyn to write this prose poem?

2. What are some similarities between the situations of the narrator of "Freedom to Breathe" and Yoshitaro in "The Real Inada"? What are some differences?

3. What do gardens and flowers mean to the main characters of these two works?

4. What things do you think you would miss the most if you were in prison? Why?

Activities

Writing Creatively

1. Think of the most beautiful garden you have ever seen. Write a poem, prose poem, or prose description of this garden.

Writing a Dialogue

2. Create a dialogue between the narrator of Solzhenitsyn's prose poem and Yoshitaro. Use details from the works in your dialogue.

Illustrating Literature

3. Make an illustration to accompany one of these works. Share your illustration with the class.

Before You Read

The Seventh Street Philosopher

Toshio Mori
1910–1980

"[Toshio Mori] took the responsibility of founding and maintaining the tradition of Japanese American literature."
—Lawson Fusao Inada

About Mori

Toshio Mori was the first Japanese American to publish a book of fiction. *Yokohama, California* is a collection of stories set in Oakland. Mori wrote most of them in the 1930s. He would work about fourteen hours each day in his family's flower nursery, then go home to write for at least four hours. A publisher accepted his manuscript in 1941, but the book didn't appear in print for eight years. Mori continued to write even while he was held in an internment camp during World War II.

Influenced by writers such as Sherwood Anderson and Anton Chekhov, Mori focused on the lives of ordinary people. He hoped that his realistic and gently humorous portraits of Japanese Americans would overcome stereotypes in popular fiction of the time. Although critics praised his book, it sold poorly. Mori was unable to publish another collection of stories until the year before his death.

Asian and Western Philosophers

Motoji Tsunoda, the hero of "The Seventh Street Philosopher," is a follower of Akegarasu Haya, who actually visited Oakland in 1929. Although Toshio Mori probably heard this great Buddhist philosopher speak on his trip to the United States, he was more interested in American thinkers such as Ralph Waldo Emerson and Henry David Thoreau. At one point, Mori wanted to follow Thoreau's example and live like a hermit in nature, but his mother discouraged him. Instead he became a writer, which he felt was the "next closest thing."

The Seventh Street Philosopher

— *Toshio Mori*

He is what our community calls the Seventh Street philosopher. This is because Motoji Tsunoda used to live on Seventh Street sixteen or seventeen years ago and loved even then to spout philosophy and talk to the people. Today he is living on an estate of an old lady who has hired him as a launderer for a dozen years or so. Every once so often he comes out of his washroom, out of obscurity, to mingle among his people and this is usually the beginning of something like a furor, something that upsets the community, the people, and Motoji Tsunoda alike.

There is nothing like it in our community, nothing so fruitless and irritable which lasts so long and persists in making a show; only Motoji Tsunoda is unique. Perhaps his being alone, a widower, working alone in his sad washroom in the old lady's basement and washing the stuff that drops from the chute and drying them on the line, has quite a bit to do with his behavior when he meets the people of our community. Anyway when Motoji Tsunoda comes to the town and enters into the company of the evening all his silent hours and silent vigils with deep thoughts and books come to the fore and there is no stopping of his flow of words and thoughts. Generally, the people are impolite when Motoji Tsunoda begins speaking, and the company of the evening either disperse quite early or entirely ignore his philosophical thoughts and begin conversations on business or weather or how the friends are getting along these days. And the strangeness of it all is that Motoji Tsunoda is a very quiet man, sitting quietly in the corner, listening to others talk until the opportunity comes. Then he will suddenly become alive and the subject and all the subjects in the world become his and the company of the evening his audience.

When Motoji Tsunoda comes to the house he usually stays till one in the morning or longer if everybody in the family are polite about it or are sympathetic with him. Sometimes there is no subject for him to talk of, having talked himself out but this does not slow him up. Instead he will think for a moment and then begin on his favorite topic: What is there for the individual to do today? And listening to him, watching him gesture desperately to bring over a point, I am often carried away by this meek man who launders for an old lady on weekdays. Not by his deep thoughts or crazy thoughts but by what he is and what he is actually and desperately trying to put across to the people and the world.

"Tsunoda-san, what are you going to speak on tonight?" my mother says when our family and Motoji Tsunoda settle down in the living room.

"What do you want to hear?" Motoji Tsunoda answers. "Shall it be about Shakyamuni's boyhood or shall we continue where we left off last week and talk about Dewey?"

That is a start. With the beginning of words there is no stopping of Motoji Tsunoda, there is no misery in his voice nor in his stance at the time as he would certainly possess in the old washroom. His tone perks up, his body becomes straight, and in a way this slight meek man becomes magnificent, powerful, and even inspired. He is proud of his debates with the numerous Buddhist clergymen and when he is in a fine fettle he delves into the various debates he has had in the past for the sake of his friends. And no matter what is said or what has happened in the evening Motoji Tsunoda will finally end his oration or debate with something about the tradition and the blood flow of Shakyamuni, St. Shinran, Akegarasu, and Motoji Tsunoda. He is not joking when he says this. He is very serious. When anyone begins kidding about it, he will sadly gaze at the joker and shake his head.

About this time something happened in our town which Motoji Tsunoda to this day is very proud of. It was an event which has prolonged the life of Motoji Tsunoda, acting as a stimulant, that of broadcasting to the world in general the apology of being alive.

It began very simply, nothing of deliberation, nothing of vanity or pride but simply the eventual event coming as the phenomenon of chance. There was the talk about this time of Akegarasu, the great philosopher of Japan, coming to our town to give a lecture. He, Akegarasu, was touring America, lecturing and studying and visiting Emerson's grave, so there was a good prospect of having this great philosopher come to our community and lecture. And before anyone was wise to his move Motoji Tsunoda voluntarily wrote to Akegarasu, asking him to lecture on the night of July 14 since that was the date he had hired the hall. And before Motoji Tsunoda had received an answer he went about the town, saying the great philosopher was coming, that he was coming to lecture at the hall.

He came to our house breathless with the news. Someone asked him if he had received a letter of acceptance and Akegarasu had consented to come.

"No, but he will come," Motoji Tsunoda said. "He will come and lecture. Be sure of that."

For days he went about preparing for the big reception, forgetting his laundering, forgetting his meekness, working as much as four men to get the Asahi Auditorium in shape. For days ahead he had all the chairs lined up, capable of seating five hundred people. Then the word came to him that the great philosopher was already on his way to Seattle to embark for Japan. This left Motoji Tsunoda very flat, leaving him to the mercy of the people who did not miss the opportunity to laugh and taunt him.

"What can you do?" they said and laughed. "What can you do but talk?"

Motoji Tsunoda came to the house, looking crestfallen and dull. We could not cheer him up that night; not once could we lift him from misery. But the next evening, unexpectedly, he came running in the house, his eyes shining, his whole being alive and powerful. "Do you know what?" he said to us. "I have an idea! A great idea."

So he sat down and told us that instead of wasting the beautiful hall, all decorated and cleaned and ready for five hundred people to come and sit down, he, Motoji Tsunoda would give a lecture. He said he had already phoned the two Japanese papers to play up his lecture and let the world know he is lecturing on July 14. He said for us to be sure to come. He said he had phoned all his friends and acquaintances and reporters to be sure to come. He said he was going home now to plan his lecture, he said this was his happiest moment of his life and wondered why he did not think of giving a lecture at the Asahi Auditorium before. And as he strode off to his home and to lecture plans, for a moment I believed he had outgrown the life of a launderer, outgrown the meekness and derision, outgrown the patheticness of it and the loneliness. And seeing him stride off with unknown power and unknown energy I firmly believed Motoji Tsunoda was on his own, a philosopher by rights, as all men are in action and thought a philosopher by rights.

We did not see Motoji Tsunoda for several days. However in the afternoon of July 14 he came running up our steps. "Tonight is the big night, everybody," he said. "Be sure to be there tonight. I speak on a topic of great importance."

"What's the time?" I said.

"The lecture is at eight," he said. "Be sure to come, everybody."

The night of July 14 was like any other night, memorable, fascinating, miserable; bringing together under a single darkness, one night of performance, of patience and the impatience of the world, the bravery of a single inhabitant and the untold braveries of all the inhabitants of the earth, crying and uncrying for salvation and crying just the same; beautiful gestures and miserable gestures coming and going; and the thoughts unexpressed and the dreams pursued to be expressed.

We were first to be seated and we sat in the front. Every now and then I looked back to see if the people were coming in. At eight-ten there were six of us in the audience. Motoji Tsunoda came on the platform and sat down and when he saw us he nodded his head. He sat alone up there, he was to introduce himself.

We sat an hour or more to see if some delay had caused the people to be late. Once Motoji Tsunoda came down and walked to the entrance to see if the people were coming in. At nine-eighteen Motoji Tsunoda stood up and introduced himself. Counting the two babies there were eleven of us in the audience.

When he began to speak on his topic of the evening, "The Apology of Living," his voice did not quiver though Motoji Tsunoda was unused to public speaking and I think that was wonderful. I do not believe he was aware of his audience when he began to speak, whether it was a large audience or a small one. And I think that also was wonderful.

Motoji Tsunoda addressed the audience for three full hours without intermission. He hardly even took time out to drink a glass of water. He stood before us and in his beautiful sad way, tried to make us understand as he understood; tried with every bit of finesse and deep thought to reveal to us the beautiful world he could see and marvel at, but which we could not see.

Then the lecture was over and Motoji Tsunoda sat down and wiped his face. It was wonderful, the spectacle; the individual standing up and expressing himself, the earth, the eternity, and the audience listening and snoring, and the beautiful auditorium standing ready to accommodate more people.

As for Motoji Tsunoda's speech that is another matter. In a way, however, I thought he did some beautiful philosophizing that night. No matter what his words might have meant, no matter what gestures and what provoking issues he might have spoken in the past, there was this man, standing up and talking to the world, and also talking to vindicate himself to the people, trying as hard as he could so he would not be misunderstood. And as he faced the eleven people in the audience including the two babies, he did not look foolish, he was not just a bag of wind. Instead I am sure he had a reason to stand up and have courage and bravery to offset the ridicule, the nonsense, and the misunderstanding.

And as he finished his lecture there was something worth while for everyone to hear and see, not just for the eleven persons in the auditorium but for the people of the earth: that of his voice, his gestures, his sadness, his patheticness, his bravery, which are of common lot and something the people, the inhabitants of the earth, could understand, sympathize and remember for awhile.

Responding to the Selection ——————

Questions for Discussion

1. Is Motoji Tsunoda someone you would like to have for a friend? Why or why not?

2. **Tone** is the attitude that a writer takes toward the audience, a subject, or a character. What tone is used to portray Motoji Tsunoda?

3. In the story's last paragraph, the narrator speaks of Motoji Tsunoda's bravery and "patheticness." In what way is Motoji Tsunodo brave? In what way is he pathetic?

4. Why might Mori have decided not to paraphrase or quote any part of Motoji Tsunoda's speech in the story?

5. Apart from Motoji Tsunoda, do the people in the narrator's neighborhood seem unusual, or is it a fairly typical American community? Explain.

Activities

Interpreting the Story

1. The narrator says that Motoji Tsunoda was "a philosopher by rights, as all men are in action and thought a philosopher by rights." What do you think he means? Write an interpretation of this statement.

Writing a Letter

2. Write a letter from Motoji Tsunoda to Akegarasu in which Motoji Tsunodo tells the great philosopher about his experience lecturing at the Asahi Auditorium. Use details from the story in your letter.

Designing a Flier

3. Even the most fascinating lecturers need to advertise their appearances. Design a flier announcing Motoji Tsunoda's upcoming lecture at the auditorium.

Television Transcript

In this interview, Bill Moyers talks with poet Li-Young Lee about his life, his homeland, and the process of writing poetry.

A Feeling of Disconnection

from The Language of Life: A Festival of Poets, *based on the 1995 PBS series by Bill Moyers*

Moyers: Your journey—China, Indonesia, Hong Kong, Macao, Japan, Seattle, Pittsburgh—is a story of the twentieth century, the century of refugees.

Lee: In a way, I feel as if our experience may be no more than an outward manifestation of a homelessness that people in general feel. It seems to me that anybody who thinks about our position in the universe cannot help but feel a little disconnected and homeless, so I don't think we're special. We refugees might simply express outwardly what all people feel inwardly.

Moyers: Do you feel yourself an exile?

Lee: In my most pessimistic moods I feel that I'm disconnected and that I'm going to be disconnected forever, that

I'll never have any place that I can call home. For example, I find it strange that when I go to visit my father's grave I look down and there on his stone is the Chinese character for his name and, when I look up, there are all these American flags on the other graves. So I feel a little strange, but I don't know what it is. I don't feel nostalgic because I don't know what to feel nostalgic *for*. It's simply a feeling of disconnection and dislocation.

Moyers: What is there about exodus and exile that gives some poets a special power?

Lee: I don't know. Exile seems both a blessing and a curse. A lot of my friends who are writers have said to me, "You're so lucky to have this background to write from," and I guess in a way I *am* lucky, but I wouldn't wish that experience on anybody. The literature I love most is the literature of ruins and the experience of exodus. I don't know why but, for example, the Book of Exodus is very important to me—the wandering of the children of Israel has a profound resonance for me. I don't feel as if those stories are about a primitive tribe in some distant desert. That struggle for belief and faith in the face of humiliation, annihilation, apostasy—all of that seems to me really what I go through and what we *all* go through, finally....

Moyers: Will you ever return to China?

Lee: I wonder about China, but I have no immediate plans to return there. My mother returned and found the family graves dug up, and she was told the bones were scattered—that happened during the Cultural Revolution—so in a way I feel there's nothing to return to. From what I understand, everything has been confiscated. They lived in a huge mansion, which has been turned into a small hospital, and certain parts of the land they owned have been turned into public parks, so I don't have any ruins to go back to, and it seems to me important that I should have ruins....

You know, I don't know if I believe in a heaven or a hell. But there's a longing in me for heaven. Maybe my longing for home comes from a longing for heaven....

Moyers: Let's talk about the craft of writing poetry.

Lee: For me, all the work *precedes* the actual writing of the poem and requires a kind of supplication, assuming a vulnerable posture, keeping open. It's like prayer. I think one has to do a lot of struggling before one actually kneels and says the words. Then after that, of course, there's a lot of revision; but I do a lot of reading and mental, spiritual, and emotional struggling before I actually come to the page.

Questions for Discussion

1. How might people overcome what Lee calls "a feeling of disconnection and dislocation"?

2. How does Lee describe his feelings about China and his past? How do you think you would feel if important parts of your past disappeared or were destroyed? Explain your answer.

Before You Read

The Gift, I Ask My Mother to Sing, and A Story

Li-Young Lee
Born 1957

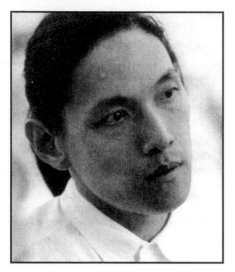

> *"A new poem requires a new mind."*

About Lee

Li-Young Lee was born in Indonesia of Chinese parents. He fled the country with his family in 1959 to escape political persecution. After living in various parts of Asia for five years, the family arrived in the United States. Lee spent the rest of his childhood in a small town in Pennsylvania, where his father was the pastor of a Presbyterian church. He feels his experience of exile has been both a blessing and a curse; it provided rich material for his poetry but also gave him a lingering sense of dislocation.

Lee has published a memoir and two books of poetry. His father, who would often recite Chinese poetry and passages from the Bible, taught Lee to love literature. Lee still turns to the Bible as a literary model and source of wisdom. "Writing poetry is absolutely religious for me," he says. "I happen to believe that everything we do or say finally is a dialogue with the universe, or God."

Family Relations

Many of Lee's poems were inspired by his parents and explore the relationships of parents and their children. Lee describes his mother, a member of what was once China's royal family, as an "incredibly resilient woman." He also often writes about his father, who had been a personal physician to Mao Zedong, China's ruler for many years. Lee admits to feeling in awe of his father, a scholarly and "infinitely tender" man.

The Gift

— Li-Young Lee

To pull the metal splinter from my palm
my father recited a story in a low voice.
I watched his lovely face and not the blade.
Before the story ended, he'd removed
5   the iron sliver I thought I'd die from.

I can't remember the tale,
but hear his voice still, a well
of dark water, a prayer.
And I recall his hands,
10   two measures of tenderness
he laid against my face,
the flames of discipline
he raised above my head.

Had you entered that afternoon
15   you would have thought you saw a man
planting something in a boy's palm,
a silver tear, a tiny flame.
Had you followed that boy
you would have arrived here,
20   where I bend over my wife's right hand.

Look how I shave her thumbnail down
so carefully she feels no pain.
Watch as I lift the splinter out.
I was seven when my father
25   took my hand like this,
and I did not hold that shard
between my fingers and think,
Metal that will bury me,
christen it Little Assassin,

The Gift

30   Ore Going Deep for My Heart.
And I did not lift up my wound and cry,
Death visited here!
I did what a child does
when he's given something to keep.
35   I kissed my father.

I Ask My Mother to Sing

— Li-Young Lee

She begins, and my grandmother joins her.
Mother and daughter sing like young girls.
If my father were alive, he would play
his accordion and sway like a boat.

5   I've never been in Peking, or the Summer Palace,
nor stood on the great Stone Boat to watch
the rain begin on Kuen Ming Lake, the picnickers
running away in the grass.

But I love to hear it sung;
10   how the waterlilies fill with rain until
they overturn, spilling water into water,
then rock back, and fill with more.

Both women have begun to cry.
But neither stops her song.

A Story

— Li-Young Lee

Sad is the man who is asked for a story
and can't come up with one.

His five-year-old son waits in his lap.
Not the same story, Baba. A new one.
5   The man rubs his chin, scratches his ear.

In a room full of books in a world
of stories, he can recall
not one, and soon, he thinks, the boy
will give up on his father.

10   Already the man lives far ahead, he sees
the day this boy will go. *Don't go!*
Hear the alligator story! The angel story once more!
You love the spider story. You laugh at the spider.
Let me tell it!

15   But the boy is packing his shirts,
he is looking for his keys. *Are you a god,*
the man screams, *that I sit mute before you?*
Am I a god that I should never disappoint?

But the boy is here. *Please, Baba, a story?*
20   It is an emotional rather than logical equation,
an earthly rather than heavenly one,
which posits that a boy's supplications
and a father's love add up to silence.

❖

Responding to the Selection

Questions for Discussion

1. After reading these poems, what thoughts do you have about relations between parents and children?

2. What has the speaker of "The Gift" learned from his father?

3. In the last stanza of "The Gift," the speaker describes what he did not think about when the splinter was removed. Why are these absent thoughts significant?

4. Why do the mother and grandmother in "I Ask My Mother to Sing" begin to cry during their song? Do you think they are crying because they are sad? Why or why not?

5. How does the father in "A Story" react to his son's request? What concerns are suggested in the father's vision of the future?

6. Which of the three poems most directly addresses the experience of immigration? Explain your response.

Activities

Analyzing Poetry

1. Write an analysis of one poem by Li-Young Lee. Discuss the development of the poem's theme or examine elements of style such as imagery, figurative language, and tone.

Writing Poetry

2. Think of a time when you had a strong emotional reaction to music that you were performing or listening to. Write a poem about this experience.

Listening to Music and Poetry

3. Choose a piece of music you feel reflects the meaning and feeling of one of these poems. Read the poem aloud to the class, using the music you have chosen as accompaniment.

Index of Titles and Authors

❖

Index of Titles and Authors

❖

Acknowledgments

❖ *cont. from page ii*

"Waiting for Papa's Return" copyright © 1987 by Cecilia Manguerra Brainard, from *Woman with Horns and Other Stories* (New Day, 1987) Reprinted by permission of the author.

"Water Names" from *Hunger* by Lan Samantha Chang. Copyright © 1998 by Lan Samantha Chang. Used by permission of W.W. Norton & Company, Inc.

"My Rough Skinned Grandmother" by Tina Chang. Reprinted by permission of the author.

"Asian-American WWII Valor Honored" from the *Chicago Tribune*, June 22, 2000. Copyright © 2000 Chicago Tribune Company. All rights reserved. Used with permission.

"Seventeen Syllables" from *Seventeen Syllables and Other Stories*, copyright © 1988 by Hisaye Yamamoto DeSoto. Reprinted by permission of Kitchen Table/Women of Color Press.

"Talk to Me, Milagros" from *Her Wild American Self*, copyright © 1996 by Evelina Galang. Reprinted by permission of Coffee House Press.

"Assimilation" and "Milkfish" by Eugene Gloria. Reprinted by permission of the author.

"The Bread of Salt" from *The Bread of Salt and Other Stories* by N.V.M. Gonzalez. Copyright © 1993 by the University of Washington Press. Reprinted by permission of the University of Washington Press.

"Beetle on a String" and "Dance of the Letters" by Vince Gotera. Reprinted by permission of the author.

Excerpt from "The fabric of their lives: Beauty, tragedy captured in Hmong needlework" by Carol Guensburg. *Milwaukee Journal Sentinel*, June 16, 1999. Reprinted by permission.

Poems from *Songs of Gold Mountain: Cantonese Rhymes from San Francisco Chinatown* by Marlon K. Hom. Copyright © 1987 The Regents of the University of California. Reprinted by permission of the University of California Press.

"Kubota" from *Volcano* by Garrett Hongo. Copyright © 1995 by Garrett Hongo. Reprinted by permission of Alfred A. Knopf, a Division of Random House, Inc.

"Eruption: Pu'u O'o" from *The River of Heaven* by Garrett Hongo. Copyright © 1988 by Garrett Hongo. Reprinted by permission of Alfred A. Knopf, a Division of Random House, Inc.

"As the Crow Flies" by Henry David Hwang. Reprinted by permission of the author.

"The Real Inada" from *Drawing the Line*, copyright © 1997 by Lawson Fusao Inada. Reprinted by permission of Coffee House Press.

"Foreseaking the Mists" by Lady Ise, from *The Penguin Book of Japanese Verse* edited and translated by Geoffrey Bownas and Anthony Thwaite (Penguin Books, 1964) translation copyright © Geoffrey Bownas and Anthony Thwaite, 1964. Reprinted by permission of Penguin Books Ltd.

"Obasan in Suburbia" and "Hambun-Hambun" by Susan Ito. Reprinted by permission of the author.

"The Water Faucet Vision" from *Who's Irish?* by Gish Jen. Copyright © 1999 by Gish Jen. Reprinted by permission

Acknowledgments

of Alfred A. Knopf, a Division of Random House, Inc.

"Hybrid" by Persis M. Karim. Reprinted by permission of the author.

"Crossings" from *Lost Names: Scenes from a Korean Boyhood,* copyright © 1998 by Richard Kim. Reprinted by permission of the University of California Press.

Excerpt from *China Men* by Maxine Hong Kingston. Copyright © 1980 by Maxine Hong Kingston. Reprinted by permission of Alfred A. Knopf, a division of Random House, Inc.

"Was it that I went to sleep" by Ono Komachi from *The Penguin Book of Japanese Verse* edited and translated by Geoffrey Bownas and Anthony Thwaite (Penguin Books, 1964) translation copyright © Geoffrey Bownas and Anthony Thwaite, 1964. Reprinted by permission of Penguin Books Ltd.

"Mango" by Christian Langworthy is reprinted by permission of the author.

"Coming Home Again" copyright © 1995 by Chang-Rae Lee. Reprinted by permission of International Creative Management.

"A Story" copyright © 1990 by Li-Young Lee. Reprinted from *The City in Which I Love You* by Li-Young Lee, with the permission of BOA Editions, Ltd.

"The Gift" and "I Ask My Mother to Sing" copyright © 1986 by Li-Young Lee. Reprinted from *Rose,* by Li-Young Lee with the permission of BOA Editions, Ltd.

"Encounter" from *Bells in Winter* by Czeslow Milosz. Copyright © 1978 by Czeslaw Milosz. Reprinted by permission of HarperCollins Publishers, Inc.

"The Chessmen" and "The Seventh Street Philosopher" from *Yokohama, California,* by Toshio Mori. Copyright © 1949 by the Caxton Printers. Reprinted by permission.

Interview with Li-Young Lee from *The Language of Life: A Festival of Poets* by Bill Moyers. Copyright © 1995 by Public Affairs Television, Inc. and David Grubin Productions, Inc. Used by permission of Doubleday, a division of Random House, Inc.

"My Father and the Figtree" and "Linked" by Naomi Shihab Nye. Reprinted by permission of the author.

"Lipstick" from *American Visa,* copyright © 1994 by Wang Ping. Reprinted by permission of Coffee House Press.

"Trailing on the Wind" by Priest Saigyo, from *The Penguin Book of Japanese Verse* edited and translated by Geoffrey Bownas and Anthony Thwaite (Penguin Books, 1964) translation copyright © Geoffrey Bownas and Anthony Thwaite, 1964. Reprinted by permission of Penguin Books Ltd.

"A Lost Memory of Delhi" from *The Half-Inch Himalayas,* copyright © 1987 by Ali Agha Shahid, Wesleyan University Press, reprinted by permission of the University Press of New England.

"Freedom to Breathe" from *Stories and Prose Poems* by Alexander Solzhenitsyn, translated by Michael Glenny. Translation copyright © 1971 by Michael Glenny. Reprinted by permission of Farrar, Straus and Giroux, LLC.

"Easter: Wahaiwa, 1959" from *Picture Bride,* copyright © 1983 by Cathy

Song. Reprinted by permission of Yale University Press.

"Trailing the wind" by Tairi Tadanori from *The Penguin Book of Japanese Verse* edited and translated by Geoffrey Bownas and Anthony Thwaite (Penguin Books, 1964) translation copyright © Geoffrey Bownas and Anthony Thwaite, 1964. Reprinted by permission of Penguin Books Ltd.

"I Remember Fermin 1930" by Jeff Tagami. Reprinted by permission of the author.

"Two Kinds" Copyright © 1989 by Amy Tan. Used by permission of Amy Tan and the Sandra Dijkstra Literary Agency.

"A Delicate Balance: An Interview with Wayne Wang about The Joy Luck Club," by John C. Tibbetts, *Literature and Film Quarterly*, vol. 22, no. 1, 1994. Reprinted by permission.

"When I went to visit" by Ki Tsurayuki from *The Penguin Book of Japanese Verse* edited and translated by Geoffrey Bownas and Anthony Thwaite (Penguin Books, 1964) translation copyright © Geoffrey Bownas and Anthony Thwaite,

1964. Reprinted by permission of Penguin Books Ltd.

"A Gift in Wartime" by Tran Mong Tu. Reprinted by permission of the author.

"Anchorage" from *Talking to the Dead* by Sylvia Watanabe, copyright © 1992 by Sylvia Watanabe. Used by permission of Doubleday, a division of Random House, Inc.

"Can't Tell" and "From a Heart of Rice Straw" from *Dreams in Harrison Railroad Park*, copyright © 1977 by Nellie Wong. Reprinted by permission of the author.

"The Tonle Sap Lake Massacre" by Ronnie Yimsut, from *Children of Cambodia's Killing Fields*, copyright © 1997 by Tale University. Reprinted by permission of Yale University Press.

"Seoul, Korea" by Jean Yoon is reprinted by permission of the author.

"The World of Our Grandmothers" by Connie Young Yu. Reprinted by permission of the author.

Excerpt from "The Iron Road" produced by Neil Goodwin, Peace River Films, from *The American Experience*, copyright © WGBH. Reprinted by permission.

Photography Acknowledgments

Cover *In Resting Mood*. Bharati Chaudhuri (1951–). Bharati Chaudhuri/SuperStock.

vi Diana Ong/SuperStock; **1** Collection of the artist; **2** Linda Ciscero/Stanford News Service; **8** Neil Davenport; **12** Seattle Art Museum/CORBIS; **19** Miriam Berkley; **28** (l)Archive Photos, (r)Joseph Sohm/ChromoSohm Inc./CORBIS; **30** ©Asian Art & Archeology, Inc./CORBIS; **44** L. Linkhart/Globe Photos; **45** (t)Philip Gould/CORBIS, (c,b)National Archives/Woodfin Camp & Associates; **46** David Weintraub; **56** Philip Gould/CORBIS; **64** The Cleveland Museum of Art; **68** Gerardo Somoza/Outline; **74** Zifen

Qian/SuperStock; **75** Tony Freeman/ PhotoEdit; **76** CALYX Books; **89** file photo; **92 93** CORBIS; **94** Courtesy Alfred A. Knopf Inc., photo by Shuzo Uemoto; **106** AFP/CORBIS; **107** Bettmann/CORBIS; **108** Haruko; **113** Seattle Art Museum/CORBIS; **119** Henry McGee/Globe Photos; **134** Courtesy Tina Chang, photo ©Robert Cusido; **138** Courtesy Sylvia Watanabe, photo by William P. Osborn; **150** Courtesy Cecilia Manguerra Brainard; **157** Courtesy Sharon Hashimoto; **160** Bharati Chaudhuri/ SuperStock; **161** National Museum of American Art, Washington DC/Art Resource, New York; **162** Courtesy Alfred A. Knopf Inc., photo by Shuzo Uemoto; **166** Marc Ancheta; **169** file photo; **184** Courtesy Gary Goddard & Associates; **187** Asian Art & Archaeology, Inc./CORBIS; **190** Courtesy Christian Nguyen Langworthy; **193** Peter Breslow; **208** Wolfgang Kaehler/CORBIS; **209** Collection of The Wing Luke Asian Museum, Seattle WA; **210** Bettmann/CORBIS; **211** (t)Bettmann/CORIS, (b)David Butow/Saba Press Photos; **212** Courtesy Ronnie Yimsut; **221** Dina Gona; **224** Asian Art & Archeology, Inc./CORBIS; **228** Heather Conley; **232** Bharati Chaudhuri/SuperStock; **233** The Seattle Art Museum. Gift of Seattle Art Museum Guild; **234** Milan Ryba/Globe Photos; **245** Courtesy Persis M. Karim; **249** Mahmoud G. Afkhami; **259** Kristen Lindquist; **264** James M. Kelly/Globe Photos; **265** Aaron Haupt; **266** Andrea Renault/Globe Photos; **278** Photo by Steven Y. Mori; **286** Boleslaw Edelhajt/Liaison Agency; **289** Gaytana Carrino; **306** PhotoEdit; **307** (t)The Mariner's Museum/CORBIS, (b)Kevin R. Morris/CORBIS; **308** Courtesy Vince Gotera; **314** Courtesy Tran Mong Tu; **318** Collection of The Wing Luke Asian Museum, Seattle WA; **319** National Museum of American Art, Washington DC/Art Resource, New York; **320** Brenda Iijima; **328** Tom Lyles; **332** Courtesy of Hisaye Yamamoto; **345** John Eddy; **350** Bettmann/CORBIS; **351** (t)SuperStock, (b)David Muench/CORBIS; **352** Nancy Crampton; **362** Sakamoto Photo Research Laboratory/CORBIS; **366** Courtesy Lawson Fusao Inada, photo by Paul Schraub; **374** Vyto Starinskas/Rutland Herald/Sygma; **377** Photo by Steven Y. Mori; **384 386** William Abranowizc.